Palisades

HUDSON VALLEY HERITAGE SERIES

Robert F. Jones, series editor

Palisades

100,000 ACRES IN 100 YEARS

ROBERT O. BINNEWIES

FORDHAM UNIVERSITY PRESS AND
PALISADES INTERSTATE PARK COMMISSION
New York
2001

Hudson Valley Heritage Series, No. 1
ISSN 1534–1399

Library of Congress Cataloging-in-Publication Data
Binnewies, Robert O.
  Palisades : 100,000 acres in 100 years / Robert Binnewies.—1st ed.
   p. cm. — (Hudson Valley heritage series ; no. 1)
  Includes bibliographical references (p.) and index.
  ISBN 0-8232-2127-X (hardcover)—ISBN 0-8232-2128-8 (pbk.)
  1. Palisades Intersate Park Commission—History. I. Title. II. Series.
  SB482.N5 B56 2001
  333.78'3'09749—dc21

                  2001023805

Printed in the United States of America
01 02 03 04 05 5 4 3 2 1
First Edition

*This book is dedicated to Aaron Gastellum,
who, for a moment, before a careless driver
struck him down, brought brightness and
passion to our continuing search for
environmental wisdom.*

CONTENTS

Greeting   ix
   Laurance S. and David Rockefeller

Foreword   xi
   Carol Ash and Barnabas McHenry

Acknowledgments   xv

1   Boss Blaster   1

2   The Commission   5

3   Upriver   22

4   Harriman   38

5   Legend and War   57

6   Welch   69

7   Bear Mountain   80

8   Perkins   100

9   Jolliffe   124

10 Trail and Bridge   141

11 Uncle Bennie   157

12 Black Thursday   171

13 The Compact   189

14 The Palisades Parkway   213

15 Storm King   239

16 Minnewaska   269

17 Sterling Forest   304

18 Looking Ahead   355

Appendix A
   Palisades Interstate Park Commission
   Parks and Historic Sites   357

Appendix B
   Commissioners of the Palisades
   Interstate Park Commision   360

Appendix C
   The Hudson River Valley Contingent for
   the Preservation of Sterling Forest   362

Sources   365

Index   397

GREETING

LAURANCE S. AND DAVID ROCKEFELLER

When we were children, our father, John D. Rockefeller, Jr., spoke to us often about the importance of conservation and the critical leadership that individuals would have to provide if places of great beauty were to be preserved for future generations. We had a great object lesson literally in front of our eyes—the magnificent Palisades stretching north along the Hudson from just opposite Manhattan all the way to Haverstraw Bay. The Palisades were not only beautiful and irreplaceable, they had also been threatened by development and saved from this fate only by a coalition of concerned and far-sighted individuals, a group that included both Father and our grandfather, John D. Rockefeller.

For that reason we are delighted that Bob Binnewies has written *Palisades,* a thoughtful and precise recounting of the history of the Palisades Interstate Park. Binnewies is particularly well qualified to tell this story. An official with the National Park Service for many years, Bob has extensive experience in the not-for-profit sector as well.

The most important part of this story is that the century-long campaign to protect the Palisades has been successful. An effort that began when Teddy Roosevelt was governor of New York State as a decidedly ad hoc effort to protect a portion of the Palisades has grown into an internationally acclaimed park with 100,000 acres and more than 8 million visitors a year. It is a grand story and a work in progress. Succeeding generations need to remember that the preservation of the Palisades did not happen by chance. Rather, it was the work of dedicated citizens who were willing to invest their time and substantial funds to achieve a worthwhile public goal that has benefited the residents of New York

City and the lower Hudson Valley for decades. It is a story that can be repeated across the country and the world.

We congratulate the commissioners and staff of the Palisades Interstate Park Commission and Fordham University Press for publishing this important book.

FOREWORD
CAROL ASH AND BARNABAS McHENRY

The publication of *Palisades* marks our centennial, and we are delighted to celebrate with this book that tells the history of our park. Our colleague, Bob Binnewies, has written an elegant chronicle that spans the twentieth century and tells of the battles, skirmishes, and acts of valor by citizens, powerful and not, that culminated in the creation of the Commission and the Palisades parks.

The private citizens who illuminate these pages are on the honor role of American conservation. The Rockefellers, Harrimans, Perkinses, Borgs, and Hansons appear in this book as advocates, donors, and hereditary commissioners. Here they receive proper recognition for their passionate labor in solving the complex tasks associated with building and protecting a one hundred thousand–acre park within sight of the Empire State Building. *Palisades* is the story of how this park was created by more than one thousand real estate transactions, and since one real property closing is agony enough, the conservation world should know how these enlightened men and women suffered through unending closings and how they scrambled, begged, borrowed, and eventually found the dollars to pay for the land.

Parks are about open space, and *Palisades* is about the struggle to acquire the land for the parks. The aesthetics of open space for outdoor recreation are a glamorous aspect of this history, and the end result includes an inn and restaurant, 350 miles of hiking trails, four large public beaches, 12 swimming pools, two golf courses, 42 miles of bike trails, ten sewage treatment plants, two police forces and a court, highways, parkways, and bridges requiring almost one thousand employees in the summer season.

Palisades is meant to be read by the first generation of the twenty-first century meritocracy in the hope that some will join the continuing conservation celebration in the Hudson Valley. There is so much more to be accomplished.

Tangible and enduring benefits abound in becoming involved with the Palisades Commission, besides the obvious one of acquiring a tax-deduction. Binnewies describes some benefits and how the aesthetic dividends are declared and paid to those volunteers who derive a sense of accomplishment in the acquisition and protection of open space. This is an approach to regional planning that discourages development in open space and encourages development in the already developed cities and towns of the lower Hudson Valley. Binnewies acknowledges the extraordinary work of volunteers, notably the trail maintainers from the New York–New Jersey Trail Conference. The 350 miles of trails in the park are their responsibility, and we could not operate without them.

Conservation of parkland is to be distinguished from environmental advocacy because environmentalists are often required to battle industry, government, and occasionally their compatriots to achieve an objective. The business of conservation is about finding ways to protect land and finding the funds to pay for it.

Governors George Pataki and Christine Whitman supported the Commission. Governor Pataki is passionate about open space and biodiversity, and Governor Whitman was able to persuade the New Jersey Legislature to invest $11 million for land in New York State to protect a watershed for northern New Jersey. Actually there is a precedent—in 1900 the New York Legislature appropriated $400,000 that was spent to buy land in the New Jersey Palisades.

"NIMBY" always plays a role in conservation, and it has usually been constructive for the park. George Perkins was concerned with more than just the ruckus from the Carpenter Brothers' quarry blasts across the Hudson from his front yard in Riverdale. John Rockefeller, Sr., wanted his view from Kykuit protected against the blight of dynamiting at Hook Mountain across the river. And Mrs. E. H. Harriman's desire to avoid a prison at the base of her mountain property was understandable—and she cared about the land. These aristocratic landowners were sensitive to the parks' proximity to metropolitan New York and its 20 million residents and were concerned with the aesthetic value of land conservation. The result includes a parkway and the protection of the twenty miles of the west bank of the Hudson Highlands.

The park budget for the operations at Palisades Park comes from the general funds of the respective states. It requires a bond act (or an occasional direct appropriation from the federal government) to provide the public portion of the capital for land acquisitions and improvements. Private support has always been crucial in park acquisitions in the Palisades, and one does not have to be a Rockefeller, a Harriman, a Perkins, or a Borg to be a player; one has only to be committed, and *Palisades* tells how. And if a campaign to add some acres of parkland does succeed, there will be no increase in local tax assessments on weekend hideaways in the Ramapos. The vision of George Perkins and the Rockefellers has protected the local tax base for those communities lucky enough to have a Palisades Park within their borders. There is no diminution in local real property taxes paid when the Palisades Commission becomes the owner; New York State will pay the full property tax for lands acquired in New York.

There are many reasons to be excited about *Palisades,* and we hope you will appreciate the marvelous energy of Hudson Valley conservation and want to participate in our twenty-first century adventures.

Bear Mountain

January, 2001

ACKNOWLEDGMENTS

Midge Binnewies volunteered for two years to research the story of the Palisades Interstate Park Commission. In the process, our dining room disappeared under a clutter of files stacked in the vicinity of a much-abused copy machine. She was joined in this task by PIPC historian Sue Smith. Together they rediscovered thousands of pages of long-forgotten documents and news articles, many of which were found discarded in a dark, mice-infested warehouse. Barnabas McHenry decided that this book would speak on the occasion of the PIPC's centennial and brought his delightful verve and wit to the adventure. Malcolm Borg voluntarily set aside guidance of his large corporation for several days to help edit the book, confirming once again that he holds the PIPC high among his personal and public priorities. Carol Ash, Ken Krieser, Mary Thomas, Jack Focht, Kathryn Brown, and Elizabeth VanHouten of the PIPC's staff were exceptionally encouraging (and tolerant). Professional editor Janet Foltin looked at the first chapters and pronounced them "promising," thus inspiring hope. Saverio Procario agreed to publish the book as part of Fordham University Press's welcome series on the Hudson River Valley. Anthony Chiffolo brought the mastery of his editing pen to the text. To these colleagues and to all who have kept the PIPC alive for a century, I am grateful.

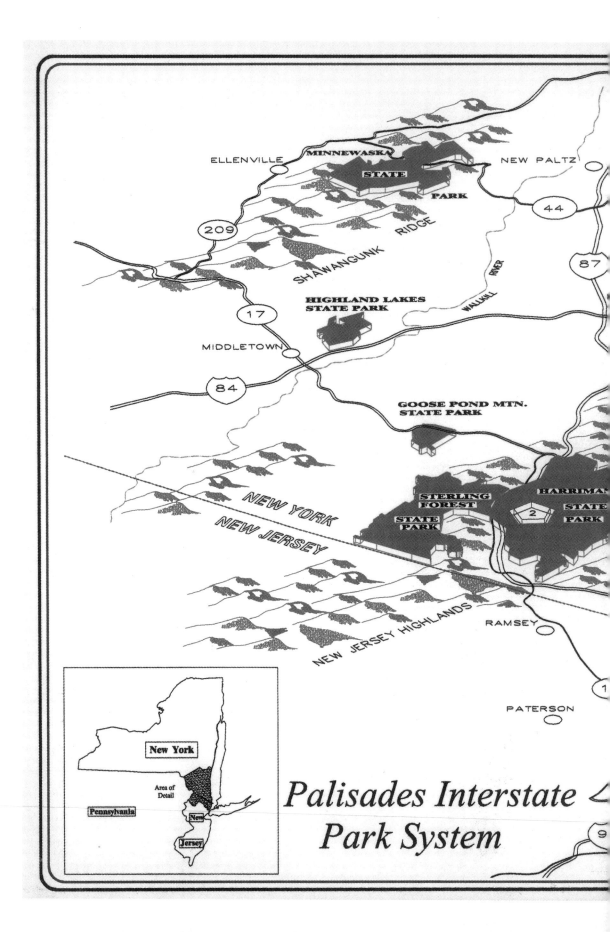

Palisades Interstate
Park System

PARKS SHOWN

1. SENATE HOUSE STATE HISTORIC SITE
2. GEORGE WASHINGTON HEADQUARTERS STATE HISTORIC SITE
3. NEW WINDSOR CANTONMENT STATE HISTORIC SITE
4. KNOX HEADQUARTERS STATE HISTORIC SITE
5. STONY POINT BATTLEFIELD STATE HISTORIC SITE
6. HIGH TOR STATE PARK
7. HAVERSTRAW BEACH STATE PARK
8. HOOK MOUNTAIN STATE PARK
9. ROCKLAND LAKE STATE PARK
10. NYACK BEACH STATE PARK
11. BLAUVELT STATE PARK
12. TALLMAN MOUNTAIN STATE PARK
13. FORT LEE STATE HISTORIC PARK

PARKS NOT SHOWN

14. BRISTOL BEACH STATE PARK SAUGERTIES
15. LAKE SUPERIOR STATE PARK MONTICELLO

FAMILY ESTATES

1. PERKINS ESTATE
2. HARRIMAN ESTATE
3. ROCKEFELLER ESTATE

1.
Boss Blaster

The land was pleasant with grass and flowers and goodly trees as ever seen, and very sweet smells came from them. We went on land to walk on the west side of the river and found good ground for corn and other garden herbs, with great store of goodly oaks, walnut trees, yew trees and trees of sweet wood in great abundance, and a great store of slate for houses and other good stones. Hard by was a cliff that looked of the color of white green as though it were either copper or silver mine, and I think it to be one of them by the trees that grew upon it. For they were all burned, and the other places were as green as grass.

Robert Juet, aboard Henry Hudson's *Half Moon*, 1609

Alice Haggerty was the winner. According to a report in the March 5, 1898, edition of *The New York Times,* "This slip of an Irish girl had been chosen for the distinction of destroying one of the most widely known and splendid pieces of scenery in North America."

This piece of scenery was known as the Indian Head, a massive two-hundred-foot vertical spire of diabase rock, a distinctive geological feature estimated to weigh 350,000 tons, hanging high on the Palisades cliff. The Carpenter Brothers, quarrymen who were dynamiting away more than a thousand cubic yards of the Palisades cliff each day, "owned" the Indian Head, which was their next target.

Forty shafts, each two inches in diameter and twenty-five feet deep, had been drilled downward from the summit of the cliff into this unique rock formation. "Eighty feet below," according to the *Times*, "a tunnel was dug from the face of the precipice. It was five feet in diameter, and ran back into the rock one hundred feet. From the inner end of this, two shafts were sunk twenty-five feet deep. Fifty feet above the base, another five-foot tunnel one hundred feet was run, and from the inner end of this, two five-foot shafts descended almost to the river's level." These shafts and tunnels were packed with seven thousand pounds of dynamite.

During the Triassic period, 30 million years ago, semimolten igneous rock had been forced up through a fissure in the earth's crust. Overlying the fissure was a layer of sandstone thousands of feet thick. The buried rock slowly cooled, shrank, and solidified into giant vertical crystals of diabase lava, consisting of silica, feldspars, magnetite, and pyroxene. Over eons, as the crust of the earth

Palisades Cliffs, Hudson River.
(Courtesy of PIPC Archives)

shifted and eroded, the flint-hard diabase was exposed to form a sweeping thirty-mile-long cliff face ranging to a height of 550 feet on the western shoreline of a river later to be named in honor of Henry Hudson. In 1524, when Giovanni da Verrazano sailed the French ship *La Dauphine* into what would become known as New York Bay, he was so amazed by the looming cliffs that he proclaimed the newly discovered land "La Terri de L'Anomee Berge"—the country of the Grand Scarp. The cliff is a geologic phenomenon also noted in 1609 by Hudson when he sailed past in the *Half Moon* on his attempt to find a sea lane through the New World to China. The Palisades cliff is easily seen from the northern end of Manhattan Island and has been considered a scenic wonder by generations of river travelers, artists, and naturalists.

Almost three centuries later, Alice Haggerty stood on the summit of the cliff admired by Verrazano, held in view by the expectant crowd. She was looking at a small wooden box, about twelve inches square, placed before her on a flat rock. The box was adorned with two electric terminals and a *T*-shaped plunger. Wires from the terminals snaked off for a long distance through grass and forest duff to dynamite charges secured in the Indian Head. One quick pulse of hand-generated electricity from the box promised to deliver explosive power that could blow almost anything into oblivion.

Haggerty was not a popular contest winner. Other young women whispered that she had won the contest with "pull." She was a friend of Mrs. Hugh Reilly, wife of the Boss Blaster. Second only to the Carpenter Brothers, the Boss Blaster was overall commander of the on-site quarry operations, and his word was supreme. So Haggerty had been chosen, and all was ready. The Carpenter Brothers floated in a boat at a safe distance out on the Hudson; and the cliff-top crowd, who had come by foot, horseback, and carriage, waited. Other spectators bobbed in boats of their own well out in the river.

If all went well, one push of the plunger and the electric current would speed to explosive caps embedded in the dynamite, setting off a gigantic blast that would bring the Indian Head crashing down into a dust-swept, jumbled pile of broken rock at the base of the cliff. Italian stone workers, swinging sledge hammers and using more dynamite and machinery, would further pulverize the rock in preparation for its shipment on barges across the river to New York City. Rock blasted from the Palisades was being used as base course and macadam for streets, fill for building foundations, and other common, unglamorous needs. Diabase rock was too brittle and hard to be used for anything other than the most utilitarian purposes; no diabase would decorate the city skyscrapers or otherwise capture the creative attention of architects—marble, granite, and sandstone were preferred for these purposes. The Palisades rock was generally being buried out of sight.

All did not go well. Haggerty "dabbed coquettishly" at the plunger, "then swept her skirts around with an involuntary movement of one hand and fled." A trickle of electricity found one or two of the distant explosive caps. From a lower tunnel, a dull thud and puff of smoke dislodged a few pieces of rock that clattered down to the base of the cliff. Then silence. The Indian Head held fast, looming over the river as it had for fifty thousand years, since the last great ice-age glaciers had receded.

Blasters describe a partial explosion as dangerously "hanging fire." At the very least, Haggerty's delicate electric current had damaged various connections that would require repair; at worst, a blasting cap somewhere in the network of tunnels and shafts might still go off unexpectedly. The Carpenter Brothers, Boss Blaster Reilly, the quarrymen, and the crowd waited. Finally, Reilly gathered four of his men and approached the edge of the cliff. The Carpenter Brothers rowed in toward shore for closer observation. With a rope around his waist, the Boss Blaster scaled down the cliff and for an hour toiled to inspect connections and reset wires.

Spectators still waiting, the Carpenters rowed back to midchannel. Reilly walked to the plunger. "The brawny arm of the Boss Blaster flew high as he drew the plunger out to its full length," the *Times* reported.

> Then he forced it back with a quick, vicious thrust. The ground for hundreds of yards back from the brink of the cliff shook and trembled. There was an enormous all-pervading crash and roar. The solid face of the cliff bellied out at the middle and then the whole great surface collapsed and crumbled with a rush. Echoes of the explosion and fall reverberated along the cliffs and shores for six minutes. Where the Indian Head had been there was a huge, raw-looking concavity in the side of the Palisades, with a great pile of broken rock heaped at the bottom.

The crowd cheered the destruction of the Indian Head. The Carpenter Brothers rushed ashore to congratulate the Boss Blaster. Haggerty's moment of fame floated away in the dust.

2.
The Commission

After the Civil War, even before the quarrymen arrived, enterprising merchants used the great vertical faces of the Palisades for patent medicine signs, painting letters twenty feet high on the cliffs, large enough to be read from across the river, almost a mile away. Fishermen had settled at the base of the cliffs, where they made their living by taking enormous catches of shad from the river. Wealthy men and women who could afford to routinely cross the river by private yacht sought out properties on the flat summit of the Palisades to escape the city's congestion and enjoy the spectacular views. A popular hotel-resort, the Palisades Mountain House, occupied one of the most desirable locations on the summit. Ownership of the Palisades had long since been divided into scores of private holdings.

The nation was in the midst of a postwar industrial boom. The iron, textile, shipping, mining, railroad, and oil industries were providing fortunes for adroit and skilled entrepreneurs, regardless of any environmental consequences. In California, three-thousand-year-old sequoia trees were being cut to produce fence posts and other low-grade lumber products. On the Great Plains, remnant herds of buffalo were being shot for sport. Buffalo Bill had moved East to regularly present his circus-like Wild West Show in New York City, reminding audiences of the glamour and danger of a frontier that had all but disappeared. A tremendous increase in the demand for crushed stone occurred when the new technology for paving streets with asphalt was combined with the use of stone aggregate mixed with concrete for building the foundations and skins of the nation's first steel-framed skyscrapers. Nowhere was this demand greater than in New York City.

Long before quarry operators started blasting the Palisades to meet market demands, Native Americans used the cliffs for shelter, observation, and protection. The Sanhikan, Hackensack, Raritan, and Tappan nations are said to have named the cliffs "Wee-awaken," rocks-that-look-like-trees. From the summit, they were able to observe any threat from their cross-river enemies, the Manhattans. In 1643 Native Americans destroyed the DeVries Colony on the western shoreline of the river at Sparkill and a farmhouse on the Hackensack River, in a hopeless attempt to stem colonial settlement in their territory. Native Americans' resistance, coupled with the Dutch policy that favored the establishment of large manorial estates on the New York side of the Hudson River, discouraged settlement near the Palisades. In 1683 what was to become Bergen County, New Jersey, was described as a "howling wilderness with scarcely a single settler located within it."

Control of the Palisades by Native Americans remained only in legend by the time the first colonial farmers and woodcutters gained a foothold on the summit in the early 1700s, and it was not until a century later that the first house was erected there. The house was framed in Boston, sent by ship to New York, floated to the base of the cliffs, and then moved inland piece by piece by its "active and enterprising" owner, Nathan T. Johnson. Johnson was followed by other settlers who scorned "anything as useless as aesthetics" and found a ready market after the Civil War for the three-hundred- and four-hundred-year-old trees that dotted the top of the Palisades. The trees were cut to provide millions of ties for the hungry railroad industry. They were felled by axemen, stripped of their branches, then literally "pitched" from the cliff summits to the talus slopes below. The Palisades, once heavily forested, were "stripped practically clean" of old-growth hardwood trees.

But not all was exploitation. The Hudson River School of art was born in 1825 when three New York City artists spotted two paintings by Thomas Cole in a frame maker's shop window. New York City Mayor Phillip Hone promptly purchased the paintings, confirming their market potential. Cole, unlike many of his peers who concentrated on European-style portraits, religious interpretations, heroic scenes, grand architecture, and the female body, began painting scenes of "sublime natural beauty." His paintings, capturing the scenic charm of the Hudson River Valley, tempted others to join in. Jasper Francis Cropsey was especially inspired by the Palisades. In loose company with Cole and Cropsey, Albert Bierstadt, Asher Durand, Willam Bartlett, George Inness, Frederic Church, Victor

Audubon, Winslow Homer, and Thomas Moran were among the artists who presented a new and inspiring view of natural landscapes that others had judged to be "useless aesthetics."

It was the rolling explosions, though, touched off by quarrymen on the Palisades that most dominated the river shoreline across from New York City at the end of the nineteenth century, prompting Rudyard Kipling to muse,

> *We hear afar the sounds of war,*
> *as rocks they rend and shiver;*
> *They blast and mine and rudely scar*
> *the pleasant banks of the river.*

Public outrage about the dynamiting began to find voice in newspapers, prodding politicians to take note. In the meantime, the Carpenter Brothers, Brown & Fleming, the Treavor Brothers, P. Gallagher, and other quarry operators were increasing production. The Carpenter Brothers could produce 1,500 cubic yards of crushed stone each day at a market price of $1 per yard. For $25,000, they purchased about one-half mile of cliff face and shoreline from the mayor of Englewood, New Jersey, guaranteeing enough raw material to ensure a steady business for decades to come, even if they found methods to double or triple production. By 1894 New Jersey's governor, George T. Werts, was actively engaged in the public debate over the future of the Palisades. Joined by New York State Senator Lexow, the governor was searching for a tangible answer to the challenge of how to protect the Palisades. His state geologist, John Smock, suggested the passage of a "park condemnation act" to take possession of the river's edge, thus denying quarrymen any access to the cliffs.

A few successes for conservation had already appeared on the nation's map, most notably the creation of Yellowstone National Park in 1872. Members of the Washburn-Langford-Doan Expedition visited the remote Yellowstone wilderness after the Civil War and recommended to Congress the novel idea that such a grand area of geysers, hot pools, bubbling mud pots, plentiful wildlife, meadows, mountains, lakes, deep gorges, and waterfalls be protected for the public, not left to be claimed for personal gain.

Even earlier, in 1864, Congress had acted to cede protection of Yosemite Valley and the Mariposa Grove of giant sequoias to the State of California "for public use, resort, and recreation." Frederick Law Olmsted, whose most prominent monument to landscape architecture is Central Park in New York City, probably influenced this little-noticed congressional action. By chance, Olmsted was staying with Gen. John C. Fremont in the Sierra Nevada foothills near the mining town of

Mariposa in 1860 when miners "discovered" Yosemite Valley while chasing "hostile" Native Americans. After Congress acted to protect the valley, Olmsted was appointed to a three-person commission to study how the new state park could be managed. (Yosemite was declared a national park in 1890.)

The nation's first publicly designated historic site had been established in Newburgh, New York, in 1850 to commemorate the Revolutionary War triumph of Gen. George Washington and the Continental Army. The New York Legislature created the Niagara Falls Reservation in 1885, following soon thereafter with the establishment in 1892 of the magnificent Adirondack State Park, the largest park in land area in the lower forty-eight states. Six million acres are included within the Adirondack State Park's "blue line."

Still, the concept of parks and historic sites remained vague and lacked direction in the late 1800s. Outside of urban centers, park-management agencies did not exist. The common assumption was that military need should be the primary reason for protecting large wilderness landscapes. By default, Yellowstone and Yosemite were turned over to the U.S. Cavalry. Army officers, using wit and invention, began setting the first management standards by which these and future parks would be passed from one generation to the next. In Yellowstone, laws did not provide the necessary authority for the Cavalry to protect the park's resources. Under orders to guard the buffalo, the troopers would catch poachers, beat them senseless, and deposit them at the park's boundary with advice to trespass no more. In Yosemite, the Cavalry, including segregated African American troops, chased sheepherders away from the fragile alpine meadows by using similar persuasive techniques.

With no particular model to follow, Governor Werts was grappling with the fact that the residents of New York were much more concerned about the destruction of the Palisades cliffs than were his own constituents in New Jersey. New Yorkers could see and hear the blasting, and the cliffs faced east toward New York. From New Jersey, the view was of a wild summit landscape, not of the cliffs. Some members of the New Jersey Legislature, whose votes would be essential to any conservation action, confessed no knowledge at all of the location of the Palisades. Still, growing public alarm about the quarrying activities was increasing the pressure on Governor Werts to act. In November, 1894, the governor hosted a boat trip on the Hudson River to allow his political associates a firsthand view of the problem. The wounds of quarrying prompted New Jersey Senator H. D. Winton to suggest that the governor appoint a commission at the opening of the next legislative session to determine the speediest means of preventing further destruction of the Palisades. Despite opposition from Repub-

Carpenter Brothers Quarry, Palisades Cliffs, 1909.
(Courtesy of PIPC Archives)

licans, Democrat Werts appointed three members to a Palisades study commission soon after delivering his annual message to the legislature on January 8, 1895. One of the New Jersey appointees, J. J. R. Croes, may not have fully understood his mission. He stated a personal belief that quarries "were capable of adding to the picturesqueness of the shore."

In February, *The New York Times* reported that on a "light legislative day," New York's Republican governor, Levi P. Morton, followed suit by appointing three commissioners to confer with their New Jersey counterparts, "for the purpose of securing action by the government of the United States of America in acquiring and setting apart the west shore of the Hudson, as designated, for the purpose of fortification and reservation in order that the brink of the precipice may be securely held and defended against attack and hostile occupation." One of the New York appointees was Waldo G. Morse, described as a moving spirit in the early efforts to protect the Palisades. Senator Winton chaired the study commission, and New York provided $1,000 for expenses. The first tentative step had been taken toward interstate cooperation to protect the Palisades.

Confirming the press's increasing interest in the subject, fourteen articles on the fight to save the Palisades appeared in *The New York Times* in 1895, including a lengthy feature article on September 29 in which a local New Jersey resident commented about the idea of fortifying the cliffs against an imagined enemy attack:

> It would take a pretty bold invader to threaten New York from the direction of northern New Jersey. It has been suggested that an enemy approaching New York from Boston by way of Albany might be checked by forts on the Palisades. It is certain, however, that such an emergency would greatly surprise the Naval War College at Newport, which has been engaged in the study of the defense of the eastern entrance of Long Island Sound under the conviction that an enemy from the east would surely try to get at New York that way.

From Washington, D.C., the Secretary of War reinforced this local opinion, tersely commenting that fortification of the Palisades "does not meet with favor" in the War Department. Most military officers ridiculed the idea of a military reservation in the Palisades.

But minority voices, too, were raised. One officer, more familiar with the details and beauty of the Palisades, suggested that, like Yellowstone, the area should be conserved as a national park. Another officer said, "I think the best course to pursue would be to secure from Congress authority and an appropriation for the purchase of the land and quarry plants and turn the whole thing over to the Interior Department." Still another said, "I favor the idea of making a great public park out of the Palisades."

In response to the initiative taken by the New Jersey and New York governors, a bill was introduced in the Fifty-fourth Congress in 1895 to cede the Palisades to the federal government. The bill died in committee. Three years later, with Spanish-American War paranoia gripping the Hudson River Valley, a second attempt was made to transfer the Palisades to the War Department, but with similar results.

In the style of the conservation battles that would reverberate through the nation in the twentieth century, lines were quickly drawn as the military-reservation idea foundered and failed. A Palisades property owner said, "If Bergen County prefers swamps and rattlesnakes and a dozen denizens on top of her miles of cliffs, and a half dozen dynamite fields along their face, she ought not to be disturbed and her rights infringed on." The Carpenter Brothers and other quarry operators were wasting no time in seeking out politicians who would defend their rights to do as they pleased with their properties. Even as *The New York Times* took up the plea for the creation of a national park, quoting scores of influential civic leaders, the initiative taken by Governor Werts to find a practical answer to such a vexing problem was forced back to square one. Werts and his New York colleague, Governor Morton, left office in 1896 with the future of the Palisades still unresolved.

A few months earlier, seventeen women had gathered at the home of Mrs. John A. Wells to form the Englewood Women's Club, a new chapter of the statewide New Jersey Federation of Women's Clubs. Led by Adaline Sterling, Elizabeth Vermilye, and Mrs. Chester Loomis, the club was formed "for the purpose of bringing together women interested in intellectual and cultural advancement, to stimulate inquiry concerning questions of public significance, to be a potent factor in the development of the community, and to promote its well-being through a program of philanthropy." Their "inquiry concerning questions of public significance" was focused sharply on the Palisades. The women intended to find a way to stop the quarry operators and save the cliffs in perpetuity. At the close of the nineteenth century, the Englewood women were ignoring the odds stacked against them. They had no voting rights and were expected to stay at home while tending to their knitting. But just before the first automobile rolled off the Ford assembly line in Detroit and while the Klondike gold rush was under way in Alaska, the Englewood women formed a subcommittee on the Palisades, chaired by Vermilye. A retrospective published years later in the *Rockland Journal News* captured Vermilye's love for the Palisades:

> In the 1860's, when she was a child, she would hike up Englewood's steep Palisades Avenue to the edge of the cliffs and roam the trails skirting the brink and the shoreline. She would clamber over the Indian Head and peer into the old tavern at Alpine where Cornwallis holed up as his British and Hessian troops scaled the cliffs to chase the Americans from Fort Lee. She marveled at the spectacular drops of Forest View, Bombay Hook, and the Giant Stairs. She watched the trains work their way up and down the opposite shoreline through Riverdale, Yonkers, and Hastings, silent as ships and barges at that distance.

Vermilye and her friend Cecelia Gaines, with encouragement and support from their Women's Club members, set out to enlist women from throughout New Jersey in the cause of the Palisades. They started writing letters to every newspaper in the state, accepted any invitation to speak before interested groups, and started lobbying legislators.

In 1897 the Englewood women won the privilege of hosting the third annual meeting of the New Jersey Federation of Women's Clubs. Fifty women went aboard the yacht *Marietta,* made available by its owner, Harrison B. Morse, for a river-view inspection of the quarry operations. Accompanying the women were several members of the newly formed American Scenic and Historic Preservation Society, chaired by Andrew H. Green. Green strongly shared the belief that the quarrying must be stopped, and as comptroller of Central Park and president of the New York City Board of Education, he brought strong and influential credentials to the issue. On board the yacht, Englewood club member Mrs. K. J. Sauzade said that the practical duty of women was to "conserve the beauties of nature." She found no disagreement from Green, whose Preservation Society included as part of its mission the need to "promote public parks by private gift or the appropriation of public funds for the health, comfort, and pleasure of the people."

At the conclusion of the cruise, the women arrived unannounced at the Carpenter Brothers' quarry just when midday blasting was scheduled. The scene can only be imagined—tough, grimy quarrymen faced by genteel ladies, men who likely held firm opinions about the place of women in society: that place was not at a quarry interfering with honest, purposeful work; church sewing societies were fine places for disenfranchised women to chatter; politics and commerce should be left to men who understood these complicated matters. The women obviously had a different opinion. Before the annual meeting of the New Jersey Federation of Women's Clubs was adjourned, a resolution was approved that stated, "This famous Hudson River scenery which the citizens of New Jersey hold in trust for all the world will eventually become a thing of the past to their lasting shame and disgrace. As it is, the glorious heritage of the people of the State is being trampled under the foot of man and beasts in the streets of Gotham. Will the State Federation realize its power for good in this matter?"

In partial answer to that question, New Jersey Governor Foster M. Voorhees, Republican successor to Governor Werts, felt enough pressure from the press and public to save the Palisades that he agreed to meet with Vermilye and the Englewood women. His message was anything but promising: "Ladies, this is a hopeless task. I have tried for ten years to save the Palisades; it cannot be done." Voorhees said that the state had no money to buy the Palisades and that no support or interest in protecting the cliffs existed in "south Jersey."

Voorhees had not counted on the 1899 arrival of Theodore Roosevelt in the New York governor's chair. No government leader would bring more energy and sense of mission to the cause of national conservation than this legendary man.

Before ascending to the governorship, Roosevelt had been Police Commissioner in New York City and, drawn as always to the outdoors, had become an active member of an Englewood, New Jersey, rod and gun club. With gun in hand, Roosevelt roamed the Palisades in search of small game, gaining a detailed knowledge of the area and an appreciation for its bold, natural beauty. Early in his term as governor, and urged on by Green, Roosevelt conferred with Voorhees and agreed that preserving the Palisades would benefit both states.

Based on the legal authority granted the previous year by both state legislatures, the governors appointed a second study commission to review the matter and recommend action. Five citizens were appointed to represent New York, and five to represent New Jersey. Vermilye and Gaines were appointed to the New Jersey contingent. Meeting every week, this commission rushed to report back to the governors as quickly as possible, even as the Carpenter Brothers accelerated their blasting schedule. By the end of the year, the study commission revisited an old idea, urging action by the two states to "take" a 737-acre strip of land along a fourteen-mile stretch of the Palisades between the base of the cliffs and the low-tide mark in the river, thus denying access to the quarry operators. The commission estimated the cost at $350 per acre; total price, $260,000.

Unknown to them, a resident from across the Hudson was about to join their cause and would become crucial to their task. From his Glyndor (Wave Hill) Estate on the eastern shoreline of the river, George Walbridge Perkins was keenly aware of the Palisades. The cliffs were boldly within his view. He could hear the blasting, see the smoke and dust, and feel the tremors. The reverberating explosions would awaken Perkins's napping two-year-old child. The destructive activities of the Carpenter Brothers and other bluestone quarry operators would draw Perkins along a path of civic duty that would span two decades and involve his family for a century. He would establish precedent-setting momentum for the creation of parks and historic sites—actions that would bring energy and skill to the nation's fledgling conservation movement and place him squarely between two giant achievers whose opposing philosophies were legend, John Pierpont Morgan and Roosevelt.

According to biographer John Garraty,

George Perkins is a man little known today but was one of the most successful, controversial, and interesting Americans of the early twentieth century. The story of his rise from obscure beginnings to wealth and power would have strained the credulity of Horatio Alger's most devoted readers. Son of the warden of a boy's reformatory, he never went to high school but was invited to lecture at Columbia University. His father thought him slow in the head, but he revolutionized the insurance business, mastered the most complicated problems of corporate finance, developed the Palisades Interstate Park, guided creation of the International Harvester Corporation, made millions of dollars—and helped to organize and run Theodore Roosevelt's "Bull Moose" Progressive Party.

So compelling was his personality that Morgan offered him a partnership (plus $125,000 for a worthy cause close to Perkins's heart) the first time they met. The jealous leaders of the hotly competitive farm-machinery industry, unable to agree about the value of their properties, asked Perkins to assess them and promised in advance to accept his decision. The Russian Finance Minister, the shrewd and powerful Sergei Witte, was so captivated that he refused to license American competitors of Perkins's life insurance company. Wall Streeters called him a socialist and Western reformers considered him a tool of Wall Street. A fierce competitor, he devoted his last years to arguing for the concept of industrial co-operation. He was a striking figure because he differed in so many respects from his business contemporaries; yet, we can see now, he also typified his times. Many of his fellows shared his interest in public service, but few formed ways of expressing their interest so forcefully and imaginatively.

George Walbridge Perkins, Palisades Interstate Park Commissioner, 1900–1920. *(Courtesy of PIPC Archives)*

Born in Chicago in 1862, Perkins died at age fifty-eight in Stamford, Connecticut. During his lifetime, and almost by accident, he became one of the nation's great environmental champions. A glimpse of the Perkins's style occurred in 1911 when he appeared as a witness before a congressional committee investigating Morgan's alleged manipulation of the stock market. "What do you say to the statement that the panic was started to get rid of certain undesirable bankers, and that you gentlemen later were unable to manage it?" Congressman Charles L. Bartlett asked Perkins. In an article in the *New Yorker*, Perkins was reported to have stood up in "high theatrical dudgeon," slammed his fist on the table, and retorted, "I say that there never was a more infamous lie started than that. There is not a scintilla of truth in it.

You might just as well say that a certain group of gentlemen made a contract with Mrs. O'Leary's cow to kick over the lamp that set Chicago on fire."

Perkins had wanted to be a missionary, but thin family finances prevented him from gaining the necessary training. Instead, he joined the New York Life Insurance Company as a clerk at age seventeen. In his mid-twenties, Perkins was selling insurance from Wichita to Denver. By age thirty, he placed his net worth at $51,000 and had arrived as third vice-president at the head office in New York City, where he assumed direct supervision of New York Life's branch-office system. He and his wife, Evelyn Ball Perkins, searched for a home in the metropolitan area and found a very pleasing property in Riverdale-on-the-Hudson with a commanding view of the Palisades. This view would prompt the first contact with Morgan, putting Perkins on an unforeseen path leading to great personal wealth. By age forty he would be a millionaire many times over. But even more, the thunder of dynamiting in the Palisades would draw Perkins along as an unexpected participant in the scenic and historic conservation movement. In the process, he would learn that conservation and controversy are almost interchangeable words.

In 1900, when the second Palisades study commission was reporting to Governors Roosevelt and Voorhees, Perkins had other issues on his mind. For him, the decade of the 1890s "had been one long triumph," according to his biographer. Perkins reached an annual pay level of $30,000 and as second-in-command of the world's largest insurance company enjoyed the allegiance of New York Life agents across the country. He had instituted a pension plan for the agents, favored steady sales over high-pressure tactics, believed in profit sharing. Reasoning that local agents could best serve their clients if they were given better financial incentives and confined by less red tape, Perkins took steps to eliminate forty-four regional agencies in favor of 208 local offices. Old-guard middle managers were eliminated and their traditional profit cuts went, instead, to the local agents, all of whom reported directly to Perkins. As far as the agents were concerned, their loyalties rested squarely with the young vice president in New York City.

In the 1890s, when the massacre of Sioux Indians at Wounded Knee in Dakota territory was seen juxtaposed against the founding of the *Wall Street Journal,* the construction of Carnegie Hall, and the opening of an immigration center on Ellis Island, the nation was still struggling to come of age and find its way in the international arena. With limited success, American insurance companies were turning toward Europe and had established footholds in England, France, and Russia. But the lucrative German market, that held the Swiss, Austrian, and Polish markets in its orbit, was closed to American insurance companies. The financially conservative Germans were leery of upstart insurance vendors from the United States. Competition among American insurers was intense, and a breakthrough into the German market would be an impressive feat. Perkins took it upon himself to break through. On several transatlantic trips, he negotiated with German insurance regulators and invited them to visit New York Life to examine the books. In response to German concerns, he convinced his corporate colleagues to forsake stock-market investments in favor of the safer investment harbor of bonds. With this assurance of financial stability, New York Life won the sole privilege to sell insurance in Germany, to the exclusion of its competitors, Mutual and Equitable Life Insurance companies.

It was this success in Germany that brought Perkins face to face with Governor Roosevelt. The competing insurance companies were seeking passage of a so-called "Limitation Bill" that, if approved by the New York Legislature and signed by the governor, would place a $1.25 billion cap on the amount of insurance-in-force that any company could carry. Ostensibly, Mutual and Equitable argued that the Limitation Bill would encourage competition and reduce insurance costs for working men and women, but the real purpose was to box in New York Life so that the smaller companies could gain a larger market share. Perkins said the legislation was "enough to make a man's hair turn white" and sought a meeting with the governor.

On March 7, 1900, the two men met. The directness and clarity of Perkins's presentation to Roosevelt convinced the governor that the Limitation Bill should not become law. The governor signaled to legislative leaders that he would not sign the bill, and it was withdrawn.

Whether Roosevelt and Perkins touched on the punishment being visited by quarry operators on the Palisades during this meeting is unrecorded, but the second study commission, including Vermilye and Gains, had effectively accomplished its work. Fifteen days after the Roosevelt-Perkins meeting, on March 22, 1900, legislation reached the governor that would "establish the Commissioners of the Palisades Interstate Park." As authorized by the legislation, the commissioners could "provide for the selection, location, appropriation, and management of certain lands along the Palisades of the Hudson River for an interstate park, and thereby preserve the scenery of the Palisades." The legislation allowed the governor of New York to appoint ten commissioners, five of whom must be residents of New York and five residents of New Jersey. The legislation included $10,000 in operating funds. Similar legislation was making its way through the New Jersey Legislature, but Roosevelt's signature was first on record, marking the initial step in what, for him, would become a national conservation legacy of immense proportions.

Perkins was vacationing in Lakewood, New Jersey, when the Palisades bill was signed. Roosevelt telephoned Perkins to say that he wanted Perkins to serve on the newly authorized interstate park commission. When Perkins asked for time to "think about it," the governor responded by saying, "I did not call you up, Mr. Perkins, to ask you to consider this thing; I called you up to tell you that you are President of the Commissioners of the Palisades Interstate Park."

One arm of the interstate commission was in place, but New Jersey Governor Voorhees was contending with opposition from landowners on the summit of the Palisades and quarry operators who warned about the loss of tax revenues, restrictions on development, and job loss. To counter these contentions, the New Jersey Federation of Women's Clubs swamped the legislature with letters, news articles, and personal visits. In various attempts to head off the women, the Palisades legislation was rewritten several times. A particular sticking point was the word *appropriation,* which had been included in the New York version of the legislation. This word, if included as well in the New Jersey version, meant that the commissioners of the interstate park would have the power to condemn and take privately owned land over the objections of landowners. Advocates for protection of the Palisades considered this power to be essential if the legislation were to have any real force at all. In a victory for Vermilye and her women's club collaborators, opposition to the legislation was overcome. Several weeks after Roosevelt signed his bill, Governor Voorhees did the same, with the power of condemnation intact and an appropriation of $5,000 for operating expenses.

Vermilye and Gaines hoped that their persistence, their service on the second study commission, and the hard-won legislative victory in New Jersey would propel them to appointments on the newly authorized interstate park commission, but the wisdom of the day was that "some male members would be less free in their deliberations if women also served." Vermilye and Gaines were denied. Appointed to the Palisades Interstate Park Commission by the two governors were Perkins, New York; Nathan Barrett, New York; D. McNeeley Stauffer, New York; Ralph Trautman, New York; J. DuPratt White, New York; W. A. Linn, New Jersey; Abram S. Hewitt, New Jersey; Col. Edwin A. Stevens, New Jersey; Franklin W. Hopkins, New Jersey; and Abram De Ronde, New Jersey.

Colonel Stevens was chosen as the first president of the Commission but soon deferred to Perkins, surely to the delight of Roosevelt. Technically, there were two separate ten-member commissions, but the membership was identical. The commissioners would meet on New Jersey matters, adjourn, and then call to order a meeting on New York matters. Their agenda was self-evident. Facing the newly appointed commissioners was increasingly aggressive quarrying and a patchwork of 147 privately owned land parcels scattered over about three thousand acres stretching along the Palisades for fourteen miles from Fort Lee, New Jersey, to the New Jersey–New York border. Land on the summit of the cliffs was generally valued at $3,000 per acre; land along the shoreline at the base of the cliffs was slightly less. Perkins and his fellow commissioners had $15,000 and the authority to receive, control, and invest money, purchase land and property, construct facilities, maintain and operate parks, and take legal action as needed. They had inadequate funding, no staff, no office, and no clear understanding of park stewardship. They knew only that they somehow were to conserve open space and natural beauty in the nation's most densely populated metropolitan region.

Ownership of Palisades land was constantly changing. Ulysses S. Grant had once owned a Palisades parcel, and Susan B. Anthony still did. She would find herself negotiating with the commissioners for its purchase. At the northern end of the Palisades, near Piermont, New York, a terminus of the "underground railroad" prior to the Civil War, former slaves had established Skunk Hollow. At one time, seventy-five black farmers wrenched a marginal living from the rocky soil before selling out and moving on. At the base of the cliffs, a few elderly widows, the last of more than eight hundred fishermen, boat builders, and their families who had settled after the Revolutionary War in the loosely defined community of Undercliff, lived in small shacks to which they had no legal claim, always fearful of eviction.

In 1858 Joseph Lamb built Falcon Lodge, the first of many summer homes along the Palisades summit that would be dubbed "millionaires' row." To reach his lodge on summer weekends, Lamb would ride up the east side of the Hudson on the New York Central Railroad line until opposite his property, ask for a special train stop, debark to be met at a prearranged rendezvous point by a shad fisherman who would row Lamb across the river, and from the shore he would climb a rugged trail to his lodge. A three-hundred-room hotel, the Palisades Mountain House, had been constructed in 1860 at a choice summit location, offering expansive views, landscaped grounds, bowling, billiards, fine dining, and music. The Mountain House was a favorite of well-to-do city dwellers who found respite there from crowded, pungent New York City. Atop the cliffs, William Dana, publisher and editor of the *New York World,* had built Greycliff in the 1850s. Cuban sugar baron Manuel Riondo arrived on the Palisades in 1904, four years after the interstate park commission was formed, and built an estate home on his two-hundred-acre Rio Vista property, complete with a one-hundred-foot-high water tower. Charles Nordhoff, editor of the *New York Herald,* who had sent Henry M. Stanley to Africa in 1869 in search of Dr. David Livingston, had a home on millionaires' row, as did John Ringling of Ringling Brothers, Barnum & Bailey Circus. A much later arrival was Anthony Fokker, the Dutch engineer who had designed the tri-wing airplane flown with such deadly success by Manfred von Richthofen, the "Red Baron," during World War I.

The eclectic collection of owners on the summit and along the base of the Palisades was of interest to Perkins as he assumed command of the Palisades Interstate Park Commission (PIPC). He and his fellow commissioners, who began meeting regularly at Perkins's office, 346 Broadway in the city, used $3,000 of the meager financial war chest to retain the services of C. C. Vermule, a reputable engineer from Englewood, New Jersey, who was charged with surveying the Palisades to untangle questions of ownership and property lines.

But Perkins's primary target was the Carpenter Brothers. He was determined to end their battering of the cliffs and the resulting assault on the sensibilities and quality of life of residents in the lower Hudson River Valley. In October, 1900, Perkins contacted George and Aaron Carpenter, beginning a negotiation that would span several weeks. Many highly successful, socially astute, patrician businessmen of the day might not have been willing to sit down with two hard-scrabble, blue-collar, tough-minded quarrymen to try to hammer out a deal, preferring, instead, to defer to lawyers. Not so Perkins: he sat across the table from the Carpenters and their lawyer to seek a purchase agreement.

The asking price started at $200,000, then was "shaded" to $190,000. Perkins offered $100,000. The Carpenters countered. They boosted the price back to $200,000 but said they would contribute $25,000 to the PIPC if the deal was made. By mid-December, after several sessions, the Carpenters were flirting with $145,000 and the commissioners were pushing for $125,000. Blasting was continuing apace. The Carpenters were racing to produce as much crushed rock as possible before a sale agreement was reached. Finally, Perkins secured an option-to-purchase for $132,500, using the $10,000 of New York money for the down payment. No one bothered to ask whether spending New York money to buy land in New Jersey was legal. That detail aside, Perkins was short $122,500 to bring the transaction to closure.

While the negotiations were under way, James Stillman, president of the National City Bank of New York, had tapped Perkins to join the bank's board of directors. In a letter to Stillman many years later, Perkins said, "You were the first man from the financial district to invite me to be connected with any of the important financial interests downtown, and I have always felt that this led to openings that have given me exceptional opportunities to broaden my education and better equip me for the work of the world." How right he was. One of the "financial interests downtown" was J. P. Morgan, who had quietly taken note of Perkins when New York Life started investing in bonds as a result of the insurance agreement with Germany, and again when Perkins joined the board of one of the city's major banks.

Perkins was searching for private funds to complete the purchase from the Carpenter Brothers. Morgan, logically, was on his list of potential donors, although Perkins did not know the legendary financier and industrial magnate. In December, Perkins asked Robert Bacon, a fellow member of the National City Bank's board, and a Morgan partner, to act as an intermediary in arranging a meeting with Morgan. Though unaware of Morgan's interest in him, Perkins was certainly aware of the giant reputation of the man he was about to meet.

Morgan controlled railroads, steel mills, and shipping at the very core of America's industrial revolution. Reputed to be brusque, hardheaded, demanding, and distrustful of publicity, Morgan was also renowned as a philanthropist. On his personal list of charitable projects were the American Museum of Natural History, the Metropolitan Museum of Art, Madison Square Garden, the Morgan libraries, the Cathedral of Saint John the Divine, the American Academy of Rome, and the Harvard Medical School.

At the meeting in Morgan's 23 Wall Street office, Bacon introduced the two men, then left them to their private conversation. As biographer Garraty chronicled the conversation:

> Perkins launched at once into the story of the Palisades, but after a moment or two Morgan interrupted.
>
> "I know all about that. You are Chairman of the Commission. What do you want?"
>
> "I want to raise $125,000."
>
> "All right, put me down for $25,000. It is a good thing. Is that all?"
>
> Perkins, delighted but probably off balance by the rapid exchange, asked Morgan whom else might be approached for a contribution. Morgan suggested John D. Rockefeller, Sr. Expressing gratitude for the fund-raising pledge and advice, Perkins rose to leave.
>
> "I will give you the whole $125,000 if you will do something for me."
>
> "Do something for you, what?"
>
> "Take that desk over there."
>
> "I have a pretty good desk up at New York Life."
>
> "No, I mean come into the firm."

With lightning speed, and on first meeting J. P. Morgan, Perkins was being offered a breathless leap to the very pinnacle of the financial world.

"I'll have to think about it."

"Certainly. Let me know tomorrow if you can."

The decision was not easy for Perkins. Morgan was a notorious taskmaster, and friends, family, and professional colleagues were giving Perkins mixed advice. New York Life responded by raising Perkins's annual salary from $30,000 to $75,000. Incredible as the conversation had been with Morgan, Perkins made an equally improbable decision. He said no.

Two months later, Perkins found himself having breakfast with the persistent Morgan at his mansion on Park Avenue. Morgan appealed to the young man by saying that Perkins's management skills were needed to respond to complex social and economic problems, that relationships between corporations, their employees, and the public must be improved, and that Perkins was the man for the job. On agreement that he could continue part-time with New York Life, Perkins acquiesced and joined the Morgan partnership, placing him near the summit of turn-of-the-century America's robust banking and corporate structures.

The Morgan check for $125,000 put Perkins and the commissioners of the Palisades Interstate Park in the position to close the deal with the Carpenter Brothers. On Christmas Eve, 1900, the dynamiting of the New Jersey Palisades ceased. The silence was a wonderful holiday gift for thousands of Hudson River Valley residents. Boss Blaster Hugh Reilly, who symbolically and actually represented all that caused the interstate park commission to be formed, was not a witness to the finish of the Carpenter Brothers' quarrying. Earlier in the year, while walking at night along a narrow trail at the edge of the Palisades precipice, he had slipped and fallen. His body had been found the following morning at the base of the cliffs.

3.
Upriver

In addition to raiding New York Life of its star executive, J. P. Morgan had one other condition in mind when he startled George Perkins with the offer to donate the entire $125,000 to save the Palisades. Morgan wanted to leverage the money. Years of looking for the maximum benefit in any transaction had honed his financial touch, and his response to the needs of the fledgling Palisades Interstate Park Commission was in keeping with his usual course of action. Morgan instinctively saw an opportunity to seek further appropriations from New York and New Jersey in response to his generous and, incidentally, anonymous gift. He advised Perkins that his gift was conditioned on further action by the legislatures and governors of both states to provide "sufficient funds," estimated at $450,000, to acquire various properties on which the Commission had obtained willing-seller options. Even while the negotiations with the Carpenters were under way, Perkins, J. DuPratt White, and their fellow commissioners had obtained options on other properties from a variety of owners who either shared the concern for the future of the Palisades, saw a chance to cash in, or both.

Although Perkins could claim impressive success by reeling in the anonymous donation to silence the Carpenters, and enjoyed continuing public and media support for the Palisades initiative, the challenge presented to him by Morgan was daunting. In November, 1900, Perkins momentarily lost direct access to the executive chamber in Albany when the effervescent governor of New York, Theodore Roosevelt, only two years in office, was chosen at the Republican National Convention to run as the vice presidential candidate on the successful William McKinley ticket.

Succeeding Roosevelt as governor of New York was Republican Benjamin Odell. Odell was a pragmatic politician who knew that the defacement of the Palisades had jangled the nerves of many voters in his state, but to him, the fact remained that the cliffs were in New Jersey. Governor Voorhees of New Jersey, now approaching his last year in office, would have to take the lead in response to Morgan's financial challenge. In mid-January, 1901, Perkins assisted in preparing an article about the Palisades for *The New York Tribune.* He then purchased two thousand copies of the paper and arranged for their delivery to each member of the New Jersey and New York Legislatures. Spreading around loads of newspapers with Perkins's article was not going to be enough. On January 27 a special article in the *Times* cautioned, "Palisade Plans in Danger." Legislators from central and southern New Jersey, who had resisted the original bill that created the Commission, were resisting again. "The prejudice that exists is as fixed as the rocks of the Palisades are now, and worse still, there is a widespread disinclination to be informed on the subject. The newspapers in the lower part of the State have treated the proposition flippantly and have prepared the legislators to resist any attempt that will be made to secure an appropriation for the Palisades scheme." New Jersey legislators, always suspicious of New York motives, did not want to be drawn into an extended financial commitment that seemingly brought no benefit to their constituents. The two states had once almost come to military blows over an early boundary dispute, and despite a closely shared history and common commercial and cultural ties, New York had the reputation either of bullying or ignoring its smaller, more rural neighbor. Of the eighty-one members of the New Jersey Legislature, no more than twenty favored more money to buy land on the Palisades.

Elizabeth Vermilye, denied a position on the Commission because of her gender, and largely redirecting her energies elsewhere, nonetheless was about to pull yet another political rabbit out of the hat. In February, 1901, she presided over the first meeting of the League for the Preservation of the Palisades. Formed only eight years after John Muir formed the Sierra Club in California, this citizen's group of activists became a forerunner of the many advocate organizations that would arise in later years to push for federal and state conservation projects. The National Audubon Society, The Nature Conservancy, the New York–New Jersey Trail Conference, Scenic Hudson, the Environmental Defense Fund, the Open Space Institute, the Natural Resources Defense Council, the Adirondack Mountain Club, the Passaic River Coalition, the Open Space Institute, the Trust for Public Land, the Appalachian Mountain Club, the American Canoe Association, the National Trust for Historic Preservation, Trout Unlimited, and many similar organizations, all with deep roots in New York and New Jersey, would have found kindred spirits among the League's volunteers. Among the many people joining Vermilye were Mrs. Ernest Thompson-Seaton, wife of the respected writer, naturalist, and scientist; her friend and colleague Cecilia Gaines, now married to John Holland; Mrs. W. A. Roebling, whose husband presided over the construction of the Brooklyn Bridge; and cliff-top property owners Mrs. Frederick Lamb and Mrs. Ralph Trautman. Frederick Lamb had served on the first Palisades study commission, Ralph Trautman on the second. The Lambs and Trautmans would remain watchful of the Palisades and the PIPC's activities from generation to generation.

This influential group assertively made its wishes known at legislative hearings in Trenton. At the same hearings, Commissioner Franklin W. Hopkins testified on behalf of the PIPC. (The Reverend) Doctor Laidlaw, spokesperson for the Federation of Churches, appeared at the hearings and urged the protection of nature's beauty. Governor Odell had already signaled Vermilye that an appropriation of $400,000 might be forthcoming from New York if New Jersey took the lead. Press reports to the contrary, the New Jersey votes were found. Governor Voorhees signed a bill on March 22, 1901, that appropriated $50,000 more for the Palisades and included a reiteration of the eminent-domain authority, should the Commission need to force the sale of privately owned land to protect the cliffs and shoreline.

In April, legislators in Albany followed New Jersey and appropriated $400,000 to the Commission, conveniently ignoring again the matter of how these funds could legally be spent to buy land in another state. Governor Odell approved the bill. Thanks to the Morgan challenge, the PIPC's funding leaped from $15,000 to $465,000 in state appropriations, plus the $125,000 "anonymous" gift, allowing for closure on options already negotiated by Perkins and his colleagues. The creation of a park and historic-site system began. Controversy followed immediately.

During the debate in Albany, legislators were left with the impression that the State of New Jersey was donating riparian (underwater) land, estimated to be worth over $1 million, to the PIPC as a major supplement to its appropriation of $50,000. Based on this assurance of "handsome" generosity by New Jersey, New Yorkers promptly acted to support the PIPC, only to discover after the fact that the PIPC's claim to title for New Jersey riparian lands was seriously in doubt. PIPC Secretary White felt the heat. A New York assemblyman, quoted in the *Hoboken Observer,* said, "Now, Mr. Secretary White can take either horn of the dilemma he pleases—he is sure to be impaled. If his inter-state commission has a gift of $1,270,000 worth of riparian lands from the state, it has something the state can't give. If his inter-state commission has no gift of riparian lands, as he says, then New York State has been what the sports call 'conned' out of $400,000." New Jersey officials who served on the state's Riparian Board were amused. They hadn't been involved in legislative actions regarding the Palisades and did not know of the assurances given in Albany about lands they owned and controlled. The secretary of the Riparian Board was in doubt about whether legislation that directed the PIPC to "improve the water's edge" included riparian land beyond the water's edge. After due deliberation, the Riparian Board concluded that the New Jersey Legislature must have "contemplated" that the river view from the Palisades shoreline would be preserved, and that riparian lands adjacent to the cliffs, therefore, should not be sold for the development of docks or industrial sites.

As events would prove, White was anything but a con man. He had attended Cornell University on a scholarship; he had been admitted to the New York Bar in 1892 and had co-founded the law firm White & Case. He later demonstrated gratitude to his alma mater by serving for many years on Cornell's Board of Trustees and led a fund-raising campaign that raised $6 million for the university. At his death almost four decades later in 1939, White was serving as the Commission's president.

Fortunately for White and his fellow commissioners, timely acquiescence by the New Jersey Riparian Board on the question of underwater rights along the Palisades shoreline took the bite out of this first controversy. It was promptly forgotten by politicians and the press.

With funds in hand, the PIPC commissioners hired their first employee in

J. DuPratt White, Palisades Interstate Park Commissioner, 1900–1938. *(Courtesy of PIPC Archives)*

April, 1901. Not surprisingly, Leonard Hull Smith was a lawyer: annual pay, $1,200. Moving quickly through the summer and fall, concentrating solely on the cliff face and shoreline of the Palisades, Perkins was able to report at a Commission meeting in mid-October that lands had been purchased from the estate of George Green, the Mahan heirs, Charles W. Opdyke, E. Ellen Anderson, John S. Lysle, the estate of William Walter Phelps, Jacob S. Wetmore, the Allison Land Company, the estate of George S. Coe, the estate of William B. Dana, Henry W. Banks, the Van Brunt Properties, and, of course, the Carpenter Brothers.

Soon after this meeting, a small article appeared in *The New York Times* under the interesting headline "A Landscape Engineer Employed to Study and Preserve the Rocks." The PIPC had retained Charles W. Levitt, Jr., civil engineer and landscape gardener—who, later in his career, would win kudos for landscape and design projects at the Saratoga and Belmont Park horse racetracks. Levitt's arrival signaled that the Commission was not content with a preserved view of the Palisades from the Hudson River and the eastern shoreline. The PIPC wanted to develop public access to the summit of the cliffs and build a carriage road along the base. It intended to invite an urban population to seek out and enjoy this wild and rugged land, though it as yet had no idea what rules should apply to public visitation.

By early 1902 the Commission was in the process of acquiring thirty-four additional properties, spending funds from New Jersey and New York almost as rapidly as money arrived in the bank account of the PIPC's land-acquisition arm, the Perkins-organized Palisades Improvement Company. Perkins used this subsidiary "company" to avoid government red tape and move quickly when land-buying opportunities beckoned. The strategy of Perkins and White was to enlist the support of property owners in the worthy purposes of the PIPC. They did so by encouraging the donation of the vertical cliff face, while offering $500 per acre for land between the base of the cliff and the shoreline, avoiding, if possible, the mention of their authority to condemn and take land against an owner's wishes. Many of these properties had been owned by the same family for several generations and were held in small, undivided interests by widely scattered children, grandchildren, and other heirs. In one instance, the Commission had to acquire a 1/240th interest in a 2.25 acre parcel from a person living in the State of Washington. During this transaction, questions were raised about the wording in the first deed after its delivery on the West Coast via train and horse carriage. Back came the flawed document. After the wording was corrected, a second deed was sent across the country and the necessary owner's signature affixed—purchase price, $3.28. Some of the properties included houses or cottages that the PIPC began to rent, always searching for ways to build its income to meet day-to-day staff and management expenses. But the PIPC made an exception to this rental policy for a property operated as a carcass-filled, smelly fat-rendering plant on the Hudson River shoreline: the commissioners demanded immediate possession and scheduled the removal of the plant.

Because of all the focus on the New Jersey Palisades, quarrying activities started sprouting upriver in New York at Nyack, Haverstraw, and Hook Mountain. The quarry operators, shut down in New Jersey, simply moved beyond the PIPC's grasp, but not for long. The same citizen hue and cry that had stopped the Carpenter Brothers was heard again, this time in Albany. With the media already attuned to the problem and reporting success in New Jersey, the New York Legislature responded to the new quarry threat by passing legislation expanding the PIPC's activities into Rockland County, just north of the New Jersey–New York border. The bill included a provision to transfer stewardship of the Revolutionary War Stony Point Battlefield from the American Scenic and Historic Preservation Society to the PIPC. The Society had acquired this spectacular and historically dramatic site in 1898 and favored its transfer to the fledgling park-management agency. This action, and an earlier initiative taken by the PIPC to gather information about the Fort Lee Revolutionary War Site in New Jersey, began to suggest that historic preservation, as well as the protection of scenic lands, might share the banner of the PIPC's conservation experiment.

The legislative invitation to the PIPC to step across the border into New York did not guarantee that the upriver quarry operations would disappear overnight. Blasting at Nyack and Hook Mountain could be seen and heard across the river in Tarrytown, New York. One observer, who owned a 3,500-acre estate high in the Pocantico Hills above Tarrytown, was John D. Rockefeller, Sr. From Kykuit, his baronial home, Rockefeller had a direct view of Hook Mountain and Nyack. The view was so compelling that Alfred Bierstadt, among the most famous of the Hudson River School artists, captured the scene from a location near where Kykuit stands today. The scene is of meadows decorated with ancient trees, gently sloping downward to the shore of the Hudson, edged by the broad river, and held by the soft, hazy background of Hook Mountain and a blue, cloud-touched sky.

Kykuit was constructed under the watchful eye of the elder Rockefeller's son, John D., Jr., but Rockefeller, Sr., known for his immense success in business and interest in economics, had personally designed the landscaping plan that emphasized "bursting views of river, hill, cloud, and the great sweep of the country." This sense of design and appreciation for natural beauty was accepted

John D. Rockefeller.
(Courtesy of the Rockefeller Archive Center)

by Rockefeller, Jr., in a way that would leave an eloquent legacy of conservation for the nation, from Maine to the Caribbean, from Williamsburg to the redwood forests of California, and down through the Rocky Mountain region, encompassing Yellowstone, the Grand Tetons, and Native American cultures. In *John D. Rockefeller, Jr., A Portrait,* Raymond B. Fosdick stated that Rockefeller, Jr., "had known and loved the Palisades since his boyhood days when he often used to take his horse across the Hudson on the Fort Lee ferry and ride for hours beneath the cliff and through the woods to the top." Rockefeller, Jr., tracked with growing interest the effort by Perkins, the New Jersey Federation of Women's Clubs, and their allies to stop the blasting farther downriver. Now his family could hear, see, and feel explosions almost at the doorstep of their Tarrytown estate.

In letters of March 18 and 31, 1902, to Lieutenant Governor Woodruff and Governor Odell of New York, Rockefeller, Jr., took up the PIPC's cause by championing an expansion of its activities into New York. Perkins was communicating with Governor Odell at the same time, and he and Rockefeller, Jr., were exchanging letters on the subject. But a red flag fluttered in a mid-March letter to Rockefeller, Jr., from James P. McQuaide, a Nyack resident: "There has been strong opposition by the people who have stone crushers in Haverstraw, the principal being General Hedges, who, for many years, was the leading Republican politician in Rockland County." McQuaide's concern was well founded. When the legislation to expand the PIPC's activities arrived on the desk of Governor Odell, he vetoed it. For the time being, the drive to expand the PIPC into New York was dead.

Struggling with the demands of property negotiation, ill political winds in New York, growing public enthusiasm for access to the Palisades, and budding interest in the Fort Lee Revolutionary War site, the PIPC was startled by the death on January 19, 1903, of one of its founding members, Abram S. Hewitt.

Hewitt's father had been a mechanic and his mother the daughter of a farmer. Born in 1822, Abram attended public schools in New York City and opened his first door to opportunity by successfully competing for a scholarship to Columbia University, where he earned a Doctor of Law degree in 1857. During his undergraduate days, he and his friend Edward Cooper toured Europe and luckily survived a shipwreck when returning to America. Hewitt landed ashore in a borrowed sailor's suit with three silver dollars in his pocket. The two Columbia classmates, now related by the marriage of Edward's sister, Sarah, to Abram, formed the firm Cooper & Hewitt, specializing in the manufacture of iron and laying the cornerstone for Cooper Union Institute in 1854. Hewitt served as permanent secretary for the board of trustees of the Institute, eventually donating about $1 million to the college.

Skilled in the techniques of iron manufacture, Cooper & Hewitt predictably was pulled into the Civil War by the demand for armaments. Traveling to Birmingham, England, in 1862, Hewitt was mistaken for an agent of the Confederacy and willingly encouraged this misconception. England was sympathetic to the South, and Hewitt, playing on this sympathy, succeeded in purchasing every gun, sword, and pistol in Birmingham, then discreetly arranged for their shipment to Union troops. In the best cloak-and-dagger style, Hewitt was suspected in the United States of being a Copperhead, a Yankee who worked secretly for the Confederacy. One person who knew otherwise was President Abraham Lincoln. While at the home of his father-in-law, Hewitt received a dispatch from Lincoln, printed on a strip of paper said to be 150-feet long, lamenting the fact that Gen. Ulysses S. Grant urgently needed twelve mortars for an attack on two Confederate fortifications. The Ordnance Department had promised delivery within one year—could Hewitt do better? He delivered the mortars in twenty-eight days.

Inspired by his friend Cooper, who became mayor of New York City, Hewitt entered politics and was elected to the House of Representatives in 1874, serving until 1886. He developed a strong reputation as a skilled strategist and adept debater who effectively convinced Congress to approve the creation of the Geological Survey, an agency whose purpose is to measure the natural wealth of the nation. But other political goals beckoned. At the end of his term in Congress, Hewitt ran as a Democrat for New York mayor and prevailed over the Labor candidate, Henry George, and the Republican, Theodore Roosevelt. After his term as mayor, Hewitt switched his legal residency from New York to New Jersey in 1898 and was subsequently appointed to the PIPC by Governor Voorhees. His business interests expanded in many directions, including railroads, mining, banking, and bridge building, but the American Geographic Society, the Museum of Natural History, and other scientific institutions remained steadily at the core of his interests.

Sudden illness at age eighty took Hewitt from his newest avocation, the PIPC, and left unfulfilled the promise of seasoned political aptitude and scientific prestige that he brought to the Commission's table. William Dana, owner of the *Financial Chronicle* and land on the summit of the Palisades, was appointed to succeed Hewitt.

Problems of property title, squatters, obscure owners, outright resistance, and slow action by New York's comptroller to dispense appropriated funds continued to plague the PIPC's land-acquisition initiatives. Still, the PIPC minutes continued to confirm progress and success, including the acquisition of a parcel owned by eighty-four-year-old Susan B. Anthony. In March, 1905, the Commission offered $2,300 for the property. Anthony thought her land to be worth $2,400. The Commission paid $2,400.

As landholdings accumulated, so too did interest in camping, canoeing, picnicking, and hiking. The Commission held properties, some disconnected from its other holdings, sprinkled along fourteen miles of shoreline from Fort Lee, New Jersey, to Piermont, New York. Several key holdings remained for the moment beyond the PIPC's grasp, including an old, weatherworn house rumored to have been briefly commandeered 125 years earlier by Lord Cornwallis, whose British troops had struggled up the Palisades in a vain attempt to capture Gen. George Washington. Warned in time, Washington retreated into New Jersey. Those few fishermen or their widows who continued to cling to squatter's shacks along the river shore were convinced that the ghost of Cornwallis returned every November. To shouted orders for king and country, the supernatural Cornwallis would beseech his phantom troops to briskly gouge out a rough road to the top of the cliffs so that the redcoats could rush forward in a single dramatic action to capture the upstart rebel general and his so-called officers, thus putting a swift end to an irritating peasant insurrection.

Ghost or no ghost, the use of newly acquired PIPC-owned lands was beginning to flourish. Members of the American Canoe Association applied for and received permission to camp under the cliffs. Four hundred canoeists, paddling across from New York City, took advantage of the opportunity. Hundreds of others decided that this idea of camping was grand and availed themselves of cost-free permits from the PIPC, even as the commissioners began to debate the merits and purposes of the park they were creating.

The need for this debate was underscored by a fast-developing perception that the Palisades was a "lawless" place on Sundays and holidays when great crowds came to recreate outside the usual police controls by which a metropolitan population lived. In 1905 the PIPC managed to retain the services of only one law-enforcement marshal, stationed at the Alpine ferry landing, who was supposed to patrol the entire fourteen-mile river frontage. The assumption was that a few well-behaved people might occasionally wander along the rugged shore; the reality was that the preserved, wild open space was a magnet for city dwellers, and the crowds were beginning to overwhelm the commissioners, who had been thinking in terms of a static, protected scene, not a dynamic, much-in-demand people's park.

Perhaps it was the sudden popularity of the work-in-progress park or the burden of continuing the complex property transactions, or both, that caused the PIPC to decline a suggestion made by Mrs. E. B. Miles, who proposed that the PIPC join with the New Jersey State Federation of Women's Clubs by securing a site on the Palisades to honor and memorialize the role of women in the fight to save the cliffs. In a ponderous response, the Commission advised Miles that it "was not in a position to take official action in that direction." Subsequent Commission minutes confirm a flow of "communications" on the matter of a women's memorial. The battle-tested women, who had successfully confronted the Carpenter Brothers and the New Jersey Legislature, were not about to take no for an answer from the very Commission they had helped create. For their part, the commissioners, on further consideration, referred the matter to White.

For parallel reasons, the 1902 veto by Governor Odell of legislation to extend the jurisdiction of the Commission into New York could not and would not be forgotten—could not because every morning and evening dynamite blasts from the quarries at Hook Mountain could be heard for twenty miles up and down the Hudson River, and would not because Rockefeller, Sr., John Speyer, and other wealthy residents were offering to help pay the expenses for Commission activities if New York would extend the PIPC's jurisdiction to the Stony Point Battlefield, fifteen miles upriver from the New Jersey–New York border. In January, 1906, a new bill was introduced for this purpose, ironically by a New York senator named Carpenter, no relation to Aaron and George. Governor Odell had left office in 1904; it would be up to his successor, Frank W. Higgins, to judge the merits of the new legislation.

The hint of financial support from wealthy New Yorkers prompted Governor Higgins to suggest that written guarantees from private individuals to cover whatever funds might be needed for the PIPC's future acquisitions would be required in order to gain favorable consideration by the new legislation. This induced Starr J. Murphy, a Rockefeller staff member, writing jointly on behalf of Rockefeller, Jr., and Morgan, to urge Timothy L. Woodruff, an influential businessman and banker with close ties to Higgins, to seek the governor's reconsideration. According to Murphy,

This suggestion seems to indicate an entire misconception as to the nature of the pending bill to extend the limits of the Palisades Park. The beauty of the Hudson River is one of the great scenic attractions of the eastern part of the United States; it probably draws more visitors to this State than any other single feature outside of Niagara Falls, and the movement to preserve it is of the same public character as the movement to preserve the Falls, or the Yellowstone Park, or the Yosemite Valley. When the original Palisades Park was established no such assurances were required, and yet, outside of the original appropriation which I understand was spent entirely for acreage property and has not yet been exhausted, whatever funds were needed for acquiring business properties the Commission was able to procure. All that is asked in this bill is an extension of the powers of the Commission so as to enable it to acquire additional lands. These lands are just as much needed for the preservation of the scenic beauty of the Hudson as the lands taken under the original act.

Based on further detective work, Murphy wrote to Rockefeller, Jr., on March 22, 1906, and reported,

I met Mr. Woodruff (President of the Smith Premier Typewriter Company) at the Club today and had a little talk with him. He said he expected to attend a meeting of your Bible Class tonight and thinking that you might perhaps see him there I thought I would give you the situation up to date. He tells me that he thinks former Governor Odell is really back of the opposition. Odell is the member of the State Committee from Rockland County and the quarry owners are therefore his direct constituents.

Odell was fanning the rumor that Rockefeller, Sr., and Morgan had pledged to fully fund the 1902 bill. Their alleged failure to keep their pledges forced the veto. Senators allied with Odell were repeating this rumor as gospel to their colleagues and had obviously influenced Governor Higgins. Without using the phrase, Odell was accusing the Rockefellers and Morgan of being deadbeats.

The Hook Mountain quarry owners were also advancing another enterprising argument. They contended that if the Commission's authority were to be extended into their territory, a "cloud" would be cast on title to their land. They argued that the value of their property would decline because of the PIPC's suspected intent to use the power of eminent domain to force them from their quarry-site holdings. (This argument resonates to this day when property-rights promoters claim that zoning controls and similar development restrictions reduce land values. The reverse is consistently true.)

Lining up against Odell and his cohorts were, in addition to the PIPC, the Rockefellers, Morgan, Speyer, and other equally concerned Hudson River Valley property owners, the American Scenic and Historic Preservation Society, the Albany Day Line Steamers, and the New York Central Railroad. Collectively, these confederates, reflecting the earlier contest in New Jersey, wanted to rid the valley of the six quarries now scarring the riverside landscape in New York.

Among those joining in the cause to shut down this latest quarrying insult was Cleveland H. Dodge, one of the founders of Phelps-Dodge, a company that operated huge mines in the western United States. Destructive mining in remote sections of the West was one thing, but Dodge and his father, who lived on the eastern shoreline of the Hudson in Riverdale, New York, had low tolerance for the abusive tactics they were witnessing across the river. Just before the PIPC was formed, the Dodges headed off the quarry company Brown & Fleming by purchasing $25,000 worth of land that blocked the extension of the Brown & Fleming operation. They later donated some of this land to the PIPC and sold the rest at a loss. Dodge thought New York political leaders made a great tactical mistake in dissembling about the need to include vulnerable sections of New York shoreline in the original act that created the interstate commission. He added his considerable stature and influence to the debate about how to rectify this botched opportunity.

The combined force of advocacy overcame the Odell contingent. Chapter 691 of Laws of New York, 1906, extended the PIPC's jurisdiction to Hook Mountain. With the door open to New York, Perkins could take comfort in the fact that almost 80 percent of the fourteen-mile New Jersey shoreline had been acquired, despite the fact that New Jersey appropriations to cover the PIPC's expenses had dried up. In June, 1906, he and his fellow commissioners took a trip up the Hudson on the yacht *Mermaid* and dined that evening at a riverfront restaurant, surely relishing their accomplishments. With the acquisition of two rock-crusher plants owned by Delaney & Galligan, White, speaking for the Commission, was able to claim that "almost all danger points" along the New Jersey Palisades had been removed. Their volunteer efforts included the grand and the mundane. Among bills paid by the Commission was $9.34 to Standard Oil of New York for naphtha, $6.70 for two flags from the Warnock Uniform Company, a printing bill for $7.35, and $73.00 paid to John Jordan to take down the old fat-rendering factory. By the beginning of 1907, the Commission had expended $470,534.80 to purchase land.

White, who took on responsibility for the day-to-day operations of the experimental park on behalf of the widely traveling Perkins and the other commissioners, found himself grappling with a spectrum of issues that hinted at challenges to come. He was assisted by one legal assistant, paid $1,500 per year, and a law-enforcement marshal, retained for $15 per month. White paid the bills, always with the signature of a New York and New Jersey commissioner on each check, issued camping permits, dealt with the myriad details of land acquisition, hired surveyors and land appraisers, prepared leases, evicted squatters, responded to complaints, prepared reports, and began to define acceptable park uses. One man wanted to use the forests for random target practice. White thought that the unpredictable flight of rifle bullets through forested areas visited by park patrons was a bad idea. He said no. Two brothers, Obediah and John Older, held side-by-side leases to houses owned by the Commission. White ordered both brothers to vacate, explaining to one, "There has been so much trouble between your family and your brother's family that the Commissioners have decided that this is the only way to settle the whole matter." In a letter to Perkins, White suggested that "the PIPC needs a receptacle for its files and papers. The Commission has never bought any furniture, and owns none." Money was a persistent problem. Perkins and White continued to encounter difficulty with New York's comptroller, an official elected independently of the governor; this official responded slowly and sometimes disdainfully to the PIPC's vouchers sent forward for reimbursement.

The New Jersey women remained steadfast in their hope that a memorial would be erected to honor their cadre of pathfinding conservationists and, in the absence of progress toward this goal, collected $3,000 with the intention of buying a suitable site and donating its title to the Commission. Treasurer of the New Jersey arm of the PIPC, Abram De Ronde, came to the aid of the women, represented by Elizabeth Demerest, president of the Englewood Garden Club.

De Ronde, a native of Teaneck, New Jersey, started work while still a boy in New York City, attending school at night. He won early success in chemical manufacturing, then founded the Palisades Trust and Guarantee Company in Englewood, New Jersey. While serving a stint in the New Jersey Assembly in 1889–91, De Ronde, a Democrat, proposed an idea whose time had not yet come: the construction of a bridge across the Hudson from New York City to New Jersey. A charter appointee to the Commission, De Ronde's tenure with the PIPC would extend for thirty-seven years. This self-made man, who knew the value of a dollar, strongly objected to the idea that the women be forced to spend their own money to purchase a site for the women's memorial. He convinced Perkins, White, and his other Commission colleagues that the PIPC should set aside land for the purpose, thus allowing the women to reserve their funds for "immediate" construction of the memorial. For the women, this small victory was welcome, but the memorial itself would remain tantalizingly beyond their grasp for years.

In July, 1907, White posted a long memorandum to his colleagues in which he summarized the many complex issues that deserved further careful deliberation, including the Commission's role in the anticipated 1909 tercentenary celebration of the "discovery" of the Hudson River. In addition to property-acquisition challenges, primarily focused on entrenched owners who were not at all inclined to deal with the PIPC, White suggested the "construction of a continuous driveway from the Park south, connecting with the State roads of New Jersey, with the view of making the outlet for the great system of good roads in New York down through the Palisades Park. . . ." Perhaps unintentionally, or perhaps thinking conceptually, White floated the idea that a park driveway (parkway) might meander from urban center to urban center, through protected open space, giving travelers a respite through natural, uncluttered scenery—a journey through a linear park. In the early years of the twentieth century, this concept suggested the eventual achievement of the George Washington and Baltimore–Washington Parkways in the nation's capital; the Blue Ridge Parkway, from Virginia to North Carolina; the Natchez-Trace Parkway, from Tennessee to Mississippi; and the parkway network that fans out from New York City—roadways designed to rest easily on the land for the pleasure of motorists. A hint of the Palisades Interstate Parkway, now accommodating 65 million cars a year, cherished and cursed by New York and New Jersey motorists, was a glimmer in White's mind, even in an era when horse-drawn carriages still far outnumbered mechanically fractious cars.

White also lamented the PIPC's dilemma at Hook Mountain, pointing to the lack of appropriations even as New York extended the PIPC's authority northward, predicting that "it is exceedingly doubtful if it will ever be possible to accomplish the purpose of the act by an absolute purchase of the properties, and the destruction of the trap rock industry." He closed by stating, "Whatever is done should be formulated and undertaken without delay, as at the present time the Commission is being severely criticized for inaction and neglect. It is not important that such criticism is unjust. The fact is, that it exists and must be met."

Only weeks later, in November, 1907, an article appeared in *The Outlook* magazine entitled, "The Preservation of the Highlands of the Hudson First Publicly Advocated by Edward Lasell Partridge, M. D." In his article, Partridge looked far beyond the trap rock quarries, those lightning rods of smoke, thunder, and defacement that had galvanized conservation action along the Hudson. He looked at a spectacular twenty-mile segment of the river where it cut though the Highlands, the northern extension of the Appalachian Mountains. Rising near Mount Marcy in the Adirondack Mountains, the Hudson cascades and descends for about a hundred miles to Fort Edward, New York, then leisurely drifts south for another hundred miles until it encounters the Highlands bulwark near the U.S. Military Academy, West Point. The river drops so imperceptibly in its journey to the sea that ocean tidal flow is measured at Albany, 150 miles upstream. But at Storm King Mountain, just north of West Point, about fifty miles from the ocean, the river changes dramatically. Following a course bulldozed through the Highlands by glaciers, the Hudson narrows, deepens, gains speed, rushes past the Military Academy in a sweeping *S*-turn, and surges onward past Bear Mountain. Early Dutch voyagers, tacking under sail against tide, current, and wind, with soaring mountains close abeam on both rocky shores, referred to the narrows of the Hudson as the "Devil's Horse Race." Henry Hudson sailed through to the upstream "gate" of the narrows, anchored, briefly explored, then turned back, ending his quest for the fabled northwest passage to China. Hudson River School painters found this portion of the river irresistible, as did American defenders who tried to stop the British by fortifying the heights of the narrows, hoping that a few well-aimed cannon shot and chains cast across from shore to shore in this strategic gorge would halt any shipborne river assault.

Partridge proposed that a sixty-five-square-mile section of the Highlands, with the Hudson River Narrows as its centerpiece, be declared a national park. He noted that the Civil War battlefields at Gettysburg, Chickamauga, and Shiloh had been preserved by the United States in a manner that included the protection of scenery, forests, fields, and historic buildings, and he argued that the military installations at West Point and nearby Iona Island justified similar congressional attention. In his vision of a park, Partridge proposed nature-education programs, scenic roads, easements and tax incentives to encourage the protection of private land within the park boundaries, and preservation of the "wild woodland." He was careful to emphasize that the rights of one landowner in particular, who owned thousands of acres in the Highlands, not be threatened in any manner by the national-park concept. The owner was the legendary Edward Henry Harriman.

Partridge's conservation plea carried with it the weight of his reputation as an honored leader and teacher within New York City's medical community and his love for the Highlands, confirmed by his residency on the northern slope of Storm King Mountain at Cornwall-on-Hudson, New York. Frederick Law Olmsted had designed the grounds of the Partridge estate. His home, set with a view northward to the Hudson's Newburgh Bay, was filled with local art and historic objects. In addition to holding the Chair of Obstetrics at the College of Physicians and Surgeons and serving many other professional associations with hospitals and medical societies, Partridge had broad interests and philanthropic activities that extended to the New York Institution for the Education of the Blind, the Washington Square Home for Friendless Girls, the Huguenot Society, the American Scenic and Historic Preservation Society, the Society of Colonial Wars, the Garden Club of America, the Constitution Island Association, the Grant Monument Association, and the New England Society of New York. From the moment he graduated from the College of Physicians and Surgeons, Columbia University, in 1873, this robust man, who relished "light" lunches of two sandwiches, a thermos of coffee, and pie, took great delight in opportunities to pursue and influence public policy. Partridge would die with his boots on at the age of seventy-seven while participating in an evening dinner event in honor of a lifelong friend, Dr. D. Bryson Delavan. By then, he had firmly left his mark on the PIPC.

Mr. and Mrs. Edward Henry Harriman, who knew Partridge as an acquaintance and neighbor in the Highlands, took careful note of *The Outlook* article. A subsequent action by Mrs. Harriman, only two years after Partridge's article appeared, would sweep the PIPC forward to new achievements that would ripple outward, influencing conservation initiatives across the nation.

4.
Harriman

As Edward Partridge urged consideration of his national park concept, the PIPC commissioners found themselves pressed by more basic concerns. Serving by default as field commander for the PIPC, J. DuPratt White was dealing with a variety of issues spawned by the increasing popularity of the public holdings along the New Jersey shore. Ferryboats were regularly delivering day-trippers and campers from 125th Street in New York City to Fort Lee, New Jersey, and from Yonkers, New York, to Alpine, New Jersey. While a handful of camping parties had appeared along the Commission's strip of shoreline when the first lands were acquired, upwards of two thousand tents now blossomed along the shore on sunny weekend days. White sought advice from the commandant of faraway Fort Yellowstone about how to regulate park visitors but found that the Army officer posted in the Wyoming wilderness, where few people ventured, could offer little practical help. White struggled to gain money from New Jersey to strengthen the meager police patrols, while George Perkins and the New York commissioners sought a small amount from Albany simply to survey Hook Mountain and determine how best to begin carrying out the imposing new responsibility for its protection.

White and Leonard Hull Smith, the PIPC's only salaried employee, handled most of the PIPC's correspondence. In one exchange of letters with a park patron, White returned $5.00 that accompanied a request for a camping permit, explaining, "It would not be proper, under any circumstances, to accept any money." In the midst of overseeing an increasingly successful city-based law firm and spending many hours commuting to his home in Nyack, New York, White still found time to respond to an aspiring camper who sought his advice on exactly what types of equipment, tents, and food to purchase to ensure a comfortable park visit. Public sanitation, accidents, the risk of forest fire, trespass by park visitors onto adjoining private property, and rowdy behavior by campers after dark were among the many problems finding their way to White's desk. In the absence of policy guidelines about how the park should be managed, a matter that White urged his colleagues to address quickly, he invented park regulations to counter the more persistent and frequent challenges.

He defended the PIPC against the Alpine, New Jersey, tax collector, who thought that the PIPC's lands should be a convenient and continuing source of revenue for the town, even though the town provided no police or fire-protection services to the PIPC. White, seeking a compromise that would allow for an exit from the immediate problem, advised the tax collector, "Of course, if these taxes are paid by the Commission, it is not to be in any way construed as a willingness on their part to pay any taxes on this property in the future." Compromise proved unnecessary; the PIPC refused to pay. White must have found irony, too, in a communiqué from New Jersey State Treasurer Daniel S. Voorhees, son of the former governor, who sought lease payments from the PIPC for the very riparian lands that had supposedly been ceded to the Commission eight years previously in 1901. Voorhees learned that his invitation to collect taxes from the PIPC for lands submerged in the Hudson River was declined.

Pressed by local residents and historians to build a battle monument on the PIPC's land at the site of historic Fort Lee, White explained that "there is a dispute over the bills of H. A. Jaeger, who hauled several large boulders which were to be used for the monument. All agree that the bill is absolutely exorbitant and out of all reason, but the party is very stubborn and has declined to make any concessions." The promise of a monument, consisting at the moment of a pile of overpriced boulders, remained unfulfilled.

At one point, White set aside his legal and community activities and went tramping along the river shoreline in a vain attempt to track down a tent missing from a river campsite. He recruited unpaid volunteers, designated them as wardens, assigned them districts along the river shoreline, and asked that they preserve order and report unlawful incidents to the marshals. They were directed to make their own "Park Warden" signs to hang on their tents. Two enterprising local boys saw an opportunity for quick profit and began selling camping supplies from their rowboat. On due consideration, White decided that these entrepreneurs could continue, not seeing in these two young men the type of conflict that would eventually develop in parks throughout the nation between those who saw an opportunity for commercial profit and those who would seek to keep development at a minimum in favor of preservation. On the environmental front, the Commission sent a letter to the Sisters of Peace advising that "the break in the sewer pipe runs over park property. This must be fixed, and in attending to it we would like to have the pipe continued further in the river so that the refuse will be carried out beyond the low water mark."

As camping increased, the PIPC found itself drawn to the idea that parklands could be used for worthy social purposes, especially in cooperation with churches and charitable organizations that served underprivileged children. Working with representatives of the Hamilton House Settlement, a charitable organization located in New York City's notoriously crowded and impoverished Lower East Side, and local church pastors in New Jersey, the Commission began issuing special long-term camping permits that allowed for the "relay of poor boys" to and from camps set up for the summer on Commission property. Social work such as this would become an increasingly important aspect of PIPC enterprises in years to come.

Most of these experiments in park stewardship went unnoticed or prompted criticism from those who for various reasons opposed the concept of public parks. But, on occasion, the Commission won praise. "I remember you very well in connection with the purchase of your property underneath the Palisades," White wrote to J. H. Magee; "the Commissioners appreciate letters written to them in the spirit of your letter as they are glad to receive suggestions and assistance from outsiders, but we find that there are not so many public spirited citizens who will take the trouble to write about matters of this kind."

The Commission, whose 1908–1909 membership included Perkins, White, William H. Porter, D. McNeely Stauffer, Edwin A. Stevens, Franklin W. Hopkins, William B. Dana, William A. Linn, Nathan T. Barrett, and Abram De Ronde, struggled to close the final land-purchase deals in New Jersey. To the north, the PIPC was on the defensive for not doing enough to rid Hook Mountain of quarry operators. In reply to a concerned citizen, White asserted, "The reason the Commission has not acquired the Hook Mountain, and the only reason, is that the Commission is without funds—I can assure you that exhaustive efforts have been made to accomplish this end in every way that the ingenuity of the Commission has been able to devise." The commissioners in general, and White in particular, were learning about the vagaries of park management, as taught in the school of hard knocks. They were learning that people eagerly responded to the availability of open space but did not necessarily appreciate how or why it was available, or who must provide for its care. The commissioners were also learning that, in the public sector, criticism gushed and praise was rare; that their investment of volunteer hours and hard work was unknown beyond a small circle of family, friends, business acquaintances, and a few government leaders; and that politics was even more fickle than they realized. They had no benchmarks to help them determine how best to be good stewards of wild and rugged parkland perched near the epicenter of the New York City colossus. Theirs was no Central Park or Boston Common with manicured lawns, gardens, landscaped ponds and hills, an urban pace and mood, and high public awareness and watchfulness. Nor were they dealing with grand, remote wilderness areas like the Adirondacks or Yellowstone. The commissioners were on their own, inventing a new type of park for an urban population, finding their way as they went along.

Perkins and his fellow commissioners saw an opportunity to raise the profile of the PIPC and gain needed public support for the growing crisis at Hook Mountain by joining with those who were planning to celebrate the three hundredth anniversary in 1909 of Hudson's "discovery" of the river named in his honor, combined with the centennial of Robert Fulton's development of steam-powered ships. Upriver, Partridge saw a similar opportunity to promote his idea for a large national park in the Highlands. The 250-member Tercentenary Commission that had been charged with the responsibility for planning and holding the Hudson-Fulton celebration consisted of a veritable who's who of business and community leaders, including Gen. Stewart L. Woodford (president), Andrew Carnegie, Joseph H. Choate, Maj. Gen. F. D. Grant, Seth Low, J. P. Morgan, L. P. Morton, Alton B. Parker, Gen. Horace Porter, Frederick W. Seward, Francis L. Stetson, Oscar S. Straus, William B. Van Rensselaer, and Gen. J. G. Wilson.

The Morgan connection did not guarantee the PIPC easy access to those who were planning the details of the Hudson-Fulton celebration. Perkins advanced the idea that the celebration be combined with a dedication of the Palisades Interstate Park in New Jersey, arguing that protection of the scenery as it existed during the voyage of the *Half Moon* was a fitting tribute to the great explorers of the river and should be the centerpiece of the celebration. He received a friendly hearing and encouragement from General Woodford. In the meantime, Partridge succeeded in winning the appointment of a Hudson-Fulton subcommittee to study the national park idea. The subcommittee never met formally but provided enough clout to advance the park idea to Albany, where it sputtered and flamed out.

Perkins, who was planning a two-month summer trip to Alaska as a respite from heavy business demands involving the United States Steel and International Harvester corporations, the Cincinnati-Hamilton & Dayton and Pere Marquette Railroads, and the management of various private investment portfolios, all under the flag of the House of Morgan, was anxious to lock in General Woodford's commitment to allow the PIPC to share prominently in the celebration spotlight. Perkins's persuasive powers, and donations from himself and Morgan totaling $20,000 to help fund the celebration, amounted to an appeal that the general could not ignore. Perkins was appointed to the Hudson-Fulton Tercentenary Commission "so that there might be the fullest possible interchange of views between the two bodies, PIPC and Tercentenary Commissions." Even so, when an announcement of the pending Hudson-Fulton celebration appeared in newspapers on August 31, 1909, no mention was made of the Palisades Park dedica-

Dedication, Palisades Interstate Park Commission, Alpine Headquarters, 1909. *(Courtesy of PIPC Archives)*

tion. Perkins strongly objected. General Woodford ordered the Army colonel who had arranged for the newspaper announcement to amend, print, and distribute more than 500,000 copies of the original announcement to ensure that the Palisades dedication was included.

On September 27, 1909, in conjunction with the week-long Hudson-Fulton celebration, a crowd of one thousand gathered on the New Jersey shoreline at the old tavern building known locally as Cornwallis Headquarters, now owned by the PIPC, to witness the dedication of the Palisades Interstate Park. Thirty-five musicians had been transported to the site aboard the *Waturus,* Perkins's private yacht, along with many dignitaries who responded to special PIPC invitations printed by Tiffany & Co. Among those in attendance were Governors Charles Evans Hughes (New York) and J. Franklin Fort (New Jersey). Elizabeth Demarest and other members of the New Jersey Federation of Women's Clubs were also in attendance, but White had declined their most recent request that the long-sought women's memorial be raised as part of the dedication, claiming, "Everyone is overwhelmed with the work in connection with the celebration in general." Attending, too, was a group representing the Iroquois Nation, invited to perform a ceremonial dance as part of the dedication event.

Back from Alaska in time to participate, Perkins announced to those assembled that a "Member of the Commission" (meaning himself) had made a $12,000 donation to the PIPC, supplemented by a gift of land worth $16,000 from Cleveland H. Dodge. He went on to say that since its inception, the Commission had raised $284,000 in gifts of land and money, primarily from Morgan, Dodge, Mrs. Lydia G. Lawrence, himself, and Mr. and Mrs. Hamilton Twombly. The Twomblys had donated sixty acres of land, including a dock and three thousand feet of riparian rights. Perkins noted that in the intervening nine years since New York and New Jersey had appropriated funds to begin purchasing land, New York had provided an additional $20,000 and New Jersey $17,500. Referring to the fact that the PIPC had acquired almost all of the 175 parcels needed to guard the cliff face and river shore for fourteen miles, from Fort Lee to the New Jersey–New York border, including twenty-one houses, Perkins said, "Here, within sight of our great, throbbing city is a little world of almost virgin nature, which has been rescued for the people and now stands as a permanent monument to the discovery of the river by Henry Hudson." Perkins credited the leadership efforts of Elizabeth Vermilye, Cecelia Gaines Holland, Franklin W. Hopkins, William A. Linn, S. Wood McClave, Andrew H. Green, Frederick W. Devoe, Frederick S. Lamb, Abraham G. Mills, and Edward Payson Cone for the creation of the PIPC. He extended special praise to Dr. George F. Kunz, president of the American

Scenic and Historic Preservation Society, Senator Edmund W. Wakeley (New Jersey), and the late William E. Dodge for ardent and effective work in support of the initiative to protect the cliffs. Perkins closed by saying, "Man can do no more than preserve its natural grandeur and make the Park accessible to one and all." The Navy warship *Gloucester* boomed a salute from the river, and the band struck up "The Star-Spangled Banner."

Perkins did not mention one man who, more than a year earlier, had become a highly unlikely and unwitting ally of the PIPC. Charles E. Howard was not a park advocate, but his influence would be tremendous. Howard, superintendent of New York State Prisons, thought that Bear Mountain, an undeveloped wildland in the Hudson River narrows just south of West Point, offered an inexhaustible supply of stone that could be used for the construction of public highways and proposed to mine the mountain with prison labor. To do so, he first needed a site on which to construct a prison. Howard convinced the Prison Commission to purchase seven hundred acres of property at Bear Mountain from C. E. Lambert in 1908. Perkins was anxious to talk with Governor Hughes about this unanticipated and unfortunate turn of events and made sure that the governor accompanied him aboard the *Waturus* at the conclusion of the dedication.

Partridge, also concerned about the prison, ended his effort to convince Congress that a national park should be created in the Highlands but succeeded in winning the New York Legislature's approval on May 22, 1909, of the "Highlands of the Hudson Forest Preservation Act." Spurred on by the prediction of Gifford Pinchot, later to be credited as the founder of the U.S. Forest Service, that at the present pace of logging all the mature trees in the nation would be cut down within twenty-five years, the Forest Preservation Act was a way for Partridge to enter a legislative side door in his crusade for conservation of the Highlands. Urgency was on his side. *Diaporthe parastica,* the "Chestnut blight," had spread into the Highlands forest from New York City. Brick manufacturing was consuming seven thousand cords of hardwood each year—clear-cutting was the standard practice. Most of the iron mines in the Highlands had long since been shut down, but the Forest-of-Deane Iron Mine at Highland Falls, between Bear Mountain and West Point, was still in operation, consuming wood in large quantities for its furnaces, and would continue to run until 1931. And the prison loomed. Trees at the site had already been clear-cut.

The Forest Preservation Act declared that "perpetuation and improvement of forest growth is declared to be in the public interest." To secure a great park in the Highlands, the act called for the designation of a resident forester who would be charged with the development of protective and regulatory principles for public and private land, the construction of a magnificent highway along the river to provide access to the park, and the prevention of forest fires. Excluding the giant E. H. Harriman estate, Partridge pointed out that private holdings in the Highlands ranged from fifty to five thousand acres, and that five-hundred- to one-thousand-acre "lots" were common. The average per acre cost of these properties was estimated to be between $25 and $50; property taxes ranged from $4 to $8 per acre.

Careful forest practices designed to protect rather than exploit forest resources had already been implemented at the U.S. Military Academy, West Point, and on the Harriman estate only a few miles away at Arden, New York. The Academy controlled sixteen thousand acres; Harriman's twenty-thousand-acre estate benefited from the management services provided by nine members of Yale's School of Forestry senior class. The Harriman estate had grown large, in part, to pull land from the market before the woodcutters got it. But Prison Superintendent Howard was not thinking of good forest practices. A stockade prison, made

Prison Stockade, Bear Mountain, New York, 1908.
(Courtesy of PIPC Archives)

of logs cut from the nearby forest, was erected at Bear Mountain in 1908. During construction performed by prison labor, so many convicts escaped from the site that the residents of nearby hamlets were reported to be in a "state of terror." Soon, 1,500 to 2,000 convicts, formerly confined at Sing Sing, would be moved to the new stockade. Except for the Sabbath, they were going to be marched daily to Bear Mountain, pick axes, pry bars, and shovels in hand, to begin wrestling rock from its slopes.

The Harrimans had taken note of the entreaties of Partridge, their Highlands neighbor, to create a great park in the region. The prison was a sharp contradiction to this vision. On the matter of conserving the Highlands, the wishes of Harriman, in failing health when the prison stockade rose at Bear Mountain, would be the incentive for a rare alliance with two men who had opposed him in the world of business, Theodore Roosevelt and Morgan.

Born in 1848, Edward Henry Harriman was one of eleven children, who, according to his biographer, Rudy Abramson, "started with nothing" and became the "mightiest" of the railroad barons. Harriman built a railroad empire, including the Union Pacific, Southern Pacific, and Illinois Central, that ultimately controlled seventy-five thousand miles of track and employed more men than the standing Army of the United States. Named for a great uncle who was forced to walk the plank during a pirate raid in the Caribbean, E. H. was the son of a minister who settled in West Hoboken, New Jersey. His father became rector of St. John's Episcopal parish after returning from a misadventure in the California gold fields. E. H.'s father was paid $200 a year, when the parish elders could scrape together the money. In addition to the steady influence provided by his mother, Cornelia, E. H. and his brother, as sons of a parish rector, could attend the Trinity School in Manhattan. They would rise before dawn, walk two miles to the ferry, cross the Hudson, and walk another mile to school. The future businessman ranked first in his class at Trinity but dropped out at the age of fourteen to begin working as a $5-per-week copyboy at the D. C. Hays brokerage firm. His earnings were dutifully turned over to his family. Promoted to "pad boy," the fleet-footed Harriman raced from office to office, calling out the latest stock quotes to brokers. He favored his memory over the quotes scribbled on his pad and quickly won the admiration of the brokers for never making a mistake. Within eight years, by 1870, E. H. had ascended in the Wall Street environment to the point of being able to buy a seat on the New York Stock Exchange. During the next ten years, Harriman gained a reputation as an outstanding broker but was found to be a "loner—secretive and relentless" by some of his peers.

Mr. and Mrs. Edward Henry Harriman. *(Courtesy of Orange County Historical Society)*

After a lengthy courtship, E. H. and Mary Averell were married in 1879. Biographer Rudy Abramson wrote,

> About the same time he was courting Mary, he struck up an equally fortuitous friendship with Stuyvesant Fish, who would eventually help him get his start in big-time railroading. It was, to put it mildly, an unlikely alliance. Fish's family had been pillars of New York commerce and society for two hundred years. Stuyvesant's father, Hamilton Fish, had been Governor of New York, a U.S. Senator, and more recently President Ulysses S. Grant's Secretary of State. Grandfather Nicholas Fish had served under General Washington from the Battle of Long Island to Yorktown.

The aristocrat, Fish, was physically large and easygoing. E. H., the former pad boy, was "scrawny, near sighted, and cunning as a wolf," according to Abramson.

Through family and business connections with financier William Henry Osborne, the young Fish was on the board of directors of Illinois Central Railroad when he met Harriman. The Illinois Central extended through America's heartland from Lake Erie to the Gulf of Mexico. Harriman took advantage of a general stock swoon in 1881, caused by the assassination of President Garfield, to buy heavily into Illinois Central, where he subsequently joined his friend, Fish, on the board. Together, they began renovating the system and going after more routes. In the process of expanding the railroad company, Harriman confronted the legendary Morgan over the fate of an obscure Iowa railroad company, the Dubuque-and-Southern. Morgan and a pool of investors seemingly controlled enough stock and proxies to dictate the fate of Dubuque-and-Southern at the annual shareholders meeting, either by retaining control of the board of directors or by driving up the price, should Morgan and his associates decide to sell their holdings. Harriman checkmated this strategy by flooding the annual stockholders meeting with more than enough small investors to wrest control of the board from Morgan. With the election of a slate of Harriman-allied board members accomplished, Morgan's proxies were declared invalid. Thereupon followed approval to sell Dubuque-and-Southern to Illinois Central. Morgan reacted by taking the matter to court but finally acquiesced to the "little man" and sold his pool of shares at a compromise price set by Harriman.

Harriman would go on to gain an incredible degree of control of America's railroad system, so much so that at the turn of the century his name was often mentioned in the same elevated realm with those of Rockefeller, Carnegie, and his business rival, Morgan. Though he and Morgan remained rivals, their large fortunes, influence, and intertwined social contacts, and the fact that Morgan, too, maintained a grand weekend home on the western shore of the Hudson at nearby Highland Falls, just north of Bear Mountain, would continue to bring the two men together. They eventually found themselves in partnership in 1901 in a merger between the Northern Pacific, Great Northern, and Burlington Railroads.

This transaction, which promised to greatly increase Harriman's personal grip on national railroading, sent him into conflict with President Theodore Roosevelt. Through the Department of Justice, the trust-busting president sought to prevent the merger. In a five-to-four antitrust vote by the Supreme Court, Roosevelt prevailed, forcing Harriman to unload the stock he held in the merged companies—at a profit of $58 million. Ironically, Harriman had raised $250,000, including a personal $50,000 contribution, for Roosevelt's 1904 campaign and was already disappointed in the result when the president declined to appoint a Harriman friend to an ambassadorship. The subsequent antitrust vote did nothing to improve matters.

Complicating the issue even more, Congress failed to reimburse Harriman's Southern Pacific Railroad Company for a heroic $3-million emergency rescue of the flood-ravaged Imperial Valley in California. The Colorado River had flooded into the agriculturally rich valley through a gaping break in a water-diversion dam. Southern Pacific boxcars delivered thousands of tons of rock to stanch the flood. Roosevelt sought reimbursement for Southern Pacific from Congress but did not succeed. Harriman thought the president did not try hard enough.

That these three disparate men, Roosevelt, Morgan, and Harriman—with Perkins standing in the middle—became united in the vision of creating a great park in the Hudson River Valley and adjacent Highlands testifies to the universal appeal of saving beautiful places.

Harriman's arrival at this intriguing unity of purpose with Morgan and Roosevelt was rooted in a decision he had made in 1885 to purchase land from iron maker Peter Parrott. Parrott had gained accolades during the Civil War by producing the "Parrott Rifle," a rifle-barreled cannon of improved range and accuracy that gave important strategic advantage to Union troops. After the war, Parrott continued to produce iron from mines in the Sterling Forest area of the Highlands, only to see his enterprise fail when abundant iron ore, discovered in Minnesota, abruptly destroyed the New York market. Harriman and Parrott were friends and hunting partners, but the collapse of Parrott's iron business led to an irreparable rupture of their friendship. At a distress auction of Parrott's assets, Harriman stepped forward to successfully bid $52,500 for the entire 7,863 acres of land placed on the block, including four iron mines and a furnace. Parrott had hoped that the land would be divided among competing speculators bidding for valuable timber rights, thus driving up the sales price to the financial benefit of his family. Harriman saw the matter in the opposite light. He successfully bid for the entire block of land to prevent it from being subdivided and timbered. His bid was far below Parrott's expectations. Within two years, Harriman had expanded his holdings to twenty thousand acres by buying about forty additional properties. The estate was named "Arden," in honor of Parrott's wife, but the schism between Harriman and Parrott never healed.

E. H. and Mary Harriman cherished the country lifestyle at Arden and probably sought solace in the Highlands after their first-born son, Henry, died tragically of diphtheria in 1888, just before the age of five, while the Harrimans were temporarily living in Chicago. They had two additional sons, William Averell

(1891) and Edward Roland (1895), and three daughters, Mary (1881), Cornelia (1884), and Carol (1889).

In 1898 Harriman, showing fatigue from the press of business, responded to his doctor's recommendation to take a family vacation. His approach to the vacation mirrored his approach to business. He decided to make the vacation into a meaningful scientific expedition to Alaska. When the day came to depart, the Harriman family was numbered in a traveling party of 126 entrained from New York, to be joined by others on the West Coast. Included among twenty-five scientists recruited for the adventure were the eminent naturalist John Burroughs and the founder of the Sierra Club, John Muir. In a retrospective written in 1912, Muir said,

> Of all the great builders—the famous doers of things in this busy world—none that I know of more ably and manfully did his appointed work than my friend Edward Henry Harriman. He was always ready and able. The greater his burdens, the more formidable the obstacles looming ahead of him, the greater was his enjoyment. He fairly reveled in heavy dynamical work and went about it naturally and unweariedly like glaciers mining landscapes, cutting canyons through ridges, carrying off hills, laying rails and bridges over lakes and rivers, mountains, and plains, making the nation's ways straight and smooth and safe, bringing everybody nearer to one another. He seemed to regard the whole continent as his farm and all the people as partners, stirring millions of workers into useful action, plowing, sowing, irrigating, mining, building cities and factories, farms and homes.

Speaking more personally of Harriman, Muir added,

> In general appearance he was said to be under-sized, but though I knew him well I never noticed anything either short or tall in his stature. His head made the rest of his body all but invisible. His magnificent brow, high and broad and finely finished, oftentimes called to mind well-known portraits of Napoleon. Every feature of his countenance manifested power, especially his wonderful eyes, deep and frank yet piercing, inspiring confidence, though likely at first sight to keep people at a distance.

Returning aboard the chartered ship *George W. Elder* after a two-month, nine-thousand-mile voyage, including a stop on the Siberian coast, Harriman rushed back to the railroad business, leaving to Burroughs, Muir, and the other scientists the task of sorting out and eventually publishing a rich treasure trove of data.

In the first decade of the twentieth century, Harriman's stamina and health continued to falter. Muir joined the family again during the summer of 1907 at

Harriman's wilderness lodge on Pelican Bay, Klamath Lake, Oregon, persuaded, in part, by Harriman's pledge to "show you how to write a book." Harriman made available a stenographer who spent many summer days recording Muir's ideas and reflective musings. "To him I owe some of the most precious moments of my life," reminisced Muir.

By the time the New York Prison Commission initiated the Bear Mountain project, Harriman was losing an excruciating personal struggle with cancer. Even so, encouraged by Partridge, Harriman had confided in Mary his strong interest in the creation of a park in the Highlands and had expressed the same wish to New York Governor Hughes, spurred on by the threatening prison project just over the hill, so to speak, from Arden. Harriman proposed to donate thousands of acres and $1 million to the PIPC if Hughes would direct New York's New Prison Board to move the Bear Mountain stockade somewhere else, preferably on the opposite side of the Hudson River. On August 9, 1909, less than two months before the Palisades Interstate Park was dedicated at the Cornwallis Headquarters, and before the prison matter could be resolved, Harriman died at the age of sixty-one. Nevertheless, Mary and his son, William Averell, would soon express his hopes for the great park in a dramatic manner.

Perkins knew of Harriman's interest in donating land for a park in the Highlands. After the September 27 dedication, Perkins briefed Governor Hughes while the two sailed upriver on the *Waturus*. Dialogue continued with both the governor and Mary Harriman, finally prompting Perkins to call a meeting of the commissioners for December 16, 1909, accompanied by the message that "Mr. Perkins particularly asks that every member of the Commission will endeavor to be present, as matters of great importance to the Commission will be brought before the meeting."

The minutes of the December meeting include a reference to a letter from Vermilye urging the acquisition of the "Clinton Point" property, but due to a lack of funds, the commissioners declined to act. A bill for $294.17 was presented to cover the cost of purchasing and mailing to every member of the New York and New Jersey Legislatures 357 copies of the book *The Palisades of the Hudson*, written by Arthur C. Mack. Perkins submitted personal receipts for $45, representing his expenses for recent trips to Albany; he added that the expenses should be considered a contribution to the Commission.

Then, according to the bland minutes of the meeting, "Mr. Perkins announced that Mrs. E. H. Harriman had signified her willingness to deed 10,000 acres at Arden, New York, to the Commission, together with $1,000,000 in cash, provided others would contribute to the extent of $1,500,000, and all of the contributions to be conditioned upon the State of New York contributing an equal amount of $2,500,000." Perkins added that he had about completed negotiations "for a plan which would permit extension of the jurisdiction of this Commission to West Point." The plan would also "permit construction of the boulevard and the acquisition of such lands between the present jurisdiction and the proposed jurisdiction as might be considered necessary." Perkins confirmed that anonymous pledges that were already in hand had reached the $1 million mark. The minutes give no feeling for the magnitude of these few words—the PIPC was leaping to a level far beyond the dreams of those who had originally sought only to stop the quarry operators.

In a follow-up meeting on December 23, the details of the Harriman proposal were spelled out:

1. That in order that the Palisades Park Commission may carry out the proposed plan and receive and hold the land and money offered the State by Mrs. Harriman, its jurisdiction shall be extended to the northward along the west bank of the Hudson river to Newburgh, and to the westward as far as and to include the Ramapo mountains, giving the Commission the same powers granted to it at the time it was created and at the time its jurisdiction was extended in 1906, including the right to condemn land for roadway and park purposes.

2. That the State of New York appropriate $2,500,000 to the use of the Commission for the acquiring of land and the building of roads and general park purposes.

3. That the State discontinue the work on the new State prison located in Rockland county, and relocate the prison where, in the judgment of the Palisades Park Commission, it will not interfere with the plans and purposes of the Commission.

4. That in addition to the aforesaid appropriation from the State, a further sum of $2,500,000, including Mrs. Harriman's pledge of a million dollars, be secured on or before January 1, 1910.

5. That in addition to the above $5,000,000, the State of New Jersey appropriate such an amount as the Palisades Park Commission shall deem to be its fair share.

On motion, the meeting adjourned. Perkins and White had already scheduled a visit the following day with Governor Hughes. They carried with them to Albany compelling information and a promise—more than the $1.5 million in private funds needed to respond to and support the Harriman gift had been pledged; their plea to the governor was for New York to do its part by immediately appropriating $2.5 million to the Commission.

Perkins, joined by John D. Rockefeller, Jr., had used the magic of personal contacts at the highest levels of New York society to develop an impressive list of contributors to the PIPC. Of those contacted, only Andrew Carnegie declined to provide a major financial gift, explaining to Rockefeller that he was engaged in raising $5.5 million for libraries in New York City and could not extend his philanthropic activities until the library project was completed. But Governor Hughes surely must have been impressed with the list of donors presented to him:

John D. Rockefeller, Sr.	$500,000
J. Pierpont Morgan	$500,000
Margaret Olivia Sage	$ 50,000
William K. Vanderbilt	$ 50,000
George F. Baker	$ 50,000
James Stillman	$ 50,000
John D. Archbold	$ 50,000
William Rockefeller	$ 50,000
Frank A. Munsey	$ 50,000
Henry Phipps	$ 50,000
E. T. Stotesbury	$ 50,000
E. H. Gray	$ 50,000
George W. Perkins	$ 50,000
Cleveland H. Dodge & James McLean	$ 25,000
Helen Miller Gould	$ 25,000
Eileen F. and Arthur Curtiss James	$ 25,000
V. Everitt Macy	$ 25,000

Perkins and Rockefeller exceeded Mrs. Harriman's fund-raising challenge by $150,000. With this information in hand, the governor delivered a message to the New York Legislature on January 6, 1910, urging that the state provide a positive response to the proffered Harriman gift. Instead of seeking quick action by the Legislature to appropriate the necessary funds, Governor Hughes, claiming a lack of tax revenue as well as other financial obligations, recommended that a $2.5 million bond be issued for the purpose of ensuring that the Harriman gift would become a reality. The bond would require approval by the New York electorate.

News of the pending Harriman gift was also carried to Trenton. The commissioners were seeking $500,000 from New Jersey, specifically for the purpose of building a road along the base of the Palisades cliff, a cherished project that had been on the PIPC's wish list almost from the moment the first properties had been purchased. The road would greatly enhance the public's use and enjoyment of the park, contended the commissioners.

With vigor, the commissioners and their allies pursued the fits and starts of the political processes in New York and New Jersey all during the following year. Then, on a beautiful autumn day, October 29, 1910, eighteen-year-old William Averell Harriman, acting on behalf of his mother and family, and speaking publicly for the first time, handed a deed for ten thousand acres to Perkins, along with three checks in the aggregate amount of $1 million. Simultaneously, the seven-hundred-acre tract that had been acquired for the prison was turned over to the Commission. As *The New York Times* reported,

> Nature itself had provided the setting. On three sides of the little plateau (where the ceremony was held) were the hills which form the rugged group clustering about Bear Mountain; just across the Hudson towered Anthony's Nose, jutting out into the river, and over the foothills shone the top of Storm King, the highest and most rugged of the mountains. All were colored red and gold by the Autumn foliage, a natural picture on which the group of men and women on the plateau gazed in admiration during the hour or more of the ceremony.

All that was artificial about the scene was the platform which had been constructed at the edge of the plateau, a flagstaff which had been reared and a gun from West Point which fired the salute to the flags of New York, New Jersey, and the Nation as they were raised by the daughters of Mrs. Harriman and of Mr. Perkins (Carroll Harriman and Dorothy Perkins) over the land which was being given as a playground for the public.

Mrs. J. Pierpont Morgan and her daughter, Mrs. Herbert Satterlee, sat with Mary Harriman on the platform, the memory of conflict between husbands dimmed to invisibility by the mood and meaning of the ceremony. Mrs. Perkins and Henry Phipps and his wife were nearby. One of the regular morning passenger trains that operated on the west side of the Hudson had made a special stop at Bear Mountain to accommodate guests from the city. Others arrived by car from neighboring country estates. The weatherbeaten Warden's quarters at Bear Mountain provided a provincial setting for the guest luncheon.

Ironically, William J. McKay of the New Prison Commission opened the ceremony by alluding to a retreat of Hessian soldiers during the Revolutionary War from the "very spot where the ceremony is being held." (McKay had his facts

W. Averell Harriman (right) hands $1 million in checks to George W. Perkins, Bear Mountain Dedication, 1910. *(Courtesy of PIPC Archives)*

slightly mixed—an overwhelming British and Hessian force caused the retreat of American militiamen from fortifications at Bear Mountain.) McKay added that the Prison Commission, too, welcomed the opportunity to retreat in favor of the interstate park. The Prison Commission's retreat was not without a price tag. Assets sold to the PIPC included a railroad bridge, fifty thousand bricks, the barracks and stockade, furniture, plumbing fixtures, and seventy rails, each thirty feet long and weighing forty-two thousand pounds. The PIPC was charged $1,083.40 for cattle left behind. The New Prison Commission gave without charge the flagpole, a barn and old sheds, and one set of ice tools.

White accepted the seven-hundred-acre tract on behalf of the Commission. "I shall avail myself of this, my first opportunity to speak of the work of George Perkins as Commissioner," stated White. "His time, his thought, his advice, and his energy have been unstintedly devoted toward the accomplishment of what has been done." White then read letters from Governors Hughes and Fort. Hughes confidently predicted that New Yorkers would approve the $2.5 million bond issue within a matter of days; Fort verified that the New Jersey Legislature had appropriated the requested $500,000. (Hughes's prediction proved to be accurate, only because the vote in New York City and surrounding counties outnumbered a universally negative vote upstate.)

After the governors' letters were read, Sgt. H. C. Lieb, in command of the West Point field gun, ordered nineteen rapid-fire salutes, to the startled delight of those in attendance. Then young Averell Harriman took center stage:

> In accordance with the long-cherished plan of my father to give to the State of New York, for the use of the people, a portion of the Arden estate, and acting in behalf of my mother, I now present to the Commissioners of the Palisades Park the land comprising the gift. I also hand you my mother's contribution to the expense of future development of the Harriman Park. It is her hope and mine that through all the years to come the health and happiness of future generations will be advanced by these gifts.

Perkins graciously accepted, reminding the audience that the great park would be larger than the Island of Manhattan and predicting that the day marked "the beginning of what will certainly become one of the largest, most beautiful, and practical recreation grounds in all the world."

Among the participants at the event were Partridge and ex-Governor Odell. Partridge's Forest Preservation Act had been rescinded as part of the political strategy to win approval of the bond issue, but Partridge was happy. His vision of a Highlands park was taking shape, and within a matter of years, unknown to him at the time, he would be appointed to the PIPC and would serve for fourteen years, until 1929. Ex-Governor Odell, who first supported the Commission as Roosevelt's successor, then opposed its expansion when he became a lobbyist for the quarry operators, must have been amazed at the sweep, authority, and financial clout conferred on the PIPC on that October day. Hook Mountain was clearly in the commissioners' sights, and the boundaries of the Commission's activities had been pushed into new and amazing territory.

Kunz of the American Scenic and Historic Preservation Society collected the brass casings from the first five shells fired from the West Point gun, polished them, and sent them to Mary Harriman to be used as flower vases.

5.
Legend and War

Those in attendance at Bear Mountain to celebrate the Harriman donation were within a stone's throw of a bloody and strategically decisive Revolutionary War battleground. Far downriver in New Jersey, the PIPC had, while in the process of purchasing the Palisades, become custodian of important historic sites. In 1906 the New York Legislature extended the PIPC's authority to include the Stony Point Battlefield, New York, the "Gibraltar of the Hudson," where, in a daring and successful midnight raid in July, 1779, Brig. Gen. (Mad) Anthony Wayne and 450 soldiers of the Continental Army's Corps of Light Infantry surprised and captured a British garrison, dealing a blow to British military pride and strengthening Patriot resolve to win the war. On the Highlands land being donated by Mary Harriman, historic legend and fact were intertwined, awaiting examination by scholars, archaeologists, and anyone else interested in the rich heritage of the Hudson River Valley. By the accidental consequences of stopping the quarry operators and the prison at Bear Mountain, the PIPC was becoming a steward of priceless Revolutionary War history as well as of fine parks.

The Highlands is an extension of the Appalachian Mountains, a one-thousand-mile-long geologic "fold" in the earth's crust extending northeastward from Alabama through the Blue Ridge Mountains of Tennessee, the Great Smokies of Virginia and West Virginia, across Pennsylvania to the New Jersey–New York Highlands, and on to the Berkshires of Connecticut. "Old" is the one-word description of these mountains, worn down by eons of water, wind, and glaciation.

Early in the eighteenth century, according to the 15th Annual Report of the New York State Forest, Fish and Game Commission, the Highlands was "a wild and shaggy wilderness, densely covered with forests of white pine and hemlock, the haunt of bears and wolves" that was largely bypassed by Dutch colonists who favored more gentle lands on the eastern shoreline and north of the Hudson River Narrows. Native Americans of the Algonquin Nation found good hunting and trapping in the Highlands, but by the 1700s almost all of the Native Americans were gone. Only a few rustic cabins were clustered on the western bank of the river at the base of Dunderberg Mountain, marking the southern gateway to the "Devil's Horse Race," the narrow six-mile defile of water, current, and wind that voyagers must navigate in order to proceed upriver as far as Albany, one hundred miles to the north.

The cluster of cabins was known as "Caldwell's," named for the family that first settled there. One of the cabins had been converted into a primitive tavern, the "last oasis" used by ships' passengers and sailors while awaiting favorable winds and tides, for fortifying their courage before tackling the unpredictable narrows. But a ship that called at Caldwell's landing in the summer of 1720 was not the typical Dutch or English vessel. Its rigging and lines were alien, nothing like those of craft common to river commerce. "From it landed a party of dark, bearded, fierce looking men," old residents of the Highlands remembered. Heavily armed members of the crew remained aboard the ship to discourage the curious.

The landing party carried picks, shovels, and sacks, told no one of their business, and asked no questions. They started west along an old indian trail that led through the pass between Bear Mountain and West Mountain, and seemed to know where they were going. No one saw them during the summer, but in the fall they came back, each staggering under a heavy load in his sack. Before boarding their ship, they stopped at Caldwell's for some cheer, and, one of them, in his cups, showed the contents of his sack, loaded with rich silver ore.

They made sail, and disappeared down the river. During the winter, hunters and trappers searched the woods and on the north slope of Black Mountain, found a rude log cabin. It was a two-room, saddle back affair, and the porch in the middle was oriented toward the summit of the mountain, as if the occupants had wanted to keep the heights under observation. Those who discovered the cabin suspected a mine, but further searching revealed not the slightest trace of any opening.

A year later, the Spaniards came back again in the same ship, and made their way to Black Mountain. Their fierce appearance discouraged interference. They worked unmolested, again coming out in the fall to sail away, sacks full.

According to the legend, these fierce-looking men, suspected of being Spanish pirates, returned again the next year and were confronted by the scruffy clientele at Caldwell's, who wanted to know their business. After a brief altercation, the locals were convinced to control their curiosity and chose not to follow as six of the mystery men disappeared into the Highlands.

But that fall, only two of the six came out and returned to their ship and sailed away, never to return. Soon after, a search party explored Black Mountain. They found the cabin and the bodies of two men inside. In the ribs of one was a Spanish dagger. The other had a broken skull. There was no sign of the other two. It was getting dark, but the searchers climbed higher on the mountain, looking for the opening to a shaft.

Late the next day, the haggard and terror stricken search party staggered into Caldwell's with a fearful story. As they approached the summit of Black Mountain, they were met by the ghosts of two men, sheeted in a light of phosphorescence. When they tried to flee, they couldn't move. They huddled under a great tree and shivered in fright until dawn, with the luminous ghosts whirling madly about. At the first light, the spirits disappeared, the searchers recovered command of their arms and legs and hurried down the mountain.

No silver was ever discovered in the Highlands. According to the tale, the cabin finally rotted away after being occupied for many years by a farmer and his family. Ghosts, lights, and strange noises are said to persist near the summit of Black Mountain.

Hidden treasure in the Highlands, guarded by ghosts from a mystery ship that sailed away into misty legend was one thing, but the presence of Gen. Sir William Howe, with his red-coated troops and Hessian mercenaries, and the British fleet in New York Harbor in June, 1776, was undeniably real. Both the British and Patriots knew the strategic value of the Hudson River—if war came, control of the Hudson by the British would divide New England from the rest of the colonies and doom any revolt almost before it began. Sir William Clinton explained this scenario in dispatches to His Majesty, King George III. For the Patriots, the logical and only way to defend the Hudson against a superior force was to fortify the Palisades and control the narrow river gorge of the Highlands, forty miles north of New York City. The Hudson River was the keystone, the centerpiece on the strategic chessboard of maneuver, countermaneuver, and pending combat that would determine the fate of a fledgling nation. According to historian Adrian C. Leiby,

When the revolution came, New York City was to be, for all but the first year of the war, the chief citadel of the British invader. In the mountains to the north and west there were to be thousands of armed Continentals, waiting and maneuvering for a chance to drive the hated redcoats into the sea. On Manhattan, Britain was to gather the largest army it had ever assembled in America, an army that lashed out at the surrounding rebel forces when it could, now and then striking out somewhere else in an effort to draw the American forces from the protecting mountains, but never forgetting that New York City was the great target and prize of the Continental army and that the Hudson Highlands were its base.

These facts were not lost on Gen. George Washington, who ordered the fortification of the Palisades, originally named "Fort Constitution," then renamed "Fort Lee" in honor of Charles Lee, a British general who switched allegiance to the Patriots, was a victor at the Battle of Charleston, South Carolina, and became Washington's second in command at the beginning of the war. (Lee was eventually court-marshaled for command failures.) Again according to Leiby:

> The site was almost a natural fortification. A clove in the Palisades, where a farm road from English Neighborhood twisting its way from the heights down to the river landing, left a high promontory standing out from the Palisades, inaccessible from three sides because of precipitous rocks, which fell off hundreds of feet to the river on one side and far enough on the other to discourage any assault. Ten acres were cleared, partly on this promontory and partly on the high land to the west, all rocky and heavily wooded wasteland on the farm of Peter Bourdet, whose farmhouse and cultivated land lay to the west, along the road to Bergen.

An "abatis" of felled trees, sharpened into giant spears pointed toward a possible enemy approach, was thrown across the vulnerable northern entrance to the fort. Scores of small log huts were built in the interior of the stronghold to house hundreds of troops. From the high cliffs, cannons were targeted to fire on any hostile warships. The British tested Washington's cannoneers in October, 1776, by sending the *Phoenix* and *Roebuck* upriver past the fort. Salvos from the Palisades caused no discernible damage.

Despite the events of April 19, 1775, at Lexington and Concord, Massachusetts, the British had no intention of being dragged into a land war with rebels in New England. "New England and the colonies to the south are entirely separated from each other by the River Hudson," observed a British general after the war, "the possession of that river would secure to Great Britain a barrier between the southern and eastern colonies." The British evacuated Boston and transported the army on troop ships to New York Harbor. On August 22, 1776, Howe ordered the attack. British and Hessian soldiers went ashore on Long Island to sharply engage an outmatched rebel force. In progression, the British drove the Patriots from lower Manhattan on September 15, established footholds on Paulus Hook and Bergen Neck across the river in New Jersey, and confronted Patriot muskets in the Harlem Heights (125th Street). After a hotly contested, but inconclusive, encounter at White Plains in late October, where the outgunned and ill-trained Patriots stiffened their resistance, Howe temporarily pulled back, leaving the Patriots guessing about his strategy and next move.

In mid-November, General Washington, sensing that the British might attempt to expand their position in New Jersey before they were locked into winter encampments, led his troops from the battle lines at White Plains. Washington's troops marched northwest to the east bank of the Hudson, crossed the river at Kings Ferry, between present-day Crugers and Stony Point, New York, then marched twenty-five miles south to join Gen. Nathanael Greene, commander of 2,400 soldiers stationed at Hackensack and Fort Lee, New Jersey. General Lee remained at White Plains with 7,500 men. Another Continental Army force of three thousand men was positioned farther north at Peekskill, New York. "Fort Washington," manned by 1,200 troops under the command of Col. Robert Magaw, on Manhattan Island (where the modern-day George Washington Bridge connects to the east side of the Hudson, directly across from Fort Lee), continued as a foothold of resistance against the British presence in the city.

Howe provided an answer for the guessing Patriots. On November 16, 1776, Fort Washington was attacked. General Greene, observing the attack from the heights of the Palisades at Fort Lee, brought the crushing news to Washington in Hackensack that more than two thousand of the most promising troops in the Continental Army, including the reinforcements Greene had sent across the river unknown to Washington, had been captured or killed. Such a swift and severe blow to the Patriots placed Washington's position on the Palisades in grave danger, but before ordering a withdrawal of the remaining troops at Fort Lee, estimated at no more than two thousand men, Washington wanted to remove as many of the supplies stored there as possible. The task would be slow.

Sensing a crucial opportunity, Howe next sent Lord Cornwallis on a secret mission to capture Washington and the Fort Lee defenders. The British clandestinely positioned twenty flatboats about ten miles above Fort Lee. Under overcast nighttime skies on November 19–20, the "portly and awkward" Cornwallis, who was later to meet Washington under very different circumstances at Yorktown, ordered the flatboats to begin ferrying battalions of British and Hessian troops across the river to a landing at an old house under the dark Palisades cliffs. Cornwallis commandeered the house as his "headquarters." The corps was in place on the landing by nine in the morning but faced the daunting challenge of gaining the summit of the cliffs up a narrow, half-mile-long, precipitous path. Night had shielded the British maneuver, but daylight revealed the expeditionary force to Continental sentries. By ten o'clock, Washington had been warned of the landing.

One of the fascinating coincidences of the Revolutionary War is that Washington's route of escape from Fort Lee and Cornwallis's route of advance passed exactly the same place, Liberty Pole Tavern, roughly midway between the two forces. Cornwallis was delayed while his troops struggled to drag cannons to the top of the cliffs. Nevertheless, he apparently assumed that Washington would stay in place to defend Fort Lee. But Washington waited no longer. He promptly withdrew, marching his men in good order past Liberty Pole Tavern within hours of the British arrival there. In the span of these few hours, Cornwallis missed an opportunity to deal a staggering, perhaps fatal, blow to the Patriots. Washington slipped beyond his grasp and would spend a harrowing winter at Morristown.

With the capture of Forts Washington and Lee, the way was clear to effect the British strategy of dividing the colonies. Winter, and further British campaign preparations, slowed the action for several months. By the following summer, commanders, tactics, and armies were in place. From Montreal, British Gen. Johnny Burgoyne would drive south, take Fort Ticonderoga, and continue into the Hudson River Valley. Lt. Col. Barry St. Leger would transport troops up the St. Lawrence River from Montreal to Fort Oswego on the southern shoreline of Lake Ontario, then loop back, marching east down the Mohawk River to the Hudson. Howe's army would move north up the Hudson to meet Burgoyne's and St. Leger's forces.

Standing against this strategy were Patriot forces in the vicinity of Albany, New York, under the command of Gen. Philip Schuyler, later succeeded by Gen. Horatio Gates, and small, rustic fortifications in the Hudson River narrows manned by militiamen, consisting primarily of tenant and freehold farmers from the surrounding counties. The principal fortifications were Forts Clinton and Montgomery, both located at Bear Mountain on the western side of the river, complemented in spectacular fashion by a great chain, forged from iron ore mined in the Highlands and drawn across the Hudson from the river's edge below the forts to the opposite shore. Farther upriver, where it widened and became more shallow, the Patriots positioned a "chevaux-de-frise," a submerged line of stone-filled, wooden cribs hiding sharp-pointed iron poles designed to rip at the hull of any passing ship. These defenses, ordered by the Continental Congress, were of great concern to Washington. He placed his trust in George Clinton, a lawyer-farmer from Ulster County, New York, who showed great natural ability to inspire trust and confidence in his fellow citizen-soldiers. Appointed to the rank of brigadier-general in the militia, Clinton was given active military command in the Highlands. He joined his brother, Col. James Clinton, who had already been posted to the forts at Bear Mountain. They organized what had been a chaotic and fitful attempt to prepare defenses in the narrows. Using boulders, logs, and earth, the Patriots erected Fort Montgomery—named in honor of Brig. Gen. Richard Montgomery, who had died in a freezing blizzard during an unsuccessful assault on Quebec in December, 1775—on the north side of Popolopen Creek, a tributary of the Hudson. Across a deep gorge cut by the creek stood the second and smaller fortification, later named Fort Clinton. One of the most dramatic and profound confrontations of the war was about to take place at these two forts.

In June, 1777, Burgoyne and St. Leger began their advances against the Patriots according to plan. But Howe, seeing a chance to take Philadelphia, and with Washington held in check in Morristown, New Jersey, divided his New York City forces and sailed for the Chesapeake Bay, leaving to Sir Henry Clinton (perhaps a distant relative of the brothers Clinton) the duty of executing the three-pronged strategy devised to vanquish the rebels in the Hudson River Valley. Sir Henry hesitated, waiting for reinforcements from England. On September 25, the reinforcements arrived, three thousand troops on sixty ships. On October 3–4, Sir Henry moved north. Earlier in the year, George Clinton's title had changed from general to governor. While overseeing the Highlands fortifications, he had been elected New York's first governor, would be reelected six more times, and would finally cap an esteemed political career as vice president of the United States. With brother James in charge at Forts Montgomery and Clinton, the governor had assumed his duties in Kingston, the provisional seat of New York government. On hearing of the British move, he rushed back from Kingston to join his brother and the militia at the forts.

The efforts at fortification and gun-positioning were centered on the obvious objective, using the narrow and swift river, the "Devil's Horse Race," in combination with the targeted guns, to throw an insurmountable block in the path of the British. To the rear of the forts, a four-pointed redoubt, incomplete earthworks, and abatis of felled trees provided some protection for the six hundred militiamen. Two Patriot frigates, a privateer, and two row galleys were anchored just above the chain.

For conspicuous reasons, Sir Henry determined not to confront the narrows head-on. On the morning of October 6, covered by an opportune fog, using the same bid for secrecy and surprise attempted by Cornwallis at the Palisades, British troops, strengthened by Loyalists under the command of Beverly Robinson, landed at Kings Ferry on the western shore of the Hudson, well downriver from the narrows. The British had shrouded their plans by making a feint the previous day on the opposite side of the river. Robinson, a wealthy landowner and loyal subject to the crown, knew the Highlands region. From his home near present-day Garrison, just across the river from West Point, Robinson had roamed the Highlands on hunting trips. He helped Sir Henry plan the flank attack, choosing a narrow trail that led through the rugged Highlands to Mountville (later renamed Doodletown), an isolated hamlet settled by woodcutters that was tucked in a small valley within two miles of Forts Clinton and Montgomery. Men from the hamlet were among the militia gathered to defend the forts. So, too, were tenant farmers from across the river who paid rent to Robinson.

To reach Mountville, the British, Loyalists, and Hessians, numbering more than two thousand troops, filed unchallenged through a pass on Dunderberg Mountain that, had it been guarded, would have raised havoc with Sir Henry's plan. At Mountville, the British forces were split into two columns, one of which looped around Bear Mountain, following the same route alleged to have been used by the mysterious Spaniards, to assault Fort Montgomery from the rear. The second column waited at Mountville. Their signal would be the sound of firing when the Fort Montgomery attack began. The movement of so many British troops had not gone entirely undetected by the Patriots. Governor Clinton could not be certain of the size of the force being brought against him, but he sent an urgent message asking for reinforcements to his commanding officer, Gen. Israel Putnam. No reinforcements would arrive. The battle started with a skirmish at about 10:00 a.m. between a Patriot scouting party and the British at Mountville. Clinton's one piece of field artillery was positioned on the Forest of Dean Mine road about a mile from Fort Montgomery, facing toward the British column that had taken the harsh route around Bear Mountain.

A crucial moment in history had arrived. Six hundred poorly armed militia and a handful of regular Continental Army soldiers faced a disciplined British force of greatly superior strength.

The battle was fierce. Grapeshot from the field piece drove back the advancing British until the gunners were outflanked. When British soldiers charged with fixed bayonets, the retreating gunners spiked the cannon, making it useless. For several hours, the opposing forces were locked in a desperate struggle. Musket fire was unrelenting across a "no-man's land" separating the contending forces. The British rushed the walls of the two forts, only to be beaten back. By late after-

Diorama, Battle of Forts Clinton and Montgomery, 1777.
(Courtesy of PIPC Archives)

noon, British galleys were close enough to begin bombarding the forts from the river. Patriot artillerymen returned fire. As the day faded, the British demanded surrender of the forts within five minutes under a white flag of truce. The Patriot response was to demand a British surrender. The lull ended with the most powerful British attack of the day. British regimental commander Mungo Campbell, who only moments earlier had demanded the Patriot surrender, died in the assault.

The first British soldier to breech the abatis and earthworks at Fort Montgomery was George Turnbull, a Loyalist. British soldiers at Fort Clinton were pushing one another up over the works, where they were met hand-to-hand with bayonets and bullets. Count Grabouski, a Polish nobleman and aide-de-camp to Sir Henry, was killed. The savage struggle turned from the defense of the doomed forts to a slashing escape for those Patriots who survived. In the dusk, Governor Clinton and his wounded brother managed to reach the river and cross by boat to the opposite shore. Militiamen, covering the escape by their comrades, fired last volleys and threw down their guns. Forty-one British lay dead; 142 were wounded. According to Col. Jim Johnson, a faculty member at West Point, seventy Patriots died, forty were wounded, and 240 were taken prisoner. The Patriot ships above the chain, unable to be sailed from harm's way upriver against a strong ebb tide, were set on fire. Several months later, a chaplain, visiting the site of the battle, reported that the bodies of the Patriots could still be seen where they had been dumped into a nearby pond.

Within a stone's throw of the place where, years later, Superintendent Howard wanted to build a prison and the PIPC celebrated the Harriman gift, the twin forts in the Hudson River narrows were lost to the British in one of the most gallant stands in the annals of U.S. military history. Sir Henry captured the forts and then sent his ships busting through the chain three days later, and past the chevaux-de-frise on October 11. But the ferocious action at Forts Montgomery and Clinton seriously delayed his advance toward Albany.

St. Leger, attempting the Mohawk River route to the Hudson, was driven into retreat at Oriskany, near Fort Stanwix, New York. Sir Henry's forces were in Kingston, New York, on October 17, still forty miles from Albany, when Burgoyne's army was defeated and surrendered to General Gates at the Battle of

Washington's Headquarters, Newburgh, New York, 1782–1783.
This is the nation's first publicly designated historic site.
(Courtesy of PIPC Archives)

Saratoga—a crushing blow to the British cause. The British strategy to divide the colonies through control of the Hudson River was in shambles. The British, who considered Kingston "a nursery for every villain in the country," torched the entire town the day before Burgoyne surrendered. By the end of October, British ships and troops were back in New York City.

George Perkins and his fellow commissioners would find themselves holding title to and managing the historic sites of Forts Lee, Clinton, and Montgomery, and the Senate House in Kingston where Governor Clinton and the New York Legislature had established a temporary seat of government. This was a far cry in terms of purpose and responsibility from the mission of protecting natural beauty that they had undertaken. They were finding that the nation's history and its natural beauty were not separate, distinct portfolios. The Harriman gift and acquisition of land on the Palisades also gave to the PIPC the stewardship of bloody soil that had nurtured the very roots of the United States. To add to these historic sites, the PIPC would also assume responsibility from the American Scenic and Historic Preservation Society for Stony Point Battlefield, where Brigadier-General Wayne and his soldiers made their daring midnight attack.

An icon of historic preservation is Washington's Headquarters in Newburgh, New York, recognized in 1850 as the nation's first publicly designated historic site. Washington had just missed capture in 1776 at Fort Lee. In 1782–83 he and his wife, Martha, occupied the Hasbrouck House in Newburgh, less than sixty miles upriver from Fort Lee. The Continental Army was encamped at nearby New Windsor. Washington was awaiting the Treaty of Paris and the end of the Revolutionary War. His officers and troops were restive. Farmer-soldiers wanted to return to their families and lands; officers were leery of a civilian government that seemed to be ignoring their rightful claims to back pay. Washington's test at Newburgh–New Windsor was to keep the army intact and ready if the Paris negotiations failed. At one point, he delivered the famous "Newburgh Address" by which, by force of personality and conviction, he convinced his officers to hold firm. For the men in ranks, Washington directed that a "Badge of Military Merit," made of purple cloth in the shape of a heart, be awarded for bravery to deserving soldiers. Three badges, the forerunners of the Purple Heart, were awarded, marking the first occasion that military awards were given to men below the rank of officer.

On behalf of the State of New York, the PIPC would assume responsibility for Washington's Headquarters at Newburgh, New York, the nearby New Windsor Cantonment where the northern wing of the Continental Army had camped during the winter of 1782–83, and the John Ellison House, used as headquarters by Maj. Gens. Henry Knox, Greene, and Gates. The Fort Lee and Black-ledge–Kearney House historic sites in New Jersey, the Stony Point Battlefield, Forts Clinton and Montgomery at Bear Mountain, Knox's Headquarters, New Windsor, the Senate House in Kingston, and the icon, Washington's Headquarters, have vested in the PIPC a special charge to keep faith with events that formed the very foundation on which this nation's democratic form of government stands. Collectively, these nine sites speak to a fragile moment in the history of international conflict, when the outcome for Washington and his army was almost always in doubt but their cause was never abandoned.

6.
Welch

April 15, 1910
Mr. Frank E. Lutz
Assistant Curator
American Museum of Natural History

Dear Sir:

Replying to your favor of the 14th instant, I beg to advise you that the Commissioners gladly extend permission to you to collect insects in the Interstate Park.

Yours very truly,
J. DuPratt White

Scientific study of moths, beetles, ants, mosquitoes, ticks, fireflies, crickets, and insects in general seems so esoteric to most people that it usually wins nothing more than amused and fleeting curiosity. An eccentric person in a pith helmet, romping through fields with a butterfly net, is the popular image of the entomologist. Frank Lutz may have used a butterfly net, but his work with the American Museum of Natural History established him as a major presence in the nation's scientific and educational community. Before his career ended in 1943, Lutz had developed a museum collection of more than 2 million specimens of insects, one of the great baseline scientific collections in the world.

Lutz was drawn to the open space being protected by the PIPC for its potential as an outdoor laboratory. Where others saw recreational opportunity, he saw in the Highlands an environment that might add important findings about insects to the repository of scientific knowledge. Lutz needed only a few acres for his research, and like almost all environmental scientists, he needed a location that was rent free, or nearly so. Budgets for his type of work ranged from meager to nonexistent. In addition to cost considerations, he was lured to the PIPC-owned land because it was close to the Museum of Natural History and promised stability; Lutz could develop baseline data while knowing that he could revisit his control points year after year.

Additionally, a scientific site in the Highlands could be used for educational purposes. Lutz enjoyed delivering educational messages in a manner that had staying power. Once, he tried to make a wager with the director of the Museum of Natural History that he could find more than five hundred species of insects on his seventy-five-by-one-hundred-foot yard in Ramsey, New Jersey. When the director declined the wager, Lutz countered by proposing that his salary be raised by $10 per year for every species above five hundred that he could find. Still the director declined, but Lutz made the count anyway. He found 1,402 insect species on his small lot. The story of the attempted wager was told over and over again.

Lutz would not realize his wish for an insect field station until 1925. In that year, W. Averell Harriman, now a PIPC commissioner, made a grant that allowed Lutz to establish the "Station for the Study of Insects" on a forty-acre plot of land in the Highlands. He used the station as a classroom by allowing young students to work and stay in the camplike setting during the summer. One of these young students was David Rockefeller, who, at age twelve, became fascinated by the universe of insects, so much so that he became an expert in beetles. In his later travels as a banker, statesman, and business leader, Rockefeller could go anywhere in the world with a certainty that the interest he developed at the station would serve him well while he personally assembled what has become a spectacular, comprehensive, and scientifically meaningful collection of beetles. In young Rockefeller, Lutz found a student who discovered the best of educational values—enjoyment, expertise, and commendable achievement.

To encourage his students, Lutz developed a trail around the station and posted small signs to identify interesting plants, insect haunts, and other natural features. In so doing, he created the first nature trail in the United States. At the beginning of the trail, the first sign read, "The spirit of the training trail: a friend somewhat versed in natural history is taking a walk with you and calling your attention to interesting things." In 1926 Lutz transplanted his educational techniques and scientific interest to Bear Mountain by establishing the Trailside

Museum in cooperation with the American Museum of Natural History. The Trailside Museum and Wildlife Center remains a significant asset for the PIPC.

By bringing the prestige and integrity of the Museum of Natural History to the woods and meadows of the Highlands, Lutz confirmed the scientific and educational benefits of parks. He recognized the potential of these lands to engage the intellect as well as the senses. Research and educational activities aimed at a better understanding of the environment, so widespread in parks throughout the nation today, can be traced, in part, to a little patch of land tucked into a remote corner of Harriman State Park.

George Perkins may have been somewhat aware of Lutz's initiative to bring practical science under the PIPC's banner, but he had other concerns on his mind. At the end of 1910 Perkins retired from J. P. Morgan & Company. His reasons for this decision were many: an increasing personal interest in the problems caused by the rapid growth of corporations; the related effect of profit-sharing on relationships between employers and employees; and the fact that he had worked hard, won significant business victories for Morgan & Company, and gained great wealth. The Harriman gift, too, was a motivating factor. Perkins had been continually at the helm of the PIPC but had not been immersed in the many day-to-day details that were rapidly transforming its assumptions and needs. In a memorandum that accompanied his retirement announcement, Perkins explained, "I have long felt that it is not wise to leave all our public affairs to the politicians, and that business men of sufficient leisure and means should for patriotic reasons give their attention to great public problems." His retirement from active business life also reflected growing stress in his relationship with Morgan. Perkins's biographer, John A. Garraty, reports that Morgan's "increased irascibility and distrust" had found its way to Perkins himself. The business association with Morgan that was started with a requested donation for the PIPC had lasted for a decade. The break was stormy but not irreparable; although a professional coolness thereafter existed between the two men, Morgan would continue to respond to the PIPC's funding pleas, and Perkins always used the quaint phrase "dear Senior" in a respectful and affectionate manner when referring to the elder financier who had catapulted him to the top of the business world.

Perkins's more focused attention on PIPC matters came none too soon. The commissioners were under criticism for not responding to the demand that Henry Hudson Drive, envisioned for the base of the Palisades in New Jersey, be extended northward along the river shore, perhaps all the way to Bear Mountain, thirty miles north of the New Jersey–New York border. J. DuPratt White again served as the lightning rod. In a lengthy letter to the editor of *The New York Times* on March 19,

1911, White defended the PIPC and explained the practical difficulties of the road project, adding that "as is usually the case with writers of letters to newspapers for the purpose of correcting supposed public wrongs, your said correspondents are hopelessly ignorant of their subject matter. They show no knowledge whatsoever of the laws creating or governing the great Interstate Park, of the plans of this Commission, or of the topography or geography of the region." Controversy swirled around the question of roads. Perkins was accused of bowing to the wishes of Mrs. Lydia G. Lawrence by refusing to condemn her property on the border of the two states to make way for the road project. A New Jersey assemblyman wrongly denounced Commissioners William A. Linn and Abram De Ronde, both appointed in 1900, for cashing in on PIPC projects through the National Bank of Hackensack and the Palisades Title and Guarantee Company of Englewood, New Jersey, controlled, respectively, by Linn and De Ronde.

Despite these criticisms, on March 11, 1911, a headline in the *Rockland Journal News* proclaimed, "COMMISSION BUYS THE HOOK." "What a few months ago seemed to many like an impossibility, or a difficult proposition at the least, has been accomplished really in a few weeks by the Palisades Park Commission." Five years after the Commission's authority had been extended north of the state line to include Hook Mountain, the Barber Asphalt Company sold its subsidiary, the Manhattan Trap Rock Company, to the PIPC for $415,000, including a large concrete power house subsequently converted to park use at Nyack Beach. Attorney Irving Hopper of Nyack, New York, assisted in settling the details of the purchase. Although two additional quarries, the Rockland Lake and Clinton Point Trap Rock companies, remained in operation, the hard-fought contest with the quarry operators was clearly coming to an end.

The heightened profile and success of the PIPC led landowners to approach the Commission in the hope of selling their properties at inflated values. Proposals were advanced, only to collide with the time-tested business and legal skills of the commissioners. Publicity caused by the Harriman gifts of land and money, and the associated increase in private and government funding for the PIPC, did not change the basic style of Perkins, White, and their colleagues—each dollar was squeezed for maximum benefit. Those looking for quick windfall profits were firmly discouraged, including Addison Johnson, who owned five hundred acres at Bear Mountain. Johnson proposed to sell his land to the PIPC for $100 per acre, total price $50,000. The commissioners learned that Johnson had purchased the property two years earlier for $7,500 and refused further contact with him for several months. When Perkins did reopen the negotiation, he offered Johnson $10,000 and gave the owner two weeks to accept. Johnson accepted.

Steven Rowe Bradley of Nyack, New York, made a much more attractive offer.

Quarry site, Hook Mountain, New York.
(Courtesy of PIPC Archives)

Bradley proposed to donate 212 acres on South Mountain to the PIPC, to be designated "Rockland Park." Bradley was a community leader who was instrumental in forming the Nyack National Bank in 1878, the Nyack Library in 1879, and the Nyack Hospital in 1895.

South Mountain is a high ridge above Piermont, New York, offering a sweeping, forty-mile view of the Hudson River. The ridge accommodates Tweed Boulevard, named for the infamous "Boss" William M. Tweed, master of New York City machine politics. Tweed sponsored a road connection from Hoboken, New Jersey, to Nyack, New York, and the narrow road on the summit of the ridge was testimony to his influence, for he was a powerful man who could make things happen. Tweed ultimately fell from a commanding position in the rough-and-tumble of his political world when he was convicted of fraud and sent "up the river" to Sing Sing Prison to spend his last days behind bars. But Tweed Boulevard, providing access to present-day Blauvelt State Park, remains a fixture on the ridge summit only a few steps away from the all-but-forgotten final resting place of John C. Fremont.

Fremont, the great western pathfinder, controversial explorer, and U.S. Army general, first governor of California, first governor of Arizona, first Republican candidate for president of the United States, gold miner, and adventurer, died in a hotel room in New York City while trying to recoup a lost fortune. Ironically, Fremont's one connection with parks was the fortunate accident of being host at his Mariposa, California, ranch to Frederick Law Olmsted when Yosemite was "discovered" in 1849. The PIPC commissioners and Bradley had no idea that a park, about to be created on South Mountain, would have a symbolic connection with the wildest of the Wild West in the remains of a man lying nearby in his grave.

At the May 1, 1911, meeting of the PIPC, the commissioners accepted Bradley's generous offer to begin the creation of a park on South Mountain. But the donor was in ill health. Before the transaction could be completed, he passed away at the age of seventy-five. His children immediately took up the cause, and title to the Bradley property was transferred to the Commission in October. In a prophetic letter to the commissioners, the Bradley heirs expressed their collective expectation that the land "shall be deeded for a natural park, to be held for the benefit and enjoyment of the public at large, open at all times for their use—to secure the perpetuation of the birds, animals, plants, trees and other natural features—and to restrict and govern the admission of motor vehicles." On behalf of their father, and so early in the century, S. R. Bradley, Mary T. Bradley, Augusta B. Chapman, and William C. Bradley were recommending guidelines for park stewardship that would become the focus of constant debate between preservation advocates and proponents for the exploitation of parks. Their concern about "motor vehicles," at a time when horse carriages still outnumbered automobiles, is reflected ninety years later in many hotly contested park debates. Today, Yosemite Valley, near the ranch once owned by Fremont, suffers traffic gridlock on summer days; sightseeing aircraft flights plague the Grand Canyon; off-road vehicles scar fragile desert habitat; snowmobiles shatter winter quiet; and motorboats and powered jet skis dominate many lakes and river segments. While preservationists urge a reduction in the impact of motor vehicles on parks, vendors see profit in the ever-increasing numbers of cars and recreational machines and in as much commercialization as possible.

Concerned about other matters, the Bradley heirs did not happen to mention rifle fire. A state rifle range existed on the summit of South Mountain adjacent to the Bradley property. Samuel Broadbent, president of the Board of Health, Village of Grand View-on-Hudson, New York, wrote to Perkins to urge the PIPC to acquire the range should it be abandoned by the state as Broadbent predicted. As it was, there were definite problems with the rifle range. It was aligned in a manner that faced shooters directly into the morning sun. Errant bullets, some caused by the sun's glare and others the result of poor shooting, would fly across the ridge line and fall among houses in Grand View and the adjacent villages. White, as usual, responded for the PIPC:

In the form of affidavits, I suggest that you gather as much evidence as you can of actual trespass of bullets upon the properties of residents in the villages. It is common talk that bullets have entered houses through the walls or roofs and the windows, and that bullets have also been seen to strike the ground within the limits of the several villages. These circumstances, it seems to me, should be run down and proper evidence embodied in affidavits before any Legislative committee is asked to pass upon a bill.

In other words, the PIPC was interested and willing to help, if the residents of the village could provide convincing proof that bullet holes in their houses had come from the rifle range. With facts in hand, and by an act of the Legislature in May, 1913, the five hundred–acre rifle range was transferred to the PIPC. Bullets flew no more.

Almost in concert with the Bradley gift, Dr. James Douglas of New York City offered to donate to the PIPC several tracts of his land atop the New Jersey Palisades. This proposal, too, was accepted, drawing the commissioners ever closer to involvement with the rolling lands and elegant estates that capped the cliffs. These properties had escaped the attention of the PIPC during its battle with the quarry operators, but the spectacular river views from the summit lands, their inherent and exquisite wildness, and the need to improve access to increasingly popular park holdings were proving to be irresistible to the commissioners.

The subject of developing a boulevard to connect urban residents with the evolving park system had been under discussion almost from the inception of the interstate initiative. The Henry Hudson Drive had been given a major financial boost when New Jersey appropriated $500,000 in response to the Harriman gift. The boulevard idea was gaining momentum as the PIPC acquired each new property. The commissioners were seeking a connection from the city all the way to Bear Mountain, forty-two miles upriver. Charles W. Leavitt, Jr., chief consulting engineer for the PIPC, recommended that the services of consulting engineer Alfred Nobel, famed as the inventor of dynamite and later to endow the Nobel Prize, be retained to study the boulevard question. The commissioners agreed, and Nobel was hired. Among the options considered by Leavitt and Nobel for road access to passengers arriving by ferry was a route to the top of the Palisades through a tunnel drilled in the cliff face at the Carpenter Brothers' old quarry site. At the invitation of Perkins, the commissioners looked forward to further discussion of this and other road options at their next meeting, to be held aboard his yacht, *Thendara*. A meeting on the yacht was timely because another concern much on the minds of the commissioners was the obvious and increasing pollution of the Hudson River.

Raw sewage was being dumped into the river from every village and municipality along its shores. Ships and boats plying the river commonly jettisoned whatever they wished. Driftwood was a menace to small craft and was clogging the New York Harbor shoreline. The river, popular for swimmers, canoeists, sailors, yacht owners, and anglers, had become a handy disposal system for all of the Hudson River Valley, including New York City. Even the Sisters of St. Michael's Convent, a handsome facility built at the edge of the cliffs, continued to dump "slops" into a small stream that cascaded down the cliff and burbled through talus rocks at the base, over a tiny beach, and into the river, much to the dislike of the commissioners. White corresponded with the Mother Superior, asking that this practice be stopped. In more general terms, the PIPC began petitioning Governors John A. Dix, New York, and newly elected Woodrow Wilson, New Jersey, to clean up the river.

While the commissioners grappled with an increasingly broad menu of park concerns, a significant problem of moral responsibility persisted. In July, 1911, White responded to a resolution critical of the PIPC that had been approved at the annual convention of the New Jersey Federation of Women's Clubs. Incredibly, as White stated in a letter to Mrs. Joseph M. Middleton,

> the resolution is a protest against the present condition of the park, and a demand by the Federation that the original idea of the Federation be given consideration, but I do not know what the Federation's original idea was. The resolution further provides that measures shall be adopted to make the tract a true park, with a fitting memorial approved by the women of New Jersey. Will you kindly inform me whether or not the Federation is under the impression that this Commission has ever undertaken to expend any money on said Memorial Park?

Obviously, a misunderstanding had occurred. After more than a decade, the women of New Jersey still did not have their monument.

Another vexing challenge was about to surface. In 1912 people who wished to establish a summer camp to be supervised by the National League of Urban Conditions Among Negroes contacted the PIPC. The commissioners promptly approved the camp in concept, finding logic and appeal in the idea that parklands could benefit any child, regardless of race. But they were to confront the racial attitudes of the early twentieth century and would struggle to open wide the park door to all people of all races.

Matters large and small came to the table for PIPC decisions. In one meeting, the commissioners focused the majority of their discussion on choices for the width of the steep road planned from the Palisades summit at Englewood, New

Jersey, to the shoreline below. Facing the commissioners and their chief consulting engineer Leavitt was a precipitous drop down the cliff face that would be a daunting test for any road builder. The middle-aged and elderly bankers, lawyers, and businessmen on the PIPC scheduled a field visit to the road site, where they scrambled up and down the proposed route to determine the width needed to allow automobiles to get through the hairpin turns.

In November, 1912, Perkins wrote to John D. Rockefeller, Jr., to report the following developments: the quarries at Hook Mountain were being acquired either through willing-seller transactions or by condemnation; the Henry Hudson Drive in New Jersey was under construction; docks had been built along the river to improve public access, including a very large dock at Bear Mountain; the Bear Mountain site itself would be opened to the public the following year; water supplies, sanitation facilities, and picnic and camping areas were being installed to meet increasing visitor demands; and forests were being cleared of deadwood. Perkins concluded the letter by reminding Rockefeller, Jr., of his financial pledge to the Commission: "The amount of your subscription is $500,000; you have paid $200,000, leaving a balance of $300,000. The Commission will very much appreciate receiving a check for this amount on or before December first of this year." Rockefeller willingly complied.

While adjusting to his retirement from Morgan & Company, and grappling with the increasingly complex PIPC agenda, Perkins took on another demanding extracurricular task, as described by Garraty:

It is the evening of June 20, 1912; the scene, a large room in the Congress Hotel in Chicago. About twenty men are present. Perhaps a dozen of them are seated around a large table. Others sprawl wearily in armchairs or lean against the walls. One, a solid, determined-looking fellow with thick glasses and a bristling mustache, paces grimly back and forth in silence, like a caged grizzly. He is Theodore Roosevelt, and these are his closest political advisers. All of them are angry, very angry.

In a nearby auditorium, the Republican National Convention is moving with the ponderous certainty of a steamroller toward the nomination of well-fed William Howard Taft for a second term as President of the United States. All of the men in the hotel room believe that this nomination rightfully belongs to Roosevelt—.

It is growing late, and everyone is weary. Conversation lags. But gradually attention is centered on two men who have withdrawn to a corner. They are talking excitedly in rapid whispers. One is the publisher Frank Munsey; the other, George W. Perkins. Neither has had much political experience, but both are very rich and very fond of Theodore Roosevelt. Now everyone senses their subject and realizes its importance. All eyes are focused in their direction. Suddenly the two millionaires reach a decision. They straighten up and stride across the room to Roosevelt. Each places a hand on one of his shoulders. "Colonel," they say simply, "we will see you through." Thus the Progressive party—"Bull Moose," some will call it—is born.

Munsey's involvement in the Progressive Party was brief, but as with all previous ventures, Perkins made a commitment and intended to do exactly as he said, see it through. He became campaign manager for Roosevelt's bid for another presidential term. Perkins's ideals and philanthropic activities were suggested to reporters in those rare moments when he nudged open the door to his personal thoughts. "Shall I go on and pile up a few more millions on top of those I have already acquired and make a big money pile the monument to my memory? A man should ask himself, what is this all about? Where is my work going to lead me?" By his actions, Perkins, at age fifty, was answering these questions for himself.

He and Roosevelt seemed the odd couple—Roosevelt the trustbuster joining with Perkins the monopolist. But there was no contradiction in Perkins's alignment with the Progressive movement. The PIPC had formed a Roosevelt-Perkins bond, and both the PIPC and this new venture into politics provided avenues that promised social benefits for working men and women, values long championed by Perkins. From the very beginning of his business career, he had maintained a strong interest in socially beneficial government policies and regulation. His involvement with the Progressive Party was an extension of this long-held interest.

The candidates in the 1912 election were President Taft, former President Roosevelt, and New Jersey Governor Wilson. The popular Wilson prevailed in the election. Roosevelt carried six states and finished strongly in second place. Even after the loss, Perkins remained involved with reform politics in the Progressive and Republican Parties, but his duties as president of the PIPC were the central focus of his public work.

That work was not going well. Within the PIPC, controversy developed over the performance of chief consulting engineer Leavitt. The New Jersey commissioners sought Leavitt's removal from direct supervision of the Englewood approach-road project. As a result, Leavitt remained in charge of general engineering work for the PIPC, except for the Englewood project. Commissioner De Ronde resigned as chair of the Roads Subcommittee in favor of Col. Edwin A.

Stevens, who had raised objections about Leavitt's performance. During his career, Leavitt would claim many laudable accomplishments, including the construction of the Yale Bowl, but his relationship with the PIPC was becoming untenable.

On Leavitt's staff was young engineer William Addams Welch. Welch had caught the eye of Perkins, who recruited him to the PIPC. Before Welch concluded his career with the Commission forty years later, he would blaze a path in park development and management second to none in the United States. A Welch connection to the Hudson River Valley was represented by "Welch Island" in the headwaters of the Hackensack River, named for an ancestor who had settled in the region in 1695. The Welch roots extended even further back to Plymouth, Massachusetts, where John Welch had landed soon after the *Mayflower* colonists. The Welch family migrated west to New Jersey, then westward again before the Revolutionary War. The family settled in Kentucky, where William Welch was born in 1868. Welch's father had ridden with Morgan's Raiders during the Civil War. His mother, Priscilla Addams, was descended from John Adams, second president of the United States. An extra *d* had been added to the name when the Southern branch of the family disagreed with the policies of John Quincy Adams, sixth president.

Welch attended college in Colorado and Virginia. On graduation, he worked on engineering projects in Alaska for six years, then in the Western states, Mexico, and South America. Yellow fever caused Welch to return to the United States, where, in private practice, he designed the beautiful Havre de Grace racetrack in Maryland and built the boardwalk at Long Beach, Long Island. When he was tapped by Perkins to join the PIPC, Welch stepped into untested territory. Long before his career ended, park advocates from all over the United States and Europe were seeking him out for advice and guidance at his small, secluded Bear Mountain cabin. Welch, who granted no interviews with the press and sought no personal accolades, became the "father" of the state-park movement and greatly influenced the creation of the National Park Service.

One of his passions was the construction of camps for children in Harriman Park. Eleanor Roosevelt attended the dedication of one of these camps. Given the honor of breaking a bottle of champagne over a boulder, Roosevelt swung hard and missed, hitting Welch instead. As reported in *The New York Times,* "After he came to, the ceremonies were resumed."

Welch's experiences and accomplishments with the PIPC would be many, but at the moment of the Leavitt controversy, unknown to himself and the commissioners, Welch was exactly the right person to join in the park experiment.

7.

Bear Mountain

March 1, 1913
Hon. William Sulzer
Governor of New York
Albany, New York

My dear Sir:

The situation existing in New Jersey, relative to the appointment of Commissioners of the Palisades Inter-State Park is such that I feel it incumbent on me to offer you my resignation.

I hereby resign as a Commissioner of the Palisades Inter-State Park of the State of New York to take effect at your pleasure or upon the appointment of my successor.

Very truly yours,
Abram De Ronde

Politics and mortality were taking a toll on the PIPC. The signal from Democrat Governor James F. Fiedler of New Jersey, who succeeded Woodrow Wilson in the November, 1912, election, echoed the former governor's opinion that Abram De Ronde, an active participant in conservation activities since the inception of the PIPC thirteen years previously, was no longer politically acceptable. De Ronde, a member of the New Jersey Democratic Committee, had apparently stepped on the wrong toes within the power structure of his own party. With his resignation, De Ronde's named disappeared from the commissioners' roster, ironically to resurface nineteen years later when he was reappointed to the PIPC by Democrat New Jersey Governor A. Harry Moore. De Ronde thereafter served until his death in 1937.

Two other charter members departed the PIPC in 1913: William A. Linn, a second political casualty in New Jersey, who, like De Ronde, submitted his resignation, and D. McNeely Stauffer, who passed away. Four years earlier, death had also taken William B. Dana. Succeeding Dana was Richard V. Lindabury, who, having grown up on his family's farm in Peapack, New Jersey, chose to become a lawyer and was a founding partner of Lindabury, Depue, & Faulks in Newark, New Jersey. Through various legal proceedings, including a successful challenge directed at the American Tobacco Company for the restraint of trade, and a defense of the United States Steel Corporation against trust-busting, Lindabury gained a distinguished reputation in his chosen profession. He served as a director and counsel for the Prudential Life Insurance Company and, a lifelong Democrat, was urged by party leaders to run for governor. Lindabury declined, preferring, instead, to return to his farming roots by creating and devoting attention to "Meadowland," his six hundred–acre estate near Bernardsville, New Jersey. Lindabury brought sharp legal talent to the PIPC and would serve as a commissioner for fourteen years until a tragic equestrian accident took his life.

Succeeding De Ronde was Frederick C. Sutro, a Harvard University graduate and campaigner for Wilson, who helped found Sutro Brothers Braid Company, a textile manufacturer. Sutro's avocation and true love were history and park conservation. He was elected president of the New Jersey Parks and Recreation Association, a post he held for twenty years. His service with the Commission extended from 1912 to 1940. Within the PIPC, Sutro performed the impossible in 1931 by stepping down from his appointment as a commissioner to assume the task of executive director for the next nine years, answering as a paid manager to the very men with whom he had shared authority as a volunteer and peer.

Appointed to succeed Stauffer was Charles W. Baker, an engineer with ties to Theodore Roosevelt and William Howard Taft. Baker played a significant role as a consultant on the Panama Canal project and was a champion for municipal ownership of utility companies. Baker's tenure with the PIPC would extend for thirty-five years. He joined his PIPC colleagues at just the right moment to provide important guidance in the construction of the Henry Hudson Driveway at the base of the Palisades cliffs.

Filling a fourth vacant slot was Dr. Edward L. Partridge, who was promptly elected treasurer. Partridge would hold that office and serve with the PIPC until 1929.

The remaining commissioners were George Perkins, Edwin Stevens, J. DuPratt White, Franklin Hopkins, Nathan Barrett, and William Porter. These men and their predecessors, successors, colleagues, and employees seemed to share a common affliction: once bitten by the park bug, always bitten. The idea of serving for two or three years in dutiful public service was alien to most commissioners. Several of them, as already demonstrated, were and would be carried feet-first from their PIPC responsibilities.

March 6, 1913
Mr. George F. Perkins
Hotel Raymond
Pasadena, California

Dear Mr. Perkins:

I enclose copy of a letter just received from Senator George A. Blauvelt in regard to certain proposed legislation hostile to Park interests. Hagar has plenty of nerve to attempt legislation of this kind. The exception of the Conger property would be a fearful breach of good faith on the part of the State with the people and the large private contributions.

Yours very truly,
Leonard Hull Smith
Assistant Secretary, PIPC

New York State Senator Hagar, otherwise unknown to the PIPC, appeared to be representing a holdout quarry operator at Hook Mountain, New York. The senator was attempting by legislative maneuver to exclude the quarry site from the PIPC's acquisitive power. Hagar attempted a clever legislative tactic by seeking to legally mandate expansion of the PIPC to twenty commissioners, with the obvious intent of diluting the influence of Perkins, White, and their eight fellow commissioners. Fortunately for the PIPC, it had a staunch, watchful, and influential champion in Albany in the person of New York State Senator George A. Blauvelt. Senator Blauvelt, a senior and respected Republican in the state legislature from Rockland County, New York, quickly smothered this bit of political smoke and mirrors.

While the PIPC had its guard up in Albany, the tax collector for the Borough of Alpine, New Jersey, put two PIPC properties on the block for sale, claiming tax delinquency. And the New Jersey comptroller was holding up $200,000 of the $500,000 appropriation made to the PIPC at the time of the Harriman gift for construction of the Henry Hudson Drive. He claimed that the funds should not be made available until the PIPC purchased the "Lawrence" property, so that the drive could be extended to the Village of Piermont, New York, ignoring the fact that he had no authority to mandate such a requirement across the border in another state.

Then on the New York side of the border the commissioners encountered reluctance on the part of Governor William Sulzer to approve legislation intended to clarify the PIPC's prerogative to establish fish and game regulations, including a restriction against hunting on parklands. Sulzer expressed concern that the legislation would undercut the authority of the New York Conservation Department.

Dr. Edward L. Partridge, Palisades Interstate Park Commissioner, 1913–1929. *(Courtesy of PIPC Archives)*

These challenges were met and overcome, only to be replaced by new challenges. Perkins succeeded in acquiring the E. I. DuPont de Nemours Powder Company property on the shoreline in New Jersey near the Carpenter Brothers' old quarry site after years of negotiation. Despite the PIPC's earlier claims that all necessary properties had been acquired to protect the cliffs, the DuPont property, including a narrow, 3,400-foot strip of land and riparian rights on the river shore and eight acres on the summit of the Palisades, was an exception. The $142,500 purchase price was tucked out of sight into the paper shell of the PIPC's subsidiary corporation, the Palisades Improvement Company, to ensure that the high per-acre cost would not come back to haunt the PIPC's future acquisition initiatives.

One of these initiatives was taking place in New York. Charles T. Ford, the estate manager for Mary Harriman, managed to win agreement from a "Mr. Cunningham," who boasted that he once stood gallantly alone and "blocked E. H. Harriman" from acquiring even more land in the Highlands. Ford took it upon himself to negotiate with Cunningham, setting a $15 per acre price for three thousand acres, and $30 per acre for an additional four hundred–acre parcel. The proposed route for a road intended to connect the PIPC-owned Bear Mountain property with land donated by Harriman went right through the Cunningham holdings. Ford's offer was accepted and promptly paid with PIPC funds, opening the way for the construction of a road later to be named Seven Lakes Drive, one of the most delightfully scenic byways in New York.

May 2, 1913
Mr. S. Gilchrist
Upper Nyack, New York

Dear Sir:

I have your note of the 29ᵗʰ about Dr. Helm's cows. I did not know of any such arrangement which you state was in force last season. I really feel that this coming season it would hardly be just the thing to allow this because the land will be more and more used by the general public and such action might be criticized, unless, of course, Dr. Helm was willing to pay some small amount for the privilege. It may be when Mr. White gets back we can take the matter up with him again.

Yours very truly,
Leonard Hull Smith
Assistant Secretary

May 9ᵗʰ, 1913
Mr. A. M. Herbert
Iona Island, New York

Dear Mr. Herbert:

Mr. Legien tells me of the manner in which he has been paying off some of the laborers. I don't think the arrangement is desirable, from many standpoints. In the first place, he tells me that it is really dangerous to take up the amount of money that we now have each month and pay off possibly two hundred laborers in the small shed which is now in use. In other words, some arrangement must be made at once whereby the man paying off can sit behind either a railing or at a door, so that they cannot be crowded or jostled. Furthermore, I think each man should receive his envelope personally, open it and count it, and if he cannot write, at least make his mark, and the name can be filled in by someone else, as is now the practice.

Yours very truly
Leonard Hull Smith
Assistant Secretary

May 10, 1913
Mr. Chester C. Platt
Secretary to the Governor
Albany, New York

My dear Mr. Platt:

I am exceedingly anxious that the Governor sign a bill that is now before him and about which I telephoned him the other day, that gives the Palisades Commission the right to accept or reject any award which may be made to purchase property which the Commission is condemning and may condemn along the west bank of the Hudson. This bill was introduced by Senator Blauvelt and I have just heard that the Governor may be inclined to hold it up or veto it because it is a Blauvelt bill. Of course, I am sure the Governor would not be actuated by any motive of this kind if the bill is all right. If there is the slightest doubt remaining in the Governor's mind as to whether he should sign it, won't you please telegraph me at once, because in that event I will come to Albany on the first train possible and see the Governor about it.

Sincerely yours,
George W. Perkins

Work at Bear Mountain was in full swing, accomplished by laborers being paid a daily wage of $2.00. Under the supervision of Andrew M. Herbert, the PIPC's superintendent, the labor force came primarily from New York City. Within months, the force expanded to 563 foremen, firemen, mechanics, drill runners, carpenters, helpers, and laborers. An additional eighty-six woodcutters were clearing the forest of dead trees and underbrush. Each day, the men would embark on the ferry to Weehawken, New Jersey, then board a West Shore Railroad Company train for the forty-five–mile ride to a special Bear Mountain stop arranged by the PIPC with the railroad owners. Ticket costs came from the pockets of the workers. Upon arrival at 7:00 a.m., this small army set to its tasks. Land was cleared and roads were being built. Baseball diamonds, lawn tennis courts, a running track, and a huge lawn were under construction.

The commissioners were also grappling with the question of how to deal with "refreshment concessions." They wanted to encourage competition and bids, control prices, and maintain quality. Any concessionaire who failed to live up to the PIPC's standards risked summary eviction, with no right of appeal. One vendor proposed to provide chewing-gum machines and weighing scales for visitors. F. D. Lockwood proceeded to sell sandwiches for ten cents that were "too thin" and lacked ham, and "small glasses" of milk for five cents. The PIPC was quick to learn that concessionaires liked profit first and service second, assuming that most customers would probably never be seen again. Correction was demanded; Lockwood's sandwiches gained weight and substance, and his milk glasses increased in size.

The McAllister Steamboat Company was planning summer excursions from the Battery in New York City to Bear Mountain at $.50 per passenger, round-trip, with a rule imposed by the PIPC that no intoxicating beverages could be taken ashore. This restriction did not include intoxicated passengers. To accommodate the steamboat passengers, a tunnel was dug under the railroad tracks, allowing easy pedestrian access from the dock to the playfields and refreshment stands on the plateau above. Beginning with the first trip, the steamboat carried six hundred to eight hundred people daily on excursions up the Hudson River from the city. In the minds of the commissioners, what some people had called a "worthless wilderness" at Bear Mountain was being transformed into a park. On many fronts, the PIPC's experiment seemed to be moving forward, until Governor Sulzer demanded an immediate halt to all activities.

As stated in the *Newburgh Daily News,*

Governor Sulzer's object in appointing a "commission" to investigate the Palisades Interstate Park Commission is tolerably plain. He wants to "reorganize" the commission[,] the members of which have been reluctant to rise up and declare him the anointed one, the fount of wisdom and the oracle of the people. Sulzer is convinced a lot of perfectly good money is not being distributed in patronage in a commission that should be responsible to political exigencies. Fully half the funding the commission possesses was subscribed by individuals, some of whom, including Chairman George W. Perkins, are members of the commission. No "investigation" is required to establish the fact that commissioners who are spending funds which they in part subscribed are not squandering them.

Publicly, the governor's primary complaint centered on his impression that the commissioners, "who were very, very busy men of large private interests," had not been giving their personal attention to the PIPC's activities, but owners who complained that the commissioners were less than generous in their offers to buy land actually prompted his criticism. Perkins hotly countered in *The New York Times* that the PIPC had asked the governor to appoint a committee to consider the PIPC's "request for more liberal powers." He pointedly added that the commissioners do not turn over their responsibilities to subordinates, and that "no lands have been bought or condemned that are not absolutely necessary to the preservation of the Palisades."

While the commissioners were struggling with Sulzer's reproach, a matter that was quickly put aside, an even more complex quandary faced them. Miss May Milne, an unmarried, unescorted woman, wanted to camp at Bear Mountain! Then, on top of this amazing request, Mrs. Albert W. Staub, wife of the headmaster of Riverdale Country School, proposed a camping trip for herself and ten Campfire girls. The commissioners had an answer for these unprecedented requests: women and girls could camp at the old rifle range on South Mountain, twenty-five miles downriver from Bear Mountain, now referred to as Blauvelt Park in recognition of Senator Blauvelt's constant presence as the PIPC's steadfast political champion. But the commissioners would not easily escape the issue. When camping was first opened in Harriman Park, their answer was that wives could accompany their spouses, so long as they separated from their husbands on arrival and stayed in a women-only section of the campground. Single women need not apply.

Group camping activities reflected the gender dilemma. The Young Women's Christian Association (YWCA) was given primary use of the old rifle range at Blauvelt Park, and a large central camp for Boy Scouts was established in 1913 at "Car Pond" in Harriman Park. As with other initiatives, Perkins and his colleagues could only guess at the eventual scale, diversity, and benefits of the group-camp program. Vacation habits have proven that most rural parks are accessible to a mobile population with money to spend, private transportation, and time for leisurely travel. City parks offer and protect small patches of green surrounded by the machines and structures of humankind. The transition between city and rural parks was and still is rare for lower-income urban residents. However, on the doorstep of the nation's most densely populated metropolitan region, the PIPC was determined to make this transition possible. The group-camp program would evolve into an unmatched connection between inner-city children from low-income families and the tranquil natural beauty of a preserved landscape, stretching for thousands of acres in every direction. For many children, the PIPC's parklands afforded a first opportunity to step away, even for a moment, from the crash and contest of the city to hike along forest paths; climb to scenic vistas; learn about trees, plants, wild birds and animals; swim in lakes, invent games; watch campfires blaze; listen to strange night sounds; and soak in the experience of nature.

By the end of the first summer of camp operations at Bear Mountain, Perkins was able to write to John D. Rockefeller, Jr., reporting success on many fronts.

Girls, Group Camp, Harriman Park.
(Courtesy of PIPC Archives)

"After a very long and hard struggle," Perkins was particularly pleased to report total awards of $611,235 for the acquisition, through condemnation, of the most strategic properties, including three quarries, at Hook Mountain. Thirteen years after the Carpenter Brothers' operation was shut down on the New Jersey Palisades, and even though additional months of legal maneuvers, court proceedings, negotiations with the last resistant sellers, and further payments that approached $3 million would result from the condemnations, the commissioners could claim final victory in the quarry wars. The Clinton Point and Rockland Lake Trap Rock (Foss) Quarries at Hook Mountain were the last quarries fronting the river to succumb. The letter from Perkins to Rockefeller, Jr., only hinted at the immense investment of time, energy, persuasiveness, determination, and political clout that Perkins personally brought to bear on this precedent-setting conservation achievement, symbolized always by the giant wounds left behind on the Hudson River cliff faces.

As the quarry smoke began to settle, the commissioners found themselves vested with a wide mandate to continue building a park system. Time after time, the PIPC had to explain and rejustify its purposes and legal prerogatives to auditors, government appointees, and elected officials from the two states who frowned on the quasi-independence enjoyed by the PIPC. Government officials in Albany and Trenton much preferred a more familiar style of pursuing the public's business: one in which political power, patronage, and budget priorities were usually molded to the next election and against the "other" party. The nonpartisan PIPC, a private-public hybrid that did not fit easily within preconceived notions of political privilege and leverage, was generally tolerated, not applauded.

Perkins was probably not worrying about the PIPC's image in the state capitals.

Boys arriving at Bear Mountain, going to Group Camp, Harriman Park.
(Courtesy of PIPC Archives)

More likely, he was thinking about the triumph of the first summer of visitation at Bear Mountain, mirrored by public enthusiasm for the Palisades shoreline in New Jersey. Blauvelt Park was a reality at South Mountain, the face of Hook Mountain was rid of quarries, and the PIPC was considering the purchase and operation of its own dayliner steamboat to provide visitors access from New York City to Bear Mountain—an especially appealing idea for Perkins. One vessel that caught Perkins's eye was the steamship *United States,* moored in Michigan City, Indiana, and offered for sale for $175,000. The sidewheeler could carry at least two thousand passengers. At the waterline, the vessel measured 208 feet in length. Its beam was forty-eight feet and its draft sixteen feet. A 2,500-horsepower engine provided propulsion for the two side paddle wheels. The commissioners hesitated, not quite ready to begin creating a PIPC navy, but at their annual meeting in September, 1914, hosted by Perkins at his Wave Hill Estate in Riverdale, New York, they agreed to immediately begin the construction of a "large restaurant" as a dayliner destination at Bear Mountain, patterned after the Old Faithful Inn in Yellowstone National Park.

At the same time, a sense of neighborly cooperation developed between the Army and the PIPC. This loose alliance started on a shaky note when the commissioners pressed to gain a right-of-way through adjoining land at the U.S. Military Academy, West Point, to allow for road access to the dramatically scenic Storm King Mountain that was farther upriver. While the right-of-way issue was under debate, White was reminded by H. Percy Silver, the West Point chaplain, that while officers had their privileges, enlisted men and their families at the academy had few options for summer holidays. The PIPC arranged for a special summer camp that accommodated three hundred soldiers, wives, and children over a six-week period.

In October, 1914, with development of the Bear Mountain area accelerating, the commissioners agreed to accept a generous offer from Henry V. Gilbert, representing the heirs of John S. Gilbert, to buy the "Fort Lot" at Fort Montgomery for $1,500. The Fort Montgomery site, where a crucial and bloody battle was fought during the Revolutionary War, had quietly slipped back into obscurity, shrouded by a canopy of trees and dense brush that made the old fortification all but invisible. One hundred thirty-six years after the battle, few people were aware of or gave thought to the "twin forts," or to the militiamen, soldiers, and mercenaries who died there. The site of Fort Clinton was being developed as a picnic area. Fort Montgomery, lost in the thick woods on the northern side of Popolopen Creek, was at last added to the list of PIPC properties, but more as a footnote than as a site the commissioners had determined to honor and open to the public.

The "large restaurant" was envisioned to occupy a site on the old Fort Clinton battleground next to a small lake, known variously as Sinnipink, Highland, or Hessian. Architects from the firm Tooker and Marsh were retained to complete the design for the restaurant. The PIPC's workers were expected to handle the construction, under the supervision of William A. Welch, who had been promoted from assistant engineer to chief engineer, succeeding Ernest D. Bean. The cost for construction was estimated at $95,000, but Perkins and Welch thought the cost could be scaled back to about $65,000 if certain efficiencies could be achieved, chief among them the avoidance of government-contract procedures. Perkins was leery of asking for state funds to cover the cost, knowing that delays and cost increases would probably result. He wanted the building up in a matter of months, and each dollar squeezed to the maximum. Perkins turned to his fellow commissioners and won their unanimous approval for the use of privately donated gift funds, largely his own, to construct the Bear Mountain Inn.

Unity among the commissioners was not so easily maintained on the New Jersey side of the border. Challenged by the Appalachian Mountain Club (AMC) about the pending construction of the Henry Hudson Drive under the Palisades cliffs, which the AMC members feared would become an "ugly gash in the landscape," Perkins was quoted in *The New York Times* as saying, "We are not building any automobile boulevard along the shore." The *Times* headline proclaimed, "No Road For Palisades." This came as a surprise to Commissioner Sutro, who had been working hard for two years to convince the New Jersey Legislature that the Henry Hudson Drive was a good idea. Perkins quickly corrected the record by explaining that "a great many people seem to think that the Commission has been determined to make out of this drive a great broad boulevard near the water and constructed in such a way as to almost obliterate many of the trees and make a long disfiguring scar through the Palisades." Referring to the PIPC's plan to carefully avoid visible roadway impact on the shoreline, Perkins added, "We have among ourselves been referring lately to the Henry Hudson Drive as an automobile trail." Perkins and Sutro promptly settled their misunderstanding. In a follow-up letter to Sutro, the PIPC's president said, "Whatever criticisms that can be made of those of us who are on the Commission, there is one thing certain, that no half way fair man could say we are not all desperately in earnest in our work and take everything that occurs in connection with it very much to heart."

There is no better symbol of Perkins's commitment than the Bear Mountain Inn, ultimately described by the PIPC as "a rugged heap of boulders and huge chestnut logs assembled by the hand of man, and yet following lines of such natural proportions as to resemble the eternal hills themselves." In late 1914 and early 1915, Welch led the PIPC's work force in a rapid effort to open the inn to the public. For this, Perkins took criticism from advocates for contracts, government largess, and union wages, but over a matter of months, and at a bargain cost of about $100,000, a structure of more than fifty thousand square feet materialized on the shore of Hessian Lake. Complete with the most modern cold-storage utilities, the three-story inn was constructed with rubble stone gathered at the site and American chestnut trees, already being decimated by an infectious blight, cut from the nearby forest. Food services were designed to range from cafeteria to restaurant style. The commissioners insisted on high quality and very reasonable prices. The inn was officially opened on June 3, 1915, and when the summer crowds arrived at Bear Mountain was able to accommodate more than one hundred thousand patrons in the first year and made a profit of $600. The magnificent stone and log appearance of the structure presented a sensitive and functional "park architecture" design that set the standard for many construction projects to follow.

Bear Mountain Inn, 1915.
(Courtesy of PIPC Archives)

A witness to the flurry of activity at Bear Mountain was twenty-three-year-old W. Averell Harriman, recently graduated from Yale, who officially attended his first PIPC meeting on April 7, 1915, as a newly appointed commissioner. The gift of land and money provided by his mother five years earlier had prompted the young man to become peripherally involved with the PIPC's activities. Now, as a duly appointed commissioner, he would remain consistently involved with the PIPC for the next fifty-nine years. Harriman would also become known as the "durable Democrat." His credentials would eventually include service as ambassador to Russia in the Franklin Delano Roosevelt administration and ambassador to Great Britain in the Harry S. Truman administration. Through the years, Harriman came to know Joseph Stalin, Winston Churchill, Charles de Gaulle, and a host of world leaders. He was elected governor of New York in 1954 and twice contended unsuccessfully for the Democratic nomination to run for president of the United States.

W. Averell Harriman, Palisades Interstate Park Commissioner, 1915–1954, 1959–1973. *(Courtesy of PIPC Archives)*

Throughout his career, Harriman always viewed himself as a "volunteer," using the railroad wealth left by his parents to maintain personal independence and pursue goals that interested him. No other allegiance matched his commitment to the PIPC. When he was elected New York governor, Harriman appointed his brother, Roland, to the PIPC. After losing in the 1958 election to Nelson A. Rockefeller, Roland stepped aside, and the new governor reappointed Averell. He served in close harmony with his fellow PIPC commissioner and the governor's brother Laurance S. Rockefeller, proving yet again that parkland conservation provides neutral ground and common purpose for otherwise competitive people. Before Harriman completed his work with the PIPC, he would donate an additional twelve thousand acres to Harriman State Park. His constant allegiance and diplomacy brought stature and strength to the PIPC during more than five decades.

Harriman was sworn in with another new appointee, John J. Voorhees, son of the former governor of New Jersey. Harriman and Voorhees arrived just in time to hear a proposal from Mr. R. G. Hazard, president of the New England Bridge and Railway Company, who urged that the Commission accept a seventy-five–acre gift of land in exchange for a right-of-way that would allow for construction of a railroad bridge, suspended three hundred feet above Bear Mountain Park, to be connected to a tunnel dug through Bear Mountain. The commissioners declined.

In New Jersey, the increasing popularity of the river shoreline was providing another challenge. Visitors were flocking to the small beaches, docks, and riverside campsites in unanticipated numbers. More law-enforcement patrols were scheduled, but few benchmarks existed to guide the unarmed patrolmen. Like so many of its activities, the PIPC found itself inventing rules and regulations to control park use. The patrolmen watched for unattended campfires, directed that camping permits be visibly affixed to tents, and ordered that rubbish be either burned or buried before campers left. Camping permits were issued for a minimum of one week for a fee of $1.00. The commissioners reminded patrolmen that "severely injured persons must be taken to the nearest hospital as soon as possible." A PIPC regulation also directed that "bathers in bathing suits shall not be allowed to parade around amongst camping and picnicking parties, but must keep to the beaches, roads, and paths." Patrolmen were advised to keep freshwater springs from becoming polluted, to prevent boulders from being rolled from the summit of the cliffs onto the crowds below, and to enforce the rule that "all boy scout parties shall be required to leave their axes with patrolmen on entering the park." "Patrolmen will be allowed one day off every two weeks, the day to be designated by the Captain," said a PIPC personnel rule.

The commissioners discovered, too, that the New Jersey Palisades were attracting "moving picture companies." Requiring that the filmmakers have permits, the commissioners gave patrolmen discretion to stop or delay any filmmaking that might interfere with the public's enjoyment of the park. Where public use was not encumbered, cameras cranked while cars plunged from the Palisades summit, and damsels clung to the cliffs by their fingertips while villains stalked and sneered. Thus introduced into the national lexicon was the phrase *cliff hanger*.

Costs were increasing with demand everywhere in the PIPC's park system. Meanwhile, the PIPC was branching out in many directions, all aimed at creating "the right sort of healthful playground for the people," as Perkins explained in a letter to Rockefeller, Jr. In response to this letter, on February 19, 1916, the PIPC received a $1 million donation from the Rockefeller Foundation. Over the span of fifteen years, Perkins and his commissioner colleagues could take credit for raising more than $3.7 million in private funds, in addition to the $1 million Harriman gift, to advance the PIPC's cause. In today's dollars, the amount raised by the commissioners in the first years of the PIPC's existence would exceed $100 million.

Momentum was everywhere. "If you love me," Perkins pleaded with Welch, "do get the steamboat business straightened out next week. I am literally snowed under with work and it is going to be next to impossible for me to go into the differences between the McAllisters and the Albany Day Line. Please get after this and let me know as soon as possible in the fewest possible words what can be done to put us in the best possible shape for this year's travel." In 1914 almost 115,000 people had arrived at Bear Mountain aboard regularly scheduled dayliner trips, and an additional 15,500 came by special chartered excursions. Palisades-bound passengers coming over from the city on the Dyckman Street Ferry numbered 199,973 in 1915. The inadequate docking facilities at Bear Mountain were already congested, and more boats would soon be under way. One of these was the *Palisades,* built for the PIPC in 1916 by the Mathis Yacht Building Company of Camden, New Jersey. This new 120-foot-long vessel was intended to provide free outings to Bear Mountain for poor mothers and children in care of social agencies. "So far as we know," reported Welch to Perkins, "the *Palisades* is the first passenger boat in America using diesel-type engines."

The PIPC continued its initiative to bring underprivileged children to Harriman State Park. A camp was established to provide for about 425 "poor boys," one hundred of whom were segregated for a nutritional experiment. Under the direction of the New York Association for Improving the Condition of the Poor, the study resulted in an average weight gain for each well-fed child of 3.5 pounds. Welch also reported that 2,369 young women had camped at Blauvelt Park, adding that, otherwise, "no record" of women was to be found in the general camping population, but by 1916 a camp that could accommodate twenty-four girls and two chaperones was established at Bear Mountain.

Presaging demands made on park managers everywhere was the insistence of hunters that they be granted access to the PIPC's lands in New Jersey to kill foxes; their claim was that these predators were a menace to birds and other small animals. Setting an early standard on this troubling question, the commissioners rejected the request. Another use of parkland was welcomed. Herbert Whyte, representing the Outing Publishing Company, asked for permission in January, 1916, to take a two-week "walking trip" through the PIPC's lands. The vanguard of "trampers" represented by Whyte and his peers would help create a generally firm and friendly alliance between hikers and the PIPC.

Unlike the hikers, Landscape Architect Nathan T. Barrett, a charter appointee to the PIPC who served until 1914, saw the natural terrain through different eyes. After he left his post as a commissioner, Barrett recommended to Perkins that equipment acquired with the quarries be used to drill a huge tunnel from Rockland Lake through Hook Mountain. His concept was that water flowing through the tunnel from the lake would tumble down a precipice into the Hudson River, creating an artificial 160-foot-tall waterfall. The commissioners declined.

But in 1916 other commissioner-approved projects were blossoming. One example was the sale of "soft drinks" of sugar-flavored Bear Mountain spring water, produced and bottled by the PIPC. In Harriman State Park, several dams were under construction to "enhance" existing lakes and ponds. Just north of Bear Mountain, a six-hundred-foot-long steel bridge was constructed across the deep Popolopen Creek gorge to greatly improve access for automobiles and horse carriages to the Military Academy at West Point and destinations farther upriver. The Bear Mountain Inn was expanded, reaching a size of eighty-one thousand square feet. Far out in Harriman State Park, group camps continued to expand, but one camp was quarantined when two members of a Boy Scout troop who had been swimming in a nearby lake were diagnosed with infantile paralysis (polio). (Years later, Franklin Delano Roosevelt would contract polio at age thirty-nine after swimming in a Harriman State Park lake.)

Land acquisition remained high on the commissioners' priority list. With the acquisition of the "Queensboro" property between Bear Mountain and Harriman Parks, the PIPC added five thousand more acres to its holdings. In New Jersey, $100,300 was spent to acquire the 113-acre Anderson Avenue Realty Company's property known as Greenbrook Park on top of the cliffs, confirming that the PIPC was taking a strong, yet publicly undeclared initiative to control the heights as well as the shoreline of the Palisades. The PIPC now owned almost twenty thousand acres.

While most parks around the nation were counting visitation in the hundreds, more than five hundred thousand annual visitors were journeying to the PIPC's park system. This fact did not go unnoticed by Stephen Tyng Mather in Washington, D.C. Mather was just succeeding with the formation of the National Park Service and invited Welch to speak at the first "National Parks Conference" in 1917. Enos Mills from Colorado, who introduced Welch to those in attendance, said, "The subject of discussion this morning is 'The Recreational Use of the National Parks.' The first speaker on this subject is Mr. W. A. Welch, who is Chief Engineer in charge of the Palisades Interstate Park. As some of you know, we will say that this park embraces 30,000 acres of land. Altogether, $8 million have been expended in this park. More than one-half of this entire sum has been donated privately." Referring more specifically to Welch's work, Mills added, "The work that this man is doing is really evolutionary and revolutionary." Welch responded by describing himself as a "little kitten" among the "lions" and went on to describe the array of opportunities and challenges encountered by the PIPC. He offered real-world examples of solutions to park-management problems learned in the PIPC's school of hard knocks. At the conclusion of the event, the "Supervisors of the National Parks" traveled to New York at the invitation of Welch and Henry Fairfield Osborne, trustee of the American Museum of Natural History, to tour the PIPC's park system.

In his conference remarks, Welch had given strong credit to the New Jersey State Federation of Women's Clubs for its dauntless role in establishing the Interstate Park Commission, but still lost within the pace of the PIPC's events was the women's memorial project. Only a small plot of land had been set aside for the memorial at a scenic location atop the cliffs. Almost two decades had passed. "Thus, alas, for the best laid plans of women, the park is a reality, the Palisades are preserved for ever and ever, but the tall tower to commemorate the work of the women is still in the air," stated a 1917 Women's Club report. "According to Miss Demarest, the money is still in the Knickerbocker Trust Company of New York and amounts to $3,500. So although the club women of New Jersey . . . virtually saved the Palisades by bringing about the first interstate movement, their own project of a permanent monument is unfulfilled." Perkins and the commissioners were meeting every month, communicating with one another and Welch in between, and dealing with a growing public clientele and critics and partisans alike. Somehow, the women's memorial kept being pushed down the agenda. This was due in part to the constant struggle for state funding. Perkins was quick to point out to anyone who would listen that the breakdown of PIPC funding consisted of 54 percent from private sources, 40 percent from New York, and 6 percent from New Jersey. Welch was distracted from the memorial project by letters of inquiry, now arriving by the sackful, from park enthusiasts from all over the country asking for information ranging from what type of toilets to use in campgrounds to why parks were even necessary.

The biggest distraction was just around the corner. *The New York Times* announced that Norman Selby, better known as the popular prizefighter and role model "Kid McCoy," had enlisted in Company K of the Seventy-first Regiment to begin military training. In 1917 England, France, and Italy were already at war with Germany. The commissioners encouraged the PIPC's staff to enlist for military training and agreed, as a contingency, that female waiters could replace male waiters at the Bear Mountain Inn if it came to that.

Rockefeller, Jr., impressed by the continuing success of the PIPC, wrote to his father in April, 1917, proposing that a fund of $15 million to $25 million be established for the purpose of "developing parks and playgrounds in the City of New York and also in the State." He also suggested that a portion of the fund be used to "build a bridge across the Hudson River connecting the Interstate Palisades Park with Riverside Drive" in the city at an estimated cost of $10 million. "I should like to see you build this bridge yourself," Rockefeller, Jr., said to his father. The senior Rockefeller was attentive to his son and seemingly not startled by the proposition that he personally pay for the construction of a bridge where the present-day George Washington Bridge exists, but war clouds were changing many agendas. A potential major Rockefeller financial gift for parks was put on hold.

From his distant perch at Long's Peak Inn in Colorado, Mills was continuing to push his national-park agenda. Writing to Welch, he said, "It is probable that a vigorous five thousand word account of your Palisades Inter-state Park, by me, will appear in the *Saturday Evening Post*. As I told yourself and, I think, Mr. Perkins last winter, our National Park Service is not a model by any means. The inclination of those in power is to play politics and no one more than yourself knows what this means." By midsummer, 1918, Perkins was able to report to Rockefeller, Jr., that the interstate-park model that Mills found so appealing was increasingly popular. "More people visited Bear Mountain than ever before." On one day, Perkins said, "Six large steamers landed passengers at our docks, and a number of people came by way of the West Shore Railroad. Something over a thousand automobiles stopped at Bear Mountain." So many people were coming that the American Scenic and Historic Preservation Society speculated that the PIPC was having a difficult problem "reconciling its desire to preserve as nearly as possible the natural beauty of the tract and its desire to make the park practically useful to the people."

Problem or not, the inn and facilities at Bear Mountain were being given over to increasingly urgent preparations for the United States's entry into the war. The 102nd Company, U.S. Marines, was housed in a dormitory formerly occupied by park workers. Their mission was to guard an ammunition depot developed by the U.S. Navy on Iona Island. At one of the most scenic locations in the Hudson River Valley, just downriver from Bear Mountain, enough ammunition was being stored to supply the U.S. and British fleets in the Atlantic. Huge warehouses and more than one hundred other structures had been erected on the island. A causeway was constructed straight across a marsh from the Bear Mountain shoreline to Iona Island. This road, traveled by heavily laden trucks, kept sinking into the mud. Each time the road sank below the high-tide mark, more fill was added, until the base of the road finally reached solid footing, about 180 feet down. Iona Island was in an ideal location, secure from enemy attack. To reach the island, any significant enemy force would have to sail past New York City and forty miles upriver to the entrance to the narrows. With confidence, the Navy stored thousands of tons of explosives on the island, within a few feet of where the dayliners were passing to and from Bear Mountain.

War overtook the PIPC in 1918. Perkins, while retaining his position as president of the PIPC, assumed new responsibilities as president of New York's Food Control Commission to prevent war profiteering, encourage bulk purchases of food commodities from upstate farmers, maintain price supports, and urge backyard gardening. This was no small task. His food commission consisted of 130 members. Welch joined the Aviation Section of the Signal Corps and was posted to the Pacific Northwest to oversee the production of spruce-tree lumber for the construction of "aeroplanes." Perkins proudly reported to Rockefeller, Sr., that Welch, given the rank of major, had been assigned to such a crucial wartime task. While engaged in what turned out to be a mammoth duty involving legions of men, Welch was visited by Mather, who, on a swing west, stopped by to further discuss park management and development. Neither man probably considered that the old rifle range at Blauvelt Park was again being used for military training with the same result as earlier: bullets were whizzing through nearby residential neighborhoods.

A few successes were being achieved even during the war years of 1917–18. Perkins, his hand always on the PIPC's tiller, continued to negotiate purchases of land, including the purchase of the Dana property on the summit of the Palisades for $175,000. One observer wrote to Perkins, commenting that "few will ever express their appreciation of what your Commission is doing; one man wants to do so." The letter was signed by Rockefeller, Jr.

8.
Perkins

For family and humanitarian reasons, George Perkins sailed for Europe in December, 1918, even as the allied forces struggled with the remnants of a destructive war-to-end-all-wars that killed 5 million combatants. His beloved daughter-in-law had become suddenly ill, but after struggling for a matter of days and rallying at one point, she passed away, Perkins at her side. As the war wound to a close, he consoled his son, George, who was posted with the U.S. Army in France. During an extended stay in Europe, Perkins involved himself in the general effort to rebuild postwar France and Germany, bringing his special skills and access to the need to rehabilitate the German economy to ensure that its war debts were paid.

In the Pacific Northwest, Maj. William Welch was completing his wartime assignment and was anxious to return to the Palisades Interstate Park Commission, but the director of the Bureau of Aircraft Production, recognizing Welch's skills and accomplishments, was in no hurry to release him. Welch finally returned to the Hudson River Valley in late February, 1919, having been recommended by Gen. Brice P. Disque for the Distinguished Service Medal. Welch was cited for directing the construction of thirteen mainline and spur railroads through mountainous terrain "in record time," for building dozens of truck roads and sawmills, for training and supervising thousands of raw recruits and untrained officers, and for increasing the production of airplane lumber by

1,500 percent. The general noted that Welch achieved these results in spite of "agitation" by the International Workers of the World and "pro-enemy propaganda."

But even as Perkins and Welch focused on the war effort, separated by oceans and continents, the work of the PIPC remained in their thoughts. Signaling the strain of events, Perkins wrote to Welch from Paris in January, 1919, saying, "It is quite evident now that I shall not be able to sail for home nearly as soon as I had expected when I left New York. My stay in the hospital, where I still am, will have consumed two and more nearly three weeks—in addition, I find more to do over here than anticipated." Perkins went on to provide a lengthy list of concerns and ideas for the spring opening of the parks, ranging from the need to improve sanitary conditions and increase drinking-water supplies to the prospect of upgrading rather than enlarging the Harriman Park group camps. Funding, a chronic concern, would have to depend, for the moment at least, solely on New York and New Jersey appropriations. Perkins, stating the obvious, confirmed to Welch that "this is a bad time to raise new funds."

In a long letter to Commissioner Richard Lindabury, Perkins expressed great concern over continuing political and state-funding problems, particularly those being caused by New Jersey's acting governor, Walter E. Edge, who seemed unsympathetic to the PIPC. Perkins stated to Lindabury that "the PIPC should not be subject to senatorial patronage or political influence but should be filled by joint action of the two Governors." He was referring to Edge's resistance to the reappointment of Franklin W. Hopkins, who had been serving with the Commission since 1900. "I think it should be pointed out to Governor Edge that the Commissioners consider continuity in office of vital importance in the management of this interstate enterprise, especially because it constitutes a great private as well as public trust. Frequent changes in the personnel, especially if those changes would seem to be distracted by partisan or factional considerations, would tend to weaken that confidence," Perkins wrote, stating a basic belief that had guided the commissioners from the very beginning.

Theodore Roosevelt had vigorously affirmed this belief, but the great champion of conservation was gone. He died on January 6, 1919. The "lofty ideals and freedom from political influence" that Roosevelt expected of the founding class of commissioners he had appointed in 1900 were proving to be under constant trial. New York Governor Al Smith was more responsive to the PIPC and used a meeting with Governor Edge concerning a New York–New Jersey tunnel project to make the point. Welch, newly returned to his position as chief engineer, reported to Perkins, still in Paris, that

Governor Edge said (to Governor Smith) that New Jersey was ready to put up her share of the cost. Governor Smith replied, "of course you will also put up the $600,000 New Jersey owes the PIPC which you understand is a debt you owe to New York." This took Edge's breath away, and then Smith rubbed it in by adding, "you might begin by reducing your action of a few days ago, when you cut out of their appropriation $100,000 for the Henry Hudson Drive, which is several years over due." That is the best thing I have heard since my return.

Inspired by the Smith-Edge meeting, Commissioners Hopkins, Baker, and Sutro took up the challenge. They scheduled a field trip to the Palisades and Bear Mountain for New Jersey legislators. Hopkins survived the reappointment challenge and continued to serve until 1929. When New Jersey appropriations in the amount of $42,500 for operations and $100,000 for the Henry Hudson Drive were restored to the PIPC, partial credit was given to Mrs. Camille Welch, who, like many park spouses to follow, had been recruited to provide for the field trip what all participants judged to be a "very fine lunch."

Dr. Charles C. Adams, Syracuse College of Forestry, was unaware of the dialogue and concerns at the top of the PIPC's organizations but was anxious to become more involved in the still novel and expanding park system. In the 1919 edition of the *Empire Forester,* he reported that the PIPC was interested in an "inventory of natural history resources." He added that it "has not been customary for park officials to see the value of such studies." According to Adams, the study would bring several benefits, including:

1. The possibility of interesting visitors and campers in birds, fish, game, and other wild animals.

2. The capability for better protecting visitors from "intrusive" plants and animals.

3. The possible development of a balance between people and nature.

4. The opportunity to issue a publication for students of park administration.

Adams pointed out that "miles of rocky, wooded wasteland" were in existence along the lower Hudson River, primarily due to "lagging economic and social ideals." He saw the PIPC's holdings as a fitting testing ground for the budding theories and concepts of park management.

Not all the land along the lower Hudson River was "wild and wasted," as Adams put it. Property on the summit of the Palisades that had been owned by former Commissioner William B. Dana was acquired from his heirs through Perkins's persistent efforts. The acquisition brought with it Greycliff, a massive twenty-six–room mansion built in 1861 of blue trap rock and pink sandstone. Proposals for the use of this elegant Victorian structure quickly followed, including a recommendation by the Federation for the Support of Jewish Philanthropic Societies that the mansion be used as a vacation resort for working girls. Edward F. Brown, manager of the Commission's Camp Department, was trying to juggle requests for use of the Dana mansion with other camp proposals, including one from Mrs. Victoria Dyke for the establishment of a camp for undernourished girls. At the beginning of 1919, Brown was overseeing nineteen camps, including two for military training, eight for Boy Scouts, two for Girl Scouts, a camp for the Children's Aid Society, one for the Harlem & Heights Business Girls Athletic League, another listed as "The Negro Fresh Air Camp," and a YWCA camp. Children from Brooklyn, the Bronx, and Queens were trans-

Greycliff (William B. Dana House), summit of Palisades Cliffs, 1918.
(Courtesy of PIPC Archives)

ported to the scout camps, usually for ten-day adventures. By year's end, thirty-seven camps were in operation, seven more were under construction, and more than fifty thousand campers were in attendance, a tenfold increase over prewar numbers.

At Upper Twin Lake in Harriman Park, "Miss Lewis" was in charge of one of the Girl Scout camps. Her demands of Brown and the PIPC's staff were unending. She wanted twenty-four feet added to the length of the mess hall and thought that the kitchen wall should be moved outward by three feet. Roofs needed attention, the camp needed more cabins, the tents were not satisfactory, and the grounds required better landscaping. "If Miss Lewis is so insistent upon our pruning the grape vines around her camp," commented an exasperated Welch, "she will probably want someone to pick the grapes next year."

In Perkins's absence, J. DuPratt White stepped forward to again help deal with the day-to-day challenges. There were many. White focused significant effort on developing Hook Mountain, prompted by a letter from King suggesting the construction of a bathhouse and lunchroom. White thought the development of Hook Mountain would be a wonderful asset for nearby Nyack, New York, and proceeded to win concurrence from the town's leaders. Along the rugged shoreline of this mountain, British Major John André had met secretly with Benedict Arnold during the Revolutionary War to receive the plans for West Point. André was caught with the plans just before reaching the British lines, was convicted as a spy, and forfeited his life on a hanging tree in Tappan, New York. Arnold, until then a hero of the Revolutionary War, escaped to England, leaving behind his sullied name and reputation, ever after associated with the word *traitor*. White and his fellow commissioners wanted this story told in a way that would enfold visitors in the event itself by encouraging them to see and sense the very place where Arnold and André had met. Educational opportunities for park visitors, both to honor history and introduce city dwellers to the natural world, were beginning to emerge as integral to development and management of the parks.

In the meantime, Welch grappled with other issues. He turned down a request from Abram De Ronde, commissioner from 1900 to 1912, who asked that the PIPC hire his son. Welch also rejected a suggestion from a taxidermist who thought that stuffed park animals and birds would be a wonderful way to educate the public and make a profit for the PIPC. Postwar costs for labor and materials were soaring, labor by 60 percent and materials by 100 percent. A copper sulfate treatment of some of the lakes in Harriman Park to get rid of aquatic plants and algae killed fish instead. Welch and Dr. Hugh Baker, Dean of the Syracuse College of Forestry, collaborated further to find the right chemical dosage for the lakes.

Problems kept coming. Maurice M. Lefkowitz wrote,

> I have been to Bear Mountain Park twice this season, and at both times was pushed off the dance floor by one of the patrolmen for doing absolutely nothing else but proper and decent dancing. This is not my case alone, but the same incident occurs at least ten or fifteen times during each dance, and the patrolmen do not bother persons dancing the "shimmy" but seem to pick out certain people. They handle the girls as though they were common street walkers. I say this because at both times my partner was a respectable refined girl who felt deeply hurt and ashamed at being roughly pushed off the dance floor.

Welch investigated and learned that Lefkowitz was a ten-time dance champion who could make moves that the patrolmen deemed "improper." Generally, the young dancers and patrolmen maintained an uneasy truce, but a visitor to the Bear Mountain Inn was not so sure they would or should. Writing to Welch, she complained,

As to morals, I realize that it is beyond your power to pacify and check the sexual impulses brought into play in the park. Still, something should be done. When the so-called "shimmy" proved to be fatal to the morals of the young, the government saw it to be proper and necessary to interfere and stop it. And so it should be—any place where vice and immorality will flourish should be uprooted. I have seen young boys and girls of fifteen shame those of twenty in the making of love.

Welch's engineering books had not covered this particular subject, and he was getting a dose of on-the-job training. In a more serene and appropriate setting, Camp Manager Brown was able to report to Perkins and Welch the first successful "musical evening in the park," provided by Miss Ruth Linrud, who played a large harp and sang to five hundred children at Carr Pond. (The name of this pond had changed from Car to Carr and would change again, to Lake Stahahe.)

At the various road entrances, "intelligence officers" were posted to "tell occupants of automobiles that they were entering the public park and that the Com-

Palisades police officer and culprit.
(Courtesy of PIPC Archives)

mission is trying to preserve its beauty by prohibiting the picking of flowers and destroying shrubs." Steamboat companies were vying for the river traffic, including the Hudson River Day Line, the Central Hudson Steamboat Company, Steamboat Agent C. T. Mallory, and the McAllister Steamboat Company.

In the midst of this fascinating variety of daily problems, two threatening political missiles were fired at the PIPC. The first came from residents of the Town of Fort Montgomery who had heard rumors that the PIPC intended to condemn and wipe out their whole village. They sent an angry petition to Albany. The commissioners hastily reported to Governor Smith's counsel that only four properties in the town were actually being acquired, two through eminent-domain settlements agreed to by the owners and two from willing sellers.

Just as this was resolved, the second missile, in the form of the "Peck Bill," came whizzing in. Somehow, New York Assemblyman Peck had managed to cleverly move through the Legislature a bill that directed the PIPC to transfer to Conger family heirs a rock-quarry property acquired by the PIPC from the erstwhile senior Conger for $368,500. Within the Commission, shock and surprise were understatements. On its face, the bill seemed illogical and adverse to any rational financial doctrine of public trust, yet it had won majority votes in both the New York Assembly and Senate. It also carried with it a potentially damaging precedent. If the acquisition of the Conger property could be overturned, so, too, could scores of other PIPC acquisitions. The whole effort to build a park system would come tumbling down. Led by White, the commissioners scrambled to make their case directly to Governor Smith, who promptly vetoed the bill.

In New Jersey, the dangling matter of the women's memorial surfaced once more.

Miss S. Elizabeth Demarest
Passaic, New Jersey

Dear Miss Demarest:

Your letter is very interesting and after reading it, I feel quite sure that you and your associates will be able to raise sufficient money to carry out the monument project. Of course, it should be approached in a rather businesslike way. . . . You will understand that all this is very tentative and I am not in anyway [sic] presuming to force any particular sketch for the acceptance of the women who are to erect the monument, and I do not believe that the Commission will, but simply render such assistance as we can.

Yours sincerely,
J. DuPratt White

Elizabeth Demarest had been secretary for the New Jersey Federation of Women's Clubs since the mid-1890s. Representing her many colleagues, some now gone, who had fought so skillfully to save the Palisades, she was still trying to win one more victory: the realization of the long-sought women's memorial. The $3,000 memorial donation made to the PIPC by the women in 1909 had accumulated interest and stood at about $3,800, but inflation had boosted the projected cost for the memorial to $10,000. Despite his largely noncommittal letter to Demarest, White was a strong advocate behind the scenes for the women. He took the step of asking architect Henry G. Emery, a personal friend, to sketch out a design for the memorial. White posted the sketch on the wall of the PIPC's meeting room at 61 Broadway in New York City to ensure that the matter would remain visible, figuratively and literally. Another Commission committee, consisting of White, Charles W. Baker, and Edward L. Partridge, was appointed to meet with the Ladies of the Memorial Park Association to pursue the monument.

Perkins, having completed his service in the war-recovery effort, and having recovered from his hospital stay, returned from France in April, 1919. Two months later, the *State Service Magazine* published his article "Sight Seeing Buses in the Palisades." The lead paragraph captured a slice of the obvious:

> The so-called sight-seeing trip is a by-product of the early development of the automobile industry. Formerly these trips consisted chiefly of excursions into the slum districts, where misery was the object of morbid curiosity, just as the wretched cripples of the eighteenth century were exhibited at circuses for the delectation of the mob. Not infrequently in the metropolitan cities, sight-seeing explorations degenerated into trips to questionable resorts where vice careered unafraid. Gradually there came into existence here and throughout the country the sight-seeing trips which constituted a source of enjoyment and education.

Perkins went on to eloquently describe the delights of a sight-seeing trip to the PIPC's park system, assuring safety for the travelers and emphasizing the social values that the system would present. The cover photo for the article showed three women standing on the Palisades cliffs, with the Englewood boat basin far below.

Learning, too, of the demands and growing tensions between various group-camp directors on the PIPC's staff, Perkins, who referred to the staff as the "managing force," summoned the combatants to a dinner (in business dress) in a little log cabin perched incongruously on the roof of the Abercrombie & Fitch

(from left) William A. Welch, New Jersey Governor Edwards, Dayliner Captain Stout, Frederick C. Sutro, 1920. *(Courtesy of PIPC Archives)*

Building in midtown New York City. The cabin was symbolic of the outdoor equipment and clothing business in which Abercrombie & Fitch specialized. This unusual setting produced the desired result: the camp directors became more understanding and tolerant of the workload carried by Welch and his men, and vice versa.

The cabin was symbolic for another reason. Welch, who continued to search for the right equation in balancing park uses, turned down a request to build a large number of rental cabins on the parklands. His rationale was that the commissioners "always agreed that such a procedure would not be in line with the general ideals which we are following." Welch contended that the parks should be "enjoyed by all people" and favored rustic camps over more exclusive resort-style developments. Welch's belief was justified, but naive; the national parks in particular would quickly become vulnerable to commercial resort development, a predictable outcome driven by what Perkins termed "the profit motive concessionaires." He and Welch knew that parks would rapidly become hot commercial properties, confirmed by visitation that leaped from a handful, to hundreds, to hundreds of thousands, and, in the PIPC's park system in 1919, to more than 1 million for the first time.

The PIPC's experiences and crystal ball were in demand. Welch, who now held the title of general manager, as well as chief engineer, was invited to be a principal speaker at a national City Planning Conference, held in Niagara Falls, New York. Following his presentation, he received inquiries from officials in Cleveland and Boston who were eager to receive additional information about park management and to arrange for field trips to the PIPC's parks. Another attentive listener at the conference was Frederick Law Olmsted, son of the famed landscape architect. On Olmsted Brothers letterhead, he wrote, "I did not have opportunity after your talk at Niagara to express my thanks for your presentation of the importance, scale, and great value of the undertakings of the Commission." Olmsted, too, proposed a field visit to the parks.

John D. Rockefeller, Jr., continued to keep a careful eye on the PIPC, and he liked what he saw. In a letter to his father in June, 1919, Rockefeller, Jr., proposed that the Laura Spelman Rockefeller Memorial Fund provide $500,000 to the PIPC for the purchase and refurbishment of the steamboats *Clermont* and *Onteora*. Making the financial argument, he pointed out that the two vessels were available and could be purchased for $400,000. Another $100,000 would be required to refit them. By comparison, he estimated that the construction of new steamboats of similar size would cost $2 million. The PIPC's operation of the steamboats "would be a service rendered directly to the people of the city in large numbers, and would have an intimate and personal aspect which would peculiarly commend it." Rockefeller, Jr., knew that the interest income from the Laura Spelman Rockefeller Memorial Fund was not sufficient to meet the purchase price. Showing his enthusiasm for the project, he proposed that principal from the fund be used to buy the steamboats, setting aside the usual unwritten philanthropic rule: never invade the principal. In Perkins's tradition of hard

The *Clermont* and *Onteora,* Bear Mountain dock, 1920.
(Courtesy of PIPC Archives)

bargaining, the *Clermont* and *Onteora* were acquired for $340,000. They would be on the river the following summer, offering daily service from the city to Bear Mountain for a combined total of five thousand passengers, joining the privately operated *Mary Powell, Highlander, Grand Republic, Seagate, Mandalay, Hendrick Hudson, Sirius, Robert Fulton, Monmouth, Albany, Benjamin J. Odell,* and many other excursion boats that provided access to the parks. Writing years later, Capt. William O. Benson described an August, 1920, trip as a nine-year-old boy aboard the *Onteora*. The trip, held vividly in his memory fifty-two years later, had made a "tremendous impression" on Benson. He kept a written list of the names of every steamboat he saw on the river that day. "When we approached Bear Mountain," Benson reported, "I could not take my eyes off the steamboats." Several were standing out in the river, waiting for dock space. In crystal clear weather, Anthony's Nose loomed on the opposite shore. Passengers were strolling up the trail from the docks to the playfields, picnic areas, and inn at Bear Mountain. Barge-towing tugboats and river freighters vied with sailboats in the narrows. Perhaps somewhere an artist was trying to capture the classic Hudson River School scene. From the distance of a half-century, Benson could remember almost every detail of his weekend adventure, reflecting similar impressions gathered and cherished by hosts of other steamboat passengers who claimed their own personal, first-time discoveries of the river.

The *Onteora* remained in operation until 1936, when it caught fire and burned while moored at the Bear Mountain dock. The *Clermont*, renamed the *Bear Mountain* after World War II, was sold for scrap in 1950, falling victim like other river steamers to the ease of automobile access across the Hudson River on bridges and improved roads.

The cessation of hostilities in Europe did nothing to diminish the Navy's enthusiasm for its ammunition depot on Iona Island. This glorious island was only about one-half mile downriver from the Bear Mountain dock. Hikers who reached a point just below the summit of Bear Mountain were rewarded with one of the most picture-perfect river scenes in the eastern United States, letting their eyes glide southward through the river narrows from West Point, past geologically prominent Anthony's Nose on the opposite side of the river, past Iona Island nestled between the flanks of Bear Mountain and Dunderberg Mountain, then farther downriver to the Tappan Zee where the Hudson widened again on its southern course to the Atlantic. On clear days, the classic New York City skyline is visible from the Bear Mountain summit.

Iona Island is the centerpiece of this enchanting scene. On its western shoreline, the island is edged by a large two hundred–acre marsh that traces the path of an ancient horseshoe bend, bypassed when the last glacier straightened and deepened the river channel on the island's east side. Native Americans called the 120-acre island "Manakawaghkin" and left behind archaeological evidence attesting to their use of it for more than five thousand years.

Through succeeding ownerships and name changes, title to Iona Island had eventually come into the hands of John Beveridge in 1849. He promptly sold a part-interest to his son-in-law, Dr. C. W. Grant. Grant, a self-styled fruit grower and wine maker, found the gently sloping, glacial soil of the island to be greatly appealing. Touched by sea breezes from the Atlantic that created temperature ranges attractive for his purposes, Grant planted orchards and vineyards. For two decades, he struggled to develop a new high-quality "Iona" variety of grape that might produce wine that could successfully compete against French imports. The end result, a wine of mediocre taste, did not match Grant's enthusiasm, persistence, and vision. His business venture failed, one of the first attempts in the United States to produce marketable wine. New owners transformed the island into a resort and picnic ground, presaging the popularity of Bear Mountain. World Heavyweight Boxing Champion John L. Sullivan was a frequent visitor.

In 1899 the Navy arrived. By Act of Congress, the island was purchased for $160,000, primarily because the Navy had run out of storage space in New York Harbor. World War I transformed the comparatively small Navy depot operation on the island, and storage capacity reached more than 2 million pounds of explosive black powder that was being packed into cannon shells and ordinance of all shapes and sizes for the U.S. and British fleets. Submarines sailed up the Hudson, tied up against the Iona Island shore, and were loaded with torpedoes. Just next to the submarines, antisubmarine depth charges intended for the "other guy" were loaded with other ordinance on barges and seagoing transports. One hundred forty-six buildings were constructed on the island, most of them made of brick and some including architectural flourishes a step above military square-and-basic. Ammunition bunkers, designed to direct any accidental explosion upward and away from the other bunkers and buildings, were clustered against stone walls chiseled into the island's topography. At the end of the war, Iona, nature's masterpiece in the narrows of the Hudson, carried the official designation U.S. Naval Ammunition Depot. Any thought that the beautiful island might be merged with the PIPC's conservation initiative on the nearby shore was transitory, if at all.

On shore, almost within sight of Iona Island, the PIPC was busy improving its park services. The *Messenger of Haverstraw* reported,

Mothers especially throughout the state will be interested to learn about the provisions made for their comfort and enjoyment at Bear Mountain. One of the features is the mothers' rest stations maintained by the Red Cross. Here, numerous comfortable baskets are provided with covers, where babies may rest in cool, quiet spots under the kindly eye of women matrons. There is no charge, and the theory is that the mother derives a double benefit of having her children cared for in pleasant surroundings, while she herself may enjoy a brief respite from the duties of motherhood.

A tourist suggested that the PIPC should post multilingual signs to inform non–English-speaking visitors of park rules. He had witnessed a visitor "wearing an undershirt, and nothing else." The visitor was "at the edge of the water rinsing a bathing suit. Every time he leaned over to put the suit in the water, he exposed the main parts of the back side of his body, and when he turned around, the front part was not hidden. I believe some visitors may not understand our customs or be able to read English." Welch referred the matter to the sign committee.

Welch continued to field questions from distant places. The Texas State Highway Commissioner asked how the PIPC acquired its parks. "Did you have to buy them? If so, where did the money come from?" Welch responded by confirming that the PIPC now owned more than thirty-five thousand acres of land and explained the details of the financial public-private partnership that fueled the PIPC's engine. Through his friend, Enos Mills, Welch was alerted to a pending visit by Mrs. D. A. "Mother" Curry, owner of Camp Curry in Yosemite National Park. She decided to make the long journey from California specifically to learn about the Palisades parks. Welch was also making plans at the invitation of Stephen Mather to attend the Superintendents of the National Parks Conference, scheduled to be held in Denver in November, 1919. Perkins, too, had been invited but could not attend. At the conference, Welch spoke and answered questions covering many topics, including patrol services and enforcement of regulations, publicity, maps, education, museums, preservation of forests and flowers, concessions, signs, sanitation, and individual and group camping.

In his report about the conference to Perkins, Welch said, "We have gone so far ahead of all the other parks in our development that they so fully recognized this that they kept me continually answering questions and discussing these problems." Following the conference, Mather helped arrange for the governor of South Dakota to visit Perkins and Welch for the purpose of gathering information to help manage the newly created sixty thousand–acre Custer State Park near Rapid City.

* * *

The PIPC's reputation may have been gaining stature on the national stage, but closer to home the trip was bumpy.

August 30, 1919

My dear Mr. Perkins:

The terrible Mike McCabe has been vanquished. Between Judge Arnold of the Knickerbocker Press and Mike McCabe of the Haverstraw Times, it has always been difficult for me to know who was the worst enemy of the park.

The letter was signed by Camp Manager Brown. McCabe had been editorially in favor of the quarry operators during the fight to save Hook Mountain and had been a persistent critic of the PIPC since then. Brown took a leap of faith and invited McCabe for a tour of Harriman Park, something the opinionated newsman had not bothered to undertake on his own. The tour included lunch at the Bear Mountain Inn, where Brown and McCabe were when Welch and the inn manager walked in and sat at a nearby table. McCabe commented about the "desperate characters" of the two men, then left with Brown for the rest of the tour. At the end of the day, he said goodbye to Brown, not giving a hint about his reactions to the many features of the park he had seen, including several of the camps. Two days later, under the headline "Making Others Happy," McCabe published a long, four-column, front-page article in *The Rockland County Times,* singing the praises of the PIPC, Perkins, Welch, Brown, the camp program, and park activities in general. "While from a literary standpoint the thing is atrocious, the fact is that the terrible Mike is vanquished, and we have one more friend, and a powerful one," Brown claimed.

The Ramapo Mountains Water, Power, & Service Company, a utility company operating along the western border of the PIPC's holdings, was not a friend. Its directors had decided to condemn lands owned by the PIPC and take them into water-company ownership. The commissioners took the case to the Court of Appeals before winning a unanimous judgment that the water company had no legal right to condemn the PIPC's land. This was only one of the many instances when the PIPC would find itself in court defending its purposes and legal prerogatives.

As the hectic postwar year of 1919 came to a close, the PIPC could look back over its brief history and count $13,096,903 in expenditures, including $4,712,644 in cash donations and $1,862,765 in donations of land. Fifty-one charitable organizations were active in the park system. Despite surprises, demands, and crises, the PIPC was beginning to take on a certain maturity. It had no equal anywhere in the nation.

The National Geographic Society, just getting into the publishing business, was planning to devote an early issue to the national parks and asked for photographs from Welch, who willingly complied. The PIPC/national park connection became apparent when the commissioners agreed to accept seventy elk from Yellowstone National Park in an effort to help save the remnants of a herd of fifteen thousand that had been gunned down by hunters and poachers until only 750 animals remained in the famous herd. Disease could conceivably wipe out these few remaining survivors. To guard against this potential calamity, a sanctuary for some of the herd had to be found far enough away to guarantee that an epidemic in one place could not reach the other. The possibility of extinction of the Yellowstone herd prompted the commissioners to act on Welch's recommendation. A five hundred–acre fenced field was established near Arden, the Harriman estate, to accommodate the seventy head of elk. Historically, elk had ranged from Canada down through the Adirondacks into the Hudson River Valley. Arrangements for the shipment were made through Horace M. Albright, Yellowstone's superintendent. The elk, exhausted and petrified, were released into their new fenced home the day after Christmas, 1919.

As the year ended, winter snows slowed the PIPC's pace of business. Perkins planned to leave at the end of January for a well-deserved rest in Florida. He planned, too, to immediately begin preparations for a new $5 million fund-raising campaign, to be launched on his return to New York in the spring. Before leaving for Florida, Perkins found himself once again in a familiar posture: fighting to restore the funding cut by New Jersey. Acting Governor Edge had stepped down at the conclusion of the war in favor of Governor William Runyan. Runyan served only one year but managed during that brief time to cut the PIPC's budget, including the funds for the on-again, off-again Henry Hudson Drive. Now Perkins and Commissioner Sutro were meeting with Runyan's successor, Governor Edward Edwards, to explain, justify, and defend the PIPC's purposes and track record. The pattern had become all too familiar: every time a political change occurred in Trenton or Albany, the PIPC had to reinvent itself. An interstate agency with a private bank account and ownership of thousands of acres of land did not readily fit on the typical government organization chart. New governors bring with them a bevy of new and eager political appointees who are in a hurry to establish their own priorities and styles of control. New arrivals are often suspicious, even resentful, of those who might have had allegiance to a previous political administration, are deemed too independent, or enjoy legal authority that is not automatically overturned by election results. The legal structure of the PIPC is not easily understood and seems to stand somewhat beyond the immediate grasp of newly arrived occupants in the hallways of government. Perkins and his commissioner colleagues always maintained a stature that allowed them direct access to the governors, regardless of partisan instincts lower down in the ranks of political appointees, but, increasingly, it seemed that the purpose of these visits with the governors was to seek a cure for the latest bruises of the budget hammer rather than to discuss the PIPC's social and environmental purposes and achievements. If appointees and elected officials could not corral the PIPC, they could hamper it with the budget. They did and would.

As the park movement across the nation gathered momentum, an ironic budget pattern developed. The creation of parks is euphoric, but once they are established, the excitement fades. Even the greatest of parks can drift along for years, taken for granted and always perceived to be there, almost as though parks were ordained from the beginning. Parks have amazing staying power. Closing or dismantling an established park for lack of funding virtually never happens. To make the attempt would be to risk unleashing the political clout of a vast but usually silent constituency of park users who plan family vacations, weekend jaunts, daily exercise, and personal explorations on the assumption that the parks are permanent fixtures, always available, woven securely into society's fabric. So long as the gates are open and some semblance of maintenance is evident, park users usually do not complain. They may expect sturdy and freshly painted facilities, clean recreation grounds, picnic areas, and campgrounds, well-maintained roads and trails, and a friendly and capable management presence, but if the facilities are shabby and neglected, the roads are falling apart, trash is overflowing, and park rangers are nowhere to be seen, most park users just cope. This curious relationship between parks and their users is usually manifested in government's budget process. Parks are a low priority. As elections approach, appropriations for parks often increase momentarily, with accompanying claims of good deeds by those seeking reelection, but otherwise, the operating budgets for parks are usually pegged just above the poverty line. The irony is that a false economy then takes over. The parks drift along, sometimes for years, as facilities deteriorate. Eventually, a big dose of funding is required to avoid a real management crisis. The PIPC commissioners were on this budget ride. Fortunately for the PIPC, the inflow of private funding softened the government budget malaise.

On the fund-raising front, Perkins was networking in anticipation of creating the third major gift fund. His personal relationship with Rockefeller, Jr., was reflected in a brief tongue-in-cheek note that Perkins received just before departing for Florida: "Thanks for your friendly note. When the six hour day and the five day week come into effect generally, you and I will grow fat, and probably our wives will be tormented to death by our so constant presence at home." Rockefeller, Jr., was interested in the new gift fund and pledged further contact on the subject with Perkins. The fund-raising effort would be aided on many fronts, among them a major article, with photographs, scheduled for a summer edition of the monthly magazine *The House Beautiful*. Mary Alden Hopkins, who was putting the article together, exclaimed to Welch, "If the thousands of park visitors enjoy the park as much as I do, there is a tremendous amount of treasure laid up in heaven or somewhere for all you who have worked so hard to make it possible for others to play."

The strategy for the fund-raising campaign came sharply into focus in a February 11, 1920, letter from Rockefeller, Jr., to Perkins. Rockefeller, Jr., reconfirmed the $500,000 commitment made by the Trustees of the Laura Spelman Rockefeller Memorial that allowed the commissioners to purchase the two river steamboats *Clermont* and *Onteora*. This commitment assumed matching amounts from state and private sources, as already agreed with Perkins. Rockefeller, Jr., then added, "The Memorial will contribute one dollar for every two dollars contributed, one by the State, one by other contributors, up to a total additional contribution from the Memorial of $500,000. Under this pledge, therefore, the possible gift from the Memorial would be increased from the present $500,000 to $1,000,000, in the event that $1,000,000 is received from the State and $1,000,000 from other contributors." If all proceeded according to plan, the Rockefeller grants, laid down as a challenge to Governor Smith and Perkins's loyal group of private donors, would generate an additional $3 million for the PIPC, plus $1 million from the Rockefeller Memorial. From Florida, Perkins sent a handwritten letter to Rockefeller, Jr., gratefully acknowledging the "wonderful" news and enthusiastically agreeing to the terms of the challenge. Perkins added a short comment about why the letter was handwritten: "I am writing in this way as I am flat on my back in bed for a week under Doctor's orders to, if possible, get rid of a cold and some digestive disturbances. The fact is, I have been overdoing for sometime and a good rest is required—am confident I'll be myself again shortly." The health problems that had sent Perkins to the hospital in Paris were with him again. Even so, his spirits were high; the news from Rockefeller, Jr., came just before Perkins learned that the Supreme Court had ruled in favor of the United States Steel Corporation after a lengthy process of antitrust litigation. Perkins was proud of the role he had played years earlier with J. P. Morgan in creating the giant steel corporation. Despite his well-known support for Roosevelt and the Progressive Party, Perkins had always been leery of antitrust actions seemingly intended to dismantle the industrial might of the United States. In a second handwritten note to Rockefeller, Jr., in which other PIPC fund-raising matters were the primary topic, Perkins said, "I am of course very happy today over the Steel Corporation victory. I believe it may point the way for better things in our larger industrial affairs and it makes me even more keenly alive."

Almost from the moment the Rockefeller challenge grant was confirmed, the wheels were in motion in Albany to win an appropriation of $1 million for the PIPC, aided by the personal involvement and advocacy of New York Assembly Speaker T. C. Sweet. By coincidence, Mather wrote to Welch in mid-February, 1920, seeking up-to-date information about the PIPC's funding initiatives, explaining, "I am very anxious to get for the national parks the kind of authority that will enable me to develop the parks under my charge along the lines of the methods used by the Palisades Interstate Park Commission." Welch responded with the latest details, providing Mather with important facts that worked to his advantage in testimony before the House of Representatives Appropriations Committee.

At the operating level, Welch continued to encounter rough situations. Heavy winter snows collapsed buildings at Bear Mountain. Many of the camp directors were asking for extra assistance due to severe weather that was hampering efforts to get the camps ready for the coming spring and summer seasons. The PIPC's management was still operating from office space in New York City after a fruitless search to find better facilities near Bear Mountain and in New Jersey. At one point, strong consideration was given to purchasing the United States Hotel in Haverstraw, New York, just to move the PIPC's staff closer to the action. Perkins commented to Commissioner Lindabury that "regarding office room, it is a vexatious question, but one thing I am convinced—we cannot go to Bear Mountain. In the winter, the location would be impossible and at anytime the question of obtaining clerical help and getting them to and from work would be a very hard matter." The PIPC's office remained in the city, but city and rural cultures and styles were not easily mixed. Welch experienced a hard management bump when a crew from New York City was brought to the park to labor alongside the PIPC's workers on a camp project for the Boy Scouts of America. In a follow-up letter to H. A. Gordon, the B.S.A. Camp Director, Welch described the problem. "Our men, as you know, are all mountain men who have been with us for a long, long time and they have not associated with the City labor nor the City people and it is very easy for a few radicals to stir up a tremendous amount of trouble. I would very much rather get along with just the men we have than take any chances of introducing trouble-makers among them."

Despite surprises and growing pains, a great distance had been covered since March 21, 1900, when Roosevelt had signed the PIPC legislation, as confirmed by an article in *The New York Times* proclaiming, "Palisades Park Has 20th Birthday Today." Over those two decades, the small experiment in landscape protection had blossomed into a full-grown conservation mandate that would forever change the character of the New York–New Jersey metropolitan region. Without fanfare, almost invisibly, Perkins and Welch had decided on a strategic move for the PIPC that would strengthen its capabilities even more. Thousands of acres were being added to the PIPC's holdings in New York. Theoretically, these lands should have been removed from the tax rolls of local towns when acquired by the PIPC. For some towns, the tax loss would have been significant. In Rockland County, and later in Orange County, New York, legislative steps were taken to retain the PIPC's lands on the local tax rolls. Perkins and the commissioners could have challenged the legislation and probably prevailed, but they chose not to. A letter from Welch to Jay Downer of the Bronx Parkway Commission explained the rationale: "As you know, we have in some instances taken practically all of the property in a number of school districts." Welch confirmed that the commissioners "considered it wisest" not to oppose the taxation bills. To do otherwise would financially wound school districts and local governments. In time, property-tax payments for almost all the PIPC's lands in New York became a routine part of the annual state budget allocations, generating about $15 million in revenue for the local towns each year during the 1990s. Had Perkins decided to oppose the tax legislation, future PIPC acquisitions would have been placed in jeopardy because of the always controversial matter of lost property-tax revenue. Instead, the PIPC is one of the few major conservation agencies that enjoys the advantage of being a property-taxpayer. This is a double benefit for local towns: they continue to receive tax revenue, and the PIPC pays for many services that otherwise would be the obligation of the towns, such as law enforcement and facilities maintenance.

The PIPC's twenty years spanned a sensational time in the history of the United States. The Wright Brothers flew at Kitty Hawk in 1903; an assembly line for Model "T" Fords cranked up in 1908; Standard Oil was declared a monopoly in 1911; the *Titanic* went down in 1912; the League of Nations was founded after World War I; Prohibition arrived in 1920. Perkins may have dwelt for a moment on the events of the era and the PIPC's anniversary, but other matters were much on his mind, including a personal battle to regain his strength. In a letter to Rockefeller, Jr., after his mid-April, 1920, return to New York from Florida, Perkins affirmed continuing health problems:

I am a trifle better than when I wrote you from Florida but still under the doctor's care, with a strict diet and regulation as to my hours of rest, and am facing the proposition of having to go away again just as quickly as I get the Palisades Park campaign out of the way. . . . Everything in connection with the campaign just now is at the touch-and-go point. I have been soliciting a number of people here in town and so far have succeeded in obtaining pledges for $350,000. I must, if possible, get this up to at least half a million before the end of next week, because at about that time I think the Governor will act on the bill which I talked over with you and which has been introduced in Albany.

Perkins made a personal donation of $50,000 to the "third gift fund." J. (Jack) Pierpont Morgan, heir to the Morgan empire, made a donation of $25,000. Perkins's prediction of favorable action in Albany was confirmed when both houses of the Legislature authorized $1 million for the PIPC, and Governor Smith signed the bill. Perkins immediately moved to reinforce accounting procedures within the PIPC to ensure that state monies and private contributions would be tracked with even greater care, sensing that a fresh opportunity was opening up for the PIPC to significantly advance its agenda.

Within the park system, the pace of activities was hectic. Residents of nearby towns were already complaining about traffic gridlock on the roads to the parks weeks before the heavy summer visitation was expected. "I want to call your attention again to the dreadful condition of the County Highway between Fort Montgomery and Highland Falls Village. The Bear Mountain Buses run up and down it every day and have helped to wear it in great ruts and holes so that it is hardly safe for life and limb," wrote Herbert L. Satterlee, partner in the Wall Street law firm of Satterlee, Canfield & Stone. The mayor of Englewood Cliffs was irate about "the worst congestion of automobile traffic that has ever occurred" and demanded more PIPC police to direct traffic on the approach road to the Dyckman Street Ferry.

On June 6, 1920, *The New York Tribune* ran a major piece by Emma Bugbee headlined, "New York Crosses the Hudson to Get Back to Nature."

Sunday on the Palisades is an institution far more typical of New York than the Zoo. What other city in the world has a wall of mountains for a playground, within a distance of one mile and a 10-cent ferry trip, and yet as remote as roaring campfires and tumbling waterfalls? On a warm Sunday afternoon it is almost impossible to find a fallen log or a natural fireplace that has not already been preempted by those mysterious and omnipresent persons who never seem to be going anywhere, but have always already arrived. Their beefsteak is always cooking over an already perfect bed of coals before you get there;

their bathing suits are wet and their shoulders already sunburned, their victrola already singing to itself under the trees, and father is already displaying a string of infant fish which he has caught from the pier. One is frequently disillusioned in finding the cliffs more full of Girls Scouts than columbines, and in learning that aching muscles last three days, while the new moon reflected in the water lasts only to the subway.

To gather information for the article, Emma had placed herself in the knowledgeable care of a friend she described as "the best Palisader I know":

It was she who taught me that a narrow skirt, no matter how old and shiny, is not efficient in cliff scaling, and that solid alcohol will burn when rain-soaked twigs will not. She knows that a taxi will take you to the end of the Hendrick Hudson Drive, saving your legs for the harder hike over the unfinished portions of the trail further north. This is the most romantic portion of the Palisades, with a gravestone now and then to remind the visitors of a once prosperous fishing village clinging to the foot of the cliffs, and with dying honeysuckles and lilac bushes telling of the unconquerable instinct of woman to beautify her dooryard.

Her friend, too, was a fashion expert. "No matter how firm a believer in freedom a woman may be and no matter how long she may have lectured on the subject of proper clothing for hiking, the moment of her first appearance without a skirt is somewhat delicate." Emma's friend wore a skirt during the ferry crossing, but with "trouserettes" in hand, "you're sure to meet your most churchgoing friends in their best clothes," she cautioned. The two women "clung to the beach for the first mile," scanning with an anxious eye the picnicking crowd. Suddenly the friend "stopped and gazed delightedly at a particularly hilarious group of bacon toasters. 'Look,' she whispered, 'that girl's got 'em on.' Sure enough she had, in the full sight of the entire Sunday parade."

The cartoonist for the *Tribune* added his own touch to the Bugbee article. One drawing showed a generous man and woman enjoying a generous picnic with the caption "The rotund couple hiked ten miles upstream in eleven hours flat—primary idea involved being 'reduction of avoirdupois'—they then partook of food—some of which may be seen in the picture—only to find upon reaching home—that each had gained four pounds."

With lively preparations under way in anticipation of another record-breaking visitor season, including management of the group camps that were under contract to sixty-seven diverse and often demanding charitable organizations, the *Clermont* and *Onteora* were coming on line. Several months previously, Perkins

New York Herald Tribune cartoon, 1920.
(Courtesy of PIPC Archives)

had seen to the purchase of these steamboats out of his own pocket, with the understanding that the Laura Spelman Rockefeller Memorial Fund would provide reimbursement. Title to the steamers was in his name, so Perkins "loaned" the steamers to the PIPC. Welch and his staff were finding that the operation of two large steamboats on the Hudson River was vastly challenging. Firing up the engines and pointing the bows into the river were the least of Welch's problems. Finding dock space in New York City and along the Jersey shore and refitting, maintaining, and crewing leaky wooden vessels of such large dimensions were nautical tasks unlike anything that the PIPC's staff had encountered before. Among other considerations, the steamboats needed music programs to be competitive. Welch went in search of an electronic version of orchestra music, and Commissioners Lindabury and Averell Harriman used their contacts to assist him with the dock problem. Joseph B. Harris & Son offered free dock space in Jersey City, thanks to Lindabury, and the Erie Railroad Company responded to Harriman by providing temporary space at one of the company's docks in the city. The PIPC's "navy" was launched.

Except for Welch and King, the distractions of making ready for the summer caused few on the PIPC's staff to take note of the chilling fact that Perkins's health continued to fail. In a routine response to a letter of inquiry about the PIPC's activities, Perkins's secretary, Mary Kihm, wrote on May 27, 1920, "Mr. Perkins is out of town at present and is not expected to return for several weeks." Perkins's physician prescribed additional extended rest in an attempt to reverse the threatening physical ailments that were dragging him down. In a June 11 letter to Welch, George F. Kunz, president of the American Scenic and Historic Preservation Society, suggested that Welch drop by at Tiffany & Co., where Kunz held a senior management position, to discuss "a matter concerning the park," adding a postscript: "Am awfully sorry about Mr. Perkins, may he be well soon."

On June 18, correspondence was flowing to and from the PIPC as usual: Welch declined a proposal to place a "dancing tent" on the Palisades shore where the Dyckman Street Ferry delivered its passengers; by memorandum, Camp Director Brown advised Welch of a pending meeting with the staff of the Museum of Natural History to develop a nature guide for the parks; King sent a memo to Commissioner Sutro about the need to convince New Jersey Governor Edwards to approve a supplemental budget appropriation for the PIPC. Then, late in the day, King wrote to Mrs. Evelina (Ball) Perkins: "May I express to you, on behalf of every employee of the Palisades Park Commission, the deep sorrow that is felt in the death of Mr. Perkins; a sorrow that carries with it a most heartfelt sympathy for you in your loss." Within the PIPC, the assumption had been that Perkins would soon regain his strength and step back into his accustomed leadership role, but at age fifty-eight, he suffered a heart attack, rallied for a brief time, and then was gone. Welch, in shock, felt that the world "had turned upside down."

The following day, a tribute written by Frank A. Munsey appeared in the *Sun and New York Herald:* "In all my acquaintance with men, I have never known one of more generous soul; have never known a better friend, or one more ready to go far, very far, to serve another. To those of us who knew him best, who knew the true impulses and purposes in his heart, who found delight in his buoyant, cheery, strong nature, the world will be dulled by his passing." The obituary in *The New York Times* ran for four long columns. Funeral services were held in Riverdale-on-Hudson, New York, where Perkins first heard, saw, and felt the explosions on the Palisades. The man who had started his career by managing a small grocery store owned by his father in Cleveland, Ohio, left an estate estimated at $10 million.

With the passing of George Walbridge Perkins, the world of the PIPC indeed turned upside down.

9.
Jolliffe

By direction of the vice-president, a special meeting of the Commission of the Palisades Interstate Park, New York, will be held at the office of the Commission, 90 Wall Street, Manhattan, on Friday, June 25th at 2:00pm.

George Perkins had been working on the "third gift fund" only days before he died. In preparation for the June 25, 1919, meeting, Commissioner Richard Lindabury wrote to George Perkins, Jr., asking for a status report on the fund-raising initiative. Perkins, Jr., listed the pledges from J. P. Morgan's son, Jack ($25,000), Arthur C. James ($50,000), Colman DuPont ($50,000), Edward S. Harkness ($100,000), Cleveland H. Dodge ($50,000), George F. Baker ($100,000), E. E. Olcott ($15,000), and George Perkins, Sr., ($50,000). These pledges, plus the $1 million authorization from New York, placed the PIPC at about the halfway point in the "third gift fund" effort, not close enough to win the $500,000 Rockefeller challenge grant.

At the special meeting, Lindabury reported the results of his inquiry to Perkins, Jr. The commissioners reviewed a list of revenue options, including a recommendation by William Welch that the PIPC publish thirty thousand booklets containing information and a park map, to be sold for ten cents each. Just prior to the meeting, Welch challenged the vendor of "Sight-Seeing Map of the Hudson River," contending that the map was full of errors and inaccuracies. The vendor, who had printed thousands of the maps on the assumption that they would be sold aboard the river steamers, including the *Clermont* and *Onteora,* tried to brush off the inaccuracies. He complimented Welch on his knowledge of the river and invited him to suggest changes that might be incorporated in future printings. The vendor did not miss the opportunity to remind Welch, too, that the PIPC stood to make 7½ ¢ on each map sold to the thousands of passengers expected aboard the PIPC's steamboats during the summer. Welch was in no mood to be diplomatic or flattered and, despite the PIPC's financial needs, reported to the commissioners that he had refused "to allow this map to be placed for sale on our boats. I think it is an imposition on the public to sell them this thing," adding that since the vendor was in the map business for profit, he should employ someone "really familiar with the present conditions" to make the necessary corrections. Welch concluded by saying, "I am quite sure that the Hudson River Day Line will join me in insisting that the map be withdrawn from sale."

At the close of the meeting, and with no evident progress on fund-raising or revenue enhancement, a statement was attached to the minutes in honor of George Perkins. In part, it stated,

> The Palisades Interstate Park as it now exists was the conception of Mr. Perkins, and it was he and he alone who raised the money for its acquisition and development. As the Park grew in size and usefulness his ideas and enthusiasm grew with it, until in the latter years of his life he conceived a playground large enough and complete enough to afford rest and recreation to all the people of New York and New Jersey who lived near enough to enjoy it, and where all the facilities for such enjoyment should be furnished at cost without profit to concessionaires or others. To the development of this idea Mr. Perkins gave the best there was in him.

Summer activities were in full swing when Perkins was lost to the PIPC. In a letter to Horace Albright, Yellowstone National Park's superintendent, Welch predicted that visitation to the PIPC's parks would increase by more than 90 percent that year. His prediction proved to be conservative. People were pouring off the steamboats onto the narrow beaches at the foot of the Palisades and the docks at Bear Mountain. Others were arriving via the growing network of roads, including an increasing number of paved miles. Still others rode the trains. An incentive for some visitors might have been Welch's decision to purchase an "automatic orchestra" from the Rudolph Wurlitzer Company. This "orchestra" was placed in the dance pavilion at Bear Mountain, much to the delight of the younger crowd. When the numbers were added up at the end of the year, visitation stood at 2,166,455 (New York, 1,307,089; New Jersey, 859,366). Nothing of this scale in park use had ever been experienced, anywhere.

However, with the swarm of visitors came scores of complaints that were deposited on Welch's desk, ranging from botched ferry schedules to food-service problems at the Bear Mountain Inn. One of the PIPC's own, Commissioner Charles W. Baker, found need to write to Welch about his own experience; "I was over on the Palisades Sunday afternoon and had invited a friend to accompany me for a tramp, who was unable to do so. I was frankly glad afterward that he did not, for I must confess I was ashamed of the appearance of things at our front door." Baker described the scene he encountered at the ferry landing on the New Jersey shore. "The most slipshod, ragged, neglected place in the whole park that I know is right there as one leaves the ferry."

Welch responded to Baker with a lament that would be repeated time and again for years to come:

> Do you realize that we have barely had sufficient money in the New Jersey end of the park to employ three laborers from Bloomers to the New York State line and six laborers from Bloomers to Fort Lee. These nine men have had to clean up that entire twelve mile section. These men have barely been able to keep the bathing beaches, bath houses and shelters and the main path clean. The picnic groves are in shocking condition as so is much of the shore front and the whole reason is that the appropriation which we received from the State was only sufficient to allow us to keep this small force on.

Nevertheless, the vast majority of visitors to the parks found no reason to complain and many reasons to tell their friends and families about the joys they discovered in nature's playground. The visitors kept coming, and their playground kept growing.

Many of the property transactions set in motion before World War I were being completed. In particular, Commissioners Lindabury, Edward L. Partridge, J. DuPratt White, and Frederick C. Sutro stepped into the breech left by Perkins, supported by Welch, Elbert W. King, and the seemingly ageless George A. Blauvelt, long retired from his Senate seat in Albany but continually responsive to the PIPC's mission as a practicing attorney. Twenty land acquisitions and one right-of-way transaction added 32,922 acres to the PIPC's holdings in 1920, at an average per-acre cost of $26. The right-of-way, obtained in a transaction with Orange County, New York, passed along the steep shoulder of Storm King Mountain just north of West Point.

The PIPC's expansive parklands did not escape the attention of "sportsmen" in New York who began pressing to have thousands of acres opened for hunting. Welch polled each commissioner by letter about this issue, receiving a unanimous response: the hunting restrictions, set in place when this question was first raised in New Jersey almost two decades previously, should be maintained. Seeking a legal basis for this decision, Welch gained a "game and fish preserve" designation from the New York Department of Conservation.

He was not so fortunate in the matter of the delivery of one hundred thousand extra pounds of TNT. The PIPC was using TNT in road construction and had received permission from the New York State Industrial Commission to keep one hundred thousand pounds stored in a powder magazine. When an Industrial Commission representative made an unannounced inspection of the site, he discovered that two hundred thousand pounds of TNT were stored, including "100,000 pounds now stacked on the ground about 300 feet from your licensed magazine, and covered with canvas." The PIPC had received two railroad cars full of TNT, which was duly stored in the magazine. Then, due to an error in paperwork, three more TNT-laden cars arrived. Welch explained this mix-up to the unsympathetic inspector. The TNT mini-crisis prompted the PIPC to inquire about storing the extra explosives on Iona Island. The local Navy commander was unresponsive, so the commissioners turned to a friend in Washington, D.C., with the hope of influencing the commander. Unfortunately, their timing was off. Franklin Delano Roosevelt had just resigned as Secretary of the Navy and was unable to lend immediate assistance, even though this son of the Hudson River Valley and his wife, Eleanor, would later become active champions of the PIPC. The crisis was resolved when Welch pledged to complete a second powder magazine "as rapidly as possible, and to post a double force of armed guards, day and night," to watch over the illicit stack of canvas-covered TNT until it could be properly stored.

While Welch and staff scrambled to stay ahead of the parks' demands, inquiries continued to arrived from interested observers. Writing for the *Wanderer of the Pittsburgh Dispatch,* Mary Ethel McAuley asked Welch for his comments on an article "How Can We Improve Our National Parks?" she planned to write. Referencing his experience, Welch offered five simple points: Obtain more appropriations from Congress—build better roads—pay concessionaire executives well, but retain a large percentage of concession receipts for the government—operate parks solely for recreational and educational purposes—place the National Park Service under the control of a nonpartisan commission. Had even some of Welch's advice been heeded, many mistakes in the future management of U.S. national parks might have been avoided entirely, especially the eventual monopolistic grip gained in many parks by concessionaires.

Welch's friend, Enos Mills, was keeping an eye on the recently created Rocky Mountain National Park, Colorado, for exactly this reason. "The policy adopted by the National Park Service to allow for monopolistic concessionaires is wrong," he had written to Welch in October, 1919. Mills attributed this wrongheadedness to NPS Director Stephen Mather. Wrongheadedness aside, the collaborative association between Mather and Welch was strong, as demonstrated when Mather asked Welch in February, 1920, to hurry as soon as possible to the Presque Isle Peninsula, near Erie, Pennsylvania, to independently study the feasibility of making the peninsula into a national park. Mather reminded Welch that "Perry's fleet was sunk in Misery Bay, a little harbor at the edge of the peninsula." With the permission of the commissioners, Welch journeyed to Misery Bay and reported back to Mather: "Presque Isle can be made, with very small expenditure, a wonderfully attractive and useful park, and provide opportunity to make one national park close to great centers of population." Belatedly, Mather wrote back to Welch, explaining that there was "some uncertainty" about the "status" of the Presque Isle Peninsula, apparently because a key portion of peninsula land, thought to be owned by the federal government, had been returned to the State of Pennsylvania. State officials were not enthusiastic about the idea of allowing title to the land to be transferred back to federal stewards. This particular Mather initiative was dropped.

A few months later, Everett G. Griggs, representing the National Park Association of Washington State, sought Welch's advice about park projects in Washington and Oregon. Welch wrote of his "dream of an interstate park in Washington and Oregon to protect the Columbia River Gorge." Welch had made this same recommendation to political officials in Oregon while he was directing the war effort to produce spruce for the aircraft industry. This Welch dream, too, remained unfulfilled. The ultimate fate of portions of the Columbia River Gorge remains to this day a topic of intense debate between conservation advocates and property-rights proponents who oppose public ownership of land.

Those from other states who were seeking counsel from Welch about park management would have been fascinated by the debate sparked within the PIPC by Anthony H. G. Fokker, inventor of the synchronized airplane machine gun and manufacturer of the planes flown by German pilots in World War I, most notably Manfred von Richthofen, the Red Baron. Using the latest technology, Fokker and a group of financial backers thought that New York City would be the ideal market for a commercial seaplane base. Their choice of sites was the PIPC-owned dock named for Sanford P. Ross, a former owner, that extended outward from the base of the Palisades into the Hudson River.

In exchange for a twenty-year lease to use Ross Dock, Fokker's Aeroplane and Motor Company, represented by J. C. Mars, proposed to invest $200,000 for a bulkhead and $50,000 for a hangar. Company representatives proposed to pay the PIPC 5 percent of the company's first-year gross income, to be increased by increments to 15 percent annually based on future company earnings, asserting that hangars and machine shops would be attractive and of interest to park visitors. They professed that the development of aircraft should be encouraged and that devoting Ross Dock to this specialized purpose would not be any more limiting to the park's use by the general public than bridle paths were in Central Park.

The proposed seaplane base did not seem to fit with Welch's philosophy that parks should be used "solely for recreational and educational purposes," but the money and excitement of being involved in the development of commercial air transport in the United States were tempting to the commissioners. Fokker's proposal was taken under serious consideration. In the meantime, Fokker purchased a plot of land atop the Palisades and announced that he would build his house there.

Revenue from another source caused a significant change in the staff ranks of the PIPC. Rental fees from the group-camp program netted the PIPC $12,154 during the 1920 summer season. This income was promptly reinvested in group-camp expansion, but Camp Manager Edward F. Brown, looking at the profitable numbers and probably thinking of his eight-year pioneering effort to develop the camps, took the opportunity to ask for a pay raise. The commissioners declined his request, prompting Brown to submit his resignation. Brown's departure was adorned by mutual expressions of high regard and appreciation between Brown, Welch, and the commissioners. He left behind a remarkable record of personal achievement, having taken the group-camp program from an uncertain, almost accidental beginning to a level of major service to metropolitan residents. By the time of his departure, the camps were a snapshot of the urban society that surrounded Harriman Park, with special emphasis on the keystone program serving underprivileged children.

With Brown's exit, the commissioners turned to an unlikely successor named Ruby M. Jolliffe, director of Camps for the New York City YWCA. She would remain at the helm of the PIPC's group-camp program for the next twenty-eight years. "I've heard people say she was a curious mixture of dignity and devil-may-care," commented Jack Focht, director of the PIPC's Trailside Museums, many years after the person, simply and fondly known as "Jolliffe," retired. "She was the first one down the toboggan hill in the winter of 1922 when it opened, clocked at 70 miles an hour." Another time, Jolliffe hopped on an idling police

Ruby Jolliffe, Group Camp Director, 1921.
(Courtesy of PIPC Archives)

motorcycle and ran it into a wall. Staring out from a photograph taken of her in winter attire soon after she was hired by the Commission at a pay rate of $3,000 per year is a prim and proper woman, cloche cap pulled tightly down to her eyebrows, large eyes, larger spectacles, a slight, tight smile (the kind that seemingly says I hate to have my picture taken), a crisp white shirt and large striped necktie covered by a heavy wool jacket, gloves, wool knickers, socks up to her knees, and laced, polished boots. Jolliffe is standing as if at attention, the first female executive on the PIPC's staff.

Born in Montreal, she had earned a Bachelor of Arts degree from the University of Toronto and a Masters degree in Modern Languages from Bryn Mawr College. After studying in Europe and teaching in New Jersey and the State of Washington, she had assumed responsibility for the New York City YWCA camping program in 1912. When the PIPC took over the old rifle range at Blauvelt Park on South Mountain, Jolliffe was there to establish the YWCA camp, marking the beginning of group camping in the PIPC's park system. When war caused the U.S. Army to reclaim the rifle range for the duration, W. Averell Harriman welcomed Jolliffe and the YWCA campers to property he owned at Summit Lake on his family's Arden estate. She was already well known to Welch and the commissioners when Brown stepped down from his camp manager post, and the decision to hire her was prompt. Before she retired almost three decades later, Jolliffe would "meet the sons, daughters, and grandchildren of her first campers," according to a report in *The New York Times*. She became a compelling presence in the camps. A young camper named Mildred Rulison particularly impressed Jolliffe, who wrote to Rulison during the winter of 1920–21, asking that she "take over" one of the nature museums that Jolliffe had established in Harriman Park. Mildred was not inclined to accept the offer. "I drove to Bear Mountain and told her, 'I think Bess McClelland should have the job. She knows more.' Jolliffe said, 'But I asked you.' I gulped and said, 'I'll take it.'"

Florence Ball also remembered Jolliffe:

Saturday was beef stew day and the Director thought that type of meal was not the right one for so honored a guest as Miss Jolliffe. She told the chef to change the menu to the Leg-of-Lamb scheduled for Sunday. The chef became so incensed that he began slamming articles around, tried opening #10 cans with a butcher knife, kicked them all, then packed up, got his pay, and left. I was called to cook the lamb dinner. The dinner went off without a hitch and Miss Jolliffe took the time to come into the kitchen—say "hello"—and said she enjoyed the meal.

The Jolliffe presence, imposing enough to create beehive activity simply in anticipation of her arrival as a dinner guest, seemed made up of equal parts disciplinarian, confidant, health officer, storyteller, naturalist, role model, sports advocate, moralist, commander, loyalist, educator, inspector, and stern administrator. *The New York Times* referred to Jolliffe as "the hand that struck the match for more campfires than any other in the country." The scores of camps, all directed by different personalities, each pursuing its own purposes, had one common bond: they had to be "ship-shape" at all times because the directors never knew when Jolliffe might appear unexpectedly. She patrolled constantly. Like Welch, Jolliffe won allegiance for being fair and quietly charming, listening carefully, and, when necessary, acting tough-as-nails. She made clear that her duty was to ensure the well-being of the camps and campers. Her domain reached the incredible number of 102 group camps, then eventually settled in at 71 with a combined population of 6,400, a scale not even remotely approached anywhere else in the nation. Among her ardent fans were the Roosevelts, who regularly visited and participated in activities with young campers. Children, awed by Jolliffe, would carry vivid memories of her far into their adulthood. Welch would discover that he had a formidable colleague who saw no limitations to the good that could be accomplished in the parks.

Sharing this view was a group of men and women who were discovering that the vast acreage controlled by the PIPC offered an opportunity to step away, even for a moment, from the sounds and intensity of urban life, to wander along woodland paths, to pause to listen to nature's gentle voice, to stretch body and mind, and then to return refreshed to the workaday world. More and more visitors were choosing hiking as a highly personal form of recreation, far from the

Eleanor Roosevelt, Group Camp, Harriman Park, 1920s.
(Courtesy of FDR Library Archives)

crowded park picnic areas, beaches, camps, and playgrounds. In September, 1920, Welch received an invitation from Dr. John H. Finley, Judge Harrington Putnam, Albert Handy, Bayard H. Christy, and Dr. George J. Fisher to meet at the Waldorf Hotel to discuss the formation of a "League of Walkers." At the Abercrombie & Fitch Building on October 5, this discussion was extended to include the Appalachian Mountain Club, the Fresh Air Club, the Green Mountain Club, the Tramp and Trail Club, the Associated Mountaineer Clubs of America, and the New York State College of Forestry. Welch and Brown represented the PIPC. Meade C. Dobson of the Fresh Air Club, who had written several articles for the *New York Evening Post* about the PIPC's park system, and Raymond H. Torrey, editor of the Outing Page for the *Post,* attended and assured media clout for the venture. In a follow-up memorandum to the commissioners, Welch explained that the purpose "was to try and take some steps to better our trail system and make our park more useable to pedestrians and tramping organizations."

Welch continued: "I told them I was sure the Commission would be very glad to have any help they could give us to accomplish this and to take up with a Committee from the several organizations the question of the location of pedestrian trails in the Park." But Welch had cautioned the group that the PIPC "rather discouraged volunteer work on trails in the past because we did not want any amateurs marking out these trails nor attempting to clear them, but that we would be very glad to have the cooperation of experts in this sort of work." Feeling that he may have overstepped, Welch concluded the memo by asking, "Will you please give me your opinion on this question and let me know if you object to my going this far with this matter?" The reply came from Partridge: "On the contrary, I approve!" Through these gatherings at the Waldorf and Abercrombie & Fitch, the PIPC tapped into a constituency of hikers who would become volunteer planners, workers, and stewards of a trail network that would expand to more than 1,300 miles. The expertise Welch was hoping for emerged from among a spectrum of professionals, students, spouses, and young people who became devoted to spending their weekends and holidays building and maintaining trails. In the process, the trail volunteers became avid defenders of open space.

The formal organization of the trail groups began with the meetings in 1920. By 1922, a "Trail Conference" had been formed specifically to lend volunteer assistance to the PIPC, and to be watchful of the commissioners' policies and practices. Today, with a membership of 10,200 and an intimate knowledge of the PIPC's park system earned with sweat-equity, the New York–New Jersey Trail Conference is a political force to be reckoned with. Its officers occasionally demand accountability for what the members perceive to be ill-considered PIPC policies and actions, but far more frequently, the Conference stands as a skilled and dedicated defender of basic park purposes.

Welch was key to this generally good chemistry. He found camaraderie and common ground with the hikers and instantly assumed a leadership role, becoming an active proponent for opening up the parks, footstep by footstep. At a November, 1920, meeting of the hiking group, Dobson reported in the *New York Evening Post,* "Major Welch expressed heartiest cooperation of the Commission, and of himself, in the trail scheme. He made several sound suggestions, which were adopted, as to routes, blazes, markers, and shelters." Welch particularly emphasized "the great idea of a path from Delaware Water Gap, across

New Jersey and New York into New England." Dobson included a comment that Welch made at the end of the meeting concerning a "housing problem of a colony of beavers placed in the park several weeks ago. The building operations undertaken by the beavers evidently have been unhampered by strikes, for their winter quarters are in readiness, together with the necessary dams and runways." At the meeting, committee officers were chosen: Albert Britt, chairman, Frank Place, Jr., vice-chairman, and Dobson, secretary.

The year 1920, so sorrowfully marked by the loss of Perkins, but so successfully concluded by leaps in activities on all fronts, was complicated by the fact that Perkins had raised only about half the funds needed to trigger the $500,000 Rockefeller challenge grant. His fellow commissioners did not have the kind of personal access to potential major donors enjoyed by Perkins that was needed to fill the fund-raising vacuum. Ahead loomed the challenge of convincing Albany and Trenton to do more to support the parks financially. One of the financial challenges was the care of the *Half Moon,* the replica of Henry Hudson's ship that had been in the care of the PIPC since the Hudson/Fulton celebration in 1909. New York State owned the ship, but the PIPC was paying for the cost of its upkeep. One cost-cutting option under consideration was to ground the *Half Moon* close to shore at Bear Mountain and encase the hull in concrete. This option was never effected. The replica, moored at Bear Mountain for many years until eventually moved upriver to Albany, met the fate of most other wooden boats whose owners did not have the money for continuing maintenance: it fell apart and disappeared.

The PIPC's dayliner boats were receiving different attention. Commissioner Baker, who was serving on the PIPC's "Hook Mountain Committee," contacted PIPC Comptroller King to suggest "the possibility that one of the Commission's boats may be put entirely in the Hook Mountain service, making two round trips per day at a fare as moderate as to attract the really poor people." Unstated, but implied, was that the "really poor people," mostly African Americans, could be sent to Hook Mountain, physically separating them from the more well-to-do, mostly white Americans who frequented Bear Mountain and other park locations. The commissioners initiated the development of facilities at Hook Mountain for this purpose.

While planning for Hook Mountain was under way, the proposed use of Ross Dock as an "aeroplane" base was refined and strengthened. Mars, representing Aeromarine Engineering & Sales Company, the same Fokker-inspired company but with a different name, recommended a refinement to the earlier concept: a "passenger elevator" that would carry visitors from the cliff top to the aeroplane base below for a per passenger price of 5¢. Mars assured the commissioners that river-steamer passengers would not be able to see the elevator's structure, made of steel beams anchored to the cliff face. Ross Dock would offer a public flying-boat anchorage, passenger air transportation, ferryboat service, and hangar facilities. In return for the requested twenty-year lease, the company guaranteed the PIPC a minimum payment of $10,000 per year, plus liquidation of an existing $100,000 mortgage that the PIPC was carrying on the Ross Dock property. Mars suggested, too, that company representatives would be interested in inspecting the Dana mansion as a possible cliff-top assembly point for visitors who wished to take the elevator ride.

Unrelated to the Aeromarine proposal, but related to the commissioners' search for funds, was a contact from another entrepreneur about the prospect of "storing" between ten and twenty oceangoing steamships on moorings just off-shore the PIPC's beaches in New Jersey. The entrepreneur offered to pay the PIPC $1,800 annually per steamship. After brief consideration, the commissioners declined this opportunity, but the matter of the Aeroplane base remained under serious consideration. The motivation was money.

King wrote to White, now president of the PIPC, "I hate to trouble you when you are not feeling well, but we really are very short of money." The commissioners had approved several more construction projects and earmarked $25,000 to "carry" the operating departments through the winter months of 1921, "leaving me with practically no funds on hand," King reported. The "Third Gift Fund" pledges obtained by Perkins were materializing slowly in the form of checks, including $50,000 from Baker, $10,000 from James, and $12,500 from Dodge, but no new pledges were in sight. King even expressed concern about the price the PIPC was charging for cigars, worrying that the federal government might cap the price. His fear on this point proved unfounded, but a much more unsettling turn in the search for income came in the form of New Jersey Assembly Bill 546, sought by the commissioners and approved by Governor Edward Edwards, "giving the Commission powers to sell, lease, or grant easements over its properties on top of the Palisades."

The commissioners were seeking to establish a $200,000 reserve fund. Reasoning that most of the PIPC's holdings on top of the Palisades had been purchased with private funds provided by New Yorkers, they decided to "gladly consider these properties as an asset of the New York Commission." Further claiming that the cliff-top properties had been purchased only to provide for "entrance" to the beaches and shoreline below, the commissioners identified "several said properties no longer necessary for park purposes," including the

Dana property and mansion, Greenbrook park known for its lush natural appeal, and even the summit portion of the Carpenter Brothers' quarry site.

The total estimated value of these properties was $322,537, more than sufficient to create the reserve fund if sold. The commissioners' action, twenty-one years after the inauguration of the effort to save the Palisades, confirmed that the PIPC's attention in New Jersey remained riveted on the shoreline and cliffs. But the fact that the Dana property was on the hit list even though Perkins had worked so diligently to acquire it suggested that the PIPC was drifting badly off course. King, in a follow-up letter to Blauvelt, the PIPC's counsel, worried that sale of the Dana property would have to be handled with great care, reminding Blauvelt that the property had been rented for several seasons to the Brooklyn Children's Aid Society. King raised no objection, however, to the sale itself, seemingly unconcerned about two crucial considerations. One was that the PIPC was about to set an ill-advised precedent that could open the way for future PIPC-land sales to cope with budget needs. The second was that the park vision in New Jersey seemed barricaded by the cliffs of the Palisades. Sweeping views of the Hudson River and the cityscape beyond could be found at practically every point along the summit of the cliffs. Terrain extending westward from the brink of the Palisades was gently rolling and gardenlike. The "millionaires' row" houses already constructed on the summit confirmed that only time stood between the existing natural beauty and heavy development in such a spectacular location so close to New York City.

Yet the commissioners were seeing financial assets, not park benefits, on top of the Palisades. Albert S. Riker, writing from the Standish Arms Hotel in Brooklyn, was among the first to express interest in the Dana property. He introduced himself in correspondence to King as a real-estate agent specializing in shorefront properties, including Riker's Island in the East River of New York City. Riker thought that the Dana property could be readily turned into a hotel and motion-picture studio. Perhaps due to continuing concerns about the Brooklyn Children's Aid Society, the PIPC was not prepared to deal with Riker, and his interest faded.

The PIPC's search for funds might have been forever resolved by Comdr. Clellan Davis of Englewood, New Jersey. On May 5, 1921, a headline in *The New York Times* read, "May Drill For Oil Under the Palisades." Davis claimed that an "oil film" was constantly appearing on the Hudson River near Edgewater, adjacent to Fort Lee. He asserted that this film must be coming "from some underground petroleum stream." Commissioner Lindabury, representing the state and the PIPC, said, "We will do everything in our power to determine whether there is a great lake of oil under the strata of New Jersey soil." The determination was quickly made—no lake of oil was found. The PIPC's holdings atop the Palisades remained at risk.

While the commissioners grappled with problems of money and policy, the PIPC police grappled with the public. James D. Moore was appointed as a "traffic magistrate" to deal with the growing number of motorist problems. "Our troubles from automobiles are not the speeding variety," King explained to Partridge. "Principally, trouble is created by the inconsiderate, selfish types who try to jump ahead of the line waiting to take the ferry. We also have difficulty with those individuals who might be called 'chesty,' who either know a Commissioner or some other influential person." The police made certain that, "chesty" or not, motorists stayed in line at the ferry terminals. Moore's appointment established a PIPC-operated traffic court for the New Jersey section of the park system. The court became an unplanned but unique organizational fixture. Unlike the erstwhile lake of oil, the court began to produce significant revenue for the PIPC

"Canoe Beach," Palisades shoreline, New Jersey.
(Courtesy of PIPC Archives)

because the "speeding variety" of motorists were becoming more common. Fines collected from these violations began to strengthen the police budget.

Moore became the first of many magistrates to hold sway in the PIPC's traffic court. He was succeeded by Abram A. Lebson who at the remarkable age of twenty-one had already been appointed a judge in Bergen County, New Jersey; he later became co-founder of the respected law firm Lebson & Prigoff.

Not all violators of park rules faced the magistrates. Capt. James Conway, chief of the PIPC police, had an answer for "foolish canoeists" who crossed the river from the city under good weather conditions, stayed too long, and then were tempted to return in waters roiled and chopped by the wind. Conway was not interested in earning "medals for heroic life saving." He and his men took the canoes into custody and ordered the paddlers to walk to the nearest ferry for their return trips home.

Welch faced a blend of issues, as usual. To Jolliffe, he responded that a YWCA request for six four-hole latrines was "preposterous," pointing out that this number would be sufficient for 480 campers. The YWCA camp accommodated only seventy-five. At Bear Mountain, construction of a general office was under way in 1921 as recommended by Commissioners Sutro and Baker. Bear Mountain had been considered "too remote" for an office, causing Welch to spend Mondays and Fridays in New York City at the PIPC's 90 Wall Street office while his engineering staff worked from rented space at the United States Hotel in Haverstraw. Most other staff members had no office at all. The new office was intended to improve management efficiency. In New Jersey, the commissioners and Welch continued to move toward the sale of the Dana property. A restaurant owner came forward as a prospective purchaser, suggesting the construction of a large hotel "on top of the Palisades," estimated at a cost of $4 million. The idea was that the hotel would be a "show place, a very magnificent edifice copied after one of the French castles." As with the earlier Riker proposal, the commissioners put this inquiry, too, on hold.

Back on the New York side, communications were taking place about the possible donations of the 114-acre "George Grant Mason Farm," including implements, livestock, and sheds valued at $25,000, and an 800-acre property owned by Dr. Ernest G. Stillman on Storm King Mountain. Stillman's father, John, was the banker who had provided Perkins with his first entree to Wall Street. Partridge was in contact with Stillman, while Harriman expressed a hope to Welch and his fellow commissioners that the 29.5-acre Storm King Stone Company could be acquired in conjunction with the Stillman transaction to "control all of the lands between the top of the hill and the river." A gift deed was subsequently received for the Mason Farm; the Stone Company property was offered for $2,000 and was purchased for $1,500.

Partridge also alerted Welch to a pending visit by Preston Clark, "who has in mind a future park upon Cape Cod." From Albany, George D. Pratt, commissioner of the New York Conservation Department, asked Welch to help block a bill that, if approved, would gut the department by taking away its "game protectors [game wardens]." "I know that you are influential with Governor Nathan Miller," Pratt reminded Welch. Welch delivered the message, and the game protectors stayed in the Conservation Department.

Frank Mason, a highly decorated ex-Army sergeant "covered with medals, service and wound stripes, and recipient of the Croix De Guerre," presented Welch with another challenge. Welch was advised that Mason was a "Negro" but did not see that as a problem. What did concern Welch was that Mason offered to bring his six-piece jazz band to Bear Mountain to provide a free weekday concert. Welch and King debated the matter, agreeing that they "did not care" for jazz, but decided nonetheless to accommodate the highly decorated war veteran. Mason and his band played at Bear Mountain to an appreciative audience. By contrast, more "traditional" music offered on the ferry was a different matter. One passenger lamented,

I've listened to music melodic and sad,
  And music harmonious and merry;
But I never heard stuff I considered so bad,
  As that on the Dyckman Street Ferry.

There was also the matter of the Women's Memorial. Writing to White, Ida W. Dawson reminded him that she had been president of the New Jersey Federation of Women's Clubs in 1908 "when the park agreed to erect a memorial on the plot of land on which the Federation holds a deed. Can you inform me as to what has been done about it in the last thirteen years, and what is the present condition of the matter?" Acknowledging that he well remembered Dawson, White replied,

As I recall it, the Commission understood to set aside the plot in question for a Women's Memorial Park, which was done, and then to erect thereon some suitable monument when the money for the purpose should be furnished. A certain amount of money was furnished and has been carried by the Commission in a separate account ever since. I don't know the exact amount that the account now shows, but will be glad to find out and give you the information if you desire.

Dawson wrote back, proposing that the PIPC use the money on hand to at least place a token marker on the plot, "while all are living who are interested." White, referring to the plot as "that very out of the way place," worried that a marker would be vandalized. "Our experience is that the public is ruthless in its care of such offerings and it is safer and better to erect only massive, substantial structures that cannot invite depredations." White assured Dawson that he and the commissioners would give the matter further thought.

At this time, Welch was recruited for a special task that took him away from his daily activities for six weeks. He was requested to "make an inspection of all national parks in the United States." The federal government paid his expenses. Welch returned in time for the October 29, 1921, dedication of the long-awaited Henry Hudson Drive, a triumph of engineering and perseverance that allowed the motoring public to tour along the base of the Palisades for a distance of about 5.5 miles. A figure-eight loop at the northern end of the drive reversed the course for motorists. No connection existed between the northern terminus of the drive and the New York State line. Total New Jersey appropriations of $628,747 had been invested in the construction of this recreational drive. An additional $181,063 in private funding was contributed from the commissioners' New York gift fund, marking the third occasion in which substantial funding from New York was used for a PIPC project in New Jersey. "The Drive is in no sense an automobile speedway," reported the PIPC. "It is more in the nature of a trail, affording ever changing scenes of wonderful beauty." In the spirit of inventive park management, the concept of roads designed especially for leisure driving and the enjoyment of nature, as contrasted with A-to-Z speed corridors, was affirmed by the roadway under the Palisades.

Project bills had to be paid. Finally, a sign was posted on the Dana property that read:

FOR SALE

This property of about 30 acres, with 1514 feet of Cliff frontage
including mansion of 23 rooms
For Sale
Inquire — Palisades Park Commission, 90 Wall Street

10.
Trail and Bridge

The FOR SALE sign stood conspicuously on the Dana property, prompting inquiries from real-estate brokers and potential buyers. At the asking price of $200,000, progress was expected to be slow in finding a person or organization with the means to seriously pursue the property. Progress below the cliffs at Ross Dock took a different turn. The commissioners went so far as to draft a detailed lease document that would allow the aeroplane base to be established, but H. G. Fokker and his colleagues were already considering other locations. Fokker established an aircraft plant on a grassy field at Teterboro, New Jersey, and joined other pioneers in the infant stages of developing civilian aviation in America. In 1927 he also began building a home on his five-acre Palisades cliff-top property. The home was never completed. Fokker chose, instead, to purchase an estate in Nyack, New York. His Palisades acreage, including a building foundation, was later incorporated into the PIPC's holdings.

As Fokker stepped off the stage, another person, who would greatly influence the national conservation movement and the PIPC, stepped to the fore. Writing for the *Journal of the American Institute of Architects* in 1921, Benton MacKaye of Shirley Center, Massachusetts, proposed the creation of a hiking trail that would extend from Maine to Georgia, a distance of more than two thousand miles. This trail, according to MacKaye, would be "a sort of backbone, linking wilderness areas to dwellers in urban areas along the Atlantic Seaboard." He saw the trail as integral to wise regional planning, as a foil to urban pressures, and as a simple,

New York–New Jersey Trail Conference logo.
(Courtesy of NYNJ Trail Conference)

affordable means of enjoying the outdoors. Years later, MacKaye explained in an article for the *Scientific Monthly* that his advocacy for the Appalachian Trail was to encourage hikers, walkers, and saunterers of all ages and abilities to become "acquainted with scenery; to absorb the landscape and its influence as revealed in the earth and primeval life. Primeval influence is the opposite of machine influence," MacKaye contended. "It is the antidote for over-rapid mechanization. It is getting feet on the ground with eyes toward the sky—not eyes on the ground with feet on a lever. It is feeling what you touch and seeing what you look at. It is the thing whence first we came and toward which we ultimately live. It is the source of all our knowledge—the open book of which all others are but copies."

Known for his "capacity for friendship, good conversation, and intellectual exploration," MacKaye found a ready audience in the hikers who had formed the Palisades Interstate Trail Conference. On April 25, 1922, the conference members reorganized to become the New York–New Jersey Trail Conference. The first elected officers of the new organization were Maj. William Welch, chair; W. W. Bell, vice-chair for New York; C. P. Wilbur, vice-chair for New Jersey; J. Ashton Allis; trails committee; Frank Place, publicity; and Raymond Torrey, secretary. In little more than a year, Torrey and Place, joined by pen-sketch artist Robert L. Dickinson, produced the first *New York Walk Book,* a masterful guide complete with detailed maps that was intended to assist anyone who might have even the slightest interest in exploring trails in the lower Hudson River Valley. MacKaye's vision of a trail that spanned fourteen states, supplemented by a "cobweb" of connecting trails, and embellished with recreational and educational facilities, galvanized this group to action.

At the forefront was Torrey, described as a "roundish figure who could maintain a moderate hiking pace all day." Torrey, the newspaperman who had attended the first Abercrombie & Fitch meeting hosted by Welch in 1920, was a "gentle man" who at an early age had discovered the joys of woodland trails near his hometown of Georgetown, Massachusetts. His many articles in the *New York Evening Post* reflected this personal interest. Echoing the values of his wide audience of mostly urban-bound readers, Torrey captured in written words a strong philosophical allegiance with Mother Nature. Once, while hiking on a Sunday, Torrey challenged a "beetle-browed" man who was painting graffiti on rocks. Not liking the challenge, the man shouted at Torrey, "You ought to be in church!"

Torrey shouted back, "You ought to be in jail!" Torrey dutifully reported this incident to his readers. He would experience another confrontation, this time with the immovable object named Robert Moses who was just entering the park scene in New York.

Welch and Torrey developed a close and informal partnership to build trails in Harriman Park. Welch was laying out trail routes and providing logistical support for Torrey, who organized and coordinated a group of volunteers to begin building the trails. The Welch-Torrey team was quick to respond to MacKaye's vision. Welch, using his drafting skills, designed a distinct marker that would ultimately identify the entire route of the Appalachian Trail. Welch and Torrey saw the first shovel strokes taken on the first segment of the trail at Bear Mountain in the summer of 1922. This first sixteen-mile section was completed on October 7, 1923, and rose from the shore of the Hudson River to the summit of Bear Mountain, then dropped down into Harriman Park and extended westward to the Ramapo River. MacKaye's vision had been transformed into reality. These first sixteen miles represented a tiny fraction of the total mileage envisioned for the trail but confirmed that volunteers of all ages and persuasions would step forward to build and maintain it. Today, the 2,158-mile Appalachian National Scenic Trail, so designated by Congress in 1968 and administered by the National Park Service, is 98 percent complete. Torrey spent years urging on the volunteers and cajoling landowners to join in a loose alliance with the multistate Appalachian Trail Conference (A.T.C.), founded in 1925 in Washington, D.C., as a greatly expanded version of the New York–New Jersey Trail Conference. Welch and Torrey assumed accustomed leadership roles with the A.T.C., Welch as chair, Torrey as treasurer. The New York–New Jersey Trail Conference became one of many branch units of the A.T.C. until it became an independent membership organization in 1931. For many, just standing on the Appalachian Trail is to feel temptation and connection. "Thru-hikers" who commit to the full length of the trail follow Welch's markers for weeks from Maine to Georgia, or vice versa. For Welch, Torrey, and a host of volunteers spanning decades, the A.T. represents great accomplishment through sweaty deed. For MacKaye, the Appalachian Trail is his legacy.

The lowest point in elevation for the trail is the Hudson River crossing at Bear Mountain. In a sense, hikers walk downhill either from Mount Katahdin, Maine, or from Mount Ogelthorpe, Georgia, to arrive at the tidal river, almost at sea level, and then begin walking uphill. When the first shovelful of earth was turned for the A.T. at Bear Mountain, no bridge crossing of the Hudson River existed for 150 miles between the open sea and Albany, except for a railroad bridge at

Poughkeepsie, New York. Once trail sections were added on the east side of the river opposite Bear Mountain, hikers had no options other than to swim, find a boat, or cross by ferry either upriver at West Point or downriver at Nyack. The demand for automobile access across the Hudson River was to solve this problem. From May to November, 1922, the Dyckman Street Ferry carried 325,000 automobiles from New York City to the Palisades. At the Nyack, New York, ferry crossing, 107,000 autos were hauled across the river. It was obvious that the demand to cross to the parks and communities on the west side of the Hudson River was rapidly reaching beyond the capacity of ferryboats. Articles began appearing in *The New York Times* and other newspapers, speculating about the possibility of bridging the Hudson River at the narrow river crossing between Anthony's Nose and Bear Mountain.

Proposed for the crossing was what would be the world's largest suspension bridge, a structure 2,500 feet in length, with a clear single span of 1,632 feet arching 135 feet above the river's high-water mark. Two steel cables, each woven of 7,252 strands of wire to create cable bundles eighteen inches in diameter, would be slung between twin four-hundred-foot-tall towers attached to concrete anchors on each shore. The concrete roadway plates to be attached to the bridge's superstructure would be thirty-eight feet wide, including walkways for pedestrians and A.T. hikers. "Both Farmers and City Dwellers Gain By New Bridge Across the Hudson River," announced one of the *Times*'s headlines. Another confirmed: "Mrs. Harriman Backs Hudson Bridge Plan." Part of the justification for the bridge was that large portions of Westchester County, a rural area on the east side of the Hudson River, could be developed into a system of parks, poetically described as "chains of pleasure grounds," that would rival or even exceed in scale the PIPC's holdings on the west side. New York Assemblyman Seabury C. Mastick argued, "There are not a few men and women in Westchester County who own estates, and who are really public spirited and of sincerely generous feeling. I am confident that they will be glad to follow as far as expedient the splendid example set by Mrs. E. H. Harriman, who gave thousands upon thousands of acres to the public which now form so valuable a part of Bear Mountain Park." A few critics grumbled that such a bridge would simply increase the value of the Westchester County estates, but momentum was on the side of the proponents who claimed that the Bear Mountain Bridge would link motorists from as far away as Buffalo, Boston, Albany, New York City, and Philadelphia, allowing them to cross the Hudson "anytime, day or night, regardless of weather conditions."

There was one problem. The estimated cost for the bridge was $5 million, and New York claimed empty financial pockets. This problem was solved by a unique legislative maneuver. The financial force of the Harriman and Perkins families prompted the New York Legislature to approve a bill permitting the formation of a private enterprise to construct a toll bridge at Bear Mountain. A charter was granted to the Bear Mountain and Hudson River Bridge Company organized by W. Averell Harriman, his brother, Roland, and George W. Perkins, Jr., acting on behalf of their families and other investors, to build the bridge. The PIPC made available the necessary approaches to the bridge on the west bank. New York took similar action on the east bank of the river. The charter provided that the state could acquire the bridge for a sum of $4.5 million at the end of five years, or claim outright no-cost possession at the end of thirty years. In the meantime, the investors could charge tolls for bridge crossings ranging from 80¢ from small cars to $1.75 for large trucks. Ironically, a policy to "wipe out" all toll bridges in the state had been adopted in Albany only two years before the charter was granted to the Bear Mountain and Hudson River Bridge Company. Despite the fact that the state had recently purchased and opened the last three toll bridges in New York to cost-free transit, public support for the Bear Mountain venture, championed by motorists who were routinely experiencing hours of waiting at the crowded ferry terminals, overcame the policy. Construction of the Bear Mountain Bridge began in the spring of 1923.

By November of the following year, the privately financed bridge was in place, ushering in a new era in the Hudson River Valley. To the eye of almost everyone, the bridge was an artistic delight as well as an engineering success, sweeping from shore to shore just north of Iona Island and the Bear Mountain Dock, almost exactly where Gen. George Washington's troops stretched the famous chain barrier across the Hudson River from Forts Clinton and Montgomery to the opposite shore. Somehow, this suspension bridge designed for purely utilitarian purposes seemed to fit aesthetically into the bold terrain of the Hudson River narrows.

On November 26, 1924, the West Point Military Academy Band greeted invited officials, eager for a ceremonial drive across the bridge in the almost three hundred automobiles that had transported them to Bear Mountain. Wilson Fitch, chief engineer in charge of construction, "proclaimed a new record in bridge building." Praise was given to Frederick Tench of the engineering firm Terry & Tench for conceiving the bridge plan and seeing construction through to completion. The moment, though, really belonged to the Harrimans. Roland Harriman, president of the bridge company, honored his mother and gave her full credit for "accomplishment of the bridge project." The memory of E. H. Harriman was close at hand. The crowd was reminded that the elder Harriman had

Bear Mountain Bridge, 1924.
(Courtesy of PIPC Archives)

been "about to start construction of the bridge when he died eleven years ago." Perkins, Jr., W. Averell Harriman, and former Governor Benjamin B. Odell, vice chair of the Bridge Celebration Commission, participated in the ceremonies. Mrs. Mary W. Harriman unveiled a plaque dedicated to all who had participated in the project, then cut the ribbon to open the bridge.

Unknown to the dignitaries assembled for the ceremonial motorcade crossing of the Bear Mountain Bridge, newlyweds Lt. E. S. Hopewell and the former Miss Jessie Welch had upstaged them. They had been married at the West Point Chapel about two weeks prior to the dedication ceremony. The concrete roadway was already in place on the bridge, even as final preparations were being made for the official opening. Major Welch and his wife watched proudly as their daughter and new son-in-law unofficially drove across the bridge to celebrate their wedding and claim bragging rights.

In 1922, before the bridge construction project got under way, New York Governor Nathan Miller had appointed Perkins, Jr., to the PIPC. His appointment and that of George T. Smith, an executive of the New Jersey Title & Guarantee Trust Company, Jersey City, were prompted by the sudden losses of John J. Voorhees and Otis H. Cutler, who died within one week of each other. Voorhees had served from 1915 to 1922 and had been particularly effective in delivering the PIPC's message in Trenton. Cutler, who was chair of the American Brake and Shoe Company and had commanded the 14th Division of the American Red Cross during World War I, had been appointed in 1921 to fill the vacancy left on the PIPC by the death of Perkins, Sr.

King had written to Cutler at the Royal Palm Hotel in Miami in February, 1922, reminding him that the crucial second installment of the $500,000 Rockefeller pledge to the PIPC was due to expire on March 1. King had reported that New Jersey Governor Miller "did not appear to be very much impressed with my statement that we might lose the balance of the Rockefeller pledge if the State did not do something at this time" and had asked Cutler to intervene. Time ran out for Cutler before he could respond.

On March 15, 1922, Perkins, Jr., was appointed to take Cutler's place on the PIPC and, in so doing, assumed the mantle of his father. For the next thirty-eight years, until 1960, Perkins, Jr., who, as an infant at the family's Wave Hill Estate had awakened crying because of the detonations on the Palisades, affirmed a continuing family commitment to conservation and park stewardship. A graduate of Princeton University, Class of 1917, and, like his father, dedicated to the high ideals of the "dollar-a-year" businesspersons who heeded the call to public service when asked, Perkins, Jr., assumed many important responsibilities for the U.S. government. His first government assignment was not at the request of an elected official, however. He voluntarily enlisted as a private with the U.S. Army American Expeditionary Force, 1st Division, immediately after graduation from Princeton, returning from Europe at the conclusion of World War I with the rank of 2d lieutenant. After receiving a Master's degree from Columbia University, Perkins, Jr., accepted his first civilian assignment in Washington, D.C., as executive secretary to the Postmaster General. He was executive vice president of Merck & Company and director of its Canadian subsidiary when World War II intervened. Back in uniform, this time with the rank of colonel, Perkins, Jr., saw action in Europe and the Pacific and was awarded the Legion of Merit. After the war, he returned briefly to Merck but then agreed in 1948 to become chief of the Industries Division of the Economic Cooperation Administration (Marshall Plan) in Paris. In 1949 Democratic President Harry S. Truman appointed Republican Perkins, Jr., as Assistant Secretary of State for European Affairs. His principal assignment was to represent the United States in the formation of the North

George W. Perkins, Jr., Palisades Interstate
Park Commissioner, 1922–1960.
(Courtesy of PIPC Archives)

Atlantic Treaty Organization (NATO). President Eisenhower followed Truman's example by appointing Perkins, Jr., as Permanent Representative to NATO in 1955 with the rank of ambassador. Throughout these years, he remained devoted to the always struggling park organization that had been so mightily influenced by the style and commitment of his father.

The arrival of Perkins, Jr., and Smith came when both praise and criticism were being directed toward the PIPC. The praise came from more than 150 attendees at the Second National Conference on State Parks, held at the Bear Mountain Inn in the spring of 1922. Speaking for the attendees, Albert M. Turner wrote that he had experienced "pioneer work of the highest order, produced by that extraordinary combination of artist, economist, and engineer now known as Major William A. Welch." Turner reminded his colleagues that there was "no manual or guide book for park managers" but that the PIPC had provided "a working model on the scale of twelve inches to the foot." He said that Major Welch "had apologized wickedly for the joyous noises of hundreds of visitors coming from outside" while the conferees were trying to hear one another inside the inn. Turner was also impressed by the one regulatory sign he saw in the park. It read, "Please do not pick the wildflowers, others want to see them." Otherwise, Turner said, there were no posted regulations, no ponderous listing of living commissioners or "graven images of the mighty dead."

The conferees were conducting earnest business. They heard from Stephen T. Mather and park representatives from practically all the states. Resolutions were passed urging the designation of a "National Conservation Day," the preservation of the Redwoods in California by "saving" them, the purchase of more National Forest land in the Appalachians, and the retention of park revenues for development and maintenance within the parks. Welch advised the conferees of another resolution he had sponsored at a meeting of the American Road Builders Association during a meeting in Chicago. The Road Builders had unanimously resolved to "prohibit advertising signs on public highways."

Welch ensured that the conferees toured the park system. Turner was impressed:

Back in the wooded hills are twenty-seven lakes, with scores of camps . . . the campers all fed three times a day with hot food from the Bear Mountain Inn, delivered by motor trucks for distances of up to twenty miles at a cost of 25¢ a meal. The craftsmanship displayed on the round timbers of the camp buildings was especially noteworthy, for the neatness and perfection was executed by woodsman and impossible to the ordinary carpenter. Down below in the placid cove lies at anchor the replica of the Half Moon, that fragile shell of a child's toy in which Henry Hudson discovered these waters. Over the fireplace in the Inn are two shrunken links of the great chain which the optimists of '76 stretched across the Hudson to mark their dead line for the Britishers, and hanging above them the skins of a real Teddy bear—shot and presented by himself, the great Theodore. A cordial welcome was extended by the civic authorities at Washington's Headquarters in Newburgh, an old stone house, on a tract of six or seven acres on the river bank. This house was set aside as a State Park in 1849—the first State Park in these States. Its historic interest is very great, since it was here that the major strategy of the war was devised, possession of the Hudson being at all times the key to the military situation. Alarms from either Boston or New York were quickly transmitted by beacon fires, and the range across the river, known as Beacon Ridge, is easily observed from the house.

En route to Washington's Headquarters, the conferees visited the newly constructed chapel at West Point and were amazed by the daring route of the PIPC-constructed Storm King Highway. The PIPC had initiated work on the highway in 1915 by lowering survey crews down the steep face of Storm King Mountain by rope. After about seven years, at a cost of $850,000, and the removal of eight thousand railroad carloads of rock, the four-and-one-half-mile highway from West Point to Cornwall-on-Hudson was proclaimed by *The New York Times* "America's most scenic eastern road." Many of the conferees felt that it equaled in scenic splendor the most famous roadways of Europe.

Turner and the conferees were unaware that New York's official Winter Carnival ground was being moved from Saranac Lake in the Adirondacks to Bear Mountain. Bobsleds, toboggans, ice skates, and snowshoes were already being made readily available for visitors who were beginning to flock to the park during the once-quiet winter months. A ski jump to be constructed near the Bear Mountain Inn, rivaling the jump at Dartmouth College, was on the drawing boards. The longest toboggan run, measuring 1,200 feet, ended with a rocket-like hurtle across the frozen ice of Hessian Lake. For the first time, winter sports at Bear Mountain were confirming that parks could serve the public in all seasons.

Nor were the conferees advised of Elbert King's concern that "the Palisades section appears to be becoming a grave yard for stolen automobiles—two were pushed over the cliffs last Friday." Faced again with an unexpected byproduct of opening the Palisades to public access, Welch and the police took the only step available to them since they did not have recourse to the thieves: they demanded that the owners of the stolen cars remove from the base of the cliffs what was left of their automobiles.

At the concluding conference banquet, held at the Hotel Pennsylvania in New York City, Dr. Edward Partridge, speaking on behalf of his fellow commissioners, announced that Dr. Ernest G. Stillman had donated eight hundred acres on Storm King Mountain to the PIPC in memory of his father, John Stillman. None of the attendees at this highly successful gathering of the nation's earliest class of park managers could have imagined that, years later, Storm King Mountain would become the focus of an epic environmental battle that would dramatically and permanently change the manner by which the United States safeguards its natural resources. But the budding strength of the national environmental movement was already evident in the banquet room. The principal host for the evening was the American Scenic and Historic Preservation Society. The PIPC was prominently listed with other organizations that had cooperated with that society in making the dinner arrangements, including the Adirondack Mountain Club, the American Alpine Club, the American Automobile Association, the American Game Protective Association, the American Museum of Natural History, the Appalachian Mountain Club, the Associated Mountaineering Clubs, the Association for the Protection of the Adirondacks, the Bird and Tree Club of New York, the Boone and Crockett Club, the Bronx Parkway Commission, the City History Club of New York, the Explorers Club, the Fresh Air Club, the Green Mountain Club, the Sierra Club, and the Zoological Society of New York. At the conclusion of the banquet, the conferees gave the PIPC and Welch a standing ovation, pleased with what they had seen and eager to take away the lessons they had learned.

While Welch presided at the conference, King, the PIPC's assistant secretary, was dealing with a controversial problem that was prevalent throughout the country in the society of the 1920s: the use of parks by African Americans. A challenge to the PIPC on race relations came from John E. Robinson, editor and manager of the *New York Amsterdam News*. Robinson contended that he had received "many complaints" that the PIPC "discriminated against colored people." In response, King wrote, "The Palisades Interstate Park is distinctly a Park for all the people irrespective of nationality, color, or religion." To reinforce his point, King added,

> We have had a great number of excursions of colored people to the various sections of the Park. Particularly, I recall one group from a church for colored people in Harlem, who for a number of years held excursions at our Forest View Grove. This group stood out above all others in the manner in which they used the Park property, leaving it in even better shape than they found it, picking up and destroying all the papers and rubbish from the excursion, and in every way cooperating with the Commission's employees. These fine actions were brought to the attention of the then President of the PIPC, and he personally complimented this organization on its treatment of the Park. We have had a great many excursions of colored people to Bear Mountain, and we have found them very desirable.

During the first quarter century of the PIPC's life, its record of nondiscrimination was apparent. Group camps were available for African American children, and general use of the parks was available to all ethnic groups. Still, the PIPC, like other public organizations, struggled with the race issue. The "really poor people" King had in mind for the special, low-cost ferry service to Hook Mountain would, on arrival, find themselves physically separated by miles from any other group of park users. African Americans were confronted in the parks with the same attitudes that prevailed in the cities: they were welcome so long as they kept to themselves. In his criticism of the PIPC, Robinson struck a raw nerve and hoisted a warning flag that the racial practices of the PIPC would remain under scrutiny in a nation obviously tainted and infested by blatant racial discrimination.

Racial segregation was not the only separate-but-equal practice that challenged the PIPC. Writing to former Senator George Blauvelt, the PIPC's counsel, King said,

> Two years ago, the Commission determined that the mixing of the sexes in camp on any one lake in the Park was unwise and in fact a dangerous plan. In view of the dangerous situation, the Commissioners decided upon a distinct segregation of the sexes between the several lakes in the Park, reserving only one lake, Tiorati, where camps for the two sexes might be maintained, only because this lake was so well adapted to family camps.

The Brooklyn Bureau of Charities did not see it this way. At its camp on Lake Stahahe, considered by the PIPC to be strictly a "boys" lake, the Bureau was alternating use of its camp between groups of girls and boys. King explained to Blauvelt that the commissioners had made a temporary exception for the Bureau in recognition of the difficulty and cost of moving a camp but that "the exception could be made no longer, the danger was too great." With legal encouragement from Blauvelt, the Bureau moved its camp to Lake Tiorati. Despite the boy/girl policy, the group-camp program kept booming. In 1923 alone, fourteen new camps were established, including Hebrew Orphan Asylum, the Boys Club of New York Tabernacle Church, and the Association for Improving the Condition of the Poor.

Finding enough money to meet the ever-increasing public demand while continuing to build a park system was becoming a chronic problem for the PIPC. Writing to Stillman, J. DuPratt White worried that "with the exception of the amount still due from the Laura Spelman Rockefeller Memorial, all of the contributions have been exhausted by investment in construction of the great camps." Actually, there was no guarantee that the Rockefeller money would be forthcoming. Theoretically, the PIPC could claim an additional $380,000 from the Memorial Fund, but to do so, it had to match the amount. Fortunately, Governor Al Smith, newly returned to office in the election of November, 1922, was an advocate for the PIPC's initiatives. In 1923 the New York Legislature appropriated $500,000 to the PIPC for land acquisition. Among properties on the commissioners' list was a 127-acre holding on Dunderberg Mountain, just south of Bear Mountain, that was owned by Charles Edison, whose father, Thomas A. Edison, had purchased it years earlier with the intent of opening an iron mine. The commissioners agreed to purchase the Edison property for $3,000.

The costs of developing, operating, and staffing the PIPC's holdings took the PIPC in some odd directions. In New Jersey, FOR SALE signs were posted on four more plots of land. King had written to Lindabury that "to meet the Ross mortgage, we can use the balance of one of our old gift fund accounts, $30,000, and raise an additional $70,000 by selling properties on top of the cliffs." FOR SALE signs subsequently appeared on the E. I. DuPont de Nemours Powder Company, Carpenter Brothers, W. W. Phelps, and Henry Torrence properties: total appraised value, $143,500.

In New York, the PIPC's need for development funds took a truly bizarre twist. At the recommendation of Welch, and with encouragement from Governor Smith, the PIPC decided to go into the quarry business. The target was none other than Hook Mountain, still battered and scarred by the discontinued quarry operations that the PIPC had acquired in 1917 through the best persuasive and financial efforts of Perkins, Sr. Under *The New York Times's* headline "To Move A Mountain For A Great Park" were the subheadings "Palisades Commission Proposes to Transfer Hook Mountain From River Bank" followed by "To Sell Rock to Pay Cost" and "Governor Smith Approves $5,000,000 Quarrying Job Near Haverstraw." The lead paragraph in the accompanying article stated: "A proposal of the Palisades Interstate Park Commission to remove the greater part of Hook Mountain and establish in its place a beautiful playground, like Bear Mountain Park, was disclosed today to Governors Smith of New York and Silzer of New Jersey, who were guests of the commission on an all-day inspection tour." Accompanying the governors aboard the *Onteora* were 350 state senators, assemblymen, and invited guests. The rationale for dismantling a mountain was explained in a subsequent paragraph: "Hook Mountain is one of the highest peaks on the west shore of the Hudson River, just below Haverstraw. Its four and a half miles of trees and foliage are bitten into by deep quarries, defacing much of the mountain's beauty. The Commission plans to remove the remaining portion of the mountain as far inland as the deepest excavation, rounding it out to restore it to its former natural state."

Welch was quoted in the article as saying, "More damage has been done to the scenery along the Hudson above Nyack by the excavations than anyone could think of. We have to remove the rest of the rock, virtually removing the mountain, and letting the rock pay for the work." Governor Smith "assured Welch that he would do everything he could to make the Commission plans real," adding, "I don't see how there can be any opposition. Go to it, and go to it quickly." Accompanying the large group on the inspection tour were Commissioners White, William P. Porter, Partridge, Perkins, Jr., Lindabury, Franklin W. Hopkins, and Frederick C. Sutro. A letter to the editor in *The New York Times* seemed to capture the public's reaction to this proposal. Under the headline "It Seems To Be Alright," the writer stated,

> One's first thought on hearing the proposal to cut away Hook Mountain and sell its material to pay the cost of removal is apt to be antagonistic to the scheme. The case for Hook Mountain, however, is special, in that the quarrymen already have cut great gashes in its side. What the PIPC wants to do is cut the mountain back, giving it a more equal and natural surface to create a new pleasure ground, with a riverside roadway that would greatly facilitate the visits of automobiles to West Point and points north. There is nothing obviously reprehensible in this, and much to commend, especially if it can be done at no expense to taxpayers.

Dismantling a mountain to make way for a recreation ground was landscape manipulation on a grand scale, but not entirely out of character with the accepted park-engineering practices of the time. The waters of many "lakes" in Harriman Park rippled against well-constructed dams. Up in Albany, Governor Smith had delivered a special message to the Legislature soon after his return to office in 1922 that, on its face, seemed innocuous enough, but that would result in raising huge public-works projects to new heights under the guise of park development. The governor advised the Legislature, "It is clear that the time has come when we must have some central control and planning for our parks and places of scenic, scientific, and historic interest. I am sending you a bill which provides for the establishment in the Conservation Commission of a State Park Council. I suggest that this new State Park Council prepare the budget for all of the park properties in the State." According to the governor's plan, member organizations of the Council would be the Conservation Commissioner (as ex-officio chair), the Palisades Interstate Park Commission, Allegheny Park, the State Reservation at Niagara, the American Scenic and Historic Preservation Society, the State Museum, Roosevelt Memorial Park, and the Finger Lakes State Park Commission (soon to be formed).

No mention of public-works projects was included in the message, but standing behind the scene, poised to take over the Council, was Robert Moses. Governor Smith rescued Moses from oblivion, according to biographer Robert Caro, who wrote that "four years earlier, at age 30, Moses was standing in line outside City Hall in Cleveland, applying, in vain, for a minor municipal job." Born in New Haven, Connecticut, in 1888, Moses, who grew up in New York City, held undergraduate and graduate degrees from Yale, Oxford, and Columbia. Before his career effectively ended in 1968, he would be the recipient of twenty-one honorary degrees. Moses had been invited into the Smith administration during the governor's first term, 1918–20, to aid in the reorganization of the state's administration. In a newspaper article "The Master Builder," George DeWan reported that, during the governor's first term, Moses developed a lifelong friendship with Smith, a "poorly educated, gruff-voiced Irishman from the Lower East Side." Smith's return to office solved Moses's career problems. The "Master Builder" never looked back.

The concept of the State Park Council was classic Moses: establish central control and grab the purse strings. By force of personality and imposing physical presence, Moses would oversee the expenditure of billions of dollars in public funds during the next four-plus decades on "bridges, tunnels, parkways, expressways, power projects, public housing, sandy beaches, concert halls, and tens of thousands of acres of parklands," mostly on Long Island, and his association with the PIPC would extend over many years, not always to the comfort of the commissioners. The PIPC's reaction to the State Park Council was predictable, being not at all inclined to be restricted in the exercise of its budget-making or administrative powers. With a wait-and-see attitude, the commissioners were willing to cooperate as a member of the proposed Council, so long as they were "left free" to pursue policies "peculiar and inseparable in the interstate nature of the enterprise."

One of those peculiar enterprises surfaced unexpectedly in New Jersey when the Police Benevolent Association managed to move a bill through the Legislature that would require the PIPC to employ police officers on a full-time, all-year basis. No additional funding was attached to the legislation. The commissioners agreed with Welch and King that police officers employed on a seasonal basis were sufficient to maintain order in the New Jersey section of the park system. But the bill, carrying an imposing price tag, had gotten through the Legislature and was on its way for signature by Governor Silzer. Sutro, Welch, and King rushed to Trenton to head off the pending financial disaster. Aided by Col. Myron W. Robinson, who had been appointed to the PIPC in 1919, King was subsequently able to report to White that "on last Monday night, when we were just ready to retire after a very hard evening, Col. Robinson brought the Governor and his secretary to our rooms at the hotel. Conceive, if you can, the three of us in our pajamas welcoming the Governor and his secretary." The pajama discussion went well; Silzer vetoed the bill.

As a result of the police caper, the commissioners moved to consolidate all police activities under one administrative line of authority, anticipating the appointment of a Superintendent of Police for the Palisades Interstate Park. To find just the right individual for this important position, the PIPC turned for guidance to Col. Herbert Norman Schwarzkopf, Chief of the New Jersey State Police. Schwarzkopf offered to assist the PIPC "wherever needed" and recommended hand-picked candidates for the position. The salary of $2,400 per year for the position was too low. The two top candidates declined the commissioners' offer. Despite Schwarzkopf's effort, and his continuing interest in the PIPC, the strategy to consolidate New York and New Jersey police operations proved unsuccessful.

In the matters of Hook Mountain, the proposed State Park Council, and the police, money was the core of the problem. The absence of Perkins, Sr., was reflected in the status of the "3rd Gift Fund." Of the $500,000 offered as a matching grant by the Laura Spelman Rockefeller Memorial Foundation, the commissioners were able to raise only $136,573 by the end of 1923, including a $25,000 contribution from Frederic A. Julliard.

And still no women's memorial.

11.
Uncle Bennie

In a letter sent to William Welch from Washington, D.C., on July 15, 1924, Robert Sterling Yard, representing Herbert Hoover, president of the National Parks Association, said:

> The longer I think it over, the more I am convinced that I ought to write the real story of Bear Mountain and circulate it at this particular stage of recreational development. The appeal to me is two-fold. It is so wonderful a tale that my pen fingers fairly itch to get at it. That's the personal side. And I can't escape the influence it will have on recreational thinking at this formative time. Today, lunching with Butler of the American Forestry Association, I told him a little of what you were doing and he went crazy over it; demanded from me (and got the promise) an article for his forestry magazine. The point I'm making is that notwithstanding the great fame of your undertaking, no one knows the size, proportions and human greatness of what you've got. It is time that the world knew.

The world may not have known of the existence of the PIPC, but Welch's reputation as a leader in the park movement was well established among his peers. More and more, he was being invited away from day-to-day management matters to attend to policy at the national level and to share his experiences with like-minded conservationists in other states.

At the request of Stephen Mather, director of the National Park Service, Welch received an important assignment from Secretary of the Interior Dr.

Hubert Work, who asked that Welch provide his expertise in the search for suitable national park sites in the southern Appalachian region of the United States. Welch and his fellow committee members visited many potential locations, hearing from anxious proponents and opponents of the plans in various states. To reduce the number of park proposals to a workable list, the committee determined not to consider sites of less than five hundred square miles. From a list of more than sixty potential national park sites, Welch's committee recommended two to Secretary Work and Director Mather. During the process, Welch exchanged correspondence with many federal and state officials, attended public meetings, and gave numerous statements to news reporters about the benefits of park conservation based on his experiences in New York and New Jersey.

In Welch's opinion, the Great Smoky Mountains in North Carolina and Tennessee "easily" ranked first on the committee's list due to the "height of mountains, depth of valleys, ruggedness of area, and the unexampled variety of trees, shrubs, and plants." The Blue Ridge Mountains of Virginia ranked second. Writing to Col. W. B. Greeley, chief of the U.S. Forest Service, Welch explained: "I do consider that we should have a National Park or two in the southern Appalachians that we may preserve for all time typical sections of these very wonderful mountains." Work, Mather, Welch, and others were effective advocates in their testimony before various congressional committees. Congress responded by authorizing the establishment of Shenandoah and Great Smoky Mountains National Park in 1926. The Appalachian Trail, anchored at Bear Mountain, would ultimately wind its way through both parks.

Welch's inspired committee work was widely applauded. The Northern Virginia Park Association, whose motto was "A National Park Near the Nation's Capital," hosted a celebratory dinner in Washington, D.C., in 1926. The letter of invitation to Welch explained that "there will be no prearranged speeches, the occasion being one of general congratulation and jollity, but it is hoped that you will not fail to give us a few words of encouragement and advice on the subject of the celebration. Your presence will be both a pleasure and a cause for satisfaction to others present; indeed it is not too much to say that the happy occasion positively demands it."

While Welch was enjoying well-earned recognition on the national stage, back in New York, a tiff occurred between the PIPC and Robert Moses when Moses interposed himself in the line of communication between the PIPC and Senator Nathan Straus, a longtime supporter of the PIPC's activities. Moses claimed that Straus was obliged to turn to him about a camp matter "after he made numerous efforts to deal directly with the Commission through Major Welch and others." J. DuPratt White was startled by the implication that Moses had to intercede on behalf of the senator in order to get action from the PIPC. "I am sorry that you should feel irritated about having such a matter brought to your attention," Moses wrote to White. "If this irritation is due in any way to your feeling that the State Council of Parks is attempting to interfere with the administration of the Palisades Interstate Park, you are entirely mistaken." The young Moses, so new to the park scene, closed the letter by preachily reminding White, who, by then, had been involved with the park movement for almost thirty years, that "all the parks in the state owe a good deal to Senator Straus." In response, White took the obvious route by contacting his friend, the senator. Without further assistance from Moses, the two met for lunch, and the matter of the senator's inquiry about a camp was resolved.

Much more to the PIPC's benefit, the fledgling State Council of Parks decided to launch a bold initiative to place before the voters of New York a bond-issue referendum that, if approved, would provide $15 million for expansion and improvement of parks statewide. The park-bond referendum was an early hint of what would become Moses's approach to public-works projects in general—going aggressively for the big money, without wasting time on nickels and dimes. The bond referendum won strong endorsement from Governor Al Smith and a bipartisan majority of the Legislature. Prompted by the bond issue idea, W. B. Van Ingen wrote "A Wilderness Transformed" for *The New York Times Magazine.* He took the reader on a chronicled journey looping through Westchester County, across the Bear Mountain Bridge, through the PIPC's "40 square miles of recreation," as he termed the Palisades Interstate Park System, and back across the river to the city. "These accomplishments are so great that one can list them only in a bewildered sort of way," Van Ingen reported. "But it is clear that the principles of combination of effort which have made for our wealth can be applied to the service of our health: for this is exactly what has been done. We cannot live by bread alone."

Another strong voice of support, though one not usually involved with park matters, was announced by a headline in the *New York City Evening World:* "Cardinal Hayes Endorses Park As Aid To Children." His Eminence, the Cardinal Archbishop, was aware of a Harriman Park camp operated for boys by the Catholic Charities of the Archdiocese of New York and threw his considerable political weight behind the bond initiative. Statistics, too, favored this proposal. In addition to the Catholic Charities camp, eighty-four other camps were in operation in the park, serving more than thirty thousand children. In *The New York Times* article "City Migrates To Camps," a reporter captured the mood of the camps and park activities on just one summer day:

In distant groves Boy and Girl Scouts may be seen wig-wagging. Bugle calls rise and fall in echo-like cadences. Elderly matrons sitting on running boards of cars strip off their stockings and presently are wading with toddling babies. Men in their shirt sleeves lie at ease smoking foreign looking pipes. Youngsters run and shout and skitter stones over the waters. The side paths present a human stream of campers coming and going in either direction. They come out of the water in dripping one-piece bathing suits, youths and misses, and sprint for hot-dog stands. There are scores of signs bearing Indian names which designate the various camps, sometimes completely encircling a lake, with more hidden in the wooded recesses behind it. At 4 o'clock in the afternoon an entire city seems to have migrated afoot or awheel to these lakes. A polyglot Babel fills the air. The camps teem with visitors, the waters with bathers, the woods with hikers. Their language, their manners, their clothes proclaim the majority not of the aristocracy and the limousine, not of the income surtax payer, but of the commoner and the flivver, the wage earner income tax payer. To them a journey of fifty miles, with a day in the open ahead of it, is no more than a ride to Central Park. They, with thousands of others of their kind, are those who find and use new park lands as fast as they are thrown open.

In 1924 the PIPC was counting more than 5 million total visitors, had planted 4 million trees, and had ninety miles of marked trails and seventy-five miles of roads. The PIPC was in a position to demonstrate to a statewide electorate that parks were proven assets for communities. An indirect benefit was that the assessed valuation of properties bordering the PIPC's parks was rising, confirming that preserved open space was a measurable financial asset to adjoining communities.

Commissioner Frederick C. Sutro and PIPC Comptroller Elbert W. King attended a State Council of Parks meeting in September, 1924, only two months before the scheduled election, and asked the logical question, "How will the Bond Issue campaign be publicized?" No one seemed to know. The startled Sutro proposed that publicity committees be organized for western, central, and metropolitan New York and that each committee develop informational booklets, posters, and newspaper materials for the publicity campaign. The Metropolitan Committee was comprised of Moses, representing Long Island; Jay Downer, representing the Westchester County park system; and King as chair. Sutro thought that the Metropolitan Committee should produce at least 150,000 booklets, estimated at a cost of $3,000. Moses said that he had "already drawn to much extent on private contributors for previous financial needs" and could not raise a dollar for the campaign. Downer responded that as a representative of a county organization, he could promise no public funds but would attempt to accomplish some private fund-raising. Sutro and King, feeling boxed in, took their plea for bond-act publicity funding to the PIPC's commissioners, who heard the plea and agreed to fund almost the entire publicity campaign at a cost of $3,800. Downer sent in a check for $150; Moses sent nothing.

Proposition 1, the bond initiative, passed handily in November, 1924, the favorable vote in the metropolitan region outweighing the predictably negative vote in upstate New York. But winning voter approval of the referendum was one thing; dividing up the bond money was another. Under the headline "Battle Over Parks At Albany Hearing," *The New York Times* reported: "Two Long Island factions opened verbal batteries on each other today at a hearing before the combined Senate Finance and Assembly Ways and Means Committees on bills appropriating $6,000,000 for State parks. At times half a dozen speakers were shouting recriminations at one another simultaneously, and after the disorder at last caused adjournment, groups continued to wrangle for half an hour."

Writing to a friend who had left the meeting early, Sutro reported,

So far as practical accomplishment was concerned, you missed nothing. The afternoon session flouted the glories of the October sunshine by dragging along its dreary course through a maze of figures, portraying the needs of innumerable small parks and historic buildings all over the State. After four-thirty, the Council finally reached the real business of the meeting and made up the budget of the bond issue money to be appropriated by the Legislature next year. There seemed to be some hesitation on the part of Moses to agree to a substantial amount, but I think I convinced him and the rest that it was to the interest of the State to meet pressing needs, especially if money could be saved thereby, as in many cases of land purchases. My view of the meeting is that there was set up an immense and unnecessarily expensive machinery to accomplish the very simple result of collating the budget requirements of the several park systems.

When Moses called a subsequent meeting to create park regions within the state, Sutro gave his proxy to Welch and King, saying that he "had gone beyond the limit of time I can afford to spend on the State Council."

Fallout from this dispute was minimal for the PIPC, but the hot-button question of the State Council of Parks's authority to forcibly appropriate land—and, by extension, the authority of the PIPC to do a similar thing—would remain a point of caustic debate for many years. Even so, for the "extension and improvement" of state parks, bond-referendum funds were allocated according to a predetermined formula. The PIPC's share was $3.5 million. The PIPC stood to receive a first-year appropriation of $1.5 million, the rest to be appropriated in succeeding years. Half the money was earmarked for land purchases, the rest for maintenance and development projects—none, of course, for New Jersey. The commissioners hoped that New Jersey would take note of the bond referendum north of the border and smile kindly on the PIPC by loosening its purse strings in the next legislative session.

Group camps in Harriman Park were not on the list of projects that would benefit from the bond funds. From the distance of Albany, the camps were viewed primarily as revenue sources for the PIPC rather than as a unique service for children. Welch did not want to argue the point. He had many other maintenance and development projects on his plate that needed money, but he was concerned, too, that the private funds that had carried the camp program to such a high level were all but exhausted. Welch turned again to the trustees of the Laura Spelman Rockefeller Memorial Foundation with a request for $120,000 for prompt expenditure in the camps, followed by $100,000 per year for four years. He added $30,000 for a dormitory at Bear Mountain, bringing the total request to an even $550,000. The request landed on the desk of Kenneth Chorley of the foundation staff, who understandably thought that such a large request deserved careful scrutiny.

He had not looked far before reporting to Col. Arthur Woods, his superior, that the Boy Scout Foundation of Great New York was pulling out of its site in the park. Members of the Boy Scout Board gave several reasons for this decision: their location in Harriman Park was not isolated enough; the rent was too high; the buildings were not suitable for their program; park authorities were not cooperative and did not understand Boy Scout needs; and there was too much red tape involved in the PIPC's management of the camps. Chorley queried several other camp directors and found mixed complaints, mostly about red tape, but he noted, too, in a follow-up memo to Woods that very little turnover occurred, remarking that only "two or three" of the eighty-five camps had changed hands in several years. Woods added, "Miss Jolliffe impressed me as being a very efficient woman, but I still believe that she is not the sort of person who ought to be Superintendent of the Camp Department. It seems to me that the department would be much more efficiently run if there was a man at the head of it." He also stated that Welch had told him that "since the death of Mr. Perkins, Sr., there is nobody to raise funds but myself, and I do not have the time." If the Rockefeller Trustees were to be enticed to provide another major contribution to the PIPC, the commissioners and Welch would obviously have to present a better, more compelling case. Rockefeller support was not going to be automatic.

In addition to being thrown financially off balance by the less-than-eager response from such stalwart friends as the Rockefellers, the PIPC suffered the loss of former Senator George Blauvelt on October 16, 1924. Blauvelt had worked with the founders of the park system from the very beginning, providing political and legal guidance since before the turn of the century. Left in his wake was Blauvelt Park on South Mountain near Nyack, New York, named in his honor so many years earlier. (Prompted by Blauvelt's death, Commissioner Franklin W. Hopkins took it upon himself to ensure that another PIPC pioneer was not forgotten. He personally arranged for a tablet to be placed on a boulder at the base of the Palisades about one-half mile south of the Alpine boat basin in New Jersey, marking the spot where the PIPC's first police captain, John Jordan, had lost his life on February 5, 1915. Jordan was carrying the payroll along the river shore path from the Alpine boat basin to the Englewood boat basin when a boulder dislodged from the cliffs above, hurtled down to the exact place where he was walking, and struck and killed him instantly.)

Soon after Blauvelt's death, more bad news reached the commissioners. A *New York Times* article announced, "Trail Typhoid Peril to Palisades Brook." Sixty-eight cases of typhoid fever, four of which were fatal, were traced to a brook that flowed through the hamlet of Englewood Cliffs, New Jersey, tumbled over the Palisades, and flowed into the Hudson. Three cesspools on land outside the park were identified as the culprits. Most of the victims were children, including eighteen Boy Scouts from one troop. The *Times*'s reporter confirmed that signs were posted within the park warning visitors not to drink from the streams, but he added that the signs were in English, while "many hundreds" of the daily visitors either could not read English or could not read at all. The PIPC was not helped by the fact that the article placed the crisis in a boy's camp in Harriman Park, New York, rather than in the New Jersey Palisades. Welch had enough to worry about in the camps in Harriman Park: four confirmed and eighteen suspected cases of scarlet fever had been reported at a YWCA camp at Summit Lake. The commissioners and Welch were learning the hard way that streams, ponds, lakes, or rivers, however pristine and inviting in appearance, were potentially severe health hazards. A program to pipe treated water to public-use areas, a practice now taken for granted, was vigorously accelerated by Welch, his engineers, and maintenance workers in the mid-1920s and was at the time considered cutting-edge in the management of parks.

In a moment of buoyancy amidst the PIPC's struggle with health calamities and bad press, King wrote to Sutro to let him know that the new hit song, sung aboard the *Clermont* by members of the orchestra, was "Does Spearmint Lose Its Flavor On The Bedpost Overnight?"

Finding an answer to the mystery of bedpost spearmint was not high on the commissioners' educational agenda, but nature education was becoming an increasingly important aspect of the PIPC's activities. Nowhere was this more evident than in a small, third-floor space tucked in the far corner of a large room at the Museum of Natural History in New York City dominated by a huge stuffed whale suspended from the ceiling as if swimming in midair. The space was occupied by Dr. Benjamin Talbot Babbitt Hyde, a patron of the Department of Anthropology and Educational Director of the Boy Scouts Foundation of Greater New York. Hyde's corner space was partially hidden behind "exhibits of live snakes, birds, skunks, and the like," according to Eleanor Adolph, a Harriman Park visitor who first encountered Hyde on a woodland trail. Adolph was so amazed by this happenstance meeting that she captured her impression on paper:

> A heavy, measured tramp, tramp, as of many feet, beat upon the murmurous silence of the woodland road. At first faint and indeterminate, the regular clop-clop grew louder and ever nearer, until, suddenly, around a steep bend, strode the army of the Twentieth Century Crusaders. Straight little fellows of ten and twelve years, this band of Boy Scouts, perspiringly, but with uncomplaining courage, followed the lead of a tall, tireless figure at their head. A leader he was. One felt it—this gift of leadership, in every movement of the big, lithe, khaki-clad frame, in the tanned face, with its firm, kind mouth, most of all, in the observant, slate-grey eyes, humorous and sympathetic, yet keen, behind their bowed glasses.

And, she should have added, a bald dome.

"He looks like Teddy Roosevelt," Adolph remembered whispering to a companion. "He is Teddy Roosevelt in his way," was the companion's reply. "Ask any Boy Scout. There isn't one who doesn't known and swear by 'Uncle Bennie.'" Adolph was impressed by what she termed "a peculiar quality of forcefulness for he is, above all things, restful. He never seems hurried."

Hearing weeks later that Uncle Bennie's plans for future summer programs were to include women and girls, Adolph trekked to the museum the following winter to seek out and interview Hyde.

Uncle Bennie's theory of outdoor education was that children should learn to appreciate woodland inhabitants, not fear them. Snakes were his specialty. At any given moment, one might crawl out of his shirt pocket or slither from under a sleeve. He inaugurated a series of rustic wildlife "museums" in Harriman Park in 1920 in association with the Boy Scout camps. "Boys are, by nature, very active

Dr. Benjamin "Uncle Bennie" Talbot Hyde.
(Courtesy of PIPC Archives)

and curious, and they are, for the most part, much interested in natural history," he explained to Adolph. "That they really prefer the study of the natural objects about them to idling or playing town games, is proven by the fact that, last year, ten thousand boys, in camp, voluntarily devoted their time to this work." As if confirming the point, Adolph's interview was interrupted by a young Boy Scout who wandered into Hyde's office. Uncle Bennie, "stooping, unfailingly kind and interested," gave the boy his full attention. "That's the way they do, they come all day, at any time. Very often, their people don't understand or care. Some one ought to. They need it." Expanding on the subject, Hyde told Adolph that part of his purpose as a naturalist and educator was

> development of the character of boys by throwing them upon their own resources, to make them self-reliant. They are never punished for short-com-

ings, but a constructive, straight-from-the-shoulder talk is given. There are no rewards, aside from merit badges. The value of a job well-done is kept always before them and, as they develop a sense of responsibility, they are assigned to positions of importance. With work comes pleasure, with trust, responsibility, and that their duty is to give service to their homes, their community, and their country. We added forestry to the subjects in 1922 and 1923 with the interest of Mr. Franklin Roosevelt.

Hyde was emphatic.

Adolph then asked the questions foremost in her mind: "Do the girls in the camps take to the nature work as readily as the boys? Do they like it? Are they as quick?"

Hyde gave a firm, one-word answer. "Fully," he said.

This man who so fascinated Adolph had been for ten years the unfascinating president of one of America's largest soap-manufacturing companies. Heir to "Babbitt's Best Soap," which was founded by his grandfather, Hyde joined the soap company after graduating from Harvard in 1901 and rose to the top management position before stepping away a decade later. His decision to leave behind the daily routine of overseeing the manufacture of soap was not surprising. While attending Harvard, he and his brother, Frederick, were greatly influenced by anthropologist Frederick Ward Putnam. Encouraged by Putnam, and backed by their own inherited wealth, the two brothers mounted the "Hyde Expedition" to the remote western region of New Mexico known as Chaco Canyon in 1896 while still undergraduates at Harvard. This was not the first trip to the Southwest for the two native sons of New York City. In 1893 the Hyde brothers had associated themselves with Richard Wetherill, a member of the famous ranching family credited with discovering the renowned Mesa Verde cliff-dweller ruins in southern Colorado. Working with Wetherill and others in the Grand Gulch area of Colorado, Hyde coined the phrase "basket makers" to identify a particular ancient Native American culture. The phrase is permanently embraced in the lexicon and literature of today's professional archaeologists. Artifacts shipped east from the Grand Gulch venture established the first formal contact between the Hyde brothers and the American Museum of Natural History. But it was the "Hyde Expedition" in 1896 to Chaco Canyon that "opened a new chapter in anthropology at the Museum," according to J. E. Snead, who wrote extensively about the archaeological adventures of the Hyde brothers. Excavating Pueblo Bonito in the canyon, the expedition members shipped an entire railroad carload of artifacts to the museum, including many exquisite examples of Native American pottery and turquoise art. Their task was not easy. Reaching Chaco Canyon required an overland wagon trip of nine days. Once in the canyon, working conditions were severe, and water and foliage were scarce. "In subsequent years," Snead observed, "the Chaco Canyon collection has had significant effect on the relationship between the American public and the cultural heritage of Native American peoples." Hyde was not just collecting artifacts. Through his association with the Museum of Natural History, he was opening to scientists and the public an important view of Native American culture. Chaco Canyon, today, is a National Historical Park and World Heritage Site.

Mounted in his trusty Model "T" Ford, anointed the "flying squirrel," Hyde took his passion for exploration and shared discovery into the Harriman Park camps. Boys and girls were so excited when they saw him coming that they would spontaneously cheer. He remained director of nature education for the Boy Scouts and was a mainstay in the camps until 1927, when he moved permanently to Santa Fe to found the Children's Nature Foundation. Hyde reflected the same skills and ability to communicate with young people that Dr. Frank E. Lutz had earlier demonstrated at Harriman Park's Station for the Study of Insects, where hand-lettered signs marked the nation's first nature trail. Lutz and Hyde could take a beetle or a boulder and open up a whole new world of delight for young, inquisitive minds. Their mastery was in helping people simply see and appreciate the intricate and intertwined natural environment that encompassed them. With a flare for the snake-assisted dramatic, Hyde helped to firmly plant the anchor of nature education in the PIPC's park system. His influence had real staying power, as affirmed by a young Boy Scout named William Carr who encountered "Uncle Bennie" while waiting on a train platform for the journey back to New York City. Inspired by the man and his message, Carr, himself, would add immeasurably to the substance of nature education in the parks when his turn came.

At the grassroots level, blossoming educational initiatives were probably not much on Welch's mind. In the summer of 1925, twenty-eight people were rescued from drowning in the Hudson River under the Palisades. First aid was administered to thousands of visitors. Thirteen forest fires were reported in the New Jersey section alone, caused primarily by campfires left unattended. In the constant search for improved sources of revenue, the commissioners decided to charge five cents per person for each dance in the pavilion at Bear Mountain. Twenty burros were purchased for rent to aspiring urban cowboys. While continuing to count every penny to keep operations going in New York and New Jersey, King had to confess by telegram to the New York Comptroller that State

Treasurer's Check number 36144, in the amount of $62,941.84, somehow had been lost, and he needed to ask for stop-payment and reissuance. At the same time, King warned Welch that failure of the New Jersey State Legislature to approve an anticipated supplemental appropriation for the PIPC meant that the New Jersey park operations would have to be put on a "starvation" basis. Efforts to sell the Dana property continued, even though the FOR SALE sign was becoming weather-worn and drooping. King took exception to another sign posted in the New Jersey park, this one reading, "This Park Don't Extend Beyond This Point." He directed Scott R. Knowles, the New Jersey Superintendent, to correct the grammar on this sign and to take down the FOR SALE signs on the Carpenter and DuPont properties. By the end of 1925, King wrote to William Shephard Dana "that the Commissioners have sold the so-called Dana property subject to the mortgage which you hold. The purchaser is Mr. Achille Ermeti of Englewood Cliffs, who proposes to develop the property for high class residential purposes with possibly a few stores." With this action, a crucial piece of land atop the Palisades seemed to slip from the commissioners' hands, contradicting almost everything the PIPC was attempting to accomplish.

While funds for land acquisition and daily operations were almost absent from the PIPC's purse, funds for construction projects remained available in a different account. The *Nyack Evening Journal* reported in the article "Big Engineering Feat Now Going On In The County" that Welch and his staff were completing a six-hundred-foot-long dam at Sandyfields in Harriman Park that would create a 375-acre lake. The project was mundanely labeled "Dam #10." The prospects for other construction projects were reflected in Welch's letter to P. H. Elwood, Jr., at Iowa State College, in which he stated, "Last Saturday afternoon, a solid stream of motor cars from New York City, northern New Jersey, and the ferries, was not able to move more than five miles an hour, and didn't entirely clear out until 1:00am Monday morning." Welch speculated that "parkways" were needed to relieve the congestion. He may have had in mind that the Port of New York Authority had gained permission from the commissioners to erect triangulation towers and concrete baseline monuments on the Palisades as part of a mapping project for the "Hudson River Bridge," proposed to span the river from 180th Street to the New Jersey shoreline.

Private funding for the PIPC's activities was increasingly difficult to garner. The Laura Spelman Rockefeller Memorial Foundation remained the best potential source for major new grants, but the dearth of matching grants from other private sources and the questions raised about the administration of the Harriman

Park camps gave pause to Rockefeller advisers. Only two other grants were imminent: $25,000 from Edwin Gould and $100,000 offered by Commissioner George F. Baker for the construction of a camp for his bank employees in Harriman Park. The commissioners agreed that "Baker Camp" would be a suitable name.

Averell Harriman, still subordinate to his more senior commissioner colleagues, stepped forward with the idea that the hesitant Rockefeller staff should make an in-depth study of the PIPC. Responding favorably to the idea, Colonel Woods said in an internal memorandum circulated within the Rockefeller organization that

> Mr. Rockefeller has had it in mind that it might be well for him to make a substantial contribution in the form of new land. In taking these matters up with the Park people, we found some unsatisfactory conditions, and in the course of conversation with Mr. Harriman he said it would be of enormous value to the Park, and he felt that it would clear our ideas, if we could have a study made of the whole situation, showing up the weak points and making suggestions to strengthen them. In view of our interest in the Park, of their need and request for our help, and of the great service it can be to the public, if well handled, I cannot help feeling that this survey would be an excellent thing to make.

The study was launched in 1925. The results would have a significant impact on the PIPC.

With park matters ricocheting in various directions, the reach of the PIPC was captured by a headline in the *Livingston Enterprise,* a Montana newspaper. Proclaiming "Mather and Welch En route to [Yellowstone] Park Are Fresh From Dynamiting Big Saw Mill in Glacier National Park: Inspect Tetons," the article described the manner in which a saw mill owned by a hotel operator in Glacier National Park was removed to improve the scenery, much to the chagrin of the owner. The purpose of the nationwide inspection trip was to further refine and adjust the boundaries between national parks and the surrounding federally owned forest lands. Mather and Welch visited Glacier, Yellowstone, the Grand Canyon, Sequoia, Crater Lake, Mesa Verde, and the Tetons. In the meantime, King held the fort at the PIPC as best he could until Welch returned at the end of August, 1925, just in time to host the fourth meeting of the New York State Council of Parks at Bear Mountain.

With private funds depleted, increasing demands for visitor services, the honor and burden on Welch to aid with park policy at the national level, and the initiation of the Rockefeller study, the vulnerability and resiliency of the PIPC were even more severely tested when a riderless saddle horse came trotting home to a barn on the Meadowbrook Estate of Richard V. Lindabury near Bernardsville, New Jersey. Searchers found Lindabury dead beside a country lane where he had fallen or been thrown from his horse. A commissioner for fourteen years, Lindabury could open any door in New Jersey, carrying with him a well-earned reputation as an esteemed corporate lawyer, civic leader, and fair man. The PIPC had greatly benefited from his experience and access on many occasions, and his fellow commissioners keenly felt the loss.

12.
Black Thursday

Brainstorming among the commissioners to find a replacement for Richard Lindabury led to an impressive list of possible candidates. Governor Moore signaled the PIPC that he would appoint whomever the commissioners recommended. After considerable investigation and dialogue, the name of William Childs was advanced to the governor. Childs had grown up on a meager farm owned by his father in Basking Ridge, New Jersey. After he and his brother, Samuel, had roamed west in an unsuccessful search for better farming opportunities, they had returned to New Jersey, pooled their collective financial resources of $1,600, and in 1889 opened a restaurant near the family farm. Forty years later, a chain of Childs Restaurants with an estimated value of $36 million extended across the nation and into Canada, delivering an estimated 50 million meals per year to satisfied customers. Customer satisfaction was somewhat curious because Childs was a confirmed vegetarian. Reflecting his personal dietary inclinations, the meatless and partly meatless menus in the Childs Restaurants were increasingly suspected of hurting revenues, leading eventually to a stockholder revolt that deposed Childs from his own company in 1929. Despite this difficulty, Childs was a self-made, independently wealthy, and admired man and was a substantial contributor to the Democratic Party. He was promptly appointed to the PIPC to fill the unexpected void left by Lindabury.

A few months after Childs's appointment, the PIPC suffered a second loss when William H. Porter, a banker who had joined J. P. Morgan & Company just as George W. Perkins, Sr., was leaving, died suddenly of a heart attack. Porter had served as a commissioner for twenty-one years, beginning in 1905. In the spring of 1927 Frederick Henry Osborn, a Hudson River Valley resident and an investor in railroads and banking, filled Porter's chair. Standing six feet eight inches tall, Osborn was a presence wherever he went. By the age of forty he had made a fortune and retired from business, but he would remain a PIPC commissioner for forty years, pausing only during World War II when, with the rank of general, he was placed in charge of Army morale.

Childs and Osborn were joining the PIPC just as a four hundred–page critique of the PIPC's activities, compiled by Attorney Mark M. Jones for the trustees of the Laura Spelman Rockefeller Memorial Foundation, arrived on the desks of William Welch and King. Alerting J. DuPratt White to the report, King cautioned that "on a number of points, the report is highly critical," adding that he and Welch had read the document without pause from 9:00 a.m. to 6:00 p.m. Although the criticisms were hard to take, a hint of the overall message contained in the report had come weeks earlier in an internal memorandum from Jones to the Rockefeller staff in which he had offered the observation that the "Commissioners have made remarkable progress . . . considering that they have had to work through an organizational structure which in itself is an obstacle to good management." Jones reaffirmed this theme in the text of the full report:

> The Palisades Interstate Park is worthy of generous financial support. Genuine progress has been made toward realization of its main purpose of making outdoor recreation available to an urban population of over ten million at a low cost. Use of the Park is increasing steadily and the Commissioners are laboring under considerable difficulty in their endeavor to keep up with demands. . . .

Turning to financial considerations, Jones pointed out that the commissioners had raised $7.9 million in private contributions since 1900:

> Since the death of Mr. George W. Perkins, the Park has operated mainly on the amounts in hand at the time of his death, plus amounts made available from appropriations of the Legislatures of the two States. These appropriations have been secured with considerable difficulty, and the policy of the State of New York, in particular, is not such as to give assurances of the continuance of reasonable support. The Appropriation Committee . . . has aimed to restrict amounts made available by the State for the support of current operations and has insisted that the Park earn more and more of its income.

On the subject of operations, Jones added, "Development, with the attendant engineering and construction problems, has been so much the order of the day that the management of operations has not received as much attention as has recently become so necessary."

Jones recommended corrective action for these problems:

The corporate structure of the Park is such as it does not provide as much assurance of the unity and continuity of the Park as is desirable for an interstate enterprise. Either State can withdraw in a comparatively simple manner, but with serious consequences. Comity and custom alone now serve as the foundation for practices which are far too weighty and important for such a flimsy base. Beyond this, the fact that certain relationships between the States and the Park have not been sufficiently defined by law results in complications, most of which are unnecessary. It has frequently been proposed that the adoption of an interstate compact (treaty) be brought about as a means of providing greater assurance of continuity and further protection against political influence. The adoption of such a compact (treaty) requires action by the Legislatures of both States as well as by the Congress of the United States. At the time of writing, steps are being taken to formulate an instrument that might serve this purpose, with the view to presenting it to the Legislatures as soon as possible.

The State Council is an unfavorable factor in the situation. It is a comparatively new agency of New York State and was organized in 1924, chiefly at the instance of Robert Moses. Its purposes are stated to be advisory in nature, yet Mr. Moses appears to aim toward building up a supervisory organization. He has strong backing from Governor Smith. He seems to think that Palisades Park is endeavoring to escape supervision, and for that reason he may resist the interstate compact. It is my understanding that he is thoroughly disliked by the New York State Legislature and that this attitude toward him may result in favorable action on the compact by the Legislature, although such action would otherwise be difficult.

Then, in two sentences that must have chilled Welch and King, Jones said, "The interstate feature is so definitely of advantage to the Park that it should be preserved at any reasonable cost. Until the corporate structure is simplified, however, we would not consider that there is a sufficiently solid legal foundation for the Park's activities to warrant large contributions being made to it directly by private organizations and individuals."

Referring to land acquisition, Jones's advocacy was apparent: "The Park proposes that seventeen tracts, consisting of about 30,000 acres, all of which are situated in New York State, be acquired at an estimated total cost of $2,670,000. If this aim is realized, it will increase the size of the Park over seventy per cent to a total of almost 70,000 acres."

Under the heading "What Mr. Rockefeller Might Do," Jones may have considerably reduced the Welch/King chill by stating, "We should like to see the entire cost of the real estate made available to the Commissioners from Rockefeller sources." However, Jones continued, "Whatever sum is given should be conditioned upon the Commissioners' raising a substantial sum from other private organizations and individuals to cover a large part of the rest of the development program. . . . The decision as to the time when action should be taken presents a difficult problem." Returning to his earlier statement, Jones reinforced his view that "it is important to secure an interstate compact at this time, not only to assure the unity and the continuity of the Park as an interstate enterprise, but also in order that there may be assurance on continuing the interstate feature as a means of resisting political interference."

Jones felt that the public/private characteristics and successes of the PIPC set it apart from other government entities: "Of the capital investment represented by the Palisades Interstate Park about fifty-one per cent has come from private organizations and individuals either in land or cash. . . . We believe that this fact should place this Park in a different position from that of other State parks, so far as present and future State supervision is concerned."

Jones's report set wheels in motion within the PIPC and Rockefeller organizations. One result, not shared with the commissioners, was that the days of support of the PIPC's park system by the Laura Spelman Rockefeller Memorial Foundation would soon end. Further support, if any, would come personally from John D. Rockefeller, Jr. On the PIPC's side, White and Welch were eager to get on with the task of convincing New York and New Jersey State Legislators and Congress of the wisdom of legally affirming by interstate compact a unique park organization that had existed for a quarter century in substance, if not in fact. The commissioners retained the services of Judge Charles Evans Hughes to pursue the compact goal, but its achievement would prove to be anything but easy. Resistance would come from at least one predictable source: Robert Moses.

In the typically animated style of the PIPC, while major policy matters were being pondered in boardrooms and in the quiet sanctuaries of estate libraries, the park experiment was plunging forward. With a transfusion of New York State bond money, the much-debated development of Hook Mountain was initiated, but, fortunately, not as originally envisioned: the mountain would remain in place instead of being flattened to make room for recreational fields and picnic areas. Instead, development was concentrated along the shoreline and in the areas at the base of the old quarry sites. Throughout Harriman Park, bond funds allowed for construction of even more dams and roads, supplemented by the pri-

Snowshoeing, Bear Mountain, New York, 1930s.
(Courtesy of PIPC Archives)

vately funded construction of the "Baker" and "Harding" Camps. The latter camp was named at the request of donor Frederick A. Julliard in honor of former President Warren G. Harding. Under the skeptical eye of Ruby Jolliffe, the PIPC's camp director who preferred Commission-sponsored camp construction and control, the privately funded "Baker Camp," in particular, ran against her grain. It would exclusively serve employees and their families of four city-based banks: First National, New York Trust, Bankers Trust, and United States Trust.

Large crowds were beginning to gather at Bear Mountain in the winter to observe and participate in an increasingly delightful schedule of winter activities. King, writing to B. C. Wallin of the International Newsreel Corporation, described one of the many events: "One race—that on snowshoes with about twenty women competitors, no one of whom had ever been on snowshoes before—was a scream." By the following winter, a ski jump was in place, based on plans provided by the Scandinavian Ski Association. But getting the plans and building the jump were two different things, Welch discovered. He wrote to P. H. Elwood, Jr.:

> To my surprise, I find that the proper design of a real ski hill is quite a complicated matter and one on which none of the Swedish and Norwegian engineers entirely agree. About the only thing they do agree upon is the fact that the hill below the take-off should be about a thirty degree angle and that the steepness of this hill should increase with its distance from the take-off to care for the increased velocity of the jumpers in proportion to the length of their jumps.

Whatever the engineering challenges, the hill proved to be a great success. The New York State and Mid-Atlantic Ski Jumping Championships were held for the

Winter crowd, ski jumping, Bear Mountain, New York, 1960s.
(Courtesy of PIPC Archives)

first time at Bear Mountain in 1927, attracting scores of Scandinavian jumpers and hundreds of spectators. Outdoor speed-skating races were added to the venue, ranging in distance from 440 yards to 3 miles. In the first series of races, one hundred men and twenty-one women were in competition. Thrill seekers continued to hurtle down the ever-popular toboggan runs.

While Welch tried to keep up with winter and summer demands, he continued to field inquiries and requests from all over the United States to speak at hearings and attend meetings on park-management matters. In rare moments, he could focus on more basic concerns. Taking drawing pen in hand, Welch designed a rustic trail shelter large enough to accommodate a dozen or more hikers. Using boulders, logs, and flat slabs of granite gathered at the site, a park maintenance crew hand-built the prototype shelter on Tom Jones Mountain in Harriman Park. One boulder used in the construction weighed six tons. Great care was taken to position the shelter behind shrubbery slightly away from the main trail and to limit construction scars.

There was also the problem of three lovesick does at distant Allegheny State Park in western New York State. DeHart Ames, writing to Welch on behalf of the Allegheny State Park Commission, described the problem of the does: "As you will recall, we lost one of the deer which you so kindly furnished for the Park and then we procured a buck to place in the pen with the three does and he met with an accident and broke his neck and therefore we are without a buck to run with the does . . . is there anyway that we might be able to secure a buck from you?" Welch said yes, but not until summer. "Last year's fawns are pretty husky now and would be hard to catch," he wisely counseled.

Other wildlife matters arriving on Welch's desk were not so easily placed within the context of professional park management. One man wrote:

Gentlemen, I am in the market for some Beaver musk, and I saw your ad in the paper, where you had just marooned 50 Beavers in their homes for the winter. Now, I will explain myself to you. I wants [*sic*] the musk from a healthy Beaver during mating season, in the midst of the Beaver heat, before she is pregnant with young. I would like to know your price . . . and if you have got musk taken from under the jaws or throat or in the thigh of the animal, let me hear from you at an early date.

The inquiry was filed with no record of response by Welch. So, too, was a letter containing a business proposition, "I have heard through a friend that you are about to open a park of some kind in Bear Mountain. I have relations in Tampa, Florida, who would like to come north with about 250 Alligators, ranging from

10 inches to 12 feet in length and perhaps they could have space with you . . . let him know direct just what the rent will be, the license that must be paid, and what percentage he must pay you."

A more telling indicator of prevailing wildlife-management attitudes was highlighted by a *New York Times* article that announced, "Park Invites Fox Hunters To Shoot 500 Which Kill Game." In the article, Welch was quoted as saying, "Any reputable citizen with a fox hound and a trigger finger . . . can take all the foxes he can hunt," adding that foxes were considered "vermin" and could be hunted any time of the year. Responding to the article, E. Childs of the Bon Ami Company, and vice president of the Wyandanch Club, Smithtown, Long Island, wrote to Welch, suggesting the club might be interested in buying live foxes for sporting purposes. Childs counseled, too, that sending hunters and hounds into the PIPC's parks was no way to get rid of foxes and offered detailed advice on sure techniques to catch and kill foxes using steel leg-busting traps. "I use a wire cage with a chicken or pigeon in it," Childs explained: "All you need is a stick for a perch, if you use a pigeon, and a couple of tin cans and some water and some cracked corn. Set it in the middle of a field, or along an old hedge row, or fox run, and put four steel traps, one on each side, double spring. If you are after hawks as well, stick up a pole about twelve feet high, within ten or fifteen feet of the cage, with a small steel trap on the top." Childs "guaranteed" that the menacing traps would do the job. In the late 1920s, the concept of balance-of-nature had not been proposed. Welch was acting on the common scientific logic of the day. There is no confirmation that he took Childs's advice, probably preferring, instead, to stick with the local fox hunters.

In the forestry arena, friends from California shipped eastward to Welch a fine supply of redwood and sequoia seedlings for transplant in Bear Mountain and Harriman Parks. The idea was to establish redwood and sequoia forests in the Hudson River Valley, a prospect that Welch thought might prove unsuccessful due to alien soil and weather conditions. He was right.

Beaver musk, alligators, fox hunters, and redwood and sequoia trees aside, on his own doorstep, Welch reported with pleasure to the commissioners that the New York Fine Arts Commission had approved the design for an "entomological and historical museum" to be constructed on the site of old Fort Clinton at Bear Mountain. The American Association of Museums made a tentative offer to pay the estimated cost of $7,800 for the project. Part of the vision for the site was that wildlife, insect, and plant specimens could be put on public display for educational purposes at Bear Mountain as a small-scale version of Uncle Bennie Hyde's collection at the Museum of Natural History. A factor not considered in the enthusiastic rush toward this project was the possible impact of constructing a building on the very ground where the remains of old Fort Clinton could still be seen. As a parting gesture of support for the PIPC, the trustees of the Laura Spelman Rockefeller Memorial Foundation agreed to provide $7,500 to construct the museum, to the relief of the financially hard-pressed Association of Museums.

The small, masterfully constructed stone building that resulted was among three funded in 1927 by the foundation, the first of their kind in the nation. The other two museum buildings were constructed at Yosemite National Park, California, and the Grand Canyon National Park, Arizona. William Carr, the young Boy Scout who had been so impressed by Hyde during their chance meeting on the Bear Mountain train platform—enough so to follow in Hyde's footsteps—was now on the staff at the American Museum of Natural History and was appointed acting director of the newly anointed "Trailside Museum."

The parks would eventually add immensely to the wealth of knowledge about the natural world. But as with fox hunts, the understanding of and response to ecological questions pertaining to park stewardship was problematic for Welch. This was confirmed in an exchange of correspondence with Harold M. Lewis, the author of *The Regional Plan of New York and Its Environs*. Lewis alerted Welch to the search around New York City for suitable airplane-landing fields, suggesting that a field was needed at Bear Mountain. Welch replied that the commissioners were "considering seriously filling in the Iona Island marsh" for this purpose. Using his engineer's eye, Welch felt that making the necessary arrangements to fill in the marsh would take "many years to work out." Fortunately, the "work out" never happened. The Iona Island tidal marsh is an exquisite natural area, left behind in a horseshoe bend when glaciers straightened the course of the Hudson River just below Bear Mountain. The marsh nourishes the river and is home or way station for a rich variety of upland birds, waterfowl, fish, and scores of aquatic species. Today it is one of four areas that comprise the federally designated Hudson River National Estuarine Research Reserve and has been designated by the National Park Service as a National Natural Landmark.

Airports were not the only concern highlighted in Lewis's report. For seven years, this planning group, chaired by Frederic A. Delano and funded by the Russell Sage Foundation, had been studying city-growth patterns and needs within a fifty-mile radius of City Hall. The words of Ralph Waldo Emerson "Build therefore your own world" were a rallying cry for the planners, who saw around them a haphazard pattern of development and waste of aesthetic opportunity. Using only the "power of recommendation," the planners issued their findings in May, 1928, in an attempt to guide and encourage better distribution of population, a more effective balance between residential and industrial needs, and reduction of "frictions of space" by providing for parks and parkways. Looking across the river to the Palisades, and anticipating the impact of the Hudson River Bridge project (the George Washington Bridge), scheduled for completion in 1932, the planners urged construction of a parkway "for about twelve miles along the crest of the towering cliffs." "Unless immediate action is taken to place the land along the crest of the Palisades under public control, the New Jersey skyline along the entire sweep of the cliffs will be marred by apartment houses and other structures built close to their edges," the planners cautioned. Realtors and developers, already speculating in land in the vicinity of the bridge, responded even before the *Regional Plan* was published and claimed that apartment houses could be built along the Palisades without detriment to its beauty, to which Loula D. Lasker of *Survey Graphic* replied that the Palisades would turn into "a gap-toothed horizon of skyscrapers . . . billboards, water tanks, and Coney Island shows." Welch estimated the cost of acquiring a five hundred–foot strip along the crest of the cliffs at $25 million to $40 million. Anticipating "tremendous industrial growth" in northern New Jersey and a projected population of 6.5 million, the planners also urged extension of the PIPC's holdings to include a large part of the Ramapo Mountains in Bergen, Passaic, and Morris Counties, New Jersey, to provide for new hiking trails and recreation areas. One person who took careful note of the plan in general, and the Palisades Parkway recommendation in particular, was Rockefeller, Jr.

In a different sphere, Welch was grappling with the perplexing task of setting in motion the machinery necessary to raise millions of dollars for land acquisition at the proposed Great Smoky Mountains National Park, Tennessee / North Carolina, and the Shenandoah National Park, Virginia. To energize the national campaign for the two national parks, Welch visited Adolph S. Ochs, publisher of *The New York Times,* to convince him to chair the campaign. Reporting back to Senator Mark Squires of New Jersey, Welch remarked that Ochs "feels very positive it would be a great mistake for him to assume the Chairmanship for this work as it would prevent all other publications, particularly in this section of the country, from taking any interest in the matter." Welch added: "I am going to see Franklin D. Roosevelt and see if we cannot induce him to take it. . . ." Roosevelt, too, declined the fund-raising task. Even so, Welch stood at a privileged point of communication when Rockefeller, Jr., wrote to him in September, 1927, confirming a pledge of $1.5 million toward the $4.5 million fund-raising goal for acquisition of lands at the "Big Smoky Park." This was astonishingly good news. Prompted by the Rockefeller, Jr., pledge, Edsel B. Ford pledged $50,000 in support of the initiative. In January, 1928, Rockefeller, Jr., wrote in confidence to Arno B. Cammerer of the National Park Service to inform him that the two pledges to Welch were being canceled in favor of an increased pledge from the Laura Spelman Rockefeller Memorial Foundation of $4.5 to $5.0 million that was intended to match an equal sum jointly provided by the states of North Carolina and Tennessee. This extraordinary Rockefeller gift, first urged by Welch, eventually allowed for the purchase of about one-half of the eight-hundred-square-mile Great Smoky Mountains National Park.

Then, abruptly, Welch dropped out of further efforts to create the Great Smoky and Shenandoah National Parks. Writing to Daniel P. Wine of the Shenandoah National Park Association, Welch said, "It is impossible for me to take any further hand in the Shenandoah and Great Smoky Park projects . . . I cannot explain the details that make this necessary, but I simply must drop it. . . ." He officially resigned from his various southern Appalachian duties on January 24, 1928. A hint of Welch's motivation may rest in a letter he sent to a friend a month later in which he lamented the "long illness" of his daughter and the "tremendous hospital bills." Dr. Howard J. Benchoff, headmaster of the Massanitten Academy, near the Great Smokies, spoke for many when he wrote to Welch: "You have done a piece of work that will stand as long as the hills of Tennessee. You deserve the title, 'Prince of Diplomats.'"

For a different reason, Raymond Torrey, who had traded in his newspaper reporter's hat and was now handling publicity for the PIPC, also contacted Roosevelt. Torrey, whose voice for development of the Appalachian Trail remained strong and persuasive, was delighted when Roosevelt, serving as chair of the Taconic State Park Commission, steward of an evolving park system just across the Hudson River from the PIPC's holdings, had contacted landscape architect Benton MacKaye, proposing that work be started on a section of the A.T. extending from the Bear Mountain Bridge to the Connecticut border. The trail was unfolding, isolated section by isolated section. But three years after a trail crew began work at Bear Mountain, the only significant, marked, and newly constructed segment of the A.T. ran through Harriman Park. The rest of the segments consisted of existing trails that happened to be in reasonably close proximity to MacKaye's Maine-to-Georgia corridor. Through the power of his journalist's pen, Torrey made certain that the public remained informed of MacKaye's grand plan and of the progress being made. Roosevelt's credible name was a wonderful addition to the message.

With plans for major new land acquisitions to expand the New York parks under debate, the PIPC continued to display its split personality regarding the

Dana property on the summit of the Palisades in New Jersey. Title to the property finally passed to Achilee Ermeti after last-minute snags were resolved; sale price, $252,000. The commissioners also moved to clean up debts on some of their other properties and to refresh the moribund gift fund. At almost the same time, King wrote to attorney L. O. Rothschild, thanking him for his recommendation that the PIPC "purchase more land atop the Palisades to protect park resources below the cliffs," and promised to place Rothschild's views before the commissioners at their next meeting.

The PIPC also broke the mold by leasing the steamers *Clermont* and *Onteora* to the McAllister Steamship Company. Driven by the vessels' need for major refurbishment, including conversion from steam to oil power, and faced with the complexities of operating the two large boats and the difficulties in maintaining schedules and dealing with passengers' complaints, the commissioners decided to hand over the operation of the steamers to a private contractor. This was a tricky bit of business. The commissioners were keenly aware that Perkins, Sr., had won the first major contribution of $500,000 for the PIPC from Rockefeller sources specifically to purchase the steamers. At the time, he made the case that the PIPC must own and operate the steamers in order to ensure city-dwellers low-cost access to the parks. He had firmly maintained that all commercial services within the parks, except for minor vending, be operated by the Commission as a guard against profiteering. Leasing of the *Clermont* and *Onteora* ran counter to Perkins's philosophy and opened the door to other commercial concession contracts. After expressing skepticism at first about the wisdom of this significant change in the PIPC's policy, the Rockefeller trustees acquiesced and agreed to the lease arrangement, guided by the report prepared by Jones that recommended just such a shift in policy. Despite this shift, King, responding to a business inquiry early in 1927, stated, "There are no concessions for let anywhere within the Palisades Interstate Park. The Commission operates every Park facility."

On June 15, 1927, ground was broken at a ceremony on top of the Palisades to begin construction of the Hudson River Bridge (the George Washington Bridge). The Commission cooperated with the Port of New York Authority by accommodating survey parties, arranging for the ceremony, and, above all, agreeing to sell the twenty-five–acre DuPont property to the Authority, including riparian rights, so that the western segment of the massive structure could be anchored to the western shore, just north of historic Fort Lee. The only concern for the river steamers was that the bridge be high enough to allow for their unencumbered passage underneath.

At that moment, the commercial viability of the PIPC's steamers was placed in greater jeopardy by a court ruling that went against the PIPC. The commissioners had tried to reserve access to the Bear Mountain docks to the McAllister and Hudson River Day Line Steamship Companies, contending that the two companies had contracts with the PIPC that provided exclusive use of the docks. In a shouting match at the docks, the crew of a boat sent by the Delaware-Hudson Steamship Company attempted to debark 1,500 passengers, only to be chased away by a combined force of PIPC and McAllister employees. In the lawsuit that followed, attorneys representing the Delaware-Hudson company argued that any member of the public should have reasonable access to the park. In a precedent-setting ruling, Justice Joseph Morschauser of the New York Supreme Court agreed. He ruled that in conformance with logical regulations, "every reasonable opportunity should be given the public, either on the land or water, to have access to this park." The judge was careful not to randomly throw open the park to any commercial operator who happened to appear on the scene, but he concluded that exclusive commercial rights, such as the use of the Bear Mountain docks, must be based on competitive contract bids. He found that the commissioners had bypassed competition by granting docking rights only to McAllister and the Hudson River Day Line.

The commissioners were not happy with this ruling. In a follow-up letter to the PIPC's attorneys, King stated, "Our recourse now is to the Appellate Division. This matter strikes at the very root of our authority to regulate the public use of the Park, and it will be fought through to the end." The commissioners worried that Judge Morschauser's ruling would turn the parks into a commercial grab bag. The subsequent court fight did not take long. Within a few months, the Appellate Division of the New York State Court ruled in favor of the PIPC by overturning the lower court's finding. Tight-fisted access to the Bear Mountain docks was back under the control of the commissioners.

The PIPC's next legal proceeding would not be so easy. The quarry wars, dormant for so long, burst open again at Tallman Mountain, just north of the New Jersey–New York border near the village of Piermont. The Standard Trap Rock Corporation arranged with the owner of the 171-acre property to open the largest quarry operation ever envisioned along the banks of the Hudson River. On a trip aboard the *Stingrist,* Averell Harriman's eighty-seven–foot yacht, the commissioners viewed Tallman Mountain from the water. Already, the quarry company was constructing a giant crushing plant and forcing a channel through the beautiful Piermont Marsh to provide barge access to the mountain. White, taking a page from the style of Perkins, Sr., sought major financial help from

Rockefeller, Jr. The commissioners hoped to initiate a friendly negotiation with the traprock company through which the property would be acquired for about $500,000, the appraised value. Col. Arthur Woods, a senior Rockefeller, Jr., adviser, echoed White's plea. Rockefeller, Jr., was not inclined to pledge the entire amount but signaled that he would contribute $300,000 if the remaining amount could be raised from other private sources. Thomas W. Lamont, a wealthy landowner who had recently acquired property on the Palisades summit near the state border, offered to contribute an additional $100,000. Harriman then matched the Lamont pledge.

By September, 1928, the PIPC was in a position to recommend the Tallman Mountain purchase at a State Council of Parks meeting in Ithaca, New York, but there was a slight problem. The Standard Trap Rock Corporation claimed that the rock it intended to quarry was worth $2 million. The property owner who was leasing the site to the quarry company added an additional demand for $950,000 in compensation. Assuming that the Commission would not accept these prices, and knowing that the PIPC held the power of "appropriation" and could take the property if it chose to do so, the traprock operators proposed an alternative. They would "carefully" quarry the property and give it to the PIPC after their work was done. The commissioners upped their offer to $600,000, and the quarry operators countered at $4 million. In October, 1928, the PIPC served papers on the Standard Trap Rock Corporation and the Sparkill Realty Corporation and "appropriated" the Tallman Mountain property, expecting to pay no more than the appraised value. The following March, *The New York Times* announced, "Park Commission Sued." Standard Trap Rock challenged the constitutionality of the commissioners' authority to appropriate property for conservation purposes. No one at the time realized that the U.S. Supreme Court would resolve the legal odyssey on which the contending parties were embarking. In June, 1929, the PIPC lost in the New York appellate court and was enjoined from keeping control of the Tallman Mountain traprock property it had taken. In February, 1930, the *Times* confirmed, "High Court Reverses Palisades Case." Except for deciding the level of compensation, the PIPC prevailed in the Tallman Mountain case on appeal to the Supreme Court. Writing later to a friend, White put the case in perspective. The PIPC "blazed the way for development of the idea that the sovereign may assert a right to preemption for the preservation of scenic beauty quite disconnected from recreational purposes," he said. An important legal precedent was established in the *Standard Trap Rock/Sparkill Realty vs. PIPC* litigation. Preservation of scenic beauty by appropriation was deemed by the U.S. Supreme Court to be a legitimate responsibility of public park agencies. This finding would benefit park preservation nationwide. The question of deciding the level of compensation for the plaintiffs would drag on for years and finally settle near the original appraised value, but Welch ordered that roads into the Tallman Mountain property be blocked off the moment the high court ruled. As far as he was concerned, the PIPC owned the property, and he intended to defend it.

In 1928 Welch, King, and PIPC staff member Ellis Horewell traveled to the State Council of Parks meeting in Ithaca, New York, to present the PIPC's case for the appropriation of Tallman Mountain. On their return to Bear Mountain after the trip, King, the ever-careful accountant, listed the expenses: bridge tolls, $1.80; 10 gallons of gas, $2.05; suppers in Ithaca for three people, $4.35; Ithaca Hotel, four nights, three people, $30.50; breakfasts for three people, $2.55. The grand total was $41.25. Apparently, the group did not eat lunch. In 1928, a dollar was a dollar.

A horse was also a horse. Writing to Welch in the summer of 1928, Anne Tracy Eristoff inquired, "How is the horse, Harry, getting along . . . when he comes useless, I shall take him off your hands with the greatest pleasure." Sheepishly, Welch wrote back to Eristoff, "Horse Harry died of colic while I was away . . . regret that you were not notified."

Another responsibility went much better for Welch. He had been in contact for several months with Mrs. William H. Osborne (no relation to Commissioner Frederick H. Osborn) about the long-delayed New Jersey Federation of Women's Clubs Memorial project. Using his own engineering talents, Welch presented a "tower design" for the memorial that was accepted by the PIPC and the Federation. On April 20, 1929, the newly constructed Watch Tower, tucked in the woods just steps from the precipice of the Palisades, was dedicated. Frederick C. Sutro represented the New Jersey commissioners. White represented his New York colleagues. Mrs. John A. Holland (Cecilia Gaines), who had been president of the Federation in 1897, was in attendance, joined by Elizabeth Demarest and a large crowd of attentive Federation members and PIPC staffers. In a crypt within the Watch Tower, they helped place a "casket of records" attesting to the early and stubborn struggle by women of the Federation to protect the Palisades. Elizabeth Vermilye was remembered for her leadership. A bronze plaque affixed to the tower reads, "This Federation Memorial Park is dedicated to the successful efforts of the New Jersey State Federation of Women's Clubs and of those men and women who aided in the opening years of the twentieth century in preserving these Palisades Cliffs from destruction for the glory of God who created them and the ennobling of the generations which may henceforth enjoy them."

After a mere thirty years of asking and waiting for recognition, the women had their memorial.

Writing afterward to Welch, Osborne said, "Words entirely fail me in trying to express to you my feelings about our Memorial—It is dignified and suitable, standing guard over the cliffs and that noble stream, providing one a quiet, remote spot to rest and meditate right in the midst of the city's teeming millions. . . ."

Unknown to the PIPC commissioners, Welch, Osborne, and others in attendance at the Memorial dedication, memos were circulating internally within the Rockefeller organization. Perhaps largely prompted by *The Regional Plan of New York City and its Environs* report, staff member Charles O. Heydt advised his boss Rockefeller, Jr., that purchase of a large portion of land on the crest of the Palisades would probably cost about $10 million. The memo hinted that Rockefeller, Jr., might wish to pursue these purchases on his own, rather than through the PIPC. Almost at the same time, the so-called "Mandigo Property," a 836-acre mountainous piece of land west of the village of Fort Montgomery near Bear Mountain, came on the market at an asking price of $40/acre. The "New York Gift Fund" of private contributions, assembled so long ago by Perkins, Sr., was all but exhausted. Commissioners Harriman and Osborn decided to respond to the opportunity by buying this property, to be held until such time as the PIPC could reimburse them.

A management routine was appearing within the Commission. To a large extent, the park experiment had matured into park-business-as-usual, with some exceptions. One of those exceptions was an attempt by Welch to schedule the 1932 Winter Olympics for Bear Mountain. In a letter to the International Olympic Committee in Lausanne, Switzerland, Welch affirmed that daily crowds of up to 160,000 were coming to Bear Mountain to enjoy winter sports activities, including 15,000 spectators on average to watch the ski jumping. Congressman Hamilton Fish, Jr., of New York, himself an avid sportsman, strongly supported Welch's initiative. Fish cautioned that Welch should send a telegram to the Olympic Committee in addition to the letter. Feeling that he had ample time, Welch decided against the telegram, only to learn that the Olympic Committee had selected Lake Placid the day before the PIPC's letter arrived.

In the summer of 1929, Governors Roosevelt of New York and Morgan F. Larson of New Jersey made an inspection tour of the Palisades parks. Roosevelt was very familiar with the parks and made sure that he and Larson spent time with some of the children in the 112 group camps now operating in Harriman Park. An article in *The New York Times* summarized the comments Roosevelt made dur-

Women's Memorial, Palisades Cliffs Summit, New Jersey, 1929.
(Courtesy of PIPC Archives)

ing the park tour at the Bear Mountain Inn: "The successful cooperation between New York and New Jersey in the Palisades Interstate Park was cited yesterday by Governor Roosevelt as a striking example of the way cooperation might be effected in many other fields, particularly the economic." Roosevelt was also quoted on the benefits of outdoor recreation. "It will relieve us of the dangers of overcrowding in the cities, the strain on our nervous systems. In the long run, it can be seen, the park idea is essential to American civilization. The two States of New York and New Jersey have set an example for the whole country. . . ." Unmentioned was that the car provided by the PIPC to Welch was so dilapidated that he had to borrow a car from an acquaintance to transport the governors on the tour.

The pace of the PIPC's administrative affairs was reasonably stable. A large administration building, including boardroom, court, police desk, and fifteen offices, had been completed in the New Jersey section of the park system in 1928. Inquiries on everything from fund-raising to transplanting mountain laurel continued to flow to Welch's desk from park advocates throughout the United States. In December, 1928, Welch learned to his regret that his good friend, sixty-two-year-old Stephen T. Mather, was stepping down as director of the National Park Service due to ill health. Horace M. Albright, who had sent the elk to Bear Mountain from Yellowstone, would succeed Mather. The battle of the budget for the Interstate Park had become an annual ritual in Albany and Trenton, bringing with it occasional high drama when the PIPC's financial requests were slashed to the bone. These actions resulted in a contingent of commissioners making the rounds in the state capitals, usually achieving partially restored funding. Dialogue continued regarding the "treaty" between the two states that would reconfigure the identical-twin interstate commissions into one governing body. The PIPC's minutes, dated March, 1929, confirmed that "the Chairman of the State Council of Parks (Robert Moses) still is in opposition to the treaty."

Then, on October 24, 1929, "Black Thursday," the stock market fell by five hundred points. A slight recovery occurred on Friday. On the following Monday, full-blown panic set in. The onset of the Great Depression was at hand, and the PIPC would feel the result, immensely.

13.
The Compact

"On your authorization to expend not more than $10 million for property on the Palisades," Charles O. Heydt wrote to John D. Rockefeller, Jr., "we have expended up to the present time approximately $8,050,000 . . . we have come to the point where we must deal with holders of the larger tracts . . . Mr. Osborne and I have discussed the matter at length and we recommend that authority be given to bid up to $6,000,000 (in addition) for the Paterno holdings." In a follow-up communiqué four days later Heydt added, "There is an immense amount of curiosity as to who is buying the Palisades property and we have done everything possible to conceal the operations under way by operating through perhaps a dozen different corporations to confuse the issue. Representatives of the Palisades Park Commission have been to see Mr. Osborne, but he has, of course, been very evasive and non-committal."

Heydt was a senior real-estate specialist on Rockefeller, Jr.'s, staff; John A. Osborne was a real-estate broker in Bergen County, New Jersey. Through these two men, Rockefeller, Jr., had set out to purchase the crest of the Palisades from Fort Lee, New Jersey, to the New York border, a distance of about twelve miles. Prompted by his familiarity with the PIPC, and strengthened in resolve by *The Regional Plan of New York and Its Environs* report, Rockefeller Jr., was secretly buying Palisades land, including the Dana property that the commissioners had sold only a few years earlier. His respect for the PIPC commissioners and William Welch did not extend to including them in the strict circle of confidence sur-

John D. Rockefeller, Jr.
(Courtesy of Rockefeller Archive Center)

rounding his land-buying activities. At the direction of Governor Morgan Larson of New Jersey, Welch and Elbert King were busy gathering landowner information along the crest in anticipation of legislation that might be sought to allow the PIPC to extend its condemnation authority inland from the edge of the cliffs. In essence, the PIPC was running on a track parallel to that of the secret land buyer. Welch and King, along with scores of local residents, land speculators, builders, and elected officials, were wondering just what was going on. Rumors circulated as the scale and pace of the land-buying activity began to sink in. Rockefeller Jr., was prominently mentioned, but other rumors had it that a "group of public spirited citizens" was buying the land to preserve it, or that Columbia University was amassing property for a new campus. Osborne, the front man, was a human vault—the secret could not be pried from him, not by reporters, other realtors, Frederick Sutro, or the other PIPC commissioners.

If the commissioners had been privy to a letter written by Rockefeller, Jr., to Heydt as 1930 came to a close, they would have been even more astonished. Working the numbers down to the penny, Rockefeller, Jr., confirmed in writing a discussion he had had the previous day with Heydt at the University Club at which Heydt had verified that $7,508,400.23 had been expended for outright purchases. Heydt had added that contracts, mortgages, interest, and taxes "coming due year by year" until 1935 amounted to another $13,348,096.79. Rockefeller, Jr., having committed a grand total of $20,856,497.02 to the clandestine acquisition project, directed that the "buying program of the Palisades" be "terminated." In the letter to Heydt, he added this intriguing thought: "We were of the opinion that a broad motor road should be laid out along the property, safely back from the edge of the cliffs, so as not to destroy the beauty thereof—. . . ." These words were the first hint that Rockefeller, Jr., would be a champion of the Palisades Interstate Parkway. For the time being, though, he planned to stand back and await further events, being particularly encouraged by the thought that the commissioners might, in fact, succeed in gaining broad legal authority to "take" those properties that could not be obtained in willing seller–willing buyer deals. The commissioners remained in the dark about Rockefeller, Jr.'s, activities, strategies, and hopes.

A saga in scenic preservation of more human and heartrending form was unfolding in Harriman Park. Governor Franklin D. Roosevelt received a petition from fifty-three residents and allies of Sandyfields, a mountain hamlet tucked in a remote section of Harriman Park, who opposed the construction of a dam and the creation of a 250-acre lake. Claiming that the project would "flood several of our homes and completely wipe out our entire village, which has been in existence for over 100 years," the residents pleaded for help from Albany in stopping construction of the dam. In response to the petition, Welch confirmed to the governor's staff that most of the Sandyfields residents had voluntarily sold their properties to the PIPC. Only a handful of owners remained, and of these, most had expressed interest in selling. But the existence of the "mountain folk" was a poignant connection with the past. Writing for *The New York Times Magazine*, Diana Rice said, "Up Sandyfields way the mountaineers of the Hudson River Highlands, near Bear Mountain, are still singing their hymns." Acknowledging that many of the residents, feeling the pressure of park development, were selling out, Rice posed the question, "But what does cash mean to a mountaineer bereft of his mountains, his shotgun and his hound-dog?

"Sandyfields is today the center of the mountaineers' country," Rice continued.

Five miles or so west of Stony Point, which lies along the Hudson River not far from Haverstraw, the settlement boasts but a handful of houses. A general store, a little schoolhouse and a Methodist church are its gathering points. There is no post office. Mail comes by rural free delivery from Stony Point; packages by parcel post. The mountaineer is an ardent reader of catalogues, and his perusal of these thick volumes often results in heavy work for the mailman. Two hundred dollars in one day have been known to leave the mountain en route to mail order houses in the Middle West.

Womenfolk of the Highlands do not waste time shopping. Few of them ever leave their homes. They order their gingham, cotton stockings, and heavy shoes direct from the great emporiums whose advertisements read like fairy-tales. If the old folks cannot read, the young ones can. For even in the mountains, life is growing more complex as sons and daughters journey out to the strange world beyond the rim of hills and bring back stories of different standards of living.

Rice described how "nearly 200 years ago . . . a bride and bridegroom unhitched their ox team in the wilderness that was then the Hudson Highlands . . . it was before the days of land records—. . . ."

In addition to Sandyfields, the mountain settlements included Baileytown, Bulsontown, Johnsontown, Pine Meadows, Pittsboro, Queensboro, Woodtown, and Doodletown, the hamlet through which British troops marched on the attack against Forts Clinton and Montgomery. The hamlets were settled by pre–Revolutionary War woodcutters, hardscrabble farmers, and hunters. Hessian soldiers, deserters during the Revolutionary War, found their way into the Highlands to join the earlier settlers, as did runaway slaves from Manhattan and Westchester County plantations and the occasional convict looking for a remote hiding place. As described in one news article, "They set up their lean-tos and cabins in the Ramapo forests, fished in the streams for trout and pickerel, hunted cottontails and snow-shoe rabbits and deer and completely ignored the world outside. They . . . were sufficient unto themselves."

Because so many of the Sandyfields residents had already voluntarily sold their properties, the petition to stop the dam project failed. The last holdouts sold their land and moved on. In 1935 Ramsey Conklin, sixty-two years old, closed the door to the isolated cabin that his grandfather had constructed in 1779. He had never been more than a few miles from the cabin, but when waters from another of the artificial lakes began lapping at the pasture where he kept his cow and heifer, he and his family also agreed to be resettled in an abandoned schoolhouse outside the Harriman Park boundary. Referring to his new home, Conklin said: "This here is a right busy spot, right off a road with them motor cars goin' by, as many as seven or eight in a single day. It won't be good for the stock."

In a way, the hamlet of Doodletown was more fortunate. It was not immediately in the path of park development and continued to thrive, even gaining population as parklands were acquired around it. For understandable reasons, the hamlet's population sharply declined during the Depression, but Doodletown persisted and adapted, providing solitude for its residents and some fine employees of the PIPC while other hamlets and mountaineer families in more remote forest vales disappeared one by one. Still, the days of the last remaining hamlet were numbered. Park development plans in the 1960s convinced the last of the Doodletowners to sell out. The hamlet ceased to exist in 1965. It continues to live only in the pages of the book *Doodletown,* tenderly written by a former resident of the hamlet, Elizabeth "Perk" Stalter, and published by the PIPC.

In addition to the impact on the pioneer lifestyle of the Hudson Highlands, the Depression created great uncertainty for the PIPC, coupled with a search for new answers to keep the parks functioning. Welch, writing to Robert Moses, suggested a special push for funding from Albany to hire additional park workers. "The unemployment situation in the vicinity of our park . . . is most deplorable. A number of large factories have closed up . . . there is practically no State work . . . no county work and very little municipal work . . . private construction work is at the lowest ebb I have seen. . . ." Red ink began flowing across the ledger of the Bear Mountain Inn, and the commissioners voted to advertise the sale of the dayliners *Clermont* and *Onteora.* They succeeded when the McAllister Navigation Company made a bid of $300,000 for the two vessels. McAllister's timing was bad. A combination of the Depression and the 1931 opening of the George Washington Bridge was too much for the company that had begun providing river excursions to Bear Mountain in 1913. In the late 1930s the company vanished when its assets fell under the hammer of the Deputy U.S. Marshal at a bankruptcy sale.

"Retrenchment," as King referred to it, was under way in all maintenance and operating departments within the PIPC. Wages were cut across the board, and a hard squeeze was placed on part-time employees. Raymond Torrey, the newspaperman-turned-publicist for the PIPC, found his salary cut in half, from $3,000 to $1,500 per year. Torrey was fortunate, nonetheless, to have any salary at all because a year earlier, Moses had tried to strangle him. Torrey wore several hats, including service as secretary to the State Council of Parks. His strongly held environmental views clashed with Moses's vigorous push to build the Northern State Parkway on Long Island. At a meeting in Albany, the confrontation came to a head when Moses cursed at the rotund, usually gentle Torrey. Torrey lost his temper and called Moses a "big noisy kike." Moses leaped forward and grabbed Torrey by the neck in a vice-like grip. Restrained by Jay Downer, executive director of the Westchester County Park Commission, who was a long-time friend of Welch and of the PIPC, and by other participants in the meeting, Moses released his grip, only to grab a heavy smoking stand and throw it at Torrey as his antagonist beat a retreat out the door. Torrey sent a letter of apology to Governor Roosevelt and resigned from his position with the State Council of Parks. Fortunately for the PIPC, the Moses-Torrey incident was kept at arm's length. In several instances, King referred to "our good friend, Bob Moses," in correspondence on various park and State Council matters, and Moses, his wife, and their two children were regular users of a guest house at Bear Mountain, including one extended stay while Moses recuperated from a serious illness.

As the PIPC grappled with the momentous challenges of the Depression, King alerted Sutro in May, 1930, that "our dear friend, Dr. Partridge, died last Friday." Stricken while attending a dinner at the New York Academy of Medicine, Edward Partridge had served as a commissioner for seventeen years. Only vaguely remembered by those who eulogized him was his turn-of-the-century advocacy for the preservation of the Hudson Highlands as a national park. No one seemed to remember that Partridge had influenced and reinforced the thinking of E. H. Harriman, leading to the decisive donation of land and money that placed the PIPC firmly on track toward building an expansive park and historic-site system. Despite the fuzzy recollection, Partridge would have been pleased by the selection of his successor. Acting promptly, Governors Larson of New Jersey and Roosevelt of New York appointed former New York Governor Alfred E. Smith to the post. Smith, who had lent strong support to the PIPC and its mission, would serve for the next thirteen years. The commissioners, Welch, and King were delighted with the prestige of the Smith appointment.

King was attending to the various rules that guided the PIPC's activities, including the continuing restriction against single women who wanted to camp. He had consistently turned down women's camping requests, making exceptions only for married women accompanied by their husbands. This restriction was challenged when a young man, aged nineteen, who had been crippled by infantile paralysis at age two, asked that his twenty-two-year-old sister be allowed to attend him on a camping trip to Harriman Park. King turned to Sutro for advice. King and Sutro were leery of single women who seemed to expect the same freedoms in the park as men, but their practical judgment prevailed. Permission was granted; as a result, a slight dent appeared in the armor of the PIPC's men-only camping policy. King and Sutro may have been influenced by their personal knowledge of the physical challenges faced by polio-stricken Governor Roosevelt.

King had clearly become the gatekeeper for the PIPC. He was at his desk in all seasons, tightly controlling the PIPC's purse strings, responding to thousands of letters, staying in constant contact with the widely traveling commissioners, working with Welch to stamp out controversy and short-circuit criticism at the first sign of trouble, rushing to Albany and Trenton to deal with the latest budget crises, seldom away from his post for personal reasons, persnickety, precise, loyal. King had become as invaluable and irreplaceable as anyone can be in an organization.

But in response to an inquiry in May, 1931, King's assistant, Jessie A. Marvin, responded, "Mr. King is at home, ill, and may be there for some days. . . ." King, who had joined the PIPC as a clerk in 1913, died on June 7, 1931. The PIPC's minutes memorialized the man who was so dedicated to his responsibilities: "The years of his service were the years of the growth of the Park. As the Park grew, so grew his versatile ability in a wide field of unique and exacting duties, grew his enthusiasm for the park and zealous devotion to its development, grew the wide circle of his friends and the high regard in which he was held by them and especially by his Commissioners."

The vacuum left by King was filled a few months later in an unlikely manner. The Depression caught up with Sutro. His company, Sutro Brothers Braid, Inc., went under. After eighteen years as a commissioner and successor to Richard Lindabury as president of the New Jersey arm of the PIPC, Sutro resigned. His former commissioner colleagues immediately hired him as executive director, assistant secretary, and assistant treasurer of the PIPC, the same titles held by King. Sutro was making a difficult transition by stepping down from a board of directors position to become a staff member within the same organization. He would now work as second-in-command to Welch and answer to the commissioners with whom he had been a copartner for so long, and his new role as policy advocate rather than policy maker would circumscribe his wide array of contacts in Trenton and Albany.

With barely a hitch, Sutro made the transition. He began immediately to tighten the PIPC's business practices, demanding strict compliance with budgets that he critiqued in detail, department by department. Sutro cut Torrey's activities even more and discharged the PIPC's Albany lobbyist. Wages paid to the employees of the Bear Mountain Inn were reduced. Welch, who had assumed routine approval of funds to replace worn-out ice-hockey equipment, found himself closely questioned by Sutro and Commissioner Charles Whiting Baker regarding this need; this sent a signal to the staff not to assume anything and to be prepared to defend every expenditure. The businesslike Sutro greatly admired Welch and the legacy left by King, but he intended to firmly apply his own standards of corporate management. In the State of New Jersey, apart from the PIPC, Sutro used the same approach. Over the next three decades, his influence on park conservation grew to the point that his voice was always heard and his advice was never ignored.

Adding unlikely event to unlikely event, Sutro's replacement on the Commission was Abram De Ronde, who had already served from 1900 to 1912 but had fallen out of favor with his own Democratic Party associates and was not reappointed to the PIPC by then-Governor Woodrow Wilson. After an absence of nineteen years, DeRonde was reappointed by Republican Governor Larson.

These changes were taking place just as Welch received the good news that New York, through Governor Roosevelt's newly created Work Relief Program, was making available $750,000 to the PIPC to provide employment for able-bodied men. To the press, Welch stated, "This will be work, not charity." The first members of this new work force soon arrived by train from New York City. "They were as uneasy as strangers arrived in a new land," Welch remarked. And well they should be: most of the men knew nothing of vast woodlands not dissected by pavement, free of concrete walls where the sound of wind in the trees replaced the grind of traffic noise on city streets. Within weeks, 2,500 men were employed in the park system, 1,200 of them traveling daily from New York City. The urban contingent crossed the river by ferry at 6:15 a.m. to board a northbound train, arriving at Bear Mountain at 7:30 a.m. to begin walking or being trucked to the work sites. The workday ended at 4:00 p.m., followed by a contest of shoving and pushing to determine who got the seats on the train or who had to stand for the long trip back to the city. Many of this vanguard of laborers had held "white collar" jobs that had evaporated with the Stock Market crash. Their former status was confirmed by the suits, ties, and street shoes many of them wore to work at Bear Mountain during the first days of their assignment to the PIPC. These clothes were soon replaced by sturdy pants and boots commandeered by Welch. The men were grateful for the work clothes and, even more, for the $4 per day they were paid, minus 50¢ for transportation. For the first time since his days in the spruce forests of Oregon during World War I, Welch found himself in command of a small army of men whose eagerness for any kind of work superseded their questionable qualifications.

Welch and his engineers were ready with a long list of projects, ranging from the clearing of fallen and dead trees from thousands of acres of forest and the planting of seedlings, to sophisticated and complex construction projects, including buildings, dams, roads, trails, utility systems, and a variety of public-use areas. Welch even hoped to construct a "through highway" from the recently opened George Washington Bridge to Bear Mountain, reminding anyone who would listen that "now, on Sundays, it often takes eight hours to travel from Bear Mountain to New York City." At the top of Welch's list was the construction of the long-envisioned "George W. Perkins Memorial Highway" to the summit of Bear

Civilian Conservation Corps crew, 1930s.
(Courtesy of PIPC Archives)

Mountain. Now Welch had the men to accomplish the task. No heavy machinery would be used to assault the route up the mountain. Instead, Welch directed that the road be built by hand so that it could be placed as gently as possible on the steep slopes of the mountain.

The first Depression-era laborers to arrive at Bear Mountain were soon to be joined by a much larger work force. The election of Roosevelt to the presidency in 1932 brought great emphasis to publicly funded work programs. The first two Civilian Conservation Corps (CCC) camps in the eastern United States were promptly established in Harriman Park early in 1933, one at "Beechy Bottom" on an old road over which "Mad" Anthony Wayne and his troops had marched in 1779 to attack the British garrison at Stony Point. The camp occupied land once owned by another Revolutionary War hero, Isaac Van Wort, who, while serving in the American militia at Tarrytown, had helped capture the British spy Major John Andre in 1780. The second camp was farther west, located in a "wilderness" location known as "Pine Meadow Swamp." Each camp housed 185 men, but before Welch and the PIPC staff could catch their breath, nine more CCC camps were under construction, increasing the complement of men to almost six thousand. By 1934, twelve camps were in place, accommodating a work force of ten thousand men. A flurry of projects was inaugurated, extending from the Palisades of New Jersey to Storm King Mountain north of West Point. Welch marched a troop of men into the Tallman Mountain site to remove quarry equipment and begin park development, even though the Tallman case remained in court. Hook Mountain came alive through landscaping and development of the old quarry sites into picnic areas, playfields, and hiking areas. Construction of a golf course was begun at Rockland Lake adjacent to Hook Mountain. A new administration building made of stone and logs was rising at Bear Mountain. Intricate stonework was a hallmark of the PIPC's projects everywhere, ranging from huge walls built to stabilize the road cuts on the face of the Palisades cliffs to small and large buildings scattered throughout the park system.

At Blauvelt Park, Torrey, still working diligently for the PIPC despite his cut in salary, reported, "An experiment in the rehabilitation of single, homeless, unemployed men selected from thousands seeking shelter at the New York Municipal Lodging House, or in the flophouses on the Bowery . . . has attained results within two months . . . leading those responsible to believe that it may point a way to solve some of the problems of human wreckage caused by the Depression." The two hundred men at Blauvelt had been itinerant wanderers who "were driven to seek scanty meals in the breadlines." Placed in charge at Blauvelt was a thirty-seven-year-old Social Sciences graduate from Notre Dame, himself from the ranks of the jobless. The head cook, also jobless until the Blauvelt opportunity came his way, had been an instructor in the Army's Cook School. Only seven of the Blauvelt recruits dropped out or were kicked out of the program. The rest, held together by a place to sleep, square meals, and the challenge of real accomplishment, formed themselves into an effective work unit. Part of the incentive was that they could save as much as $30 over three months if they were frugal.

In addition to the resident camps, the Works Progress Administration (WPA) continued to provide a commuter work force from the city. A reporter for the *Ossining Citizen Register* spent a day with these men:

> The hardships . . . are seared in the soul of every man who goes to the WPA project at Bear Mountain. . . . It is a story of men, unused to physical labor, moving huge rocks with bare hands in bitter cold; dinners of frozen sandwiches; crowded transportation . . . rugged pioneer conditions, generations

removed from soft, Twentieth Century drawing-room life. . . . Bear Mountain is considered a "Siberia" among the WPA workers.

Despite the trauma of the Depression, highest quality results were expected. Time was not an urgent factor, so care could be taken in attendance to details, training, and project design. Talent and maturity were the common denominators among the work force. The organizational structure was military in design and expectation. The men had to measure up to a stern standard of discipline. The *Ossining Citizen* reporter thought the whole endeavor was like fighting a war. White collars merged side-by-side with blue collars; the results within the PIPC and in parks across the nation were artistic, appropriate, solid, and lasting. The stone-and-log theme of the Bear Mountain Inn, completed in 1915, was reflected in an architectural style throughout the PIPC's park system. Probably because of the hardships, many of the men who found themselves engaged in the public-works programs of the economically devastated 1930s carried the experience with them as a badge of honor for the rest of their lives, having learned much in a hard school of personal necessity and by accomplishing truly remarkable projects that have lasting public value.

William Carr, guiding the fortunes of the Trailside Museum, took advantage of the public-works programs by increasing his corps of trained naturalists to twenty-two, including geologists, botanists, archaeologists, and zoologists. He sought and won Welch's approval for the construction of new buildings, trails, and exhibits at the museum. In league with Ruby Jolliffe, museum activities were expanded to include four "regional" museums, strategically placed in Harriman Park to more effectively serve the group camps. Carr and his naturalists staffed the regional museums, allowing for direct contact with hundreds of wide-eyed children. Influenced by the style of "Uncle Bennie" Hyde, the education programs specialized in snakes. A popular technique used by Carr and his staff was to allow snakes to casually crawl out of shirt sleeves or collars while the seemingly oblivious naturalists talked about something else.

Out in Harriman Park, snakes and museums were only part of Jolliffe's constant effort to expand the thinking and joy of her campers. Her most potent educator existed in the person of Princess Te Ata, a member of the Chickasaw from Oklahoma who had once performed on Broadway. As described in *Liberty Magazine:* "Sometimes she wears blue butterflies in her jet-black hair. She is tall, very straight, very slender; voice of clear contralto, tones quietly modulated. Her name—Te Ata—means 'Bearer of the Morning.' She's an American-Indian girl; on stage she portrays dramatically the ancient arts and legends of her people." The magazine *Camp Life* echoed the allure:

Princess Te Ata modestly claims to interpret the fine spirit of the North American Indian in her artistry of dance and song and old legends. Yet she goes far beyond the limits of any tribe or any nation. It is not only the soul of the Indian which takes form in her figure, her dress, her voice and poetry of her cadenced movements. It is the spirit of man and womankind expressing in its fullness the beauty of the wild and primal world from which it sprang. This is what makes her art significant for those of us who are privileged to hear it.

This privilege was extended time and again to the young campers on Te Ata's regular tours through Harriman Park. The girls and boys would sit in rapt attention, captivated and carried along by the voice and movements of the princess. Jolliffe felt that Te Ata's importance to her young campers was such that one of the newly created CCC lakes should be named in her honor. Jolliffe was joined by her friend and compatriot Eleanor Roosevelt in this request. Welch and the

Princess Te Ata.
(Courtesy of PIPC Archives)

commissioners readily agreed. On the appointed day in July, 1932, the governor's wife, surrounded by hundreds of her cherished campers, watched the ceremonial arrival of Te Ata, carried by canoe across the lake that would perpetually bear her name. Roosevelt performed the christening by pouring a mixture of waters, collected from all the other park lakes, into "Lake Te Ata." The First Lady later invited the princess to perform at the White House and, again, for King George VI and Queen Elizabeth on their 1939 visit to Hyde Park.

Through his press releases, many of which were picked up verbatim by *The New York Times* and other newspapers, Torrey attempted to extend the educational services provided within the parks by Carr, Jolliffe, and their staffs. Writing about the wildflower bandits, he declared:

> Some are just plain dumb; they pluck laurel at the side of a sign with letters a foot high—PLEASE DO NOT PICK WILD FLOWERS: OTHERS WANT TO SEE THEM. Some are just thieves . . . and a few are innocent and honest . . . supposing that the flowers are for everybody, and walk back past the doors of the police station. . . . Visitors of foreign origin forget English. . . . Sweethearts are funny; they try to take the blame for each other . . . the judge's desk is heaped with wilted flowers.

The police desk sergeant, quoted as saying, "If we didn't pick em up this way, they'd carry off the park," joined Torry in this concern.

But on other matters of natural history, Torrey was more upbeat:

> Those who recall the condition of the forest in the Highlands a quarter century ago will have in their minds' eye a memory of sad-looking sprout lands, often burned over and set back for years, which were the result of a century of repeated cutting for saw logs, charcoal, and cord wood. . . . The forest in the park, aided and protected by man in the past twenty years, now shows what nature can do if let alone in our deciduous broad-leaf vegetation in the Northeastern United States. . . . The recovery of the larger forest trees is bringing with it the return of shrubs, herbaceous flowering plants, ferns, mosses and lichens, so that the Harriman, Bear Mountain, and Storm King sections, in particular, now present one of the richest and most interesting regions in the East for the study and enjoyment of native flora and fauna.

Reporting on the consequences of flooding caused by the many artificial lakes created in Harriman Park, Torrey observed,

> Many species of bog and shore plants did survive . . . in the curious floating island, which was formerly part of the quaking bog around Little Cedar Pond. When the water rose, the bog tore loose and floated around the lake until it

finally came to a halt near the southwest end of the present lake. The old bog plants, the insectivorous sundews and pitcher plants, the marsh fern, water loosestrife, cranberries, swamp honeysuckle, poison sumach, red maple, a few small tamaracks, a terrestrial bright yellow flowered species of bladderwort, water arims and cattails, persisted and now afford a very interesting association on the floating island.

As part-time tour guide, in addition to his public-relations specialty, Torrey hosted a visit by scientists to the Palisades cliffs, explaining his rationale to Sutro: "The fossil Phytosaur was found in this part of the Park, a primeval dinosaur, with a duck bill, about as big as an alligator."

While Carr, Jolliffe, Torrey, and most of the PIPC's staff were in the trenches, attempting to cope with and squeeze advantages from the contradictory forces of the Depression, Sutro was coping with the surreal nature of funding for the PIPC. Above the line, in the public-works arena, the PIPC had access to funding and workers beyond its wildest imagination, but below the line, in the realm of the traditional state budget process, the news was grim. Reacting to an episode in Trenton in which funding for the PIPC was almost eliminated, Sutro wrote to Commissioner Edmund Wakelee, who had succeeded Sutro as president of the New Jersey branch of the Commission:

> This incident has impressed on my mind the extreme (termity) of the hold which we, as an interstate body, have on the two States. Either Legislature could practically without notice destroy the work of almost 35 years by simply refusing to appropriate any money to the Park. All this again brings up the question of the vital importance of pushing to a conclusion a thought that has been uppermost in Mr. White's mind for years, vis: the enactment of an interstate compact.

J. DuPratt White picked up this theme in a letter to Rockefeller, Jr., in which he reiterated the need "for a treaty between the two states." White continued, "I have been met with opposition in this effort by what I think is jealousy. . . . The formation of the treaty has not received the approval of the State Council of Parks"—meaning Moses.

Even with belts tightened, the PIPC was able to host the Thirteenth National Conference on State Parks at the Bear Mountain Inn in May, 1933. The highlight of the event was a motorcade up the George W. Perkins Memorial Highway, still under construction, that allowed the attendees to be "the first to enjoy by automobile" the magnificent scene from atop Bear Mountain, including views to the towers of the New York City skyline, forty miles away, and a vista that included four states: New York, New Jersey, Connecticut, and Massachusetts. The next day, White presided over an event at the Trailside Museum at which Eleanor Roosevelt unveiled a memorial plaque in honor of Stephen T. Mather. The principal speaker was Secretary of the Interior Harold Ickes. Attending were Horace M. Albright, Mather's successor as director of the National Park Service; Mrs. Stephen (Jane T.) Mather of Darien, Connecticut; Mather's daughter, Mrs. Edward R. McPherson, Jr.; Welch; and the conference participants.

Below the cliffs of the Palisades, another dedication took place on June 8, 1933, when the old "Cornwallis Headquarters" was opened to the public, thanks to yet another public-spirited initiative taken by the New Jersey Federation of Women's Clubs. "Early American treasures of pine, oak, maple, pewter, china and glass, were given by 149 clubs, and 22 individuals . . . ," according to the Women's Clubs historical record. "The most precious relic was donated by the Commissioners, themselves, the sea chest of Henry Hudson." Mrs. John R. (Cecilia Gaines) Holland had earlier written to Sutro suggesting that the Cornwallis Headquarters be "put in order permanently as a museum." She could look back at decades of personal advocacy for the Palisades, and she was pleased by the latest, women-sparked accomplishment of the Federation. She would have been even more pleased had she known of a letter being prepared for the signature of Rockefeller, Jr., that arrived in the hands of the commissioners within a matter of days of the Cornwallis Headquarters's dedication.

> Through various real estate corporations I am now the owner of certain parcels of real estate along the top of the Palisades on the west side of the Hudson River, commencing at a point about 2,500 feet south of the George Washington Bridge and extending north to the New York-New Jersey State Line, a distance of approximately 13 miles. My primary purpose in acquiring this property was to preserve the land lying along the top of the Palisades from any use inconsistent with your ownership and protection of the Palisades themselves. It has also been my hope that a strip of this land of adequate width might ultimately be developed as a parkway, along the general lines recommended by the Regional Plan Association, Inc.

Describing his understanding of the Commission's interest in obtaining funds for parkway construction, Rockefeller, Jr., used a few simple words to affirm his enormous charitable intention:

> I am therefore now offering to give or cause to be given to you the titles to all of these parcels of property which I have thus acquired. . . . The gifts of land to be made hereunder are to be made to your Commission from time to time

for parkway purposes under appropriate conveyances as the various parcels are required by your Commission for construction of the parkway. This offer is conditioned upon your being able to obtain within a reasonable time sufficient funds to commence the construction of the proposed parkway and thereafter to continue and complete its construction. It is my understanding that the purpose will be eventually to continue the proposed parkway to the north across the State line into the State of New York and up to the Bear Mountain section of the Palisades Interstate Park. In this connection, it would be my hope that it might ultimately be possible, if the lands hereby offered to your Commission are accepted, for a treaty to be arranged between the States of New York and New Jersey for a joint commission, with appropriate powers for policing and maintenance, which would insure for all time a continuity and permanence of interstate administration for both the proposed parkway and the park areas adjacent and connected to it.

Headlines in *The New York Times* trumpeted the proposed gift. With acceptance of the offer by the PIPC a foregone conclusion, White referred to the "princely offer" and confirmed the obvious, that the suggestion of a "treaty has my hearty approval. In my opinion, the matter should receive prompt and favorable consideration of the Legislatures of the two States and the Congress of the United States." Credited with influencing the Rockefeller, Jr., decision were President and Mrs. Roosevelt; Thomas Adams, who directed the Regional Plan survey; Cleveland Dodge, Jr.; Cass Gilbert; Paul U. Kellogg, editor of *The Survey*; Thomas W. Lamont; George McAneny; the late Dwight Morrow; and many others. Walter Kidde, who had provided a report on the Palisades to the New Jersey State Chamber of Commerce two years previously, was credited with convincing Rockefeller, Jr., to begin his land purchases. Anticipating public curiosity about exactly what a parkway was, one of the *Times*'s articles explained,

> A parkway, in fact and by legal definition, differs widely from a highway or boulevard. Specifically, it is distinctive in that the right of access to it of the owners of adjacent land is restricted. This means that its park-like character can be maintained, that crossroads may be admitted only at intervals which fit into the general plan, and that disfiguring structures cannot be erected along the borders of the right of way.

Confidence by White and the PIPC commissioners that they could readily find in federal public-works monies the estimated $3.5 million needed to guarantee construction of the twelve-mile New Jersey section of the Palisades Parkway was soon dashed. Despite support, even from President Roosevelt, White encountered frustration after frustration in his attempt to convince authorities in Washington that funds were needed from the Public Works Section of the National Recovery Administration to help the commissioners keep their end of the bargain with Rockefeller, Jr. White's frustration was matched by that of Rockefeller, Jr., who at one point referred to the "slow moving" commissioners in a letter to a member of his staff. After months of effort, but no results, Rockefeller, Jr., decided to remove the original gift conditions and give the land to the PIPC anyway. In June, 1935, *The New York Times* confirmed the decision by reminding readers that the commissioners were to "obtain additional land and to construct a parkway from the bridge to the State line. Funds for this have not been obtained. No such stipulation is contained in the present gift, although the parkway idea has not been abandoned." After the remaining legal details were resolved, the Rockefeller, Jr., deeds were transferred to the Commission in late November, 1935, including the Dana land, minus the old mansion that was torn down. The Dana property had come full circle. In the realm of giant steps, Rockefeller Jr., deliberately concealing his role until the success of his land-buying venture on the Palisades was assured, had added a vital chapter to the development of the PIPC's park and historic-site system. The threat of "gap-toothed" buildings parading along the crest of the Palisades was permanently averted.

George Gyra, a public-works employee from New York City, had things on his mind other than preservation of the Palisades. Wandering away from his fellow laborers during a lunch break in Harriman Park, "and quite by accident," as later reported, Gyra and one of his co-workers discovered a crevice on the slope of Letter Rock Mountain. "It was barely large enough to admit a man, but he crawled inside. He got in six or eight feet and it was all dark. He lit matches but they made hardly a splash in that great dome of darkness. He picked up stones, when he was able to stand erect, and pitched them as far as he could, trying to hit the opposite wall, but they didn't hit. Then he crawled out." Park rangers and police officers were perplexed when they started hearing what sounded like thunder in the park on clear days with not a cloud in sight. Investigation led to the arrest of four men from the city who were dynamiting the Letter Rock crevice in search of buried treasure. Gyra was not among the culprits, and he claimed no knowledge of how they found out about his discovery. Welch affirmed in the news coverage of the arrests that "the whole territory around Letter Rock is rich in legends of buried treasure. One tells of a lode called Spanish Silver Mine, on Black Mountain, a mile east of Letter Rock, where Spaniards who came up from the West Indies were supposed to have mined great fortunes in silver." Offering his usual pragmatic opinion, Welch reckoned, "Don't think there's a dime's worth there, myself."

President Roosevelt and the First Lady were back at Bear Mountain in early September, 1934, for a private inspection of the new road to the top of Bear Mountain. On October 31, 1934, Roosevelt officially dedicated the "George W. Perkins Memorial Highway," and he applauded Mrs. Linn Perkins for her generous gift of funds that allowed for WPA construction of a memorial tower made of large blocks of granite on the mountain's summit. The sixty-five–foot tower, designed to serve the practical needs of meteorological, aircraft, and forest-fire surveillance, offers a sweeping, 360-degree view of the surrounding landscape, including the ridge lines of Sterling Forest to the west, an area of expansive woodlands and historic iron mines and furnaces just across the Ramapo River from Harriman Park that occasionally prompted entreaties to the Commission for its preservation. In one exchange of correspondence, Welch affirmed that the Sterling Iron and Railway Company, a Harriman enterprise, owned Sterling Forest, but he gave no encouragement that the land would come into the ownership of the PIPC.

President Franklin Delano Roosevelt and Eleanor Roosevelt. William A. Welch is standing, hatless, near car door. Bear Mountain, New York, 1934. *(Courtesy of FDR Library Archives)*

Perkins Memorial Tower, summit of Bear Mountain.
(Courtesy of PIPC Archives)

The persistent Depression maintained a grip on the PIPC. Sutro had long since issued instructions that no checks would be accepted as payment for the PIPC's services and programs; only "scrip" or cash would do. The PIPC issued checks to its employees but would not cash them. The Dyckman Street Ferry, so important for access by city-dwellers to the Palisades, struggled to reopen in 1935. Use of the ferry by the thousands who annually enjoyed the picnic grounds, beaches, and hiking trails under the Palisades was in jeopardy. Low-income people, especially, might lose the only access they had to the PIPC's parks. The commissioners appealed to Mayor Fiorello La Guardia for help in developing a revised city contract, minus a $25,000 security deposit, so that the financially threatened ferry operators could continue to offer low-cost services at the Dyckman Street landing. La Guardia agreed, and ferry service was reestablished in May. Despite the Depression, or because of it, group outings to Bear Mountain via the river day-liners or buses by more affluent visitors continued to hold firm. More than one hundred groups reached Bear Mountain during one July-to-September period. Among the groups were the Metropolitan Leather and Finding Club, the Yan Ye Recreation Association, the G. H. P. Cigar Company, the Mother A. M. E. Zion Church, the Sons of Italy, the Swanky Yacht Club, the Lu Lu Temple Patrol Party, the Go-As-You-Please Bowling Club, the New York Stock Exchange Glee Club, the Lithuanian Pleasure Club, the Hartford Steam Boiler Inspection Company, and the Downtown Athletic Club.

Not all groups were encouraged to voyage to Bear Mountain. Writing to Dan F. McAllister, Sutro confirmed:

> All are agreed that they prefer to have especially colored parties go to the North Dock at Hook Mountain rather than to Bear Mountain or the South Dock at Hook Mountain . . . to relieve embarrassment . . . of having colored parties mixed with . . . daily visitors from your regular boat . . . [which] also relieves difficulties experienced at Bear Mountain from having large groups of colored people mingle with the regular visitors there.

Sutro was reflecting the typical racist attitudes of the time, even though the Commission routinely fought off demands that African Americans be excluded entirely from the parks. Segregation of African Americans to avoid "embarrassment" of "regular visitors" obviously was wrong in a nation built on a belief in equality for all of its citizens, and it seems especially ludicrous given the behavior of "regular visitors." Reporting on a corporate picnic at Bear Mountain, J. J. Tamsen, superintendent of operations in the New York parks, declared:

> The outing arrived yesterday . . . [They] drank 38 barrels of beer in all . . . the beer was distributed in pitchers, gallon mayonnaise jars, paper containers, and glasses. These were left strewn over the Park. The drunks lay around on the playground, men staggered, women were falling down, girls and fellows mushing it up. . . . Ladies as well as men did not use the comfort stations. . . . A great number of people got sick. . . . Took until 9:00 P.M. to clean up.

No such report came from the North Dock area at Hook Mountain to which African Americans had been limited.

Fortunately for the Commission, most people of all ethnic backgrounds were well behaved. Good behavior was an absolute necessity in the mid-1930s in a park system attracting 14 million annual visitors representing one-ninth of the nation's population—more visitors than all the national parks combined. "We are engaged in the precarious work of attempting to please the public . . . ," Welch observed.

Dayliners, Hook Mountain dock, New York.
(Courtesy of PIPC Archives)

Commissioner Victor H. Berman, a 1935 New Jersey appointee to the PIPC and president of Onyx Oil, saw an opportunity to connect with the public by donating a fifteen-foot-tall Tiffany-sculpted bronze elk head to the PIPC. Berman felt that this spectacular piece of art was emblematic of the wild animals and native plants that the PIPC sought to preserve. The sculpture, unveiled at a ceremony by Berman's daughters, Joan and Audrey, was affixed to a rock ledge at the Trailside Museum overlooking the boat docks. There it remains, silently graceful, now hidden from view by vegetation and almost forgotten. Not so a statue of Walt Whitman, donated by Averell Harriman in memory of his father and mother; it stands prominently at an intersection of footpaths on the museum's grounds, constantly greeting strollers and Appalachian Trail hikers with words from Whitman's poem "The Long Brown Path" chiseled into the statue's rock base.

The Depression slowed but did not stop the Commission's acquisition of land. One particularly important acquisition won Torrey-inspired headlines: "Storm King Mountain Now Preserved in Interstate Park." With the addition of a 203-acre purchase, Torrey reported that 900 acres of Storm King, guardian of the northern entrance to the Hudson River narrows, was in the Commission's hands "and now stands in the way forever of any industrial development on the river front of the mountain which might mar its grandeur." Torrey's words were prophetic: Storm King was destined to become an industrial-development bat- tleground of enormous importance that would tear at the very core of the PIPC and realign the national environmental agenda.

But a much more urgent battle was looming in 1936. Under the headline "Joint Board Urged On Palisades Park," New Jersey Governor Harold G. Hoffman con- firmed his request of the Legislature to approve an "interstate compact" for the Commission. On the New York side, the Solicitor General and Governor Her- bert Lehman's counsel recommended approval of the compact, leading to intro- duction of legislation that would authorize Commissioners White, Harriman, George Perkins, Jr., and Frederick Osborn, or any three members of this group, to negotiate the final details with New Jersey representatives. Prominently absent from the list of negotiators was the fifth PIPC commissioner, Smith, who, reflect- ing the influence of Moses, was opposed to the compact. Moses's opposition and persuasive strength were made clear in a ten-to-one vote against the proposed compact by the State Council of Parks. Moses charged that the compact "would lift the PIPC out of State control and supervision, and would interfere with a uni- fied state park policy." Despite Moses's position, the New York Senate voted to approve the interstate compact by a twenty-eight-to-twenty-two margin, prompt- ing Moses to complain that New York's action, in concert with New Jersey's, would "take control of the PIP from the State Council of Parks," thus contra- dicting his oft-stated position that the State Council was an advisory body made up of representatives of the various park commissions, including the PIPC.

These first exchanges of political fire were muffled and out of the limelight. The noise level dramatically increased when, to the surprise of the PIPC's allies, the New York Assembly rejected the Senate's action. "Mr. Moses, in his own slimy way, is determined to defeat these bills but he doesn't come out honestly and openly against them," said Assemblyman Mailler, a sponsor of the legisla- tion. "Instead, Mr. Moses sends his representatives to the Capitol to urge their defeat." Responding, Assemblyman Moffat said, "No man has done more for the people of the State through park development than Bob Moses and it ill becomes a member of this House to refer to him as slimy." Looking for a compromise, the Assembly and Senate created a joint committee to further investigate the compact idea.

Moses continued to seek ammunition against the compact. Using State Coun- cil of Parks stationery that ironically listed White on the letterhead, Moses con- tacted Downer, formerly the executive director of the Westchester County Park Commission, now on the Rockefeller staff, to inquire about Rockefeller's position on the matter. "The PIP has been agitating for some time for acts of the legislatures of New York and New Jersey, ratified by the Congress, creating the PIPC . . . by treaty and lifting it out of the two states." Downer responded that Rockefeller, Jr., indeed had expressed support for the initiative but that no financial pledges or commitments were in any manner awaiting formal approval of an interstate compact.

In November, 1936, PIPC Commissioners White, Perkins, Jr., and Baker traveled to Albany to testify before the joint legislative committee. White, founder of the prestigious New York City law firm of White & Case, was serving in his thirty-sixth year of volunteer work for the PIPC, and he presented a lengthy, eloquent, and well-reasoned statement about the PIPC's purposes and accomplishments, and the benefits of formalizing a structure that had existed on a handshake for so many years. He spoke of the private donations that had been won over the life of the PIPC, amounting to almost $18 million. Stressing the advantages and efficiency of interstate cooperation, White carefully explained the details of the proposed compact, constructed to guard state control and hold the PIPC accountable to the states. He reminded the legislators that the PIPC was legally required to remain a member of the State Council of Parks and would meet a similar requirement in New Jersey, should that state form a similar state council.

Moses, accompanied by PIPC Commissioner Smith, took his turn. If the compact is approved, Moses argued, the PIPC would not be subject to state supervision. The compact would destroy the park system in the State of New York. If the PIPC became self-perpetuating behind the compact shield, eventually it "would die of dry rot," Moses said, perhaps alluding to the elderly White. Smith, who rarely attended PIPC meetings, introduced himself as a PIPC commissioner and made the remarkable statement that "as soon as one park sees another getting away from the State Council of Parks, all will be looking for some way to get out." This was not exactly a ringing endorsement of State Council's leadership. White, responding, said that some of Moses's testimony was not based on fact, propelling Moses to leap to his feet to accuse White of calling him a "liar." Mark M. Jones, who had conducted the 1925 survey of PIPC activities for the Laura Spelman Rockefeller Memorial Foundation and who subsequently recommended an interstate compact, testified that the "PIP investment hangs by a thread; in effect, the Park has a corporate existence that extends but from one year to the next."

Following the hearing, Commissioner Smith, discarding his opposition to the compact in favor of working out a compromise, met with White and the other commissioners to work on modified language. The principal change involved the manner by which the PIPC would report its financial activities to the two states and account for state appropriations. With these changes, White wrote to Thomas M. Debevoise, senior member of the Rockefeller, Jr., staff, affirming that

> the compact provides that all such land and property shall hereafter be owned by the new Commission and continue under its jurisdiction and be used only for public park purposes, and that none of said lands or any part thereof shall be sold, exchanged, or conveyed except with the consent of both States by specific enactments. The mutual pledge of the States to hold in high trust for the benefit of the public the blessings and advantages of the Park . . . would imply a pledge to the various benefactors, of whom there are many and some of whom are not living, of good faith for the future.

Rockefeller, Jr., wrote back to White, referring to a "notable step" and saying that the compact would provide "assurance of permanency of the Park."

The revised compact was approved by New York on April 5, 1937, by New Jersey on June 2, 1937, and by the U.S. Congress on August 19, 1937. The cross-border handshake that had lasted for almost four decades was replaced by the solid legal foundation of an interstate agency.

All New York and New Jersey commissioners, including Smith, were appointed to the new Palisades Interstate Park Commission. White was elected president.

14.
The Palisades Parkway

The advent of World War II understandably brought great changes to the PIPC. The public-works programs gave way to the nation's call to arms in response to Pearl Harbor. Commissioners and PIPC staff alike joined or were recruited into the Army, Navy, Coast Guard, Merchant Marine, and civilian war industry. Gas rationing made travel difficult. For the duration, the *Clermont* was taken down-river to be used as a floating cafeteria at the Brooklyn Navy Yard. The PIPC's staff, unable to provide continuing care for the forty-two elk that traced their roots to the Yellowstone herd, was directed by the commissioners either to find homes for the animals in zoos or arrange for their slaughter. Fortunately, a farmer from upstate New York decided to provide a retirement home for the herd.

Wartime travel restrictions reduced general visitation to the parks, but a fascinating new clientele arrived at Bear Mountain Inn specifically due to the travel constraints. In 1941 the commissioners decided, through contract, to place the inn under the management of a concessionaire, changing for the first time the long-standing policy of George Perkins, Sr., and William Welch to keep the inn directly in the hands of the PIPC. The new concessionaire was Jack Martin, described as a "big amiable bear of a man; a human dynamic firework." Martin was a dedicated sports fan. Seeing the need for a place not too far from New York City where travel-restricted professional sports teams could stay and practice, Martin became host to the Brooklyn Dodgers baseball team, and the New York Giants, Green Bay Packers, and Cleveland Rams (later the Browns) football teams. He made certain, too, that accommodations were available for amateur teams. The Notre Dame and Cornell football teams stayed at the inn when they came to play the Army team at West Point. Martin was also a regular host to the Eastern Golden Gloves Boxing Team. Bear Mountain became a thriving sports training camp buzzing with activity and winning the informal stamp "happy gymnasium." Jack Dempsey was a Martin guest while recovering from a serious illness. On the great lawn adjacent to the inn, Jackie Robinson took batting practice under the appreciative eye of Branch Rickey, aiming his hits at the spires of the Bear Mountain Bridge. Robinson was given his own table in the inn's dining room, where he ate alone. Notre Dame coach Frank Leahy was a frequent guest, as was Steve Owen, coach of the New York Giants.

During one season, after the Giants had checked in for three days, Martin strolled up to Owen and asked, "Know that fellow sitting at the next table there?"

Owen responded, "No, but then you don't expect me to know all my rookie players by name yet, do you. Give me a little time."

Martin, grinning, said, "Okay, Steve, I can give you all the time you want but it's costing the Giants money. That guy isn't even on the squad."

Athletes were not the only wartime visitors to the inn. In the midst of world conflict, with China at great risk, Madame Chiang Kai-shek, wife of the Chinese premier, arrived at the inn to convalesce for several weeks. There she felt safe, her privacy defended by Martin. On the wall just outside his office, Martin proudly displayed a thank-you letter from his most honored guest. Athletes and special guests intermingled with soldiers and sailors sent to the inn for rest, including a shell-shocked GI who walked up to the front desk and demanded a room, with bath. To make the point, the soldier aimed a loaded machine gun at the desk clerk. Martin helped the young man gain treatment at a veterans' hospital and later reported that the GI was "completely cured." Bands played, and food kept pace with the appetites of football and baseball players. Sports writers, among others, made sure the bar was kept open. One visitor, reminiscing years later, said, "The Bear Mountain Inn! What a place that used to be. All the big bands played there. Tommy Dorsey. Harry James. Oh, we used to dance! Kate Smith sat at a table at the Inn, composing her signature song, 'When The Moon Comes Over The Mountain.'"

Other changes came to the PIPC before and during World War II. Commissioner Averell Harriman was far away, serving as ambassador to Russia. By the time Col. George Perkins, Jr., and Lieut. Comdr. Laurance S. Rockefeller returned to civilian life from their wartime duties, White, Welch, Frederick Sutro, Raymond Torrey, and William Carr were gone. Commissioners Edmund

Wakelee, Al Smith, Charles Baker, William Childs, and Abram DeRonde were gone. So, too, was Torger Tokle, the dominant, almost legendary, prewar champion of the Bear Mountain ski jump. Tokle was killed in action while serving in Europe with the famous 10th Mountain Division.

During the war, President Franklin Delano Roosevelt once again visited the summit of Bear Mountain where, on cue, he was treated to numerous spirals of smoke rising on command above the vast forest canopy stretching all the way to the horizon. The smoke spirals were a salute to the polio crippled president from Ruby Jolliffe and the group-camp managers in Harriman Park. The president could no longer stride into the camps as he once did, so the smoke spirals reached for the sky to mark the locations of scores of camps, signaling a "thank you" from the camp managers to a national leader who had befriended and supported them almost from the beginning.

J. DuPratt White was not witness to the changes brought by the war. He attended his last Commission meeting in May, 1939, then, due to deteriorating health, resigned from the PIPC two days later, concluding almost four decades of volunteer service and leadership for the PIPC. He passed away on July 14, 1939, less than a year after the Interstate Compact received presidential approval. Commissioner and former New Jersey Senator Edmund W. Wakelee succeeded White as president. Wakelee, a key political sponsor of the original 1900 legislation that initiated the PIPC experiment, and an equally effective advocate for New Jersey's approval of the 1937 Compact, carried the PIPC through the war years until his death in 1945.

Constantly gaining power and influence, Robert Moses wrote to Rockefeller in August, 1939, urging him to accept an appointment to the PIPC to fill the vacancy left by White. Moses added,

> What this Commission needs is a complete reorganization of its administrative staff. The present Chief Engineer (Welch) should be pensioned or made the Consulting Engineer. He has a long and honorable record, and deserves a great deal of consideration, but his usefulness as active head of the organization is over. The other executive (Sutro) . . . never had the slightest fitness for his position, has rendered no service in it, and in my opinion is not entitled to any consideration whatever. He was a Commissioner and suffered some financial reverses, and [then] jockeyed himself into a paid job. A competent new executive could not possibly work with him.

Moses recommended that Kenneth Morgan, the former superintendent at Jones Beach on Long Island, a Massachusetts Institute of Technology graduate in general engineering and a Moses protégé, be hired as the general superintendent for the PIPC.

Rockefeller accepted an appointment to the PIPC within a matter of days after receiving Moses's letter. He would prove to be an exceedingly worthy successor to White, ironically serving for thirty-nine years, the same length of tenure as White. Rockefeller probably appreciated Moses's encouragement, but his real motivation was a deep and growing personal commitment to conservation, combined with recognition of the compelling interest his father held in preserving the Palisades.

Nonetheless, the caustic message Moses sent to Rockefeller about Welch and Sutro had its intended impact. In November, 1939, Perkins, Jr., wrote to Morgan on behalf of the PIPC, confirming that Morgan would join the staff on February 1, 1940, with the titles of chief engineer and general manager. "At the same time, Major Welch will retire as Chief Engineer and General Manager and will take the position of consultant to the Commission. Mr. Sutro will retire as Executive Director and Assistant Treasurer and will probably retain a nominal title of Assistant Secretary. His duties, however, will be only those directed by you," Perkins advised. Morgan was offered a salary substantially higher than that received by Welch. The PIPC staff was alerted in a brief memorandum that stated, "It is with regret that the Commission announces that Major Welch and Mr. Sutro have both asked to be relieved of the major part of their responsibilities . . . they will both be available to Mr. Morgan to assist him whenever he requests such assistance."

Welch, who had suffered bouts of ill health for several years, was politely but firmly pushed out of his job. There is no record that Morgan subsequently consulted with him. Welch died on May 4, 1941.

Sutro, not so politely removed, went on to other work, serving for twenty more years as president of the New Jersey Parks and Recreation Association, until age eighty-five. Sutro was consulted once by Morgan, who asked him to write a memorial statement in honor of Welch. Sutro wrote,

Drawing upon long training and wide experience in many fields, he wrought a miracle of transformation. By his magic touch, forests grew in waste spaces, lovely sheets of water appeared in valleys long since gone dry, roads and trails threaded the woodlands, the deer, the beaver and the elk returned to their ancient haunts in the Highlands, and camps on the banks of lakes echoed the laughter of innumerable children. He loved Nature and used her treasures to make humanity happier.

In the PIPC's minutes memorializing Welch, Sutro's words were not used.

Torrey, the ever-alert publicist for the PIPC and champion of the trails, is commemorated on Long Mountain in Harriman Park where his ashes were scattered in 1938. Carr, director of the Trailside Museum, was also dealing with health and marital problems. He left Bear Mountain in 1945 for an extended rest in a warmer climate. Hoping eventually to return to the PIPC, and encouraged to do so by Morgan, events took Carr in a different direction. Always the educator, Carr settled in Tucson, Arizona, to become one of the founders of the Arizona-Sonora Desert Museum, patterned after the Trailside Museum. Today, the Arizona-Sonora Desert Museum is host to thousands of visitors annually and enjoys international stature as a superb outdoor educational facility, reminding all who visit of the intricacies, beauty, and fragility of the desert environment.

Just after the war, Jolliffe made certain that many of her campers were present when the lake at the old Sandyfields settlement was dedicated to Welch. After almost thirty years on the PIPC's staff, and even more years actively engaged in group-camp programs, Jolliffe submitted her resignation in January, 1948, leaving behind standards of expectation and excellence that had so positively influenced the lives of thousands of girls and boys.

Even during the war years, the PIPC continued to acquire land. Perkins, Rockefeller, and Harriman combined financial resources to cause the purchase of a Standard Oil of New York property that greatly expanded Tallman Mountain Park. The craters left behind when oil storage tanks next to a highway were removed eventually filled with rain and snow water to provide a home for hundreds of frogs, turtles, and aquatic plants.

To the north, the threatened development of High Tor, a high ridge line of diabase rock in Rockland County, New York, prompted local residents to join the PIPC in a mutual effort to protect the jeopardized property. Maxwell Anderson, the playwright, had written the much acclaimed *High Tor* while living at the base of the ridge. Artist Henry Varnum Poor painted *Gray Dawn,* a scene of High Tor that hangs in the Metropolitan Museum of Art. The poet Amy Murray wrote "Looking East At Sunrise," her ode to the ridge. High Tor was known historically as well as scenically. From its summit, beacon fires provided warning of advancing British ships and troops during the Revolutionary War. The historic beacon site and surrounding land had been safe in the hands of owner Elmer Van Orden, who, more than once, had refused to sell to speculators or quarry operators. When the land and farmhouse passed to Van Orden's estate in 1942, his heirs promptly listed the property for sale for $12,000. This turn of events sparked a grassroots effort within the Rockland County Conservation Association, the

New York–New Jersey Trail Conference, and the Hudson River Conservation Society to attempt to purchase the twenty-three–acre property for $12,000 and donate it to the PIPC. In a classic example of galvanized community action, pennies, dollars, and more dollars were successfully collected to buy the Van Orden property and transfer title to the PIPC.

The Van Orden fund-raising quest led Mrs. Leonard Morgan of the Rockland County Conservation Association to visit Archer M. Huntington, a wealthy art collector living in Boston. Morgan asked Huntington for a $1,000 donation for the High Tor initiative. After briefly considering the request, Huntington agreed to the donation, but on condition that the PIPC would also accept donation of his 474-acre property, including a seventy-two–room English Tudor–style mansion on the High Tor ridge line next to the Van Orden property. The mansion had been built by Samuel Katz, son-in-law of Adolph Zukor, and included formal gardens, a swimming pool, and a pipe organ. Zukor, Katz, and Huntington had won wealth and fame in the world of entertainment and show business. The mansion at High Tor was rumored to have been built by Katz for his girlfriend. Whatever the genesis of the mansion, Huntington obviously no longer had use for it. Morgan still holds the honor of having made the most amazing fund-raising visit in the history of the Rockland County Conservation Association.

The end of the war brought renewed interest in construction of the Palisades Parkway. New commissioners were appointed, including attorney Albert R. Jube, personal counsel to Governor Charles Edison of New Jersey and a graduate of Amherst College and New York Law School. Joining Jube and the other commissioners was Horace M. Albright, former superintendent of Yellowstone National Park, director of the National Park Service, and vice president of the United States Potash Company, producer of Twenty-Mule-Team Borax. Rockefeller recommended Albright, who won quick and enthusiastic approval from Rockefeller, Jr., and New York Governor Thomas E. Dewey.

The commissioners were keenly aware of Rockefeller, Jr.'s, gift of land on the crest of the Palisades and viewed the parkway project as their highest priority. They were optimistic that the parkway, put on hold during the war, would be reactivated without difficulty. The commissioners had not reckoned with Thomas Lamont and his son, Corliss. In a letter to Perkins, Jr., Moses said:

> I was somewhat disturbed about our talk yesterday regarding the Palisades Parkway because, as you know, I have gone way out in front of this project, especially as it affects the program in New York. . . . If all this flurry about Tom Lamont amounts to nothing more than opposition on his part, that of Mrs. Lamont, and that of their son, Corliss, based upon their desire to have no traf-

fic and no travelers near their estate, it is of no importance. . . . If, on the other hand, you and Laurance are seriously thinking of deferring to Tom Lamont on the entire Parkway issue, and are prepared to discuss with him whether a parkway is needed or not on the top of the Palisades, then I think it is time to take the matter seriously, and for those of us who after all have taken great responsibilities as to this project, to reconsider the whole matter. There is nothing easier than to take a project or a group of related projects from a position at the head of the list and drop them down to a point where they won't be reached for years. . . . The day has passed when the owner of a big estate can block an important public improvement by wire-pulling, influence and similar shenanigans—that is, unless the public officials who are immediately responsible are impressed with this sort of thing. This is the problem which the members of the Palisades Interstate Park Commission will have to face if they regard Mr. Lamont's opposition as serious. . . .

Perkins, Jr., shot back:

If I were in the habit of getting mad about letters, I probably would about this one, because of the implications in it concerning Laurance Rockefeller and me are anything but complimentary. You ought to know both of us by this time better than that. Of course, we have no intention of deferring to anybody on the Parkway matter on a personal or any other basis. My interest in seeing the Parkway built is of long standing, and I suspect I was interested in it long before you were. Just because we don't agree a hundred percent with you on the way of handling the situation doesn't mean that we are weakening. My own personal policy is to avoid raising opposition whenever possible without compromising the issue. When opposition can't be avoided, then it is time enough to roll up your sleeves.

Perkins, Jr., was indeed ready to guide the PIPC through controversy, preferably by winning consensus, but with sleeves rolled up if necessary. At the June, 1945, meeting of the commissioners, Perkins, Jr., was elected president, succeeding Wakelee. His fellow officers were Jube, vice president; Rockefeller, secretary; and Victor H. Berman, treasurer. Events affecting or threatening the PIPC would require more and more of Perkins's time, to the point where he would step away from his senior management responsibilities at Merck & Company to devote himself to the PIPC's needs, just as his father had stepped away from Morgan & Company for the same reason.

The first test for the new president was fast in arriving. Opposition to the parkway from Thomas Lamont was known, but it was Lamont's son, Corliss, who fired a journalistic shot across the PIPC's bow. A month after Perkins, Jr., assumed policy leadership for the commissioners, a lengthy article written by Corliss Lamont appeared in the prestigious magazine *Survey Graphic*. After describing in intricate detail the beauties and delights of the Palisades, Lamont pointed directly at the PIPC as the misguided proponent of constructing "a new concrete super-highway, running along almost the entire thirteen miles of the Palisades. They would cut down a wide swath of woodland, slaughtering right and left the natural growth of trees, shrubbery and flowers. This would sacrifice much of the wildness of the area; and bring the sights and sounds—not to mention the fumes—of speeding automobile traffic close to the edge of the precipice." Lamont advocated that a state highway route that paralleled the Palisades slightly west of the proposed parkway alignment be widened to accommodate motorists wishing to drive north toward Bear Mountain. He recommended turn-outs and parking facilities along the state route to allow for easy access by hikers and bicyclists who wanted to enjoy the natural beauties of the Palisades. Lamont gave no credence to the difference between a parkway and a "super highway," or to the fact that the Parkway would be restricted to passenger cars only, whereas the parallel state route was already choked with truck traffic. He found eager political allies in the person of Dr. J. C. Burnett, owner of a sixty-seven–acre estate on the Palisades near the Lamont property, and among elected officials in the New Jersey towns of Fort Lee, Englewood Cliffs, Teaneck, and Alpine. Burnett was motivated by a frightful vision that the parkway would run right through his front yard. The elected officials were worried about the loss of tax revenues due to the possible reduction in property values near a noisy parkway. Lamont, Burnett, and the elected officials offered stiff opposition to the PIPC.

Moses, writing to Morgan, was not impressed with Lamont: "He is a bad actor trained in the communistic tradition and is absolutely unscrupulous in the way he handles facts. The Palisades need no saving at the instance of a phony like Lamont who never did anything for anybody except verbally, and whose mother told me twice that our Parkway should not be built because it brought people and traffic into the region where Corliss did his thinking."

Rockefeller, Jr., who, like the commissioners, assumed that a decision to build the parkway had been made before World War II and had simply been delayed, not scrapped, entered the public debate by stating to news reporters, "All my life, I have known, loved and frequented the Palisades." He reminded the press of the $21 million donation in land he had made to the PIPC to remove the threat of development, contending that construction of a carefully designed parkway, set back from the cliffs, would help ensure the permanent protection of the Palisades, not destroy them. By personal invitation, New Jersey Governor Walter E.

Edge joined Rockefeller, Jr., in a tour of the Palisades. Writing to Morgan, Rockefeller, Jr., counseled, "I am sorry that Dr. Burnett has developed into such an aggressive antagonist of the Parkway project. Perhaps it is best, however, that he has come out into the open and unburdened his mind of the hostile thoughts that have been festering there."

Perkins, Jr., appeared at various forums, including a raucous meeting attended by 350 residents of Englewood, New Jersey. He reminded his audiences that the parkway had first been proposed in 1926 and been endorsed by the New Jersey Legislature in 1933 and then by the New Jersey Highway Commission in 1935. New Jersey and New York had appropriated funds for planning in 1941. Engineering sketches of parkway landscaping, bridges, and overlooks were made available for public review. Commissioners Rockefeller and Albright joined Perkins, Jr., by describing the benefits of the George Washington Parkway, which provides a scenic drive between Washington, D.C., and Mt. Vernon; the Colonial Parkway, between Yorktown and Williamsburg, Virginia; and the Blue Ridge Parkway, constructed by the CCC to connect Shenandoah and Great Smoky Mountains National Parks. Rockefeller, Jr., and the commissioners were making headway, gathering support from many organizations and individual voters day by day, including the New Jersey Federation of Women's Clubs, but not enough to turn the political tide in Trenton. The Lamont-Burnett forces were severe in their criticism of the PIPC and had the support of several weekly newspapers, various town officials, and the ear of State Senator David Van Alstyne, Jr. Van Alstyne was the sole state senator from Bergen County, New Jersey, and he sat on the powerful Appropriations Committee. Governor Edge, mindful of the "acrimonious division of opinion" about the Parkway, advised Rockefeller, Jr., that "under these circumstances I cannot conscientiously recommend an appropriation for the Parkway at this time."

Donald G. Borg, owner of northeastern New Jersey's most influential daily newspaper, *The Bergen Evening Record*, was watching the debate unfold. His newspaper had published numerous articles about the parkway battle, focusing on the history, construction, and engineering details, as well as the effects of parkway development on neighboring communities. These articles were journalistically neutral, presenting factual information, but then, on August 8, 1946, Borg's newspaper published the tough editorial "Good Faith and Bad On Parkway."

Commenting on the tactics of the Lamont-Burnett group, the editorial stated,

Weapons commonly used by professional propagandists, persons who for money unhesitatingly further an unjust cause, are to hit and run, to distort a fact, to glamorize untruths, and to use pressure-group power in an attempt to further their own selfish interests. All of these devices and more are being used in the current campaign to convince Bergen County residents that construction of a parkway along the edge of the Palisades would be undesirable.

In a booklet being widely circulated by the parkway's opponents, a prominently displayed photograph was labeled, "This Area Closed To The Public By Order Of The Palisades Interstate Park Commission" as proof that the PIPC was heavy-handed in its treatment of visitors to the Palisades. The editorial confirmed that "the important fact is that this particular photograph was taken in New York State, not the New Jersey section of the Palisades Interstate Park. It was taken in an area owned by the Standard Oil Company, so naturally the public was excluded." The editorial writer pointed out that the commissioners, using private donations, were buying the Standard Oil property so that it could be "turned over" to the people for park purposes. "These are the same men who now by the deceptive photo are accused of trying to block natural development of the Park for public purposes." Using other examples of distorted information, the editorial concluded, "Persons who have been misled, misinformed, or self-deluded can and should rectify their error; their deceivers cannot and will not, but by that very fact are automatically discredited."

With Borg's editorial advocacy, the advantage swung to the PIPC. In April, 1947, *The Bergen Evening Record* reported that recently elected New Jersey Governor Alfred E. Driscoll had signed a bill approving the "much disputed" parkway route. With the approval came an appropriation to the PIPC of $500,000 from New Jersey to begin the project, sponsored by the same Senator Van Alstyne, Jr., who earlier had been sympathetic to the Lamont camp. With additional funds gathered from various other federal and state sources over the next several months, the commissioners accepted a bid of $834,000 for construction of the first 2.1 miles of the Palisades Interstate Parkway.

At about the same time, Josephine-the-snake returned to Bear Mountain. As chronicled in *The New York Times*, "A changed Josephine has returned here after an absence of ten years. When she made her first appearance for the campers at the Regional Museum, Twin Lakes, ten years ago, she fought her director. Today she put on a sedate show, earning her right to the title, 'the Sarah Barnhardt of the snakes.' For Josephine is a 6-foot-8-inch pilot black snake that has made reptilian history." When the museum staff had first captured Josephine, she was only three feet long but so "scrappy" that the snake was named after heavyweight boxing champion Joe Louis—before her sex was determined. Turned over to the American Museum of Natural History, Josephine went on tour, entertaining audiences as far away as Maine and, during the war, making the circuit of numerous convalescent centers for veterans. The seasoned performer "now is handled by the children who visit Bear Mountain. Not only do they pick her up and fondle her and have their pictures taken with her, but they go out into the fields and trap mice for her."

Josephine-the-snake would have approved of a cooperative agreement entered into between the PIPC and the newly formed Palisades Nature Association, a group of volunteers formed to begin managing the Greenbrook area of the Palisades in New Jersey as a wildlife preserve. The idea of preserving natural sanctuaries in a manner that would encourage humans to visit as guests, rather than as manipulators or predators of the wild plants, birds, and animals, was still in its infancy. Even in the national parks, very little was known of the dynamic relationship and interdependence among naturally occurring life-forms. Bears, vexed by a baseless reputation as dangerous miscreants, were often shot by park rangers for the slightest transgression, such as invading smelly garbage cans. Mountain lions, bobcats, foxes, coyotes, and wolves fared even worse. No transgression was necessary. They stood convicted of capital crimes even before they were born. Bullets, traps, and poisons were common tools for ridding the parks of predators. Rachel Carson's definitive book *Silent Spring* would not be published for another twenty years, and the word *environment* was not commonly in use in the 1940s. But in 1946, sensing the need for better environmental ethics, volunteers of the Palisades Nature Association persuaded the PIPC to draw a line around 165 acres at Greenbrook (a property once offered for sale by the commissioners) on the crest of the Palisades to create a restricted and tightly protected nature sanctuary. Membership would be required for access, conditioned on a willingness by the members to acknowledge that the sanctuary was created for the preservation of wild flora and fauna, not for the caprice of human visitors. Here, within the boundaries of the sanctuary, began a constant process of husbandry, scientific observation, and data collection that, along with similar long-term effort at the Trailside Museum at Bear Mountain, continues to produce a treasure-trove of baseline scientific data, knowledge of the natural world, and an increasingly sensitive understanding of the sweep and majesty of life on fragile planet Earth.

The second generation commissioner team, led by Perkins, Jr., Rockefeller, Harriman, and Jube, was quick to respond to opportunities to protect the natural environment by expanding the PIPC's holdings. They lacked the fabled ability of Perkins, Sr., to contact a few associates and friends and raise millions within a matter of days, but Perkins, Jr., Rockefeller, and Harriman were quick to reach for their personal checkbooks to maintain the momentum of building a park system. One such opportunity came to Rockefeller, who, on learning from A. K. Morgan of the availability of 640 acres on Dunderberg Mountain, just south of Bear Mountain, promptly donated $25,000 to the PIPC to cover the $40-per-acre purchase price. Unfortunately, some projects were considered just too large or remote to capture the individual or collective attention of the commissioners. Ridsdale Ellis, representing the New York–New Jersey Trail Conference, thought the commissioners might do well to look west past Harriman Park to the seventeen thousand–acre "Sterling Lake tract," which was still owned by the Harriman-family-controlled Sterling Iron & Railway Company. In a letter to Rockefeller, Jr., in October, 1951, Ellis and his Trail Conference colleagues, Louis A. Sigaud and Paul A. Reynolds, suggested that the Sterling Lake property could be purchased for $975,000. In a tactful response, Rockefeller, Jr., declined, explaining that his financial participation in the PIPC's activities was already very significant. Ellis's letter was passed on to the PIPC, but it elicited no further action.

Rockefeller, Jr's., already substantial financial stake in the PIPC was slated to increase even more in the face of the PIPC's struggle with vexing property matters in New Jersey that threatened to disrupt construction of the Palisades Parkway and wreak havoc with historic old Fort Lee, from which Gen. George Washington had learned of the capture of New York City by British forces in 1776 and began his legendary retreat to Morristown and Valley Forge. A developer wanted to build five apartment buildings, each fifteen stories high, on a fifteen-acre plot of land located just south of the George Washington Bridge at the site of the old fort. The Borough of Fort Lee had gained ownership of the land due to nonpayment of property taxes during the Great Depression. The mayor and borough council were eager to unload the land to a developer so that property-tax income would again begin to flow. The commissioners were alerted to the mood of the borough's elected officials in a letter from Ida W. Certo to Rockefeller, Jr.: "Forgive me for intruding on your convalescence. I am the only local citizen who dares to even suggest this land belongs to the people. Letters . . . received by officials . . . are greeted with hoots, catcalls, and wisecracks." The attitude of the Fort Lee mayor was that every possible dollar in property-tax revenue should be squeezed from the Fort Lee site, leaving only an undefined "small parcel for patriotic purposes," probably in the form of a plaque on a rock.

The "second battle" for Fort Lee would extend for more than four years, from 1951 to 1956, demanding the involvement of Governor Driscoll, the commissioners, *The Bergen Evening Record*'s Borg, and an increasing chorus of advocates for the preservation of the old fort. Rockefeller convinced his father to enter the fray after the PIPC was repeatedly rebuffed in bids for the property that reached $385,000. Rockefeller, Jr., through his Sealantic Corporation, proposed to purchase the property for $250,000, donate to the PIPC a crucial 7.7-acre parcel where the old fort had actually stood, and give the remainder to the Borough of Fort Lee for development with restricted building-height limitations to ensure that the roofs of any newly constructed buildings would remain below the tree line. The development strategy favored by the mayor shifted from fifteen-story apartments to ten-story office buildings to be built squarely on the old fortification, fifteen feet from the edge of the Palisades cliffs. A headline in the *Daily News* declared, "Cops To Guard Palisades Zone Hearing," and the paper further reported that the "bitterest fight in history" was taking place in the borough's council chambers. In the face of growing public outcry to save the fort, the mayor and council refused to budge. A strong majority of outraged borough residents made their feelings known in the November, 1955, election by voting the mayor and his political allies out of office.

Despite the election results, the issue dragged on for another six months. In the meantime, Sealantic upped its offer to $300,000, with the understanding that a six-acre parcel, the absolute minimum needed to preserve the historic site, would be donated to the PIPC. With height restrictions in place, this deal was approved by borough officials. Subsequently, they sold the borough's seven-acre parcel to the Washington, D.C.–based Marriott Hot Shoppes Corporation for the construction of a hotel and conference center. The height restrictions then became a point of extended and contentious combat between the PIPC and Marriott. The height restriction prevailed, however, and the hotel/conference center was never built. Historic preservation won the day, guaranteeing that the old fort would not be buried under concrete and parking lots, or tucked into the shadow of a multistoried hotel with a revolving restaurant on top.

The "second battle" of Fort Lee was taking place at almost the same time that another confrontation faced the commissioners in the persons of Dr. Burnett and his wife, Cora. "In barbed-wire isolation on the edge of the Palisades here lies the mystery-cloaked sanctuary of Dr. and Mrs. John Clawson Burnett," reported the *Newark Sunday News.* "Designed by the recluse couple a quarter century ago to shut out the world, the cliff-edge estate, fenced by metal mesh and opaque foliage and guarded around-the-clock by men and dogs, has successfully hidden the Burnetts from the general public since that time." The problem was that the Burnetts' fifty-four–acre estate stood squarely in the path of the Palisades Parkway. The Burnetts had chosen to be married on the property in 1920 and had developed it into their version of isolated perfection, just across the river from teeming New York City.

The property possessed "a variety of fairy-land-like buildings and acres of cliff top woodlands, a pear-shaped swimming pool and a reinforced concrete bomb shelter, carved by hand from the roof of the Palisades, which could accommodate almost all this [Alpine] borough's 644 residents," said William J. Kohm, the reporter fortunate enough to win agreement from the Burnetts to visit the property. Mrs. Burnett, "the former Cora Timken of the multimillionaire Timken roller-bearing family," was "in seclusion" when he arrived, but Dr. Burnett took Kohm on a limited tour, once certain rules were understood: "The doctor ruled that no photographs would be taken of him or his wife, and that no personal questions, or questions about the background of either, would be asked.

"The first . . . of many startling stops of the tour was the residence of the Burnetts. It is imposing not only because it contains all of Mrs. Burnett's personalized architectural touches, but also because it houses the principal pieces of the couple's fabulous collection of Oriental art," reported Kohm. The entire roof of the huge structure was made of copper, the exterior walls of terra-cotta tile. The house stood near the highest point of the Palisades, ten feet from the cliff's edge. Inside, in addition to a "magnificent Turkish prayer rug" and "a disorderly room crammed with art objects of all shapes and sizes," was a "complete hand-carved copy of an Indian temple." The amazed Kohm continued: "A life-sized Egyptian pharaoh stands wide-eyed before a slit-eyed Buddha; two feminine figures from the Middle East relax disdainfully beside the Grecian Sister of Venus de Milo; a Gauguin shouts its colors at the carved silence of an Indian musician. A place of honor is reserved for a plaster-of-paris head of Christ, a copy of an original in the Louvre in Paris. . . ." Though reporting that the Burnett collection was scattered through nine buildings on the property, Kohm was not allowed to see "many of the better pieces" in an off-limits house containing guest apartments. In a separate "dining building," the reporter saw one room "devoted solely to several floor-to-ceiling food lockers." The dining building included "an organ, one 12-foot statue and several figures of lesser size and a collection of Far Eastern dinner gongs." Nearby was the "service building" containing enough tools, machines, supplies, and equipment to "launch a small factory," including the estate's independent water and power systems. This building was in contrast to a softly elegant "Japanese tea-house," one of three studio buildings perched right on the edge of the cliff, where Mrs. Burnett did her artwork.

Now the sequestered world of the Burnetts was facing invasion by the Palisades Parkway. Dr. Burnett, who earlier had joined Lamont in an attempt to stop the parkway project altogether, was largely on his own in defense of his property. Construction machinery was moving in his direction. He dug in and fought. Burnett hired lawyers, sued, proposed a series of compromises that would force

Bill Miller's Riviera, Palisades Cliffs, New Jersey.
(Courtesy of PIPC Archives)

alignment of the parkway farther to the west, away from the major portion of his property, and sought public sympathy for his plight. Against him stood the two states, a project estimated at $46 million, the PIPC, perceived public good, the concept of a beautiful linear parkway that would beckon motorists along a leisurely, forty-two–mile drive from the city to Bear Mountain, and the news media, generally favorable to the PIPC and skeptical of Burnett. Moses, the undisputed champion of parkways in New York, was making sure that aggressive steps were being taken to acquire land for the Palisades Parkway route along the thirty-mile stretch through New York to the New Jersey border. He wanted assurance that Burnett would not stand in the way. Almost every other parcel in New Jersey was already in the hands of the PIPC, with one other exception.

That was Bill Miller's Riviera, an elegant supper/nightclub of yellow stucco and blue trim built on the brink of the Palisades cliffs. From a revolving dance

Donald G. Borg, Palisades Interstate Park Commissioner, 1953–1973. *(Courtesy of* The Record *Archives)*

floor, dramatic views of a twinkling, nighttime cityscape prompted many of the Riviera's clientele to ardently refer to the place as "the most beautiful nightclub in the world." Sophie Tucker, Joe E. Lewis, Jimmy Durante, Danny Thomas, Milton Berle, Harry Richmond, Martha Raye, Harry Belafonte, Jane Froman, and the Ritz Brothers were among the many stars who performed at the Riviera. But the nightclub had to go. It blocked a needed parkway off-ramp that would connect to the George Washington Bridge. (The present-day toll booths for the GW Bridge at the southern end of the Palisades Parkway stand almost exactly on the site of the old Riviera.)

Turning again to Rockefeller, Jr., the commissioners won a pledge of $500,000 to pay one-half of the purchase price of the Riviera, with the understanding that New Jersey would pay the rest. A side agreement with state officials was that New Jersey would also condemn and purchase the Burnett property for transfer to the PIPC. Newspaper owner Borg, continuing to act as an advocate for the PIPC, negotiated the deal with Miller and Governor Driscoll. On the night that Borg met at the nightclub with Miller to confirm the transaction, he was accompanied by his ten-year-old son, Malcolm, who would one day become a PIPC commissioner. Durante, Belafonte, and Froman were performing at the Riviera that night. Governor Driscoll's staff was not enthusiastic about the Burnett part of the deal. Each time the PIPC thought it had gained airtight assurance that New Jersey would condemn the entire Burnett property, the Commissioner of Transportation and his engineers would retreat in the face of furious opposition from the Burnetts. A frustrated Commissioner Morgan advised Perkins, Jr., "I can see no good reason why we shouldn't ask the Governor to stop this foolishness, and once and for all condemn Burnett and do the job right." Commenting about a meeting with New Jersey highway engineers, Morgan said, "Kilpatrick intimated that the building of the Parkway would be stopped unless the arrangement was made to build . . . around Burnett. He also said that he had a very definite idea that the Highway Commissioner could build the Parkway where he wanted to and spend the money where he wanted to"—meaning, to hell with the PIPC.

Still faltering on condemnation of the Burnett property, but otherwise sympathetic to the PIPC's activities, Governor Driscoll appointed Borg to the PIPC in late 1953. The owner, editor, and publisher of *The Bergen Evening Record* brought with him a delightfully blunt and effective style of communication. Writing to Perkins, Jr., who was serving in Paris as the Permanent U.S. Representative to the North Atlantic Treaty Organization (NATO) while still retaining his office as president of the PIPC, Borg commented on yet another property matter, the ongoing saga of settling the Allison estate. Vague language in the Allison will suggested that this important property on the Palisades was to go to the PIPC, but the trustees of the estate were dragging the matter out, seemingly for their own financial benefit.

> The Allison thing is showing signs of life too. Arthur Vanderbilt [a retired Chief Justice for the State of New Jersey] called the trustees into his office last week, and told them in effect to explain themselves to me. I . . . expect an elaborate rationalization of the previous inaction. As you know, there are two postgraduate larcenists and an honest man, Paul Hudson. I intend to ask them merely what happened to the $700,000 shrinkage between the will probate and their last accounting, also what they intend to do after they have disposed of all the real estate except Allison Park. As I see it, there are three possibilities: sit on the existing park and exhaust the $2,400,000 corpus in fees and maintenance; buy some more park land, develop it, and go out of business sooner; or get honest and turn the damned thing over to us. I shan't bother you with blow-by-blow accounts, but I think the long-term prognosis is good, especially with Arthur on our side. If it's all right with you, I'll play it gently for about a month until I get this cast off [Borg had fallen and broken his hip]. As things are, I can't fight and I can't run.

Borg, a Phi Beta Kappa graduate of Yale, whose father had bought *The Bergen Evening Record* in 1924 with funds accumulated through highly successful Wall Street investments, became editor of the newspaper at age twenty-six, immediately setting a standard for independent reporting and a passion for truth that, in later years, included sometimes unflattering coverage of himself. He was swift with ideas and decisions, and of low tolerance for verbosity. Circulation of the newspaper rose from 20,000 to over 150,000 during his tenure, and it became the most important daily news source in northern New Jersey. Working as a reporter after graduating from Yale, Borg, with two colleagues, started carrying guns for protection as they uncovered an organized-crime scandal that resulted in the expulsion of a senator from the New Jersey State Legislature. In his characteristic style, Borg, replying to an invitation to be considered for the Newspaper Boys Hall of Fame, said, "I regret my disqualification . . . I have never carried newspapers, but for quite a while, this newspaper has carried me."

For the next twenty-two years, Borg would serve with the PIPC. Even before being appointed, he had made his mark: his influence and straight talk kept the New Jersey section of the Palisades Parkway project moving forward with no compromises. Nor did he back off on the matter of the Allison estate. Borg maintained constant dialogue with the New Jersey Attorney General, urging legal action to hold the estate trustees accountable, finally preventing the trustees from selling off seventy-six acres of the property for commercial development and, instead, forcing them to deal with the PIPC, even though the "one honest man," Hudson, had been discharged by the other two trustees.

North of historic Fort Lee, the Riviera, and the Allison estate, Dr. Burnett continued to defend his bastion through the remainder of the Driscoll administration, using every legal maneuver he could think of and constantly backtracking to earlier strategies designed to reroute the Palisades Parkway to the west, away from his property. Governor Robert B. Meyner, elected in November, 1954, countenanced no further delay in the court-ordered condemnation of the property. Under continuing pressure, Burnett admitted that he and his wife were thinking about moving to a four-mile-wide island they owned in a river in Montana where "we won't have to worry about highway construction." The move never took place. Continuing to resist, Burnett appealed a condemnation award of $1,245,321 for his cherished home and land. More months went by while the appeal moved through the courts. Cora Burnett would not live to witness the conclusion of her husband's final legal battle with New Jersey and the PIPC. She passed away in January, 1956. In May, 1957, a court ruling awarded Burnett $1,585,600. He vacated the property in June, almost twelve years after Perkins, Jr., and Morgan first contacted him seeking a willing-seller, willing-buyer transaction. On a visit to the now-deserted site, a *New York Times* reporter explored the strangely designed buildings that included flaring, "elephant feet" buttresses, a gaping hole in the wall of one building through which Burnett had removed a Hindu Temple, the large underground bomb shelter, and the security fence that surrounded the entire property.

Governor Meyner was firm on the Burnett matter, in part because he had been encouraged by New York's newly elected governor. Harriman succeeded Dewey to the governorship in 1954. Harriman had been serving with the PIPC for forty years, and he took his family's long-standing commitment to the PIPC with him to Albany. Governor Harriman resigned from the PIPC on January 1, 1955, the first day of his term, but wasted no time in appointing his brother, Roland, ten days later to fill the seat he had held with the PIPC.

For five years prior to Harriman's election, Morgan and the PIPC's staff had been consumed by the property obstacles in New Jersey and the constant need in both New Jersey and New York to continually reinforce the financial commitments to the parkway project. In one instance, Morgan wrote to Rockefeller, suggesting that they take Moses in tow and call on Governor Dewey at his Long Island estate to reaffirm Dewey's promise to support a pending $9.6 million appropriation for the parkway: "I favor going [to Dewey's residence] mainly for the psychological victory which it would give Governor Dewey to have Mr. Moses seek him out for a favor." This tactic failed, but the election of Harriman as governor provided a powerful guarantee that the parkway would be completed. Further delay, if any, would be caused only by the cumbersome mechanics of appropriating funds year by year and the time needed for construction. Moses was particularly attentive to the new governor's wishes. He kept the Palisades Parkway at the top of his list of State Council of Parks priorities.

Morgan and staff were breathing a sigh of relief about the parkway when two men from Connecticut appeared at Bear Mountain with Geiger counters. The men knew of federal laws, approved by Congress in the 1800s in support of mining activities in the West, that allowed prospectors to stake claims on practically any mineral deposits found on public land. The headline in the *New York Times* declared, "Bear Mountain Uranium Hunters Put Ski Jump Among Filed Claims." Not only was the ski jump claimed, so were 320 acres, including land under the PIPC's administration building and two-thirds of the great lawn between the administration building and the Bear Mountain Inn. The prospectors were particularly interested in the administration building, where they found the "hottest" reaction on their Geiger counters. Reminding the commissioners that uranium ore was urgently needed for nuclear weapons, not to mention the fact that the men would become wealthy if they could successfully mine uranium at Bear Mountain, the prospectors sought permission to proceed with test drilling. Writing to newly elected Governor Harriman, William Kean reported that "uranium readings at Bear Mountain are higher than anything heard of by the Atomic Energy Commission, even in the west." Attorneys in Albany scrambled to find a legally sound reason why the drilling request could be denied. The prospectors were refused because the PIPC, not the State of New York, owned the land.

The commissioners were presiding over the largest land holdings in the New York/New Jersey metropolitan region, prompting constant inquiries from agencies and individuals for various uses of the land. The Borough of Fort Lee in New Jersey wanted Miller's Riviera and eighteen acres for a grade school; the U.S. Army wanted eighty acres for a Nike Missile Base; Civil Defense and the local police wanted radio antennas on the summit of High Tor; various towns wanted land for fire stations, court buildings, and police barracks; one entrepreneur wanted land for an enclosure where hunters could shoot "wild" African game for a fee. The uranium prospectors joined a growing list of disappointed people who learned that the PIPC was steadfast in its resolve to protect natural values and history, not become the vendor of land for myriad nonpark community needs, however worthy they might seem.

Moses was keen on one project that, in his eyes, was exceedingly worthy. Taking a page from construction activities in his parks on Long Island, Moses began pressing hard in 1957 for the construction of "separate but equal" picnic areas, playgrounds, and swimming pools at Hook Mountain. Construction funds for facilities throughout the New York park system were filtered through Moses's State Council of Parks, so even the PIPC could not ignore his command of the purse strings. Moses wanted separate facilities at Hook Mountain especially to accommodate visitors from "Harlem and 125th Street," emphasizing that these "groups" should enjoy the same privileges as any other park "group," but in their own designated areas of the park system. As a rationale, Moses argued that access to Hook Mountain by ferry was best for lower-income people, even though the 1955 opening of another giant bridge, this one spanning the Hudson River's Tappan Zee, all but put the ferries out of business. The ferryboat operators were clinging to a rapidly declining clientele, looking at red ink, and beginning to suggest the need for subsidies from the PIPC just to stay in operation on reduced schedules. Moses seemed unconcerned. He started pushing construction funds into the State Council's budget for the Hook Mountain project. Morgan, writing to Perkins, Jr., alluded to other construction priorities of much more interest to the Commission and cautioned: "Shouldn't you also see Robert Moses before the Commission meeting? He may blow his top again if the Commission acts contrary to his ideas." Fortunately, the Civil Rights movement and budget constraints in New York overtook Moses's insistence for separate-but-equal treatment of visitors at Hook Mountain.

Rockefeller was interested in the Hook Mountain area for a different reason. Land at Rockland Lake, adjacent to the mountain, was for sale. The natural lake, with a privately owned lakeshore area, was already a popular recreation area for nearby residents. In the late nineteenth and early-twentieth centuries, Rockland Lake had been well known as a major source of ice for New York City. The clarity and depth of the lake water were ideal for ice harvesting, with Mother Nature as the principal production specialist. In winter, large blocks had been sawn from the frozen surface of the lake, maneuvered to shore by men wielding long poles, hauled out with giant ice tongs attached to the harnesses of horse teams, dragged uphill to the top of a long wooden chute, then slid by gravity to the river's edge. Daring laborers would occasionally leap on blocks of ice and joy-ride them down the chute. Insulated by sawdust, the ice would then be transported down the Hudson to supply the cold-storage lockers of hotels, clubs, and fine homes in New York City. Handled properly in insulated lockers, the ice would last for months.

In the spirit and tradition of the PIPC's philanthropy, Rockefeller took the lead among his fellow commissioners, seeking to acquire as much land as possible around Rockland Lake. From Albany, Governor Harriman was not particularly enthusiastic about the initiative, perhaps reflecting advice from Moses, but Rockefeller was determined to proceed. He did so using a strategy that had served Perkins, Sr., so well in the early days of the PIPC. With the goal of raising $750,000 in private funds, to be matched by New York, Rockefeller turned to Perkins, Jr., and Roland Harriman, winning pledges from each for $25,000 to complement his own pledge of $50,000. Using family contacts and proof of personal commitments, Rockefeller then succeeded in convincing trustees of the family-controlled Rockefeller Brothers Fund to contribute $400,000 and had the Jackson Hole Preserve, another Rockefeller charitable trust, add $250,000. With the $750,000 of private money in hand, Governor Harriman and the State Legislature found the opportunity to bring the total to $1.5 million irresistible. Acquisition of Rockland Lake State Park was under way. As success of the initiative grew, Rockefeller donated an additional $25,000 in personal funds. Perkins, Jr., provided another $33,333.33, and Roland Harriman $66,666.67. The Rockefeller Brothers Fund matched these personal donations with an additional $125,000,

Ice harvesting at Rockland Lake, 1800s.
(Courtesy of PIPC Archives)

Palisades Parkway dedication. *Back row:* George W. Perkins, Jr., New Jersey Governor Meyner, New York Governor Harriman, Laurance S. Rockefeller, Robert Moses. *Front row:* David Harriman Mortimer, Averell Harriman Fisk, 1958. *(Courtesy of PIPC Archives)*

bringing the grand total of all private donations to $1 million. Eventually, more than one thousand acres were acquired for the park. Rockland Lake State Park ranks among the most popular and heavily visited within the PIPC's park system and, sharing a common boundary with seven hundred–acre Hook Mountain, is almost island-like as a green, natural area surrounded by a sea of suburbs. Golfers on the Rockland Lake Championship Course have witnessed coyote pups lolling and playing on the edge of fairways, seemingly oblivious to nearby hacks, grunts, and explicatives as golf balls fly off in various unpredictable directions. Bird life is abundant. The whole of Rockland Lake and Hook Mountain is a triumph, offering a great variety in outdoor recreational opportunities, swimming pools for thousands of eager kids, and wilderness-like settings in more remote locations away from the developed areas. Without timely involvement by Rockefeller and the PIPC in 1958, Rockland Lake surely would have become a developer's dream and another piece of land buried by urban sprawl.

At about the time that fund-raising for Rockland Lake was in high gear, a *Newburgh News* headline announced, "Rockefellers, Harrimans Get Praise At Parkway Dedication." In August, 1958, Governor Harriman and a large, enthusiastic crowd celebrated the opening of the last five-mile link of the forty-two–mile Palisades Interstate Parkway. Moses "lauded the generosity of the two families," and Harriman's grandsons, Averell Harriman Fisk and David Harriman Mortimer, cut the ribbon. Only a traffic circle at one road junction remained to be completed, a task accomplished in 1959. The artful link between city and park, envisioned for decades, was in place. The parkway is a design success, living up to expectations that a major roadway could be constructed in a manner that rested gently on the land, presenting motorists with a green corridor looping along the contours of rolling terrain, passing under stone bridges of elegant style, meandering through a linear park of trees and flowers, avoiding the typical recipes for road building that too often result in dull troughs. The planners and designers of the Palisades Parkway could not have fully comprehended their success. By the late 1990s the parkway has become one of the most heavily traveled commuter routes in the New York/New Jersey Metropolitan Region. Even with this traffic volume, the parkway remains a limited-access route unavailable to trucks, buses, and commercial vehicles. Thousands of travelers still find their way along the parkway to Bear Mountain. Commuters, often frustrated by gridlock on the parkway, at least have trees to look at and are heard from vocally at the slightest hint that limited-access, passenger-vehicle-only standards might be lowered.

On the fine August day of the parkway's dedication, Governor Harriman was enjoying the moment. After the ribbon was cut, he hopped into a 1928 Model A Ford, loaded it with his grandsons and other small, lively kids, and proceeded to lead a motor procession toward the Bear Mountain Inn, where he and New Jersey Governor Meyner were scheduled to join other guests at a celebratory luncheon. An alert police officer, seeing the old Model A chugging along in front of the shiny official Cadillac assigned to the governor, assumed that some enterprising spectator had broken into the motorcade, and he pulled Harriman over. The problem of identity quickly resolved, Harriman proceeded to the inn and spoke to the invited guests at the luncheon, applauding the PIPC and singling out Rockefeller, Jr., for special praise. Once again, the PIPC was providing common ground for influential people of different political persuasions and ambitions. As he spoke at the luncheon, Democrat Harriman was fighting a vigorous campaign to retain the governorship and keep it from falling into the hands of a formida-

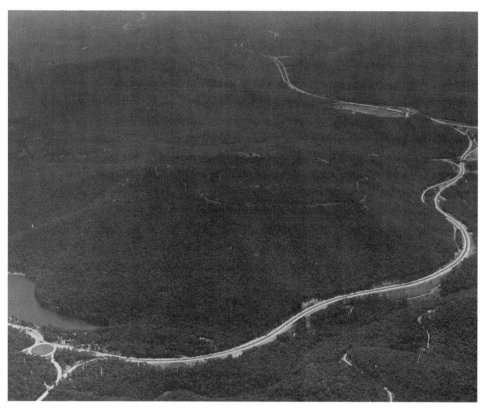

Palisades Parkway, vicinity of Bear Mountain, New York.
(Courtesy of PIPC Archives)

ble Republican opponent, Nelson Rockefeller, son of Rockefeller, Jr., and older brother of Laurance. Harriman did not succeed. Rockefeller won in a landslide in the November election. By March, 1959, Harriman had returned to the PIPC, succeeding his brother, Roland, who stepped aside so that the new Governor Rockefeller could appoint Harriman to his old commissioner's post.

Averell Harriman rejoined his Commission colleagues shortly before Morgan received a communiqué from Lt. Col. J. B. Meanor, Jr., Corps of Engineers, confirming a conversation in which Morgan had been alerted to interest by the U.S. Air Force in taking over Storm King Mountain "for a military project of a classified nature." Meanor reminded Morgan that "it is understood that you will advise the Commission of the Government requirement for the land and will avail it of the information furnished you during the discussion. Should the Commission desire additional information, attempts will be made to obtain the necessary security clearance to furnish the data it requires." Without providing any desired "additional information," Meanor pressed for and gained permission to begin making topographic surveys and subsurface test borings on Storm King Mountain. A representative of the Air Force Air Defense Command, based in Colorado Springs, met with the commissioners in June, 1959, to further explain the top secret project. Even at the meeting, the Air Force representative was vague, but in a follow-up discussion with Perkins, Jr., who, through his senior assignments with the State Department and as ambassador to NATO, had all the security clearances imaginable, the Air Force plans unfolded.

The Air Force wanted a fifty-year lease or outright ownership of six hundred acres on Storm King Mountain. Two huge tunnels were to be driven deep into the mountain. Under a rocky subterranean roof five hundred to six hundred feet thick, chambers would be hollowed out to accommodate equipment "vital to the Continental defense" of the United States. A complement of one thousand military and civilian personnel would be assigned to work around the clock, 365 days a year, within the depths of the mountain. The commissioners were assured that, except for the tunnels, the surface of the mountain would not be disturbed other than for "air vents, exhaust vents, cooling towers, and related structures made to resemble farm buildings." Prompted by the hard bomb-proof quality of the Storm King Mountain rock, and the logistical convenience provided by nearby Stewart Air Force Base at Newburgh, New York, the Air Force wanted to build a Semi-Automatic Ground Environment (SAGE) site inside the mountain. Once activated, the underground air-defense center would watch the skies, connected through a radar network to nine other SAGE installations across the nation, waiting for the first hint of a sneak attack by bombers from the Union of Soviet Socialist Republics. Should an attack be detected, SAGE would alert the Pentagon and White House through the Air Force's North American Air Defense System based in Colorado Springs. Using SAGE radar vectors, Bomarc II rockets would be launched against the incoming enemy aircraft.

The Air Force was anxious to proceed, citing the need for "early completion of this important defense facility." In 1959, the Soviet Union had already placed Sputnik into orbit. Fidel Castro was on the verge of overwhelming the dispirited forces of Cuban military dictator Fulgencio Batista. The temperature of the Cold War was dropping toward frigid. Nonetheless, the commissioners and nearby residents of the village of Cornwall-on-Hudson were not enthusiastic about this purported national security need. Some of the land wanted by the Air Force included village water-supply reservoirs on the slopes of adjacent White Horse Mountain, just west of Storm King Mountain. PIPC and village representatives asked for proof from the Air Force that other alternatives had been explored, including other mountain locations in the Hudson River Valley. The fact that local Congresswoman Katharine St. George sat as a member of the House Armed Services Committee helped ensure that the Air Force paid attention to provincial concerns. Morgan pointed out that most of the land sought for the SAGE site had been donated to the PIPC by the Stillman family with the condition that, if the land was ever used for "other than park purposes," title would automatically revert to the Stillmans. This might have presented a complication, but it posed no real barrier to the Air Force's plans. If necessary, the land needed, including the PIPC's land on Storm King Mountain, would be condemned and taken by the U.S. Department of Justice.

In fact, the Air Force was already busy studying other alternatives and fighting its own perpetual battle of the budget. In 1960, Congress cut funding for SAGE, based on the conclusion that Bomarc II missiles would be obsolete even before they were in position to be launched against incoming Soviet bombers. Soviet missiles, not bombers, had become the real threat. The Air Force's strategy shifted to other projects and locations, and Storm King and White Horse Mountains seemed secure once again. But an assault on the scenic and natural integrity of the mountains would soon come from an entirely different direction, this time shaking the PIPC to its environmental core.

Perkins, Jr., would not live to witness the second Storm King controversy. Even while engaged in high government assignments from the distances of Washington, D.C., and Paris, he had effectively retained the presidency of the Commission for fifteen years of his thirty-eight–year tenure with the PIPC, corresponding constantly with his commissioner colleagues and Morgan, attending meetings whenever in the United States, returning with undiminished enthusiasm to day-to-day involvement at the completion of his assignments, and constantly demonstrating an ability to envision, guide, and respond to the myriad details of the PIPC's projects based on intimate knowledge of the parks, historic sites, and their purposes. Between Perkins, Jr., and his father, a member of the family had been with the PIPC for fifty-eight of its sixty-year existence, when, in January, 1960, Perkins, Jr., passed away at age sixty-five. In delivering a eulogy at the Perkins Memorial Tower on the summit of Bear Mountain, Commissioner Rockefeller, after summarizing a public career that spanned responsibilities from Army private to NATO ambassador, always with the PIPC as centerpiece, closed by saying, "Those of us who knew George Perkins are also thankful for his simplicity and for his humility of spirit and his sense of service to his fellow man that marked him as a distinguished and outstanding American." An inestimable member of the Commission's second generation was gone.

15.
Storm King

Elizabeth Vermilye would have been proud. On March 21, 1960, almost sixty years after she was denied official involvement with the PIPC due to her gender, the first woman was appointed to the Commission. Linn Perkins, who married George W. Perkins, Jr., in 1921, was appointed by Governor Nelson Rockefeller to succeed her husband and, in so doing, to carry on the distinguished tradition of park and historic-site conservation that so typifies the Perkins family. Linn Perkins was the daughter of George and Friedrike Merck, thereby bringing to her marriage and personal interests the guarantee of access to a portion of the Merck Pharmaceutical fortune. Her fellow commissioners would soon learn that, like her husband and father-in-law, Linn Perkins would willingly open her formidable Perkins-Merck checkbook to provide financial support for the PIPC's objectives once convinced of the merits of specific needs and priorities. She often did so during her eleven-year tenure as a commissioner and for many years thereafter as a commissioner emerita. Averell Harriman, an advocate for her appointment, stressed in a letter to A. K. Morgan: "We are overdue in having a woman on the Commission. . . . We haven't been keeping up with the times." As so often seemed the case, Robert Moses had a different view. He agreed that a continuing Perkins presence on the PIPC was important, but in a letter to Governor Rockefeller, Moses urged appointment of the son of Perkins, Jr. The commissioners nonetheless recommended Linn Perkins to the governor, as confirmed in a letter from Laurance Rockefeller to his brother highlighting her memberships with the Hudson River Conservation Society, American Forestry Association, National Audubon Society, Save the Redwoods League, and the National Wildlife Federation. The governor did not hesitate; he acted promptly and with favor on the commissioners' recommendation.

Albert R. Jube, who had been appointed to the Commission in 1941 by New Jersey Governor Charles Edison, was elected to succeed Perkins, Jr., as president. In a little-noted move, Rockefeller, serving as the PIPC's vice president, also agreed to serve as vice chair of Moses's State Council of Parks (SCP). His move to the number two position with the SCP suggested that cracks were beginning to show in the relationship between Governor Rockefeller and Moses. Although Moses encouraged Rockefeller to accept the vice chair, he had reacted strongly to a report prepared for Governor Rockefeller by Dr. William J. Ronan, the governor's secretary. The report recommended consolidating and streamlining various departments and agencies within the structure of the state government, including the State Council of Parks. "The Ronan Report is a gratuitous public insult," Moses wrote to Governor Rockefeller. "I have no desire to interfere with your program and certainly do not propose after all these years to argue to remain in office if you have concluded that you can do better under other auspices." The governor did not accept Moses's veiled offer to resign, but the positioning of his brother as vice chair of the SCP hinted that as far as the governor was concerned, Moses, the all-powerful chair of various quasi-independent state authorities created by the Legislature—mostly at his urging and recommendation—and overseer of millions of dollars in contracts for the construction of bridges, roadways, and parks, was not indispensable.

In the realm of influence, Rockefeller was adding to his national reputation as a champion of natural-resources conservation by chairing President Eisenhower's Outdoor Recreation Resources Review Commission (ORRRC), referred to by insiders as "ork," which would result in major action by Congress to establish the Land & Water Conservation Fund (L&WCF) and create the Bureau of Outdoor Recreation within the Department of the Interior. The L&WCF was structured as a repository for funds flowing into the federal coffers from taxes levied on offshore oil production, fees collected for entry to national parks and wildlife refuges, and proceeds from the sale of surplus federal properties. Estimated inflow into the L&WCF was pegged at about $900 million per year, all to be reinvested in conservation projects throughout the nation. Part of the fund would be used to expand federal land holdings, with the rest shared on a matching basis with the states. Even though Congress often fails to appropriate the full amount of money flowing into the L&WCF, hundreds of thousands of acres of park, forest, and wildlife refuge land from Maine to Florida, from Virginia to Hawaii, and everywhere in between, have been protected over the intervening years, thanks to the visionary guidance provided by Rockefeller and his "ork" Commission. He took on the Rockefeller Family's mantle on the conservation front, honoring the interests of his father and grandfather that began with the Palisades and was now pushed outward to America's most distant horizons. Rockefeller brought these impressive credentials, plus his position with the PIPC, to Moses's turf, the State Council of Parks.

By 1960, when Perkins, Jr., like his father before him, was eulogized at the memorial tower atop Bear Mountain, the PIPC had truly come of age. The strong brother-to-brother relationship between Nelson and Laurance Rockefeller was only one factor. The long-ago battle against the Carpenter Brothers had led to ownership of 53,320 acres and control of twenty-four miles of Hudson River shore frontage. The forty-two-mile-long Palisades Parkway was meeting every expectation as a beautiful automobile corridor. In Harriman Park, forty-three group camps, though reduced in number from a prewar high of more than a hundred, were more refined, manageable, and permanent. Each year, thousands of children found the kind of magic and memories in the camps that still rank the PIPC in a class by itself as a vital link between girls and boys from inner-city neighborhoods and preserved parklands. Annual visitation to the Commission's eleven parks stood at a solid 6.3 million and was steadily increasing year by year. The rustic Bear Mountain Inn was a counterpoint to the elaborate and slick hotels and restaurants more typical of the vast urban market, attracting a steady clientele, including President Dwight David Eisenhower and his classmates from the U.S. Military Academy, Class of 1915, who held their 1960 reunion there.

Publicity about the accomplishments of the PIPC prompted a senior partner at the New York City–based law firm of White & Case to suggest to Commission President Jube that a memorial, perhaps in the form of a plaque, be placed somewhere within the park system to honor the memory of J. DuPratt White. Jube passed on the request to his fellow commissioners, commenting that White "was Secretary of the PIPC when it was formed in 1900, and later became its President around 1920 . . . I look upon the suggestion with favor." But the commissioners took little time for backward glances. The suggestion about honoring White disappeared somewhere in the shuffle of internal dialogue; no action was taken.

Iona Island, Hudson River Narrows.
(Courtesy of PIPC Archives)

Rockefeller was increasingly interested in Iona Island, nestled in an exquisite portion of the Hudson River narrows just downstream from the Bear Mountain dock. The Navy had acquired the island in 1900, ironically in the same year that the PIPC was being formed. Over the years, 144 buildings had been erected on the island's 118 acres, housing enough ammunition to make any military tactician proud. By 1958, the Navy declared Iona Island excess to its needs, choosing, instead, to disperse its store of ammunition to a variety of more remote locations and hardened bunkers rather than presenting such a single, inviting missile target so close to New York City. When the Navy moved out, the federal General Services Administration (GSA), keeper of excess properties, moved in. Despite vigorous interest expressed by the PIPC in taking over Iona Island, the GSA decided to fill up the buildings with "strategic materials," including rubber, cobalt, copper, and aluminum. At the urging of his brother, Governor Rockefeller placed the state on record in support of the PIPC's initiative to acquire Iona Island. On a trip to Washington, Governor Rockefeller gained endorsement from the New York congressional delegation for this purpose, but the GSA would not budge, claiming that the tons of natural rubber stored on the island were essential to national defense, even though synthetic rubber had clearly made the natural product obsolete.

For the moment, Rockefeller was stalemated by entrenched GSA officials who probably never had seen Iona Island, knew little about the Hudson River Valley, and were supposed to dispose of excess federal property, not hold it for their own warehousing purposes. Even the collective clout of the Rockefeller brothers could not budge the GSA, but while the question of stewardship for Iona Island remained unresolved, the PIPC found itself being pressured to assume ownership of another island, this one rich in national meaning, symbolic of America's invitation to the world to "send us your tired, your poor, your troubled masses yearning to be free." The same Dr. Ronan who had so irritated Moses by suggesting realignments and adjustments within the structure of the state government proposed that the PIPC "take over" Ellis Island in New York Harbor. Ronan accurately contended that ownership of Ellis Island was in dispute between New York and New Jersey. He argued the logic of vesting ownership of the island in the Palisades Interstate Park Commission to settle the dispute and ensure that both states would be represented in its future care. At a meeting in February, 1961, the commissioners considered Ronan's surprising notion. After due deliberation, they declined to seek jurisdiction over Ellis Island. The question of the island's ownership remained unsettled for many years, barely noticeable, like a low-grade fever, until a temporary bridge was built from the nearby New Jersey shore to the island by its present stewards, the National Park Service. The bridge allowed for access by construction vehicles and workers involved in the historic restoration of the principal buildings on a portion of the island. At the conclusion of the restoration project, the bridge was scheduled to be removed. New Jersey officials, reasoning that the bridge might be converted for pedestrian use to increase visitation to Ellis Island from its side of the river, wanted it to remain. New York wanted the bridge gone, anxious that the legions of tourists who traditionally embarked by boat from the Battery at the tip of Manhattan Island for visits to the Statue of Liberty and Ellis Island would not be distracted by a grab for tourist traffic and dollars, suggested by the option of a leisurely walk to Ellis Island from the Jersey shore. Thirty-seven years after Ronan discerningly suggested that the PIPC "take over" the island, thus settling the dispute, the matter was somewhat resolved by the U.S. Supreme Court. Ownership of a small slice of the island was affirmed for New York, a larger piece and better bragging rights for New Jersey. The National Park Service and the controversial bridge were left in the middle.

Commissioner Donald Borg had probably forgotten about the PIPC's brief flirtation with Ellis Island when a letter arrived on his desk from J. Willard Marriott, Jr. "Please accept this quarter, Mr. Borg, as a 'token payment' for taking five minutes of valuable time from your busy schedule to do me a favor." Marriott Hot Shoppes Inc. was making a market survey for the hotel it proposed to build next to the Commission's Fort Lee Historic Site. Borg was just one of many businesspeople in the Fort Lee area who received the Marriott inquiry and a shiny quarter, but the details of the marketing questionnaire caught his eye, especially since Borg had met personally with Marriott to discuss the building-height restrictions that the PIPC was determined to enforce at the hotel site. Borg had been under the impression that Marriott was willing to abide by the height restrictions that would allow for a four-story structure, but the questionnaire described a "10-story building offering panoramic views of the Hudson River, two restaurants, one located on the roof of the hotel, and 400 attractive guest rooms available at $10 for a single and $15 for a double." The estimated construction cost was $6 million. Borg answered the two questions asked of him: Would you use the facility? "No." Would you use the facility for conventions or meetings? "No." Encouraged to add a comment in a space provided at the bottom of the questionnaire, Borg wrote, "My personal interest is chiefly the height of the proposed structure and its gratuitous defacement of the Palisades." Alerted by the market survey, Borg and the commissioners began to prepare for a lengthy court fight, convinced that their effort to reach a compromise with Marriott had failed.

Farther north within the PIPC's park system, better news prevailed. Nine hundred people gathered at Lake Welch in May, 1962, to participate in the official opening of a gigantic facility designed and constructed to provide for thirty thousand visitors per day, most of them attracted by a half-mile beach of Long Island sand that had been barged up the Hudson River and then trucked to the site. Parking was available for 3,200 cars and scores of buses. This was the scale of development that fit nicely into Moses's concept of wilderness, and he was there along with Governor Rockefeller and several of the PIPC commissioners to speak at the celebration. The day was not very obliging, bringing with it blustery winds and a steady rain. As chronicled by *The New York Times*, "A ten-foot flagstaff was

Nelson and Laurance S. Rockefeller, Lake Welch dedication,
Harriman State Park, New York, 1962.
(Courtesy of PIPC Archives)

toppled by the wind and the sharp beak of a brass eagle atop it nearly struck Mr. Moses on the head . . . just after he had said some caustic things about people 'who sit in ivory towers, stuffy clubs, and cellar bistros' to judge park problems 'rather than explore the wilderness for a first-hand view.'"

Engineers for the Consolidated Edison Company of New York, Inc., (Con Ed) were, in fact, out exploring the PIPC's wilderness. Con Ed was the giant vendor of electric power serving 8.5 million customers in New York City and the suburbs of Westchester County. In September, 1962, Morgan made a note to the files to record a visit to his office by a Con Ed representative who courteously told him that the company wanted to build a "pumped storage power generating plant" on Commission property. Morgan responded that the commissioners would take an exceedingly dim view of a power plant on parkland but probably could accommodate the utility easements needed as part of the project's infrastructure. Three days later, a news headline heralded, "Huge Power Plant Planned on Hudson."

Con Ed was proposing to build the largest pumped-storage hydroelectric plant in the nation on Storm King Mountain. Morgan, already convinced that the plant would be placed north of the PIPC's property, followed up with a memo to L. L. Huttleston, the New York State Parks Director in Albany, stating: "The only thing they need from us is a permit to build a tunnel under our land"—implying that this was yet another routine utility-easement matter. The PIPC from time to time had issued permits to accommodate utility services for the surrounding communities. Morgan saw the Con Ed proposal as just the latest such request. Farther upriver, immediately north of Storm King Mountain, the little village of Cornwall-on-Hudson found itself being courted by Con Ed. The power company knew that it must persuade the local voters to give up village-owned land needed for the massive project. Not yet knowing many details, a first reaction by village residents was to wonder whether the hydroelectric plant might disrupt television reception.

A. K. Morgan and Robert Moses, Lake Welch dedication, Harriman State Park, New York, 1962. *(Courtesy of PIPC Archives)*

Company representatives described the project as like a "large storage battery" and said the village would be caused "as little inconvenience as possible." Very convenient to the village might be huge economic benefits.

Even so, one of the first cautious expressions of opposition to the venture came from members of the Cornwall-on-Hudson Garden Club. Meeting at the home of Mrs. Dale Bouton, the women voted unanimously to oppose "the transmission of power by an aerial cable across the Hudson River from Storm King," then settled in for a discussion led by Mrs. Marie Hand on the sundry uses of herbs for Christmas decorations. Once again, in the very early stage of what was to become a stupendous environmental battle, garden-club women were among the first to fire a shot across the bow of industrialists bent on exploitation of the Hudson Highlands.

Calvin W. Stillman was also watchful. Those many years ago his father, banker James Stillman, had introduced Perkins, Sr., to Wall Street, thereby opening the door for Perkins to join J. P. Morgan & Company. Much of the land owned by the PIPC on Storm King Mountain had been donated by James Stillman or by members of his family in his memory. When Calvin Stillman first heard of the Con Ed initiative, he promptly stopped by to visit company officials in New York City, advising them that the PIPC would never allow a pumped storage power plant to be constructed on its land, a message already delivered by Morgan. Stillman echoed, too, the concern of the garden club's members: stringing power lines across the "Wind Gate" of the scenic Hudson River narrows would not do. If Con Ed wished to succeed, Stillman counseled, the company must find an alternate site to Storm King Mountain. Company officials paid attention. Their revised maps placed the power plant and pumped storage reservoir on private land, just outside the boundaries of PIPC-owned property but still on the northeast slope of the mountain. Only the tunnel would remain on (or under) the PIPC's land.

Company officials listened to and took Morgan and Stillman's advice because, as reported years later by Ron Britzke in *The Cornwall Local,* "Con Ed had a problem in the early 1960s." The problem was demand for peak power in New York City. The coal-fired and nuclear-power generating plants operated by Con Ed were barely sufficient to meet the city's normal demands for power. These demands peaked in the mornings and evenings when millions of people were home turning on lights, using appliances, setting thermostats to kick on furnaces or air conditioners, and otherwise expecting "unlimited power at the flick of a switch," as Britzke put it. When too many switches were flicked too quickly, New York City experienced brownouts, menacing dips in the flow of electric power that dimmed lights, reduced cooling and heating capabilities, impacted emergency medical, law enforcement, and fire services, slowed pumps that delivered drinking water, and otherwise threatened to push the electric grid into blackout, the final stage of collapse that would force the power-dependent city to its knees. Brownouts were becoming all too common, and a major blackout in 1961 captured world headlines by shutting down five square miles of Manhattan.

The "large storage battery" Con Ed's executives and engineers had in mind for Storm King Mountain consisted of eight enormous "reversible" electric-power-generating turbines, each capable of generating 250,000 kilowatts of electric power. They were to be located at the base of the mountain on the shoreline of the Hudson River, just across from the location where Henry Hudson gave up his quest in 1609 for discovery of the fabled passage to Asia and turned back toward Europe. When reversed to gulp water (and fish) from the river, the turbines would pump 12 billion gallons of water upward through a tunnel forty feet in diameter and two miles long, to be "stored" in a 260-acre reservoir perched more than one thousand feet above the river on land to be acquired from the village of Cornwall-on-Hudson. Pumping to fill the reservoir would occur late at night and in the predawn hours when the city's power demands were low. When demand moved toward peak, billions of gallons would be released from the reservoir to be sent gushing back down through the tunnel, spinning the turbines with an immense hydro impact. Ironically, more electric power would be required to pump the water up to the reservoir in the first place than would be produced when the water came coursing back down through the turbines. But that was not the point. Con Ed could leisurely use excess nighttime power to pump the water uphill. The whole purpose was that anywhere from 900,000 to 2 million kilowatts of extra electrical energy could be injected into the Con Ed power grid in a matter of minutes by the down-rushing water, depending on how many of the eight turbines were used at any given moment. Customers in the city could flick switches with impunity during the approximately 4 percent of each twenty-four–hour period when peak demand otherwise threatened to override Con Ed's regular power service. Fish in the Hudson River, first sucked up into the reservoir through the reversible turbines, then blasted back down through the tunnel hours later, would swim no more.

Con Ed emphasized the benefits of the project to Cornwall-on-Hudson residents. In a four-color brochure that contained no technical or design information about the pumped-storage plant, but featured several photos of derelict buildings near the river's edge, Con Ed promised to

> transform nearly a mile of dilapidated waterfront property north of the plant into a park and turn it over to the Village of Cornwall. This will serve several important purposes. It will beautify the waterfront; it will provide a major recreation area on the river where none now exists; and, perhaps most important, it will preserve for all time an extensive segment of waterfront that otherwise might be redeveloped for industry or other purposes.

Con Ed's tag line proclaimed: "From electric power to serve southeastern New York State will come the means not only to conserve but to add to the beauty of the Hudson River."

With the PIPC standing aside on the assumption that its primary concern was the matter of issuing a permit to allow for the tunnel to be carved deep under Storm King Mountain, the power company offered a tax treasure chest to residents of the Village of Cornwall. If the giant power company became a landowner, power-plant developer, and taxpayer in the village, the property-tax burden on village residents might plummet by two-thirds or more, perhaps even to zero. The heady thought of letting Con Ed take over most of the property-tax burden for the village was, according to *The Cornwall Local,* like "a rainbow with the mythical pot of gold. . . ." Jobs, too, were dangled as an incentive, perhaps as many as four hundred during the construction phase. The fact that almost no one in Cornwall had any experience in hard-rock tunneling or power-plant construction was only a minor concern. Most of the village's residents began thinking that these incentives were just fine and started rolling out the welcome carpet. But a few villagers were increasingly skeptical. Britzke reported, "At the heart of it all was the mountain. Visible from virtually everywhere in the vicinity, it brooded over the river. For the first time, the mostly unspoiled Highlands would be invaded by man and his commerce. Storm King would become a symbol of ecology vs. industry." Among friends and neighbors, elected officials and family members, lines were beginning to be drawn. No one understood the full scale of controversy that would develop. No one assumed that a company with the influence and brawn of Con Ed could be stopped. About the best the skeptics could hope for was that the environmental impact of the power plant might be minimized.

At Bear Mountain, a member of the PIPC's staff alerted Morgan that Mr. and Mrs. George Brooks of Cornwall were willing to give their twelve-acre property to the PIPC if the proffered donation would somehow help stop Con Ed. The PIPC's staff advised the Brookses: "The Commission will not get involved . . . if this entails opposition to Con Ed. . . . The Commission usually works with utilities. . . . [We] suggest that you make the best possible deal and sell to Con Ed." Only a short time later, Morgan learned that Con Ed might want to dump rock spoil from the tunneling operation at the PIPC's old CCC campsite on Storm King Mountain. He responded by speculating that this "might be a good way to fill up and make usable this land."

A seemingly unrelated transition occurred in Albany in January, 1963. With the informal encouragement and consent of the governor, Laurance Rockefeller replaced Moses as chairman of the State Council of Parks. Strain between the Rockefellers and Moses had grown. Moses's departure from the SCP was an indication that his iron-fisted control of so many New York State construction activities might not survive the Rockefeller administration. He turned over the reins of the SCP to his successor, leaving behind the "advisory" organization Moses founded in 1924 to grab the budget purse strings from those he characterized at the time as "the old park men." Moses's departure from the SCP did not hinder him from commenting on the Storm King Mountain issue. In response to a request to help stop Con Ed, Moses, wearing his hat as chair of the Long Island Park Commission, said: "I have been aware of this proposed development from the beginning, and I feel that the Consolidated Edison Company has used every reasonable effort to preserve the natural scenery."

Con Ed's 1962 stock holders report brought graphic definition to the company's interpretation of what was meant by the phrase "preserve the natural scenery." Shown on the cover of the report was an engineer's rendering of exactly what Con Ed had in mind for the base of Storm King Mountain. As Britzke described it, "The rendering (by an unknown artist who should be enshrined in the ecological hall of fame) showed a rectangular chunk the size of several football fields blasted out of the foot of the mountain. The enormous notch would house the transformer and switchyard" for the eight underground turbines. People who had been generally aware and somewhat concerned about the Con Ed proposal were suddenly galvanized into action after taking one glance at the cover of the annual report. To the still small cadre of opponents, the drawing was a bombshell. Immediately realizing the consequences of its public-relations gaff, Con Ed announced that the riverfront portion of the plant would be nestled underground. Cost for the project, originally estimated at about $100 million, jumped to $150 million.

The New York–New Jersey Trail Conference, who counted Maj. William Welch among its founders and was long allied with the PIPC, stepped forward to voice opposition to the Con Ed project. In a May, 1963, letter to Dr. Ronan, but intended for the eyes of Governor Rockefeller, Leo O. Rothschild, the Trail Conference Conservation chair and an attorney, cautioned, "The threat to the northern gate of the Hudson Highlands has become far more ominous in the last few weeks."

Rothschild was reacting, in part, to a declaration by another power company, the Central Hudson Gas & Electric Corporation, that it intended to build its own new power plant on Breakneck Ridge, on the east side of the Hudson facing the Con Ed pumped-storage plant. Central Hudson served the Hudson River Valley north of Con Ed territory, and it saw an opportunity to follow along with larger Con Ed leading the charge. Ronan sent Rothschild's letter to Morgan for comment. A fault line between the PIPC and its traditional environmental constituents was becoming increasingly visible, as confirmed by Morgan's response to Ronan that the PIPC must "determine whether their [Central Hudson's] installation will be as satisfactory as that of Con Ed is expected to be." As in the days when the commissioners were trying to sell land on the summit of the Palisades

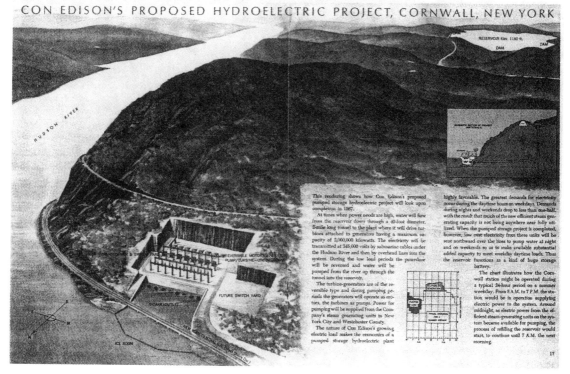

CON EDISON'S PROPOSED HYDROELECTRIC PROJECT, CORNWALL, NEW YORK

Artist's rendering of the proposed power plant at Storm King Mountain, New York, 1962.
(Courtesy of PIPC Archives)

to meet budget needs, the PIPC seemed to be losing contact with its purposes and roots. Morgan was seemingly content to view the pumped-storage power plant only from the perspective of a tunnel passing under Storm King Mountain, not in the larger context of protecting the scenery of the Hudson River narrows. The fact that the PIPC did not own the property on which Con Ed planned to build the turbines and reservoir became a factor in the PIPC's hesitancy to challenge the project, even though the commissioners had never hesitated to challenge quarry companies up and down the river or to use aggressive acquisition tactics if necessary to stop the desecration of natural beauty. Somehow, the PIPC viewed the pumped-storage power plant, potentially the granddaddy quarry of them all, more kindly.

Alerted by Trail Conference members, *The New York Times* broadcast the first of many succeeding articles: "Power Plan Stirs Battle On Hudson." In the article, a direct remark by Rothschild to Governor Rockefeller was quoted: "Knowing your interest in the scenic and historic landmarks of our State, we hope you will do everything in your power to preserve the Highlands. We would appreciate hearing from you."

Reacting to the *Times*'s article, Robert A. Roe, the New Jersey Conservation commissioner, asked of Morgan, "What does the PIPC recommend?"

Morgan responded, "We are fully aware of these two developments and have made an exhaustive examination of the probable damage to scenery. . . . The projects will not severely damage the scenery. . . . It is not the Forest Primeval. . . . The area is occupied by many old buildings. . . . The forestalling of all enterprise in this area is neither practical nor desirable. . . . The Commission will not object to either one."

Roe must have been pondering Morgan's advice when an editorial, "Defacing the Hudson," appeared in the May 29, 1963, edition of *The New York Times:*

> If any utility proposed to construct a plant in the middle of Central Park, the absurdity of such a defacement of precious natural (or nearly natural) surrounding would be immediately apparent. It is almost as bad to plunk down a couple of power installations right in the heart of one of the most stunning natural regions in the Eastern United States: Storm King Mountain and Breakneck Ridge. . . . All of us who have hiked and played in Palisades Interstate Park know what a beautiful backyard exists 50 miles north of New York City. Is it too close to home to appreciate? "This is very good land to fall with and a pleasant land to see" said one of Henry Hudson's officers, going up the river under these high blue hills. That great traveler Baedecker found the Hudson's scenery "grander and more inspiring" than the Rhine. The proposed power plants . . . would desecrate great areas that are part of the natural and historic heritage of our country, are still largely unspoiled and should remain that way.

Answering for the PIPC, Rockefeller responded in a letter to the editor that had been drafted by Morgan and approved by the other commissioners. Expressing regret that Storm King and Breakneck Ridge had been chosen for the siting of new power plants, Rockefeller said, "We have recognized that additional facility developments of this type must be made available to meet the requirements of a growing population." Then, reciting the history of the PIPC as "a strong protector of the natural beauty of the Hudson," he continued:

> For some time now the Commission . . . has been working with Consolidated Edison to make sure that the greatest consideration possible is given to scenic and other values in the construction of this power plant. . . . The plant will be at river level, facing north. Most of the plant will be below ground level and it has been designed to blend into the hillside and will be landscaped by an outstanding landscape architect.

Repeating Morgan's contention that the proposed site "is not forest primeval," Rockefeller stated that "on balance the Commission prefers to take the positive approach to insure that the esthetic, historical, and recreational values of the area are protected as much as possible."

The PIPC's staff was alerted that Con Ed might dump 720,000 cubic yards of rock spoil from the tunnel onto the old CCC site at Storm King, creating "about 28 acres of level land," and pay the PIPC twenty-five to fifty cents a yard for the privilege, producing income for the PIPC of from $430,000 to $860,000. Con Ed sweetened the offer even more by suggesting that it would donate about 160 acres on Storm King Mountain to the PIPC that would be excess to the company's needs once construction was completed.

The PIPC, champion of scenic preservation, but now advocating compromise with the power companies, was feeling growing pressure to defend its position. Rockefeller, writing in July, 1963, to Con Ed's chair, Harland D. Forbes, and to Lelan F. Sillin, Forbes's counterpart at Central Hudson, inquired:

> One conservation organization, The Nature Conservancy, has assigned a representative who is on a fact-finding mission to find among other things the necessity for additional facilities in this area. . . . Would it be possible to obtain some relative facts and figures that would illustrate your reasons for selecting this site as well as their particular method of generating power against other methods?

Forbes was quick to reply, and he referred to the "world's largest pumped-storage power plant" at Vianden, Luxembourg, as proof of proven technology, citing the "highly advantageous" economic benefits of the proposed Storm King plant, while explaining that "considerable new power capacity . . . would be ready at a moment's notice." Forbes listed various alternatives, all sites along the Hudson River of lesser elevation than Storm King and the Cornwall reservoir, and discarded the choice of depending on old coal-fired steam plants, which would cost about double the hydro option. Forbes did not mention other options for producing peaking power, such as using natural gas–fired power plants, energy conservation, or the import of electric power from other vendors.

Carl O. Gustafson, executive assistant to Rockefeller, had been appointed to the PIPC in 1961. A reputable conservationist in his own right, Gustafson nonetheless was happy with Forbes's response. "The next time The Nature Conservancy boys draw a bead on me, I'll be able to fire back," he wrote to Morgan. In the meantime, Rothschild communicated again with Ronan, challenging the content of the letter to the *Times* that Rockefeller signed. "That the Consolidated Edison plant would supply electricity in an efficient way, I assume is beyond dispute," he said. "What I do dispute is the damage to be done to the river, and my position is that the defacement of one of the finest river stretches in the world cannot be excused because an economical source of power would be developed. The proposal is on a par with a plan to dam the Grand Canyon." In further contact with Morgan, Gustafson said of the Rothschild letter, "It is my opinion that there is enough nonsense in it so that we can at least prepare a response to Ronan, pointing out where Rothschild is in error." This was not to be. Ten days after communicating with Morgan, the forty-two-year-old Gustafson, his wife, and daughter tragically died when Gustafson, a skilled World War II and Pan American World Airline pilot, failed in an attempted emergency landing of his Cessna 190 near Teterboro Airport, New Jersey.

In the Village of Cornwall, a large majority of residents were persuaded that the Con Ed project would, in addition to being a boon for the village tax base, bring improvement to the neglected waterfront through creation of the proposed fifty-seven–acre shoreline park built out of spoil material from the tunnel and reservoir excavations. Con Ed was pledged to purchase and expand the village's reservoir, allowing Cornwall to reap the benefits of upgraded utility systems at company expense. According to the *Cornwall Local,* about 1,700 residents signed a petition favoring the development; only 100 were opposed. Two of the Cornwall residents who stood in opposition were Stephen and Beatrice Duggan. They understood that any hope for success against Con Ed must be found outside the village limits. In November, 1963, at the home of Carl Carmer, writer and historian, Beatrice joined a dozen other people, including the Trail Conference's Rothschild and Walter Boardman of The Nature Conservancy, to form the Scenic Hudson Preservation Conference. Stephen, an attorney, also became a founder of the Natural Resources Defense Council (NRDC), another organization sparked to life by Con Ed; the NRDC would eventually gain impressive national credentials as a highly respected champion of sound environmental law.

What the dozen founders of Scenic Hudson did not understand at the time was that the Storm King Mountain controversy would last for almost twenty years. The conflict and results would profoundly change the manner in which the United States conducts its environmental business.

As the volume of the Con Ed debate increased, Morgan alerted the commissioners to a totally unanticipated inquiry from a deputy director of the Atomic Energy Commission (AEC). "The AEC is considering the establishment of a tunnel from the river into the rock north of West Point for the purpose of servicing atomic submarines," Morgan reported in a letter to Rockefeller, implying that

the AEC was unaware of the Con Ed controversy. The vision of submarines floating on a millpond of black water beneath a stadium-sized domed ceiling cut from
ancient diabase rock, guards marching to and fro, and technicians working by flu-
orescent light, surpassed in creativity the 1920s proposal to cut a tunnel through
Hook Mountain to form a mighty artificial waterfall plunging into the Hudson
River. "I told him I thought that the conservationists had taken about all the
defacement of the mountains on either side of the river in this vicinity that they
would take, and strongly urged him to leave our property alone and go somewhere else." The AEC listened; the atomic subs went to Groton, Connecticut.

Many other issues remained actively on the PIPC's agenda. In Orange County,
the PIPC acquired 1,600 acres to create Highland Lakes State Park. With access
to New York State bond funding, the PIPC added almost 7,500 acres to its holdings in 1963 and continued a steady pace of acquisition through the 1960s.
Among the acquisitions were 34.5 acres, donated to the PIPC by T. Dwight Partridge, son of Dr. Edward L. Partridge.

At High Tor Park, the PIPC concluded that the seventy-four–room mansion,
donated years earlier to the PIPC by Archer M. Huntington, was "rambling, dis-
jointed, unorganized, could not be used as a hotel, and had no historical value or
charm." After attempting on several occasions to find a suitable use for the structure, the commissioners voted unanimously to demolish the mansion to make
way for a scenic view out over the Hudson River toward the city. Demolishing
buildings was not unusual for the PIPC. Even the PIPC's own New Jersey office
building that was constructed by CCC workers during the Depression fell to
wrecking crews after World War II to make way for the Palisades Parkway.

An occasional outcry could be heard as some buildings disappeared, but the
commissioners were not prepared for the group of women who threatened in
midwinter, 1966, to "lie down in the road" to save the Huntington mansion. Mrs.
John R. Sarno, Jr., and thirty women confederates thought that the removal of
the English Tudor-style mansion was a very bad idea. When contractors arrived
to begin demolition, they were met by a group of determined women who literally placed themselves in the path of the wrecking ball. To outflank the
women, the workers climbed up on the mansion to begin ripping off roof tiles.
Their maneuver was short-lived. Reacting to adverse publicity, Governor Rockefeller directed that the PIPC commissioners halt the demolition and make one
more good-faith attempt to find a worthy use for the building. The PIPC held a
hearing at which the protesters and local political officials were invited to produce a sufficiently funded organization capable of guaranteeing maintenance and
public use of the Huntington house. No satisfactory organization was identified.

Despite pleas for more time, the commissioners ruled, "The house is coming down." Two months after the confrontation at High Tor, all that remained of the mansion was a flat, open site outlined by low walls, a lawn, a disconnected fountain, and a sunken terrace. Mother Nature was already in the process of reclaiming the site.

Building demolition of much larger scale became possible when the General Services Administration advised Morgan by letter in August, 1965, "Your application to acquire Iona Island is acceptable to this Agency." The PIPC was invited to close the transaction for $290,000, one-half of the appraised value for the 118-acre island. The commissioners wasted no time. Within a matter of weeks, the island and its 144 buildings, totaling 469,000 square feet, were in the PIPC's ownership. The island had been variously considered by the GSA for industrial development, a university campus, a prison, a mental-health institution, or a resort, but only months after acquisition by the PIPC, contracts were let to demolish the buildings, tunnels, web of roads, and ammunition bunkers left behind by the U.S. Navy. Only six of the old brick-and-concrete buildings remain on the island today. The largest of these, the Marine Corps barracks, is a drafty, empty relic. The PIPC uses the others for storage, and abundant wildlife and plant species have returned to the recovering island, including bald eagles that use trees along the island's shoreline during the winter season as launch pads to catch fish from the Hudson River.

The PIPC almost missed the opportunity to let Iona Island shine again as a natural gemstone. At one point, the commissioners and Morgan considered the island as a suitable site to handle "overflow" crowds from Bear Mountain. A 1,500-car parking lot was constructed on the north side of the island. An Olympic-sized swimming pool, picnic areas, tennis courts, and baseball fields were planned at an estimated cost of $20 million. Commissioners Frederick Osborn and Conrad Wirth were not convinced of the wisdom of replacing the Navy infrastructure with more of the same. The National Audubon Society also took a dim view of the PIPC's development plans, cautioning that restoration of bird habitat should take precedence. Audubon members were joined by an unlikely ally, the famous Iona Island sinking road that the Navy had built straight across a portion of the Iona Island marsh. Each time the Hudson River's high tide started to wash over the road's surface, the Navy would add more layers of gravel and blacktop to keep road access open to the island. The PIPC would be faced with the same costly problem. Thousands of visitors driving to and fro on the marsh road would continue to push it downward. This problem of access, including an at-grade crossing of Penn-Central railroad tracks near the main gate to the island, combined with budget constraints and skepticism about any further development of Iona Island, short-circuited the PIPC's plans. Now, rare plant species have been found by botanists to be growing in the abandoned parking lot.

In New Jersey, Commissioner Donald Borg was keeping track of the legal maneuvers required to convince the Marriott Company that it could not ignore building-height limitations on the Palisades. Borg, Rockefeller, Morgan, and attorney Henry Diamond, a member of Rockefeller's staff, met with New Jersey Governor Richard J. Hughes to successfully enlist his support for the development of the Fort Lee Historic Site and, coincidentally, to join in the effort to persuade Marriott to back off. The commissioners promised to provide $250,000 of the estimated $500,000 cost of developing the historic site.

Con Ed, though, remained at the center of the commissioners' attention. The company dropped off a model of the proposed project at Morgan's Bear Mountain office. The model was four feet by ten feet, came with its own aluminum platform, and was delivered by truck. Morgan had to recruit members of the PIPC's maintenance staff to help off-load the model. Forces in opposition to Con Ed were continuing to gather around the Scenic Hudson Preservation Conference, including the city-based Regional Plan Association, yet another traditional ally of the PIPC that chose to stand against Con Ed on this issue. The twelve people who had formed Scenic Hudson found themselves joined by thirty-three affiliate organizations, representing thousands of members, with the New York–New Jersey Trail Conference and The Nature Conservancy retaining prominent positions of leadership. Before the controversy ended, Scenic Hudson would receive small and large donations from more than twenty thousand people, including many Con Ed stockholders. In written statements to the Federal Power Commission (FPC), Con Ed's attorneys began referring to the Scenic Hudson advocates as "extreme conservationists." Dale E. Doty, a Washington-based attorney retained to represent Scenic Hudson in the FPC proceedings, admitted in response that his clients were "conservationists," but added that whether they were "extreme" would be left to the judgment of history.

With the consent of the commissioners, Morgan journeyed to Washington to appear before the FPC. This federal agency was at the vortex of the Storm King controversy because it had legal authority to accept or deny Con Ed's application to build the pumped-storage power plant. In his testimony, Morgan contended that "the project, when completed, would not damage the scenery," that "dual use would occur, [with] the tunnel below [and] recreation above," and that "it would be unreasonable to oppose the project provided that the company does everything within reason to minimize impact on the scenery." Morgan's comments were confined to possible impact on the PIPC's land. Even though the Con Ed turbines and reservoir dams would be only a stone's throw to the north of the Commission's property lines, the PIPC continued to break with its own decades-old tradition by hunkering down behind its own boundaries.

The FPC inquiry concluded in March, 1964, with a finding that the Storm King plant "would have little adverse effect on the scenic beauty of the Hudson River Valley." This Con Ed victory was short-lived. Opposition was becoming more vocal by the day. The most constant PIPC allies, the garden clubs, now represented by the Garden Club of America, found that a power plant with 700 feet of frontage on the river, quarried 900 feet into Storm King, standing at a height of 122 feet, and backed by five earth and rock dams, each 250 feet tall, the largest of which would extend laterally for 2,000 feet, would indeed have horrendous scenic impact on the Hudson River Highlands. Writing to Moses, who was listed on the Garden Club of America letterhead as an adviser to the Conservation Committee, Mrs. Alexander Saunders asked for his advice on how to stop Con Ed. Moses was consistent in his reply: "I think you and your Conservation Committee should reexamine your decisions." Then, quoting Morgan's testimony before the FPC, he said, "No eyesore or desecration will result," adding that there is an "urgent need for this additional power at a cheap price."

Randall J. LeBoeuf, Jr., of the law firm LeBoeuf, Lamb & Leiby, was representing Con Ed in hearings before the FPC. His firm's letterhead listed eighteen lawyers. Doty, representing Scenic Hudson, had a letterhead with a single name, his own. LeBoeuf alerted Morgan that the FPC, feeling pressure, was planning to hold further hearings, and that Doty specifically would request Morgan's appearance. A letter from Doty to Morgan confirmed the warning: "I feel that the present position of your Commission is not clear and that your testimony would be of benefit not only to the FPC but to better public understanding of the PIPC's position in this matter." Morgan drafted a written statement and sent an advance copy to LeBoeuf, asking for his comment and guidance on the text of the statement, but did not extend the same courtesy to Doty. In his further statements and correspondence, Morgan took the position that the PIPC had won major concessions from Con Ed. Construction scars and the power plant's infrastructure would be professionally landscaped, power cables would pass under the river, and 1.5 miles (of a projected 23.5 miles) of power cable on the east side of the Hudson River would be buried underground. "I feel that this type of cooperation, rather than opposition, has been worthwhile," Morgan claimed.

As an increasing number of letters reached his desk, asking that the PIPC intercede more vigorously against Con Ed, Morgan gave a standard response: "Contact the FPC."

But the political ground was shifting under the feet of those who had assumed that the best hope for protecting scenery in the narrows of the Hudson River was to win as many design and operating compromises as possible from Con Ed. In a legal brief submitted for the record to the FPC, Doty described the imposing dimensions of the power plant and contended: "To argue that such a plant will not mar Storm King and the scenery of the area is nonsense. . . . To speak of landscaping such a monstrosity is sophistry."

The Hudson River Conservation Society, long existing as a stately forum for dialogue among some of the most influential families in the lower Hudson Valley, found itself struggling with the controversy. The society's founder was William Church Osborn, father of PIPC Commissioner Frederick Osborn. Frederick's brother, William H., served as president of the Society. Mrs. Frederick Osborn served on the society's board, as did Mrs. Leroy Clark, president of the Palisades Nature Association (Greenbrook Sanctuary), Laurance Rockefeller, Calvin Stillman, Mrs. Lila Acheson Wallace (a founder of *Reader's Digest*), and Carl Carmer, one of the founders of Scenic Hudson. Hearing rumors that the Con Ed plant, once constructed, might be expanded, the Society Board sent a communiqué to its members, confirming its original position that "the best way to protect the river was not to oppose the entire project in a battle we were bound to lose . . . [but] if the protests piling in on the FPC succeed in completely stopping this project, our approach has of course been proved wrong. . . ." The board then passed a resolution that, in part, stated: "The plans of Consolidated Edison . . . will cause objectionable damage in our judgment to the natural scenic beauty. . . ."

Chairing the State Council of Parks, Laurance Rockefeller found another reason for concern. High-voltage power lines from the project were shown to pass over the Clarence Fahnstock State Park on the east side of the Hudson River. By unanimous vote, the State Council voted to oppose the alignment of the high-voltage lines. In a statement to reporters, Rockefeller announced the opposition, and he added: "New York is leading the nation in park development," citing $100 million made available for land conservation during his brother's tenure as governor. Fahnstock was the immediate concern, but perhaps the real message was that Rockefeller, dedicated absolutely to the best possible quality of life for everyone, was losing patience with Con Ed.

The *New York Times* captured the contentious issue in an editorial headlined,

"Preserving The Hudson Highlands." "If the area is to be fully protected for future generations, it cannot be most efficiently used now for a power plant or a dam, for mineral exploitation or for grazing: If it is to be used for such purposes, its particular esthetic or scenic qualities, its beauty and its silences, will be lost forever." Though the *Times* editorial spoke of Storm King, in a much larger sense, it captured the essence of park battles yet to be fought throughout the nation. *Life* magazine joined the *Times* in editorial opposition to the pumped-storage power plant, posing the question in its headline "Must God's Junkyard Grow?" Dr. Nathan M. Pusey, president of Harvard University, did not think so. Harvard had a stake in the natural integrity of one thousand–acre Black Rock Forest, just west of Storm King Mountain. The forest had been donated to the university by the Stillman family. Pusey expressed personal opposition to the pumped-storage power-generating project.

Morgan, in response to an inquiry from Rockefeller, confirmed in June, 1964, that Con Ed's plant likely would be expanded, once in place. He said that based on recommendations from the staff of the FPC, Con Ed would consider raising the dams by fifty feet and adding more turbine generators at the river's edge. Rumors of possible expansion spurred Con Ed's opponents to search for any means of blocking the project. Morgan shared engineer-to-engineer camaraderie with Earl Griffith, his principal contact at Con Ed. When Griffith alerted Morgan that Doty or Rothschild might attempt a "taxpayer's law suit" against the PIPC to enjoin it from issuing a permit for construction of the tunnel under "Stillman gift lands," Morgan wrote a note to the file: "I told Earl that the Stillman gift land was not above the area expected to be used for the tunnel. We both got a big laugh out of this."

The burgeoning grassroots effort to stop Con Ed resorted to other ploys to capture publicity. A flotilla of fifty boats moved up the Hudson River in September, 1964, led by the *Westerly,* the seventy-nine–foot flagship of the New York Yacht Club. Behind the *Westerly* came other motor-powered yachts, sailboats, outboard motorboats, two houseboats, and four kayaks. Under the shadow of Storm King, three teenage boys dressed in Revolutionary War uniforms rowed ashore from the flotilla, invaded the Con Ed site, and, playing word games with Con Ed's motto, "Dig We Must," planted a sign, "DIG YOU MUST NOT!" Cheers and boat horns echoed in the narrows.

Dig Con Ed would not. This was the reality facing the giant power company, but no one knew it in November, 1964, when 107 people appeared before a New York Joint Legislative Committee on Natural Resources that held a two-day hearing at the Bear Mountain Inn on the project. The purpose of the hearing was to examine the prospect for strengthening state control of uses along the Hudson by establishing a "Hudson River Valley Authority," but the spotlight shone unblinkingly on the pumped-storage power-plant project. Predictably, speakers delivered a mixed message. Dr. Michael J. Donahue, mayor of the Village of Cornwall-on-Hudson, expressed his continuing strong support for the project, as did the mayor of Newburgh, New York, several labor-union representatives, a handful of citizens who introduced themselves as "taxpayers," and a spokesperson for the power company. Standing against the project were Rothschild, now president of Scenic Hudson, Charles Eggert of the Sierra Club, and others from throughout the lower Hudson River Valley who urged protection of the scenic beauty of the river.

John J. Tamsen, retired superintendent of the PIPC's Bear Mountain State Park and once a contender for the position occupied by Morgan, came forward with a charge that there was a "change in philosophy of the Commission that creates a serious void in the forces which were formerly dedicated to the preservation of the Hudson." Citing a Greek adage, Tamsen reminded those in attendance at the hearing that "life is the gift of nature; but beautiful living is a gift of wisdom." Poetry and philosophy, though, however elegantly expressed, were not going to win the day against the advantages already established by Con Ed. The company was seeking a license from the FPC, not the State of New York, and the FPC clearly and firmly was in the Con Ed camp. The hearings at the Bear Mountain Inn were more allegorical than substantive. Still, proponents and opponents alike should have been paying close attention when Robert H. Boyle, a writer for *Sports Illustrated,* strode to the microphone to present his allotted five minutes of testimony.

Boyle represented a little-known local organization identified for the record as the Cortland Conservation Society. In his brief comments, Boyle said, "The very life of the Hudson, itself, is at stake." Calling the lower Hudson River "a remarkable marine nursery and spawning ground," Boyle implored that "such vital resources should not be hastily overridden by the ichthyological illiterates of the power commission." Most of those opposed to the power plant had reacted to the potential negative impact on natural scenery that would occur along the shoreline of the Hudson River as well as the power line that would cut a swath through the forest for miles from the river to a Con Ed substation in Westchester County. Boyle was raising a different issue, the impact of the power plant on fishery resources in the river. Rising in the Adirondacks, the Hudson is 315 miles in length, but, incredibly, the drop in the river's surface elevation for the last 150 miles, from Albany to the tip of Manhattan, is less than five feet. Starting as a tumbling mountain brook, the great river slows at Albany, where it is met by the tidal flow from the distant Atlantic Ocean. From this point downriver, the Hudson essentially is a fjord, a glaciated arm of the sea, that allows for the wash and mix of salt and fresh waters. This intermixing of nutrients and salinity creates the vibrant "nursery" that Boyle referred to on that November day at the Bear Mountain Inn. Shad, striped bass, and many other fish species would swim from spawning grounds in the Hudson River to the ocean. Boyle took a dim view of the power plant colossus that promised to chop the fisheries resource unmercifully. The intake to the pumped storage plant was to be located just where the broad upper river was constricted by the Highlands and made a slight shift to starboard. The natural flow would push migrating fish right into the mouths of the power plant's turbines.

Boyle's five minutes at the microphone likely became just part of the numbing verbal tabloid woven by more than a hundred speakers over two days of public hearings, but it would be the fish and the extraordinary persistence of Con Ed's opponents that finally saved Storm King Mountain. This salvation was not even glimmering on the horizon when the hearings at the Bear Mountain Inn were adjourned. No crystal ball could predict that sixteen more grinding years of litigation, hearings, acrimony, attempted compromises, redesigns and adjustments, eroding political support, and media brawling loomed ahead for Con Ed before it rid itself of the Storm King project in 1980 after estimated construction costs had risen fivefold, to about $550 million. An indistinct but telling signal that the road ahead for Con Ed was a dead end came several months after the hearing at the Bear Mountain Inn, when Governor Rockefeller, reacting to a bipartisan initiative by Democratic Congressman Richard Ottinger, Republican Senator Jacob K. Javits, and Democratic Senator Robert F. Kennedy, Jr., to designate the lower Hudson River Valley a federally protected conservation zone, issued an executive order creating the Hudson River Valley Commission and appointed Laurance Rockefeller as its chair. For obvious reasons, the PIPC endorsed the newly formed HRVC, and though still publicly maintaining the position that "dual needs" could be served at Storm King, the commissioners were beginning to move cautiously back toward their traditional environmental allies.

About a year after hearings, the newly formed Hudson River Valley Commission came forward with its recommendation about the Storm King Mountain pumped-storage electric project. The signal to Con Ed was unmistakable. In addition to Rockefeller, the newly created Hudson River Valley Commission included

Averell Harriman, Ford Foundation President Henry Heald, Lowell Thomas, IBM's Tom Watson, and Marion Heiskell of *The New York Times,* among a roster of prominent corporate, community, and educational leaders. "The HRVC strongly believes scenic and conservation values must be given as much weight as the more measurable economic values and that we should not necessarily destroy one to create another," said the HRVC. Then, narrowing its comment, the HRVC added, "The immediate case in point is the plan of Con Edison to build a pumped storage plant at Storm King Mountain. The HRVC believes that scenic values are paramount here and that the plant should not be built if a feasible alternative can be found."

A cascade of legal actions followed. The Hudson River Fishermen's Association, formed by Boyle and his colleagues, intervened to seek legal standing in the FPC licensing process by claiming that the proceedings were seriously flawed in the absence of accurate scientific data regarding the potential negative impact on fish. Secretary of the Interior Stewart Udall recommended that the plant "not be built." Then New York City, potential recipient of "desperately needed" peaking power according to Con Ed, intervened in the proceedings when city officials realized that placing the reversible turbines underground would require the removal of 580,000 tons of rock to create three underground chambers, the largest of which could accommodate a fifteen-story building. Blasting for the underground chambers would threaten the city's Moodna Tunnel, hidden in the adjacent rock formation only 140 feet from where thousands of dynamite blasts would be triggered. This was not just any tunnel. Constructed through Storm King Mountain before World War I, the Moodna Tunnel delivered more than 40 percent of New York City's drinking water from the distant Catskill Mountains into the city's vast reservoir and plumbing system. When the tunnel was constructed more than fifty years before Con Ed arrived on the scene, unstable rock formations presented an engineering challenge. Peaking power or no peaking power, the city did not want Con Ed's explosions to jeopardize its crucial water supply tunnel in any way, claiming possible "catastrophic consequences" for 8 million people if blasting for the turbine chambers either cracked the Moodna Tunnel or caused sections to collapse. The FPC, by now notorious for its disdain of environmental arguments advanced by Scenic Hudson and its allies, could not ignore this new heavyweight contender for a voice in the proceedings, nor could the power company.

In response to concerns raised by city officials, Con Ed attempted to reconfigure the pumped-storage power plant by reverting to an earlier concept that would move the plant away from the city's Moodna Tunnel and onto the PIPC's land, still with the idea of digging the enormous underground chambers. It justified this stratagem by saying that it would build the power plant "underneath" the park, as if building economically feasible industrial sites "underneath" Yellowstone, Mount Rushmore, or any other park were logical beyond dispute. It was as if parks were like icing on a geologic cake, good for decoration, but of little consequence in the exploitation of any profitable underground resources. In an "action letter" signed jointly by Scenic Hudson, the New York–New Jersey Trail Conference, the Sierra Club, and the New Jersey Conservation Foundation, Con Ed's reasoning was robustly attacked. "To concede the rights to build a great power plant under any part of the park . . . would not only set a grave precedent for the Palisades Park, but would in effect endanger all parks. . . . Such a precedent could range far and wide across parks of many states. Which then would be immune to industrial invasion if the land suited some private purpose?" As a result of Con Ed's gambit and the action letter, the PIPC and its commissioners were flooded with demands to finally step from the sidelines and join in the fight to stop the power company. The commissioners needed little convincing. In a general letter of response, PIPC President Jube said, "The Commission is taking the appropriate steps to make its opposition to the location of the proposed power plant on park land known to the Federal Power Commission formally. If the FPC opens hearings on this subject, I can assure you that the PIPC will present its opposition vigorously." Jube and the commissioners were given their chance; on November 11, 1968, the FPC, keenly aware of New York City's shadow, reopened hearings for the purpose of considering an alternate location on the PIPC's land. The PIPC legally intervened in the Storm King proceedings in December, 1968, to ensure that its "vigorous opposition" could not be ignored by the FPC.

Three months later, Commissioner Wirth was seated before the FPC's hearing officers in Washington, D.C. He testified that the PIPC was unalterably opposed to any uses of preserved parklands for industrial purposes except for essential utility easements. Wirth was distinctly qualified to deliver this message on behalf of his PIPC colleagues. He brought to the hearing a distinguished professional record in landscape architecture and resource management, marked most prominently by his service as director of the National Park Service from 1951 to 1964. Recipient of many professional honors and awards, Wirth long since had come to grips with the purposes and promise of wise land stewardship. When questioned at the FPC's hearing, in a sense Wirth was speaking for everyone who cherished precious natural places.

Question: What are the general criteria used in what you call "environmental planning?"

Answer: To be a good environmental planner one must recognize the needs of all the social, cultural, and economic values and be able to place them in balance. To do this is one of the most difficult of all tasks. One is confronted with things that are described in dollars and cents but that must be compared with human values, values that affect and govern our social and cultural growth, and, in fact, our very civilization. These are not new values. They are basic values that are fundamental in the establishment of this nation. They are references to the freedoms and the right of people not only to work for a living but to enjoy life itself. They control those things that contribute to the enjoyment of that life, as described in our Bill of Rights, Declaration of Independence, and the Constitution.

Question: How would you apply these criteria or values to the subject of parks?

Answer: Well, with respect to parks, this balance has already been struck. Parks are set aside for the enjoyment of people and to preserve some of our outstanding natural scenery as a heritage to be passed on to future generations. Things of this kind are found only where the good Lord placed them and man cannot create them. He can only destroy them in order to gain a monetary value, usually for only a relatively few years. Therefore, we in this country have decided that our outstanding natural heritages must be set aside for their true value to all the people. Park areas have been settled upon by the people and have been so set aside.

The voice of the PIPC, sought for so long by opponents of the Storm King Mountain project, was finally and eloquently brought to bear.

Con Ed was now facing legal actions by Scenic Hudson, the NRDC, the Hudson River Fishermen's Association, the City of New York, and the PIPC. Even so, the issue dragged on. The FPC persisted in its single-minded determination to license the plant, casting aside every assertion that it might cause environmental and scenic harm. In 1974, with a four-year-old FPC license in hand, and the city's concern about the Moodna Tunnel somewhat muted, Con Ed actually started construction. Hard-rock miners, mostly from the West, were moving into the Cornwall-on-Hudson neighborhood. But faced with the unprecedented success of the Hudson River Fishermen's Association's plea to the Court of Appeals to reopen hearings on the impact to the fisheries resource, construction was abruptly halted three months after it began. One miner from California, who had moved into his newly purchase Cornwall house one day, put a FOR SALE sign on his lawn the next.

The federal Environmental Protection Agency (EPA), which was not even in existence when Con Ed first proposed the Storm King plant but was at this point an important regulatory player, took a careful look in 1977 at the impact of power-plant operations on fish in the Hudson River and ruled that "closed-cycle" cooling towers would have to be built at existing Con Ed, Central Hudson Gas & Electric, and other Hudson River power plants to protect the fish. For the power companies, this ruling brought with it a staggering price tag. Con Ed had started with the idea for a new pumped-storage power generating plant, only to find itself after twenty-two years of effort, and 12,542 pages of testimony on the FPC record, faced with the unanticipated and very costly challenge of retrofitting the Indian Point Nuclear Power Plant with closed-cycle cooling towers to protect the Hudson River's fishery resource. Other alternatives for peaking power were available and more cost-effective, especially the use of natural gas to fuel smaller plants nearer to the city. Company officials decided to settle with their opponents and walk away from Storm King.

In 1980 Mrs. Willis (Franny) Reese, chair of Scenic Hudson, was among the fatigued but euphoric and proud signatories to a settlement agreement with Con Ed. Albert Butzel, by then Scenic Hudson's battle-tested counsel, looked on. Con Ed surrendered its FPC license for the Storm King project, vowing not to attempt any similar project for at least twenty-five years. Con Ed paid $12 million to fund independent fisheries research in the Hudson River and paid another $500,000 to offset the legal expenses accumulated over many years by Scenic Hudson, the NRDC, the Hudson River Fishermen's Association, and other litigators. Land on the river at Storm King, acquired for the main power-plant infrastructure, was deeded to the PIPC. Land acquired at the Cornwall-on-Hudson reservoir site went to the village. Central Hudson Gas & Electric abandoned its attempt to build a cross-river power plant at Breakneck Ridge, and it agreed to sell the site, more than six hundred acres, to the State of New York. In return, the EPA agreed that Con Ed, Central Hudson Gas & Electric, and other companies would not be forced to build closed-cycle cooling towers at their existing Hudson River power plants. Con Ed had invested more than $35 million in the Storm King venture and came away empty-handed.

The Storm King Mountain controversy had proven to be a vexing contradiction for the PIPC. The commissioners and Morgan sincerely felt that in the early years they had influenced the Con Ed project in a manner that seemed to meet larger public needs while also defending the integrity of parklands. But this "dual use" approach only weakened their credibility in the eyes of so many who supported the PIPC's basic purposes and impressive conservation track record.

When settlement was finally reached, conservation organizations from throughout the United States were greatly strengthened by the battle to save Storm King Mountain. Con Ed never lost in court, but environmental organizations nonetheless gained immeasurably. Citizens with no specific economic interest in a property had gained important standing before regulatory agencies and in federal and state courts to defend environmental, cultural, and historic values. Thanks to the fish in the Hudson River, the environmental impact statements of new development must now include precise identification, data collection and research, independent analysis, identification of alternatives, and means of possible mitigation. If the impacts are too great, and mitigation is not feasible, federal and state laws require that projects must be greatly modified, or even dropped, to protect wildlife species, plants, water and air quality, and natural beauty. Storm King Mountain stands as a permanent monument to this heightened national environmental awareness and commitment to the "wisdom of beautiful living."

For the PIPC, Storm King Mountain was a hard lesson, but the pace and good purposes of the PIPC's other activities never faltered. The day after Boyle spoke about fish at the Bear Mountain Inn, Rockefeller, Borg, Jube, and Morgan were in New Jersey with Governor Hughes to witness the firing of a vintage cannon from historic Fort Lee for the first time in 188 years. They were determined to build a wonderful museum on the site where history was made in 1776, and they were resolved even more to continue the expansion of the PIPC's park and historic-site system, wherever that path might lead.

A key member of the PIPC's staff would not participate in the journey ahead. He was Joseph Kearns McManus, a former school principal and coach from New Jersey who, for the last twelve years of his career, managed Bear Mountain State Park on behalf of the PIPC. Writing about McManus on September 5, 1967, Sports Editor Bo Gill of the *Newburgh Evening News* said: "The warmth of the fireplace,

Frederick H. Osborn, Palisades Interstate Park Commissioner, 1927–1971. Photo dated 1941.

the singing of happy ski jumpers, the spills on the slopes, the crowds and traffic jams, the snow-cleared Palisades Parkway, the recreational areas and everything that is and will be Bear Mountain will feature one thing . . . Right smack in the middle of it all will be the lovable memory of Mr. McManus. . . . His spirit always will be there." Writing to Morgan, Commissioner Osborn echoed the sentiment: "In August, we came down from Maine for a few days and I went to Silvermine [ski area] and Joe met me there long after hours. We had such a nice talk and I am glad to have that last memory of him." In the minutes of the PIPC, Osborn ensured that his own personal recollections became a part of the official record: "I want to say that I knew Joe well and considered him a very remarkable man, extraordinarily competent, with great personal qualities and a spirit about the work in the Park. He embodied the highest ideals you could wish for the Park. A very unusual man. I would like to move this resolution and ask that we vote by standing. . . ." Like so many of his co-workers, McManus worked out of the limelight but discovered a fulfilling lifestyle intertwined with his job. He worked with the moods of Bear Mountain Park rather than searching beyond its boundaries for a better paycheck. Like so many of his fellow employees, McManus seemed to find an unusual and rewarding level of personal satisfaction in the gemstone-like workplace that greeted him each day.

A hint of the path ahead for the PIPC came in early 1969 when Commissioner Osborn mentioned at a Commission meeting that "a 7,000-acre tract believed to be owned by real estate people" might be available for purchase on the Shawangunk Ridge, just west of New Paltz, New York. The tract was near the famous Cliff House, a Victorian-style hotel, vintage 1879, perched on the edge of a cliff at Lake Minnewaska, a so-called "sky lake." Osborn said the property was "scenic and might be of interest to the PIPC." With the consent of his fellow commissioners, Osborn asked the PIPC's staff "to try to find out what is proposed to be done with this tract."

Morgan was not at the meeting when Osborn recommended that the Shawangunk Ridge be investigated. In response to inquiries by the commissioners and staff, J. O. I. Williams, the PIPC's assistant general manager, advised: "Ken is feeling better and thinks he might be back in circulation soon," but Morgan's deteriorating health prevented him from pursuing the Minnewaska opportunity as recommended by Osborn. After twenty-nine years as the PIPC's chief engineer and general manager, health problems forced Morgan to retire on September 1, 1969.

16.
Minnewaska

Anticipating change at the top of the PIPC's staff organization, Laurance Rock-efeller was thinking about exactly the right person to succeed A. K. Morgan. On his many trips to Washington, D.C., to chair the Outdoor Recreation Resources Review Commission and, later, to chair the White House Conference on Natural Beauty, Rockefeller came in contact with Nash Castro. Castro was serving as regional director for the National Park Service (NPS) in the nation's capital. NPS holdings in Washington, D.C., include a treasure-trove of the United States's most cherished shrines, among them the Lincoln and Jefferson Memorials, the Washington Monument, the Mall, and the grounds of 1600 Pennsylvania Avenue—the White House. Unlike more traditional NPS operations that focused on natural areas, historic and archaeological sites, battlegrounds, and outdoor recreation areas usually far removed from city centers, Castro was responsible for a full-blown urban-park operation. At age forty-nine, he was near the pinna-cle of his profession, standing among a select few who exercised senior admin-istrative and management influence over the NPS's policies, priorities, and style. A naval aviator during World War II, Castro had a wide range of responsibilities, including service as executive vice president of the White House Historical Asso-ciation, an organization he helped found during the Kennedy administration. Castro's continuing work with the historical society led him to assist Mrs. Lyn-don Baines "Lady Bird" Johnson, who was using her position as First Lady to advance beautification projects throughout the nation. In this initiative, Johnson enlisted the celebrity and kindred interest of Rockefeller and the administrative skills of Castro.

While traveling with Johnson to visit beautification projects, Rockefeller and Castro "came to know each other quite well," as Castro later recalled. Rockefeller obviously liked what he saw in the person and competency of Castro, confirmed in 1966 when Rockefeller, wearing his hat as chair of the New York State Council of Parks, attempted to lure Castro to New York to become director of the State Park System. Castro declined, citing his work with Johnson and other professional commitments to the NPS. Nonetheless, Rockefeller remained determined. Soon after the inauguration of President Richard Nixon in January, 1969, Castro received a message that Rockefeller would be in Washington, D.C., and wanted to meet with him. "I speculated that he might wish to underwrite one or more unfunded beautification projects," Castro said. "Instead, he surprised me by inviting me to succeed Ken Morgan at the PIPC. L. S. R. said to me, 'This time don't say no. Come to the Palisades and take a look.'"

Accepting the Rockefeller invitation "more as a courtesy than anything," Castro toured the PIPC's parks and historic sites. "I did a lot of soul-searching subsequently, remembering that I filled a very satisfying niche in the National Park Service. . . . To offset this, I dwelled considerably on L. S. R.'s most commendable environmental work of 30 years in which he more than distinguished himself." Still, Castro hesitated. Mrs. Johnson was making frequent return trips to Washington to continue her advocacy for beautification. Along with Laurance and Mary Rockefeller, Castro and his wife, Bette, were included in various social events when the former First Lady was in town. Rockefeller would take advantage of these gatherings to again discuss the PIPC opportunity with the Castros. Bette Castro fondly remembers Rockefeller as being "very persuasive." In June, 1969, Rockefeller dispatched his Citation jet to Washington to transport the Castros to the Hudson River Valley. Aboard Rockefeller's boat, the *Dauntless,* a converted Canadian minesweeper, the Castros were treated to a waterborne view of the Hudson River from Tarrytown to Bear Mountain. Rockefeller escorted the Castros to lunch at the Bear Mountain Inn, where they were joined by Commissioners Linn Perkins, Averell Harriman, Frederick Osborn, Conrad Wirth, and Donald Borg. Not leaving anything to chance, Rockefeller also included Commissioner-emeritus Horace Albright. Both Albright and Wirth were former directors of the NPS. Two weeks after the visit, Castro agreed to bring his NPS career to a conclusion and join the PIPC as its next general manager. "Bette and I considered all the pros and cons about making such a big change in our lives," Castro remembered. "Every discussion recalled the prospect of working with a real star of the conservation fraternity, Laurance S. Rockefeller." In September, 1969, Castro stepped up to his second career, one that would extend over another two decades.

Castro had been on the job for only a few days when Commissioner Osborn telephoned him at the Tarrytown Hilton where he and his family were temporarily lodged. Osborn's call was prompted by an article in *The New York Times* describing the Shawangunk Ridge and its classic Victorian-style hotels at Lakes Minnewaska and Mohonk. In the 1870s, twin brothers Albert and Alfred Smiley had purchased a tavern on the shore of Lake Mohonk, a "sky lake" on a knife-edged promontory near the northern end of the thirty-mile-long ridge. Following their Quaker beliefs, the Smileys forbade the drinking of alcoholic beverages, card playing, or dancing in their newly acquired tavern,

Laurance Rockefeller, speaking. Nash Castro, Executive Director, Palisades Interstate Park Commission, 1969–1990, is second from Rockefeller's left. *(Courtesy of PIPC Archives)*

named the Mohonk Mountain House. Despite these restrictions, the brothers began to transform the mountain house into a successful mountain resort for guests primarily from New York City. The guests would journey by train to a railroad stop near New Paltz, New York, then would be transported by horse-drawn carriages to Lake Mohonk. Inspired by a carriage trip to nearby Coxing Pond, the other "sky lake" on the ridge, Alfred Smiley determined to develop a second resort hotel at the site. He renamed the pond Lake Minnewaska, borrowing a word associated with the Native American language of the region. Alfred's Minnewaska Mountain House (later renamed the Cliff House) was constructed just beyond the edge of the cliff that surrounded the lake and accommodated 225 guests. Within a decade, the Wildmere, a second hotel that accommodated 350 guests, shared the locality with the Cliff House.

The Times's article confirmed that the geologically elaborate Shawangunk Ridge was a phenomenal nursery for thousands of plant and wildlife species. Osborn said to Castro: "Let's drive up there and take a look." Enlisting Commissioner Wirth to the reconnaissance team, the three men confirmed that the

Empire National Bank was in fact threatening to foreclose on thousands of acres on the ridge owned by Kenneth E. Phillips, Sr. Phillips, an ardent spokesperson for the sensational beauty of the Shawangunk Ridge, acquired the Cliff House and Wildmere Hotels and ten thousand acres of land surrounding Lake Minnewaska from the heirs of Alfred Smiley in 1955 for a reported $75,000, a sum never corroborated by public record. The hotels retained their outward charm when the Osborn team visited in 1969, but three-quarters of a century of weather and wear and tear had taken their toll on the old wooden structures. The cost of maintenance was spiraling upward. Travel patterns were also changing. City dwellers who once provided a dependable leisure clientele for the Shawangunks, Catskills, and Adirondacks were routinely traveling to more distant places. Ownership of the old hotels, combined with a property-tax burden on so much land, was proving to be beyond the limits of Phillips's pocketbook in a faltering market.

Maneuvering to financially reinforce the Lake Minnewaska operation and avoid foreclosure, Phillips signaled a willingness to sell seven thousand acres of land while retaining three thousand acres nearest to the lake. Resting along the ridge line south of the lake, the land offered for sale was a stunningly beautiful domain of cliffs, forests, and narrow valleys. Osborn, Wirth, and Castro needed no convincing that such a place should be preserved. They quickly learned, too, that the PIPC had a readily approachable ally in The Nature Conservancy. The Conservancy was known for its businesslike approach to the acquisition of natural areas noted for biological diversity and vitality. The fact that Pat Noonan, The Nature Conservancy's executive director, was already interested in the Shawangunk Ridge ecosystem was a huge plus to the PIPC.

In November, 1969, the commissioners formally went on record in support of the initiative to acquire seven thousand acres from Phillips at a cost of $1.5 million. Castro affirmed that The Nature Conservancy was positioned to handle the transaction and was willing to transfer title to the PIPC on the handshake expectation that the commissioners would succeed in arranging for sufficient public funding to reimburse the Conservancy. If successful, the acquisition would stand among the most meaningful on the PIPC's ledger. Phillips's acreage was of sufficient scale to create a stand-alone park. Miles of carriage roads and hiking trails were already in place. A forest of rare dwarf pitch pine trees, abundant wildlife, sweeping views, and two wilderness lakes awaited future park visitors. Just south of the land being sought by the PIPC, deep fissures in the striated cliffs sheltered cavelike ice formations that grew from trickling water during the winter months and were permanently sheltered from the summer heat in naturally refrigerated alcoves. Just north of Phillips's acreage, rock climbers had discovered the "gunks" in the mid-1950s and added the hard rock cliffs to their informal network of prized climbing destinations.

Working out the details of the transaction put the PIPC and the Conservancy in a race against the Empire National Bank. The first challenge was to determine exactly how much land Phillips was actually selling. His estimate was 6,725 acres. A survey and title search boosted the figure to 7,100 acres. Phillips did not quibble; his price was firm regardless of the acreage discrepancy. With support for the transaction expressed by Governor Nelson Rockefeller, the Conservancy closed the deal in June, 1970, only days before the bank was prepared to foreclose. With signature affixed to the legal documents, the PIPC assumed management of a major new park of rare merit. Reimbursement to the Conservancy took months of concerted effort by the commissioners and Castro. Half of the $1.5 million purchase price was slated to come from the federal Land & Water Conservation Fund on condition that New York State would match the amount. Two years after Phillips sold to the Conservancy, the commissioners

Cliff House Hotel, Lake Minnewaska, New York.
(Courtesy of PIPC Archives)

commended Castro for the "infinitely painful and highly effective effort in the matter of the Minnewaska acquisition." The pain came from the after-the-fact need to convince federal and state officials that the PIPC's commitment to The Nature Conservancy was valid, justifiable, and undeniably beneficial to the public. Even with the weight of Governor Rockefeller's support complemented by the national standing of Laurance Rockefeller as a commonsense champion of conservation, the many keepers of the public purse still had to be persuaded. New to his PIPC job, Castro used diplomacy and his personal contacts in Washington, D.C., to lock in the $750,000 federal investment in the Shawangunk Ridge. The New York matching amount followed.

Commissioner Osborn was actually in a lame-duck position with the PIPC when the transaction for Phillips's land was completed. His five-year term had expired in 1969. Commissioners with expired terms could continue to serve until they or their successors were appointed to a new term. Osborn learned through Rockefeller that the governor did not intend to reappoint him. The governor's reasoning was that Osborn, at age eighty-two, was too old to be reappointed. On learning the news, Osborn commented that "this association has been one of the happiest of my life" and went right on with his volunteer work for the PIPC, including pursuit of Phillips's property, until poor health finally caused him to submit his resignation in 1972. Osborn served with the PIPC for forty-four years. Speaking on behalf of the commissioners, Castro credited Osborn with a "triumph of the first order" on the Shawangunk Ridge.

The commissioners and Castro were faced with the pleasant need of selecting a name for the new park on the Shawangunk Ridge. They preferred Minnewaska but worried that the public might confuse "Minnewaska State Park" with Lake Minnewaska and the resort hotels still owned by Kenneth Phillips. Other possibilities included "Shawangunk State Park" or "Lake Awosting State Park." After brief debate, the Minnewaska name was affirmed. Castro moved quickly to begin developing a park-management plan. One of the immediate and interesting challenges was that a rustic camp existed at Lake Awosting consisting of several "rather marginal buildings" and "more especially, a problem from a sanitation point of view," as Castro delicately advised the commissioners. Practitioners of yoga used the camp for prayer and meditation. The campers promptly launched "a highly effective letter-writing campaign" to retain camp privileges that would be almost in the geographic center of the new park. Castro knew well this type of instant demand for special-interest use of newly acquired parklands. Groups and individuals not necessarily involved in the hard political efforts to create new parks, nor particular advocates of sufficient funding to properly manage them, frequently were the first in line to insist on entitled access. Usually claiming that "our tax dollars created the park," groups and individuals motivated by singular agendas often seek to stake out territory by means of whatever political clout may be available to them. The yoga campers at Lake Awosting were no exception. They wanted not to budge or to be disturbed. Close after them, hunters, trappers, and snowmobilers made known their expectations that the new Minnewaska State Park would be immediately open for their purposes.

To find answers for the future stewardship of Minnewaska, Castro turned to a planning technique routinely used by the NPS. He imported a team of NPS experts and opened the planning process to public debate. A strong consensus quickly developed for preserving the wild character of the new park. The minority, particularly representatives of nearby communities who wished maximum economic benefit from Minnewaska-inspired tourism, expressed a contrary view. They urged rapid development that would include bus access, use of the carriage roads by automobiles, motorboats on Lake Awosting, off-road vehicle trails, and the construction of tennis and basketball courts, swimming pools, and food stands. Snowmobilers aligned themselves with the community representatives, seeking strength in numbers as a springboard to influence the PIPC and elected officials in Albany.

Claiming that the park should not be "locked up for the hardy few" who enjoyed the solitude of wilderness trails, the proponents for development of Minnewaska discovered that their voices were overmatched by the "hardy few" whose numbers far surpassed their own. Spokesperson after spokesperson appeared before the planning team to urge strict limits on development and motor-vehicle access in favor of park uses including hiking, nature education, cross-country skiing, sledding, ice skating, horseback riding, bicycling, bird-watching, photography, fishing, swimming in the lakes and streams, canoeing, rock climbing, and the simple pleasure of experiencing the sights and sounds of a natural place unencumbered by blacktop, buildings, and combustion engines.

The planning team found in favor of the "hardy few" by recommending to the PIPC that snowmobiles (later allowed), motorcycles, trail bikes, outboard motors, and automobiles not be permitted access to the carriage roads in the new park. In varying degrees the team reasoned that these activities might severely limit other uses, could be dangerous, and would be destructive to the natural integrity of the park. The team concluded that these "artificial" forms of recreation were not appropriate in such an exquisite and complex natural ecosystem.

Hunting was another matter. The NPS planning team recommended against hunting at Minnewaska State Park, taking a page from federal rules that deny hunting in national parks. But the tradition of hunting on most public lands in New York runs deep. Despite the pleas from many who participated in the planning dialogue that the sound of gunfire and bullets whizzing through the trees would be intrusive and dangerous, Castro judged that a compromise on hunting was necessary. He recommended that the commissioners approve hunting—limited to the use of shotguns only—in a 1,600-acre section of the new park .

At about the time that the Minnewaska plan was being settled, the PIPC found itself affected by a nationwide economic recession. In late 1970, Castro alerted the commissioners that Governor Rockefeller was imposing an austerity program on all state agencies, including the PIPC. A hiring freeze was imposed, and all agencies were directed to reduce operations by 40 percent. This economic squeeze caught up with the last of the side-wheel steamers still operating on the Hudson River. The *Alexander Hamilton* made its final voyage from New York City to Bear Mountain on September 6, 1971. When the steamer turned downriver from the Bear Mountain dock, the grand era of steamboat service on the river came to an end. Launched in 1924, the old and slow *Alexander Hamilton* was being replaced by the *Dayliner,* a modern four-deck vessel measuring 308 feet at the waterline and powered by two 1,750-horsepower diesel engines. The *Dayliner* could carry 3,500 passengers at a speed of sixteen knots. Constructed of nine hundred tons of steel plate at a cost of $3.5 million, the *Dayliner* made its maiden voyage to Bear Mountain on June 10, 1972, continuing the tradition of excursions from the city to the narrows of the Hudson River for the 109th consecutive year. The many side-wheel steamers that had operated on the river were memories, captured in paintings and photographs, symbolic of the Hudson's history and majesty, but ultimately consigned to scrap yards, burned, sunk, or simply run aground and abandoned in backwater coves.

While grappling with the challenges of the economic recession, Castro was also looking at the details of the operation. At his direction, the staff began changing the language on the signs that greeted the host of visitors to the PIPC's parks and historic sites. Message changes included

Old Sign	New Sign
Persons Discarding Rubbish Will Be Arrested	Please Keep Your Park Clean
No Skating	Sorry—Ice Unsafe For Skating Today
Stay On Walks	Please Use Walks
No Picnicking	Please Picnic In Designated Areas Only

User-friendly initiatives at the grassroots level, combined with Castro's bid to ensure that the public was heard on the question of the Minnewaska plan, brought well-deserved praise to the PIPC. Wirth echoed this sentiment as he submitted his resignation as a PIPC commissioner in 1972. Writing to Castro, the former NPS director said, "You are demonstrating, as I knew you would, what a fine professional park man can do. One of the most important aspects of administration (it may be the most important) is understanding people." By attempting to improve contact between the PIPC and its patrons, Castro was inviting the public to join in the care of their lands.

This invitation, though, had its limits. Park visitor Christopher J. Schubert, a geologist on the staff of the Museum of Natural History, confirmed that crystals found near Bear Mountain "are Jeffersonite, a manganese-zinc bearing pyroxene." Schubert affirmed: "These are without doubt the largest sized crystals of Jeffersonite in this region. . . . They have respectable market value and word of their occurrence should be kept to a minimum." But having cautioned the PIPC, Schubert could not resist adding, "It would be most appropriate to try to incorporate these pockets into a natural trail exhibit. So rarely does a student have the opportunity to see museum quality crystals in their natural setting." Castro heeded Schubert's first advice. The location of the crystals remained undisclosed. Even in a user-friendly park, to do otherwise guaranteed that the crystals would disappear, either as mementos or at the hands of commercial raiders.

While Castro was encouraging visitor cooperation in the care of the parks, he found himself on a collision course with the PIPC's own police force in New Jersey. The police officers were unhappy with their level of pay. They had been lumped into a general State of New Jersey pay category with game wardens and prison guards even though their duties closely paralleled those of the more highly paid State Police. The complaint of the Palisades Parkway Police was directed at the union structure within New Jersey, not at the PIPC, but their leverage was the parkway. Urged on by the Patrolmen's Benevolent Association, the Parkway Police began stopping rush-hour motorists to check driver's licenses and automobile registrations. The officers were careful and took their time, so much so that the result was a ten-mile-long traffic jam on the Palisades Parkway involving an estimated 9,200 vehicles occupied by infuriated commuters. The "job action" produced exactly the opposite result of that sought by the police officers. They generated such bad publicity for themselves that state officials stiffened their resistance to any change in the union status for the Palisades Parkway Police. The commissioners and Castro, acting to stem an instant erosion of public support, directed that key leaders of the "job action" be reprimanded and reassigned to foot-patrol duties at the Englewood and Alpine boat basins.

Nor had the user-friendly approach prevailed in the lengthy dialogue between Commissioner Borg and representatives of the Marriott Corporation. After almost fifteen years of effort, during which the PIPC had sought to reach a compromise with Marriott to preserve the character of the Fort Lee Historic Site, the corporation was finally forced from its 6.43-acre development site through condemnation proceedings by the State of New Jersey. Marriott received $1,012,500 as payment for the acreage. The PIPC's share of the payout to Marriott was 25 percent, about $253,000. Borg and his fellow commissioners might have been forgiven a sigh of relief at the departure of such a stubborn foe, but their contest with Marriott at Fort Lee was to pale by comparison with a conflict yet to come with the corporation. Marriott was about to arrive on the scene at Minnewaska.

"Dear Laurance: My resignation as a member of the Palisades Interstate Park Commission has been accepted and I am writing to tell you and the other members how very much it has meant to me to serve with you gentlemen. . . ." With this note, dated September 18, 1973, Linn M. Perkins, the first woman appointed to the PIPC, signaled a transition among the commissioners equal to the major changes that occurred in the late 1930s. Less than three months after Perkins resigned, Borg stepped down because of health reasons. He would not be participating in the second struggle with the Marriott Corporation. Then, in March, 1974, former governor and ambassador Harriman followed suit after more than a half-century of involvement with the PIPC, beginning with his first public speech, delivered as a teenager in recognition of his mother's pace-setting 1909 gift of land and money to the PIPC.

The resignations, coming so closely in line, might have opened the PIPC to political pressures of unaccustomed scale. Instead, the resignations served to reinforce family commitments to the PIPC. Governor Rockefeller appointed Perkins's son, George Perkins, Jr. (III), to succeed her. In late spring, 1974, Malcolm Wilson, who ascended to the governorship of New York when Nelson Rockefeller was affirmed as vice president of the United States in the Ford administration, appointed Mary Fisk, daughter of Harriman, to take her father's place as a commissioner, followed only a few weeks later when New Jersey Governor Brendan Byrne appointed Malcolm A. Borg to succeed his father. The PIPC commissioners representing these wealthy, influential, and independent families serve on a variety of other charitable and corporate boards of directors and could easily transfer their allegiances to still other good causes on the expiration of their unpaid, five-year terms with the PIPC. An interesting aspect of the organization is that despite other opportunities, the commissioners, almost without exception, accept reappointment to the PIPC, term after term. In so doing, they demonstrate remarkable dedication to the purposes and activities of an organization that otherwise is only vaguely recognized in the New York/New Jersey metropolitan region and among established national conservation organizations, if recognized at all. The incentive for such constancy to the PIPC apparently lies in the product of the commissioners' work. The commissioners, including sons and daughters, even grandsons and granddaughters, of the original founders, continue to create an immense public preserve surrounded by the stridency of a tough and demanding urban cityscape. The commissioners can see, touch, measure, and cherish the results. The successful conservation of land is tangible, a touchstone with the past and a timeless gift for the future. This seems enticing reward enough for the generations of commissioners.

Mary Fisk, of the Harriman family, Palisades Interstate Park Commissioner, 1974–1996. *(Courtesy of PIPC Archives)*

During the transition among the commissioners, the portion of the Lake Minnewaska property still owned by Kenneth L. Phillips, Sr., was found to be at risk. At a PIPC meeting in April, 1974, Castro recounted that the *Daily Freeman,* a Kingston, New York, newspaper, carried an article reporting that Phillips "has not arranged financing" and that he was planning to demolish the old Cliff House and Wildmere Hotels in favor of subdividing the land to accommodate motels, condominiums, and private homes. George R. Cooley, a local Hudson River Valley member of The Nature Conservancy, wrote to Castro later in the year, stating, "Word comes to me that Phillips is getting slow in making his monthly payments to the First National Bank of Highland on the $750,000 first mortgage which the bank owns. Is the ultimate acquisition of the hotel property and its 2,895 acres something which interests you and should the Conservancy step in at the right time?" An article in the *Sunday Times Herald Record,* Middletown, New York, announced, "$18 Million Project Proposed For Minnewaska" and underscored Cooley's questions. According to the accompanying article, "a 1,136-unit condominium project that would transform a large tract of wilderness land adjoining the Minnewaska State Park into a four-season resort has been proposed to Town of Rochester and Gardiner officials." Included in the development plan, said reporter Peter Kutschera, were "commercial tracts that would include a theater, motel, restaurants, service stations, retail shops and professional offices," He added that the plans also encompassed "an equestrian ranch, tennis courts, a children's recreation area, hiking trails and an expanded golf course." Subdivided lots for 110 private homes were part of the development concept. Kutschera speculated that "as word of the proposal spreads through the region, it appears that a battle may be in store." Quoted in the same article, Frederick Faerber, president of the Ulster Sportsmen's Federation, confirmed that his organization would oppose the plan, contending that the proposed development "would further threaten a continually diminishing supply of available game land." Faerber stressed, "A high-density development next to a forever wild park makes absolutely no sense to us." The Rondout Valley Sportsmen Club echoed Faerber's view. Its representative sent a letter to Ogden Reid, New York's newly appointed Commissioner of Environmental Conservation, recommending that the Phillips property be annexed to the park. "That's the only way we can see something like this being stopped cold," contended club member Steve Schwartz.

Within days of the *Times Herald*'s article, Phillips and Castro were meeting at Bear Mountain to discuss a possible willing-seller, willing-buyer transaction. As he had done once before, Phillips suggested sale of one-half of his remaining land holdings. "This would permit him to apply the funds from such a sale to the requirements of the other one-half of his property," Castro reported to the commissioners. But events were moving quickly. Less than a month later, Phillips was in Albany, meeting with representatives of the Office of Parks and Recreation, seeking, as Castro summarized it, "a State financial vehicle" that would allow him to "avoid subscribing any land for development." Before the state could respond, the *Times Herald Record* confirmed that the Ulster County Planning Board had recommended to Town of Rochester officials that rezoning of the property be denied. The proposed development "would be entirely out of character" with Minnewaska State Park, said Board Chairman Gifford Beal. He, too, urged the state to acquire the property.

In the spring of 1975, Castro and Phillips were talking again. On this occasion, Phillips proposed that the PIPC purchase six hundred acres of his property, including a marginal downhill ski facility, for $1.8 million. Castro characterized this proposal as not being "business-like." Without fanfare, the PIPC was completing businesslike transactions with various other landowners on the Shawangunk Ridge. At the May Commission meeting, Castro confirmed that an additional 1,570 acres had been added to Minnewaska State Park, bringing the total holdings to 8,644 acres.

The next item on the Commission's agenda dampened this good news. Castro confirmed that in an overheated moment of government restructuring, the New York Legislature had voted to consolidate all parkways in the state under the authority of the Department of Transportation. Most parkways near New York City had evolved into jam-packed commuter routes. Older design standards were proving inadequate to demand. The costs for maintenance and improvement were skyrocketing. Still, the fact that the Palisades Interstate Parkway was swept along with the rest came as a surprise. Unlike the other New York parkways, the Palisades Parkway formed a historic connection between two states. It existed because of the foresight of early PIPC pioneers working in alliance with John D. Rockefeller, Jr., and it was integral to the formation of the entire PIPC park and historic-site system. To summarily yank the parkway from the PIPC and turn it over to highway engineers who had little knowledge, if any, of its genesis and purpose posed a real threat to the integrity of the PIPC's operations. Commissioner-emeritus Harriman was first in line to protest. He urged recently elected Governor Hugh Carey to veto the bill, arguing that "parkways are parks and not highways and should continue to be managed as such." Harriman's plea went unheeded. Although ownership remains with the PIPC, the thirty-mile New York section of the Palisades Parkway is maintained by the New York Department of Transportation (DOT); the fourteen-mile New Jersey section of the parkway remained under the authority of the PIPC.

In June, 1975, *The New York Times* carried a bold advertisement with a photograph of the Cliff House and Wildmere Hotels at Lake Minnewaska over the lead line "Equity Partner Sought." Following a detailed description of the property, the tag line declared, "We seek an equity partner of substance to co-venture the development of what must be considered one of the finest resort locations in the world." Interested parties were invited to contact Phillips and his son, Kenneth, Jr. The search for venture capital was another race by the Phillipses against the financial clock. Time ran out in early August, as the *Daily Freeman* confirmed: "Foreclosure Action Is Filed Against Lake Minnewaska." The accompanying article gave the details: $750,000 plus interest in default to the First National Bank of Highland; $134,173 in school taxes unpaid; and a $35,000 federal tax lien. The "state financial vehicle" that Phillips sought through Castro to avoid the kind of headline appearing in the Kingston newspaper did not arrive. In response to a conversation with Castro, Phillips wrote: "Thank you for your telephone call. . . .

Although your answer is negative, we want you to know that we appreciate your efforts in going to Albany to seek funds to acquire additional lands for Minnewaska State Park. . . . Your reply leaves us no choice but to pursue alternatives." Neither Phillips nor Castro knew what those "alternatives" might be.

Phillips and his son understandably wanted to avoid losing their livelihood and the property they cherished. If foreclosure somehow could be avoided by finding venture-capital co-partners or funding from the state at a level that would satisfy the First National Bank, the Phillips family presence at Lake Minnewaska could continue in genteel style in the picturesque and historic setting. C. David Loeks, representing Mid-Hudson Pattern for Progress, an alliance of business people, recommended that funds from a voter-approved 1972 Bond Act be used to acquire the Phillips land. Loeks reminded readers of the *Times Herald Record* that only $22 million of the $66 million bond fund had been spent, leaving an obvious source of readily available dollars for the purchase. The Adirondack Mountain Club, The Nature Conservancy, and other environmental groups echoed the Pattern for Progress's plea.

These organizations found a careful listener in the person of Maurice D. Hinchey, representing the 101st New York Assembly District. Hinchey's legislative district covered a significant midportion of the Hudson River Valley. Democrat Hinchey was chair of the New York Assembly's Environmental Conservation Committee. He was known for paying close attention to the policies, presumptions, activities, and purse strings of the state's land-management agencies. Hinchey was not shy about holding accountable the Department of Environmental Conservation, the Office of Parks and Recreation, the PIPC, or any other state agency if he felt that environmental priorities were being politically diluted or short-changed. Learning that Castro's initiative to find state funding for the Minnewaska purchase had been unsuccessful, Hinchey jumped in. On September 6, 1975, he toured Minnewaska State Park and the adjoining Phillips property with Castro and Orin Lehman, commissioner of the New York Office of Parks and Recreation (OPR). Hinchey found obvious, ready partners in both men. Within four days, Lehman, who was to gain a highly respected reputation as a defender of parks during his many years of service with the state, was in contact with Peter Goldmark, Governor Carey's budget director. Lehman wanted a $2 million commitment from Goldmark to buy the Phillips property, using The Nature Conservancy as the agent to put together the deal. From that moment, Lehman and his OPR staff were determined to reel in the Phillips land, doing whatever it would take to convince the Carey administration and elected officials to approve the needed funding.

A new commissioner was appointed to the PIPC as the drive to acquire the Phillips property gathered momentum. She was Dr. Mamie Phipps Clark, a resident of Hastings-on-Hudson and the first African American to serve on the Commission. Her background was in contrast to that of the commissioners who had preceded her, but her professional skills and personal interests merged readily with one of the most basic purposes of the PIPC: to connect parks with inner-city children in need. Born in Arkansas, Clark was a magna cum laude and Phi Beta Kappa graduate of Howard University. In 1944 she was awarded a Ph.D. in clinical psychology from Columbia University. On graduation from Columbia, Clark joined the staff of the Riverdale Home for Children, not far from Wave Hill, the former estate of George Perkins, Sr. The privately funded Riverdale agency specialized in providing protection and care for homeless black girls. Realizing the "critical need" to provide psychological counseling to Harlem's black children and their families, Clark and her husband established the Northside Center for Child Development, where she served as executive director for thirty-four years. Using the Northside Center as a catalyst, Clark successfully created the 110th Street Plaza Housing Development Corporation to provide low- and middle-income housing for six hundred families.

Dr. Mamie Phipps Clark, Palisades Interstate Park Commissioner, 1976–1983. *(Courtesy of PIPC Archives)*

Clark found a kindred spirit among her commissioner colleagues. Fisk, though light years removed from Clark in childhood experiences and opportunities, had also chosen a path as educator in the inner city. Without fanfare but with quiet determination, Fisk traveled from her home on the Harriman estate to Harlem, where she taught as a volunteer for many years. Fisk and Clark stood with inner-city children along a fault line between hope and despair. Both women believed strongly in hope; they devoted themselves to the talent and promise they found in the children they assisted. Both women saw the group camps in Harriman Park as meaningful extensions of their efforts in the city. Though they were commissioners with disparate backgrounds, they made the camps their specialty, sharing in advocacy and friendship.

Ironically, a commissioner who had preceded them, a champion in his own time of the group camps, one of the great PIPC pioneers, became a victim of the hazy veils of history. The son of Dr. Edward L. Partridge offered a portrait of his father to the commissioners. Although records confirmed that Partridge had served as a commissioner from 1913 to 1930, institutional memory was vague. In the brief discussion about accepting the portrait, there was no hint of Partridge's turn-of-the-century promotion for a national park in the Hudson Highlands or of the development of a children's camp on his own property at Cornwall-on-Hudson. Nor was there mention of his contact with E. H. Harriman, in which the conservation theme for the Highlands was rung like a bell and a crucial champion was enlisted in the cause. On due deliberation, the commissioners declined to accept the portrait, reasoning that acceptance "might set a precedent which would be difficult to control."

Partridge nonetheless would have cheered an October, 1975, editorial in *The New York Times* that reflected growing public concern about the fate of the Phillips property. The *Times* confirmed that The Nature Conservancy was again standing in the wings, waiting for a signal to negotiate the purchase on behalf of the state. Noonan was quoted as saying that the Conservancy had money available and was willing to move "as soon as the whistle is blown," but Castro learned that the state had temporarily withdrawn from the bond market because of "fiscal uncertainties," even though assurance was given that Minnewaska was at the top of the list "when the freeze is off." Writing to Lehman early in 1976, Brad Northrup, the Conservancy's Boston-based regional director, reiterated Noonan's message that the Conservancy was ready to act, with the expectation that Lake Minnewaska and the surrounding land would soon be on the auction block. Phillips held a contrary view. A Conservancy representative met "amiably" with him to offer $1.2 million for the property. Phillips countered by claiming that he "had an offer in hand" exceeding $1.5 million, adding that the fair market value really was $3.5 million, the price he expected to receive. With prospective buyer and potential seller far apart on purchase price, discussion shifted to the option of acquiring two thousand acres of mostly undeveloped land, leaving the "core resort" and about one thousand acres with Phillips.

New York Park Commissioner Lehman and his staff rejected Phillips's proposal for payment of more than double the state's estimate of value and the alternative of a partial sale of land not including the centerpiece of the property, Lake Minnewaska. In the meantime, an ad appeared in the *Kruse Reports,* an Indiana-based investment journal, stating, "Lake Minnewaska, one of America's most beautiful resorts since 1879, now offered for sale. Owners will trade equity for stock. Mergers invited." Coincident with the ad, Phillips was back in contact with the local planning board, presenting a plan for a 120-unit trailer park near the location he proposed for the townhouse development, but delinquent mortgage and tax claims still stood against the property.

In late April, 1976, Castro alerted the Conservancy's staff that "the judgment will be returned today for the Judge's signature, and he will then appoint a referee for the sale. Once this is done, he can then proceed to prepare the Notice for Sale for publication. The publication will be made once a week for four weeks." The bank's attorney "looks for the property to be sold at the end of May or the beginning of June." The stage was set for the bankruptcy auction. Time, place, and date were scheduled: 10:00 a.m., June 14, Kingston, New York. Everyone assumed that the matter would be settled within a few weeks, everyone except the Phillipses.

The first rescheduling shifted the date to June 25, when the Phillips family attorney asked for a "stay" of the bankruptcy proceedings. By then, the Conservancy had a letter of intent confirming that "the State of New York will make every effort to repurchase the property known as Lake Minnewaska from The Nature Conservancy within one year of its purchase." Lehman signed the letter with the approval of Governor Carey's budget director, Goldmark. Editorial and public support in the Hudson River Valley for adding the Phillips property to Minnewaska State Park was widespread. By August, 1976, Castro was again in contact with the Conservancy's Northrup, advising him that attorneys for the First National Bank of Highland were attempting to get the "stay lifted" on the bankruptcy proceedings. Understandably, Phillips was doing everything in his power to convince the court that he had the ability to pay off his creditors. The judge continued a "stay" in the proceedings to provide Phillips more time, with the expectation that disagreements over value and financial viability would have to be settled by court trial.

While juggling trial preparations and creditor payments, Phillips maintained contact with the PIPC and Commissioner Lehman, suggesting that the state might wish to acquire the Lake Minnewaska property, then lease it back to the Phillips family to continue operation of the resort hotels. Castro was informed by memo that the state and the PIPC should "not attempt to negotiate a leaseback." Lehman's staff felt that "the odds are 70-30 in our favor of picking up the property at a foreclosure sale." Albert E. Caccese, counsel for the New York Office of Parks and Recreation, advised U.S. District Court Judge R. Lewis Townsend, "Although all parties made a bona fide attempt to arrive at an amicable and reasonable leaseback arrangement with the Phillips family, we are, unfortunately, unable to arrive at a meeting of the minds." A trial date was set for December 8. In preparation, the bank's attorneys filed an appraisal report with the court that estimated the fair market value for the property at $1.7 million. By this time, the Phillips family was claiming a value of $5.7 million based on estimates from its own "real estate experts." With the state and the PIPC contending that the purchase price would be no more than $1.5 million, the director of the federal Bureau of Outdoor Recreation, the agency created as a result of Laurance Rockefeller's work at the national level for President Eisenhower, confirmed that $500,000 was available to assist with the purchase.

The trial date was rescheduled yet again. In March, 1977, Lucille Phillips wrote to Castro: "It was so good to see you Saturday." She asked in the letter whether the PIPC might consider the idea of a "life tenancy" for the Phillips family at Lake Minnewaska. The notion was that the Phillipses would be paid for the property but could continue to live there. Phillips referred to other property owners who had made similar arrangements with the PIPC, thanks to "much kindly assistance from you and the Nature Conservancy." Castro put a margin note on the letter: "No." Public interest in the acquisition took on the characteristics of a low-grade fever as weeks dragged into months with the occasional burble of activity surfacing in the media to remind people that the property remained in jeopardy. One of those reminded was Robert M. Watkins. In one of many letters received by the PIPC, this one addressed to Commissioner-emeritus Harriman, Watkins introduced himself as a "stockbroker, not an ecologist." He described Lake Minnewaska as a

> fairy-land lake, the most beautiful I have ever seen. Its iridescent blue color and over-all beauty are such they must be seen to be believed. Of particular significance is that it is pristine, completely untouched from the time two Victorian hotels were built on its cliffs shortly after the Civil War. To expose such a piece of property now to the wrong type of private or commercial development would represent nothing short of a rape of probably the most beautiful remaining spot in New York State, if not the entire northeast United States.

Staff members for Lehman and Castro kept up a steady exchange of information, confirming that "18 separate parcels" made up the Phillips family's holdings and that these parcels might finally come under the hammer of the auctioneer more than two years after the First National Bank of Highland initiated the bankruptcy action. David Strauss & Company, Auctioneers, announced in *The New York Times* that "2,600 acres of resort land" would be auctioned, including two hotels, a nine-hole golf course, ski area, twenty miles of riding trails, and tennis courts adjacent to a "crystal clear glacial lake." The auction date was set for noon on November 9, 1977, at Lake Minnewaska. Before the auction could take place, Lehman's staff, reflecting lengthy behind-the-scenes dialogue among all parties, including the PIPC, made an offer of $1,050,000 for a partial purchase of the Phillips family property. On October 20, 1977, a press release from Lehman confirmed that the deal for a partial purchase had been struck with Kenneth and Lucille Phillips. In the release, Lehman praised the Phillips family "for conducting their resort operation with utmost concern for the preservation of the environment" and advised Judge Townsend on October 31, 1977: "We have reached agreement with the owner for the purchase of 1,300 acres of the Minnewaska property plus conservation easements on another 239 acres which include the lake."

The primary intent of the easement was to prevent the use of powerboats on the lake, but it also encompassed land on which a nine-hole golf course was located and restricted alterations to the natural landscape, including a strict limitation on tree cutting except to provide for scenic views. Any tree cutting required the PIPC's advance approval. The total purchase price, including miscellaneous costs, came to $1,110,000. The federal Department of the Interior provided $550,000 of the total purchase price, placing it in a position to legally monitor the future use of the land, including the easement, to ensure that park purposes would not suffer "conversion" to other uses. Title to the land and easement were vested in the PIPC. With proceeds in hand from the sale, the Phillipses were positioned to make temporary peace with their creditors, although the family's corporation remained in bankruptcy. An editorial in the Newburgh, New York, *Evening News* cheered, "Minnewaska Saved."

Tucked in the text of the editorial was a telling comment that would come back to haunt the PIPC: "From a conservationist point of view, it would have been better if the state had acquired the entire mountaintop. But half a loaf is better than none." The half-loaf left out of the deal was to prove very hot to handle.

With the issue of Minnewaska seemingly resolved for the moment, Castro, the commissioners, and the PIPC's staff could focus more time on the many other matters of management that made up the matrix of the organization. Good news came from Barnabas McHenry, vice president and chief counsel for the Reader's Digest Association, who confirmed that Lila Acheson Wallace and DeWitt Wallace, founders of the Digest, were committing long-term financial support to the Tiorati Workshop for Environmental Learning in Harriman Park. Money in support of environmental education was difficult to find in the 1970s, but McHenry made a persuasive case to his employers. The Wallaces needed little convincing. Their charitable legacy in the New York metropolitan area and beyond would grow to huge levels, including the establishment of a trust fund that has allowed two organizations, Scenic Hudson and the Open Space Institute, to invest more than $100 million, and still counting, in land conservation in the Hudson River Valley.

Castro and the staff had to balance the good news of the Tiorati Workshop against the startling news that sixty-four historic manuscripts, some signed by George Washington, had disappeared from a secure storage area at the PIPC-managed Washington's Headquarters State Historic Site in Newburgh, New York. Suspecting the obvious—that someone on the staff with access to the storage area had stolen the manuscripts—the Park Police questioned every member of the PIPC's staff at the site. Police Sergeant Daniel Shea was particularly persistent in the investigation. He tracked down leads that implicated a former part-time night watchman who had moved to Raleigh, North Carolina. With the arrest of the watchman, all sixty-four manuscripts were recovered and safely returned.

Even more startling than the theft was the disastrous fire, probably caused by vandals, that burned the Lake Minnewaska Cliff House Hotel to the ground in January, 1978. The Phillips family had closed the ninety-nine-year-old hotel, a tinderbox of dry wood, in 1972. With the closure, the sprinkler system was turned off and insurance coverage canceled. When the fire broke out in a second-story room, only two four-wheel-drive vehicles from distant volunteer fire departments were able reach the scene over the steep, snow-covered access road. By the time the fire fighters arrived, nothing was left of the hotel but a pile of glowing embers. (The Commission was more fortunate later that same year when a fire broke out in the kitchen of the Bear Mountain Inn. At the time, nine volunteer fire fighters happened to be having dinner at the inn. They got up from their table and put out the fire.)

About a year after the Cliff House fire, Phillips, Jr., confirmed that the Marriott Corporation wished to build a new eight-story, four-hundred–room "destination resort hotel" on the site of the old Cliff House. According to Marriott, the hotel, anticipated to cost $31 million, would employ four hundred workers and inject $16 million in taxes into the local government coffers in the first ten years of operation. The resort would offer a separate sports building, restaurants, a disco, indoor and outdoor swimming pools, indoor tennis courts, an ice rink, an equestrian center, a skeet range, and five racquetball courts. To complement the hotel's operation, five hundred condominium units were expected to be added to the Lake Minnewaska site.

Commissioner Borg, among others, must have raised his eyebrows at the thought of the Marriott Corporation's arrival at Minnewaska. He and the other

PIPC commissioners had been present in 1976 at the dedication of the new Visitor Center at the Fort Lee Historic Site in New Jersey. The commissioners had invested $3.5 million of the PIPC's funds in the Visitor Center in recognition of the nation's Bicentennial celebration, the largest amount spent on any project in New Jersey. One of the speakers at the dedication was Alfred T. Guido, New Jersey's director of Parks and Forestry, who reminded those in attendance that "we would be standing in the lobby of a high-rise hotel were it not for the Palisades Interstate Park Commission. Hotels are nice, but parks are better." Two decades earlier, Borg, as a young man, accompanied his commissioner father, Donald, to meetings with Willard Marriott during the "second battle" of Fort Lee, the contest of will that matched Borg and Rockefeller, representing the PIPC, against the resolute son of the founder of Washington, D.C.–based Marriott Hot Shoppes. In that contest, the PIPC eventually prevailed, sparing the twenty-eight–acre Fort Lee Historic Site the embellishment of Marriott's high-rise hotel.

Change was occurring within the PIPC as Marriott-Minnewaska sailed into view. After serving almost forty years with the PIPC, Rockefeller advised Governor Carey that he would step down when his term expired in February, 1979. Citing age as the reason, the sixty-eight-year-old commissioner recommended to the governor that a fourth generation Rockefeller, Larry, his son, be appointed to take his place. At his final PIPC meeting, Rockefeller said, "At a time like this, one has a lot of mixed emotions—a sense of achievement on the one hand, and gratitude to so many people for the things we have done together." Rockefeller was leaving behind a proud record. Even in the final few years of his service, he had directed almost $1.3 million in personal and Rockefeller family contributions to the PIPC. Rockefeller could claim specific credit for Rockland Lake and Tallman Mountain Parks and for wresting Iona Island from the federal government. Writing from California, PIPC commissioner-emeritus Albright stated: "From afar, my old friend, I salute you. I rejoice in your achievements."

At the same PIPC meeting in which Rockefeller offered his farewell, Castro confirmed that he was resigning after almost ten years as general manager of the PIPC to return to Washington, D.C. Castro had declined in 1974 the invitation of Secretary of the Interior Rogers C. B. Morton to accept the directorship of the National Park Service, but when a second invitation came to return to the nation's capital, he accepted the position of executive director of the White House Historical Association, the organization Castro had helped organize during the Kennedy administration in 1961. He was leaving with high praise from the commissioners for his adroit skills and graceful style.

A search committee was formed to recruit Castro's successor. The PIPC's deputy general manager, Donald B. Stewart, was charged with all responsibilities for day-to-day management pending the result of the search. Fortunately for the PIPC, the search progressed slowly. In the meantime, Castro discovered that the challenges and complexities of the PIPC far exceeded the demands of his new assignment in Washington. He reminisced, "I would arrive at the White House, get all my work done in the first two hours, and have nothing much to do for the rest of the day." To the relief of the commissioners, Castro asked to be reinstated. Seven months after he departed for Washington, Castro was back on the job at Bear Mountain. Despite additional job offers, three times to serve as New York Park commissioner and once as commissioner of Environmental Conservation, Castro remained at the PIPC's helm until he retired in 1990.

During Castro's brief absence in Washington, D.C., Stewart responded to an article in the *Gannett Westchester Newspapers* entitled, "The View Today." In the text of the article, the PIPC was taken to task for two unsightly radio towers that loomed over the New Jersey section of the Palisades Parkway, pointing out that a primary obligation of the PIPC was to protect the skyline from just such intrusions. In early 1978, Stewart could do little in response other than to explain that the largest of the two towers, a four-hundred-foot-tall behemoth with three one-hundred-foot-wide cross arms, had been constructed just off the PIPC's property in 1937 to transmit the world's first FM radio signals. The tower is so large that it appears as an official visual checkpoint on Federal Aviation Administration aeronautical charts for pilots flying in and out of Newark and Teterboro Airports. AT&T had constructed the smaller tower, also just off the PIPC's property, as part of its long-distance telephone network.

Stewart could do nothing about the towers but did act when, in April, 1978, he was advised by a PIPC staff member that "someone has remembered us in his will." In the last will and testament of Albert E. Milliken, instructions were left that if his wife survived him the residuary of his estate, including land on the Shawangunk Ridge, would go to her. If she did not survive him, 165 acres adjoining lands at Minnewaska State Park would go to the PIPC. "In order to fully understand this material," stated PIPC staff member Ron Karner, "some background information concerning Mr. Milliken's untimely demise is necessary. It is alleged that Mr. Milliken murdered his wife and then committed suicide." Further explanation followed: "Mr. Milliken had been married previously and had children by his first wife. It was these, his natural children, [to whom] he left his estate. Milliken's second wife's former husband filed a wrongful death action on behalf of his children, who had been left out of the will." By the time Castro was back at his desk, lawyers for the contending family members had settled the issue, and the land came to the PIPC.

Within days of Castro's return, he received a letter from James J. Stapleton, chair of the Ulster County, New York, Environmental Management Council, transmitting a report from Dr. Stephen J. Egemeier, chair of the council's subsidiary Land Use Committee. Egemeier had reviewed Marriott's development proposal at Lake Minnewaska and summarized his findings in the report. In his cover letter to Stapleton, Egemeier said, "I find it amusing that I'm accused in the July 7th *Poughkeepsie Journal* by Marriott's consultant of 'reflecting a typical environmental bias.' On T. V. the other night, Marriott advertised its Essex House as 'on Central Park.' The selling point was a desirable environment." Egemeier then listed his concerns: Marriott had misrepresented the geological structure of the Shawangunk Ridge, referring to "granite" rock rather than the sedimentary conglomerate that formed the ridge. This was important, Egemeier claimed, because of potential for groundwater pollution. The corporation claimed that no archaeological or historic sites existed in the area, contrary to findings of State University of New York archaeologists. Marriott denied any potential visual impact, although the hotel "would be visible all over the northern Wallkill Valley," according to Egemeier. Company officials claimed that the new hotel simply would replace the existing old hotels, but room capacity would increase from 333 to about 1,400, including the condominiums.

The most telling comments in the report involved water and sewage. Pointing out that Lake Minnewaska was a "sky lake," replenished seasonally by rainwater and snowmelt, Egemeier commented that the level of the lake would fluctuate over six feet in the wettest years, based on Marriott's projected water usage, and could not recover at all in drought years. He then described the sewage problem:

> Presently, Minnewaska sewage is pumped from a septic tank . . . and dumped on the top of a hill. From there it flows downhill, forming a pond and killing trees. This "overland flow system" is the worst pollution mess and health hazard I have seen anywhere in the county. The sewage pond is black and foul-smelling with a green scum. Gasses bubble to the surface, which is covered with flies. Remnants of toilet paper litter the ground. Approximately 600 feet downhill from the pipe I took a water sample. It gave a coliform count of 1500, an incredibly polluted sample.

Marriott proposed to use the same sewage system.

During a heavily attended public forum sponsored by the Friends of the Shawangunks and Citizens to Save Minnewaska, soon after the Egemeier report was released, Warren McKeon, a former New York Department of Environmental Conservation regional director, labeled the Marriott plan "environmentally unsound." Spectators at the meeting "erupted into applause," according to an article in the *Times Herald Record,* "when one person from the audience suggested that the state take over the proposed 375-acre hotel site and convert it into public park land." Individuals began forming themselves into activist groups in opposition to the project. A few dissident voices began to take on the characteristics of a chorus.

The PIPC commissioners and Castro were working with Lehman, Caccese, and the OPR staff in Albany to develop a strategy to ensure a maximum level of park protection on the Shawangunk Ridge. Looking north toward Minnewaska, the PIPC itself was caught off guard by a lengthy article in the September 9, 1979, *Sunday Record,* Commissioner Borg's own newspaper. "At N.J.'s Edge, A Park Is Dying," declared the headline; the subtitle was "Management Fails to Halt Decline, Detect Abuse." Investigative reporters Philip Barbara and Bruce Locklin had spent many weeks touring the PIPC's facilities in New Jersey, interviewing PIPC commissioners, including Borg, talking with present and former employees, and mingling with park visitors. The result was a seven-page article highly critical of the PIPC. To a large degree, the article was great testimony to the value Borg placed on the independence of his reporters. As owner and publisher of *The Record,* Borg was obviously responsible for the economic vitality and growth of his newspaper, but he let the news flow, wherever legitimate reporting might lead, even on those rare occasions when he found himself criticized in his own paper. The Barbara-Locklin piece was a case in point. The thrust of the article was that a beautiful park had badly deteriorated, along with severe loss of morale among the PIPC's employees, because senior managers, including the commissioners and Castro, were not paying attention. The commissioners were criticized for holding most of their meetings in a private room at Rockefeller Center in New York City, a tradition that had been followed for many years. Using the meeting location as one example, Barbara and Locklin charged that the hierarchy within the PIPC was far too remote from the guts of the operation in New Jersey. To drive home the point, vividly contrasting photographs accompanied the article. One photo highlighted a nicely remodeled bathroom in the PIPC-owned home of the park's assistant manager, a project accomplished in part with the PIPC's funds and the use of the park's maintenance force. Juxta-posed was another photo that showed a grungy, ill-maintained restroom at State Line Lookout, the premier tourist stop on the New Jersey Palisades. Two other photos, similarly displayed, contrasted a lively beach scene in the Undercliff area of the park, vintage 1925, to a then-vacant beach littered with driftwood. A PIPC employee was quoted as saying, "I was born and raised here, I love the park so much it hurts to see it going to hell."

The *Record*'s article appeared at a time when the PIPC and other governmen-tal agencies in New Jersey and New York were adjusting to new requirements for open public meetings, as mandated by both legislatures. The long-standing habit of holding many of the PIPC's meetings in a private room on the 64th floor of 30 Rockefeller Center was already being modified. The meetings were always conducted during luncheon, served from the kitchens of the famous Rainbow Room restaurant, which was located a floor above. When the meetings were first opened as required by law, a few members of the public arrived with their brown-bag lunches. They sat around the wall of the room, observing the meeting and admiring the luncheon, while they munched on their sandwiches. Barbara and Locklin had underscored the need for the commissioners to hear from the pub-lic about park management's activities, good or bad. The few brown-baggers who had the time, inclination, and determination to attend the Rockefeller Center meetings symbolized a much wider public interest, confirmed when eleven orga-nizations, representing a combined membership of 76,450, petitioned the PIPC to open its meetings to wide and unrestricted comment. Among the organiza-tions were the Environmental Defense Fund, the Hudson River Sloop *Clearwa-ter*, the Adirondack Mountain Club, the Audubon Society, the Sierra Club, the Friends of the Earth, and the Rockland County Conservation Association.

Borg and Larry Rockefeller, who succeeded his father on the Commission in October, 1979, echoed this plea. Rockefeller, a graduate of Columbia Law School, former VISTA volunteer in Harlem, and a senior member of the NRDC, saw a clear need and benefit in regular PIPC dialogue with the public it serves. He supported Borg's view that the PIPC should schedule fewer meetings in the city and more at PIPC parks and historic sites. In short time, the Rockefeller Cen-ter meetings ceased entirely.

Public input was helpful, but the core of the problem in New Jersey was money. The PIPC was caught off balance again in 1976 when it spent $3.5 million of its funds to construct the Fort Lee Historic Site Visitor Center in celebration of the Bicentennial at a moment when the New Jersey Legislature cut appropriations across the board for park operations. The net result for the PIPC was that its revenues, generated primarily from sales at two gasoline stations near the southern terminus of the Palisades Parkway, had to be shifted from projects to paychecks. Money for the restoration and improvement of facilities dried up. Priorities were given over to avoiding layoffs within an already meager staff.

In election years, parks may receive an extra injection of funds to momentarily raise them above a level of financial subsistence, but much more common is the type of false economy that results from appropriations being reduced to levels below which even routine maintenance becomes difficult. A split park-management personality results. Parks expand. Precious places are preserved. The public estate evolves to benefit future generations, attendant with public and media excitement, and grand political flourishes. Left in the wake of the creation of each new park and historic site are the professional managers struggling to make the case for continuing financial support once the excitement is over. The PIPC's split personality was dealing with peeling paint in restrooms at State Line Lookout and, at the same time, waging a conservation battle-royal to expand Minnewaska State Park.

Phillips, Jr., confirmed in a November, 1979, news article that "we are in the process of liquidating numerous antiques and artifacts that have been stored at Wildmere since it was opened for business a century ago." Marriott planned a spring opening for its new resort. The Wildmere Hotel would be torn down to make way for condominiums. Headlines started to appear in regional newspapers every few days: "Tests Polluting Stream, Opponents Say," "Marriott, Ulster Leaders Laud Resort Plans," "Minnewaska Sale Near, Marriott Says," "Archeologist Urges Study of Minnewaska Hotel Site," "Will Marriott Mar Lake Minnewaska?" "Marriott Big Issue In New Paltz School Vote," "Casinos Not Marriott's Issue," "Marriott Studies Disputed."

The New York Department of Environmental Conservation, custodian of the state's environmental regulations and sister agency to the Office of Parks and Recreation and the PIPC, appointed administrative law judge Robert S. Drew to preside at public hearings to gauge the accuracy and acceptability of data contained in plans prepared by Marriott as a requirement for obtaining the necessary water and sewage permits for its development project. Announcement of the hearings drew in the principals who would vigorously debate the issue: Caccese, representing the Office of Parks and Recreation and the PIPC: Attorney Robert Kafin, representing Marriott: Phillip Gitlen, a former DEC attorney, representing the Friends of the Shawangunks and Citizens to Save Minnewaska.

Castro received a letter in June, 1980, from a senior Marriott attorney stating, "In order to accomplish expansion of the golf course it will be necessary to modify certain portions of the Indenture (conservation easement) which limit development activities." Not knowing the exact meaning of the word "modify," Caccese asked that the DEC hearings be delayed pending more information from Marriott. Judge Drew rejected the request. A subsequent exchange during the hearing procedures contrasted the positions of the contending parties on the easement question:

Kafin: The golf course cannot be built without permission of the PIPC. We will go and ask them for permission. They can set restrictions, [but] until they do, it is very hard for us to give much detail.

Caccese: We made a motion to adjourn at the pre-hearing conference on the basis that we don't have enough information here to determine what the impact is going to be. Now, if the impact is going to be very severe and harmful to the easement area, then we're not going to act at all. We're not going to sit down. What we want to know is what is the proposal, not guess at this and guess at that. We have to know what sort of mitigation is necessary based on the environmental ills that will be caused by the project. We don't know that.

The hearings, expected to be concluded after a few days, extended into weeks, then into months. Opponents and proponents alike were astonished at a session held in August, 1980, when Joseph C. Cataldo, a hydrologist with the Cooper Institute for the Advancement of Science and Art, took the stand. Cataldo claimed that projected water use by the Marriott resort would consume 80 percent of the water in thirty-two–acre Lake Minnewaska in one decade, lowering the surface by twenty-three feet. Kafin objected to accepting this testimony into the record, contending that Cataldo had used a "mishmash of tables" to arrive at his findings. Kafin was overruled. Castro, in attendance at the hearings, labeled the Cataldo testimony "very dramatic."

At another moment in the hearings, Albert F. Smiley, grandson of the founder of the Mohonk Mountain House, found himself the target of a subpoena from Kafin. Trying to counter the apparent damage done to Marriott's proposal by Cataldo, Kafin demanded on a Friday morning that Smiley produce historic records on lake-level fluctuations at the two "sky lakes," Mohonk and Minnewaska, by 10:00 a.m. that day. Smiley appeared at the hearing as ordered.

"All right, Al, what do you have for me?" Kafin commanded.

"Nothing," replied Smiley.

"Nothing?" said Kafin. "See you in court, fella!"

On further questioning by attorneys and the judge, Kafin admitted that Marriott had never made a reasonable request of Smiley for the records, depending, instead, on information provided by the Phillips family. Water and the conservation easement held by the PIPC on a portion of the Phillips land were appearing more and more to be the blocking points to the Marriott venture. Kafin, struggling to prove that the impact on Lake Minnewaska would not be nearly so dire as that asserted by Cataldo, sought from Judge Drew and won an extended suspension of the hearings pending the development of more precise water data by engineering and hydrology consultants retained by Marriott.

Phillips, Jr., reminded the public through a news reporter that he and his family retained all the prerogatives of private land ownership. "People from the Unification Church have been up there a number of times," he said. "I even met the Reverend Moon in person." Reacting to a claim by Assemblyman Hinchey that 55 percent of his constituents favored adding the Phillips holding to Minnewaska State Park, Phillips responded by saying that Hinchey "was playing to the rabble."

The hearings resumed in February, 1981. In the interim, an editorial appeared in *The New York Times* on December 20, 1980, that proclaimed, "A Peace Treaty On The Hudson," but the editorial was not focused on Marriott and Minnewaska. It marked the agreement, mediated by Russell Train, former administrator of the Environmental Protection Agency, to finally put to rest the Storm King Mountain controversy. Ross Sandler of the NRDC, Albert Butzel representing Scenic Hudson, and Charles Luce of Consolidated Edison had agreed to and accepted the details of the long-awaited truce.

Storm King was history, but Marriott was back at the DEC hearings with new data on water consumption. It had pumped 30 million gallons from Lake Minnewaska in January, mimicking the projected water usage by the proposed resort as a test of the capacity of the lake to recover. The lake level dropped only twenty-one inches, less than the hydrology experts had predicted. Marriott contended, too, that nearby test wells demonstrated "ample capacity," independent of the lake. Caccese and Castro continued to seek more details. In a letter to Phillips, Jr., Castro said, "It is not business-like for us to treat this matter informally, and the information we have been provided thus far is precisely that, informal." Whether water consumption, golf course expansion, or other possible environmental impacts, Castro wanted plans that were not based on "guesswork, approximations, or vagueness." He and Caccese were grappling with contradictory statements and controversy and trying to nail down objective data on which to base decisions that would best serve the interests of the public.

After eight months, including lengthy delays, Judge Drew asked for closing written statements from the various parties who had participated in the hearings.

In a Statement of Proposed Findings of Fact, Issues, and Recommendations sub-mitted to the judge, Caccese contended,

> Undisputed evidence presented at the hearing has established the fact that Mar-riott proposes a mountaintop complex with a footprint at least six times as large as the historic development on this site. At this scale, the project will have dra-matic, adverse effect on scenic integrity as well as the water supply and the quality of trails, vegetation, traffic, noise and air. We find that with its massive scale and adverse impact, the project presently proposed by Marriott does not respect the natural constraints of the land nor the public interest in surround-ing parklands and affected resources. While approval of the present project would be contrary to our public trust, we believe that a project reduced in scale and more carefully sited is acceptable, given the historic presence of a resort hotel and its significance to the local economy.

Caccese recommended that an easement be granted by Marriott to the PIPC to ensure a more limited hotel and condominium development, with emphasis on protecting a ridge line on the east side of Lake Minnewaska where Marriott wanted to build three hundred condominiums.

Marriott's representatives had expected no opposition from the PIPC or the OPR. In anger, lawyers in the firm of Miller, Mannix, Lemery & Kafin submit-ted a brief in rebuttal, charging, "In an intemperate, near hysterical, unsigned, and undocumented paper entitled 'Proposed Findings of Fact, Issues and Rec-ommendations,' the Office of Parks and Recreation and the Palisades Interstate Park Commission ask the Department (of Environmental Conservation) illegally and unconstitutionally to seize by confiscation the Cliff House site to prevent the Applicant from using it for its Project."

All contestants awaited the judge's opinion. Prompted by the promise of 450 new jobs and a $6 million annual payroll in an economy with a 9.7 percent unem-ployment rate, county officials favored the development. Phillips, Jr., reaffirmed that his family's bankrupt corporation had to sell. If the Marriott deal prevailed, the Phillips family stood to receive $1.85 million in cash, 1.5 percent of the sales price for each condominium unit sold, and 35 percent of hotel revenues for twenty-nine years, a compensation package that Phillips said would "bring us out about even." If the Marriott deal feel through, Phillips suggested that the fam-ily's alternative would be to auction off the forty-seven separate land parcels that constituted its Lake Minnewaska holdings. Advocates for the preservation of the site, led by Friends of the Shawangunks and Citizens to Save Minnewaska, remained staunch supporters of adding the Phillips property to Minnewaska State Park.

Commissioner Robert Flacke of the New York Department of Environmental Conservation endorsed on June 2, 1981, a 129-page decision by Administrative Law Judge Drew allowing for the construction of Marriott's four hundred–room hotel and fifty condominiums on the Phillips property. Kafin and Gitlen, lead attorneys representing the contending parties, each claimed victory. Judge Drew found in favor of Marriott but restricted condominium development to fifty units unless and until Marriott proved that the "total supply of water from its permanent wells can provide sufficient water to meet the total yearly water demands for the entire project." The judge granted Marriott a sewage permit for discharging effluent on the planned eighteen-hole golf course but confirmed that the decision about amending the conservation easement to allow for expansion of the existing nine-hole golf course rested squarely in the hands of the PIPC. According to Marriott, the eighteen-hole course was termed "essential to the success" of the entire venture, now elevated in estimated cost from $18 million to $78 million. Kafin, representing Marriott, was pleased that DEC Commissioner Flacke had "given his general approval" to the project. The Friends of the Shawangunks and Citizens to Save Minnewaska expressed confidence that Marriott would never be able to prove sufficient groundwater supplies, thus holding the scale of development below a level considered economically viable for Marriott.

With the ruling, the *Times Herald Record* confirmed that Marriott's opponents were shifting their focus to the PIPC. Paul Lowry, president of the Mid-Hudson Chapter of the Sierra Club, charged that the PIPC had a cavalier attitude about the easement that would make or break the Marriott project. "The Commission," Lowry said, "thinks of the easement as something they can trade on, but our position is it should not be violated. It's an important tool to environmentalists. I know of no other easement that has been changed anywhere in the country." Castro, speaking for the commissioners, confirmed that, in fact, the PIPC was anticipating "negotiations" with Marriott, using the easement as a bargaining chip to win the corporation's guarantee of maximum protection of scenery and water, as well as assurances that the public would have the right of transit through the property. A key PIPC commissioner, Rockefeller, was emerging as a proponent for not amending the easement to expand the golf course unless Marriott agreed to relocate its three hundred proposed condominiums to a less visible section of the Phillips property and add to the PIPC's existing conservation easement the 750 ridge-line acres that Marriott had designated as the condo-development site. This, according to Kafin, would sink the project. Edward Bednarz, director of Hotel Development for Marriott, labeled Rockefeller's stance "hard-line," adding that Rockefeller was "making extreme demands we can't meet." Bednarz failed to say that all ten members of the Commission unanimously adopted Rockefeller's "hard-line" position.

Phillips, Jr., labeled the commissioners' position "improper," and he was quoted by the *Times Herald Record* as saying, "It's a hell of a thing. I knew there would be battles left, but I didn't expect this." In an editorial, the *Kingston Daily Freeman* chided the commissioners for being "outsiders [who] meet in New Jersey" and who "have the last word on a local issue."

The PIPC commissioners held a special meeting in June, 1981, at Bear Mountain to hear from the public about Marriott's project. It prompted Joseph Penzato, a pavement contractor and president of the citizens group Friends of Marriott, to say that "the Commission is behaving like a spoiled child crying: 'it's my baseball, so we'll play by my rules.'" Kafin added, "The PIPC had two years to get their point across; it's a little bit late to be redesigning the project now." About two hundred people attended the meeting. A large majority spoke in favor of protecting the natural beauty of Lake Minnewaska and voiced strong opposition to any change in the terms of the conservation easement. At the conclusion of the meeting, a PIPC negotiating team was appointed to continue discussions with Marriott. The team included Commissioners Rockefeller and Jon F. Hanson, Castro, Caccese, and special counsel Arthur Savage.

Within weeks, the PIPC's and Marriott's negotiators reached agreement that the easement would be amended to allow an expansion of the golf course primarily on condition that the condominiums would be set back fifty feet from the ridge line and would be limited to 150 in number. Marriott's opponents immediately expressed extreme resistance to the compromise and vowed to fight on. Castro wrote to Lehman, thanking the park commissioner for his support "throughout the interminable proceedings" and adding, "[I have] profound admiration for Al Caccese. I have not witnessed a more dedicated public servant than he."

The "interminable" proceedings were not over. The Friends of the Shawangunks, Citizens to Save Minnewaska, and Appalachian Mountain Club initiated a lawsuit against the New York Department of Environmental Conservation, contending that the DEC had violated its own regulations when it approved a "conditional" water-taking permit for Marriott. The Sierra Club and Appalachian Mountain Club filed a second suit against the PIPC, claiming the PIPC should have received approval from the Department of the Interior and the New York and New Jersey Legislatures before reaching agreement with Marriott to amend the conservation easement. Support for the PIPC came from an NPS regional director who administratively ruled by letter to Caccese that "none of the stated purposes for which the easement was acquired are defeated" by the PIPC's agreement with Marriott. The parties to the lawsuit, now joined by the Friends of the Shawangunks, disagreed with the ruling and reaffirmed their determination to "go forward." A New York State Supreme Court judge issued a temporary order on November 23, 1981, preventing Marriott and the PIPC from implementing their negotiated agreement. Then, in mid-December, the court lifted the order, but the lawsuit remained alive.

In May of the following year, New York State Supreme Court Justice Abraham S. Isseks found that the PIPC had acted properly when it granted Marriott permission to clear part of the 239-acre easement-protected property for the golf-course expansion. A spokesperson for the Sierra Club confirmed that the club would appeal.

Several months later a federal bankruptcy court judge directed the Phillips family to provide confirmation that Marriott was in fact prepared to spend $80 million to construct the new Lake Minnewaska resort. Personal liability for the Phillipses stood at about $1.5 million; $820,000 in accumulated tax bills were going unpaid; and the Wildmere Hotel had lost $15,374 in its operations the previous year. More than six years had passed since bankruptcy proceedings had been brought against the Lake Minnewaska Mountain Houses company owned by the Phillips family. Creditors and tax collectors were understandably frustrated.

The bankruptcy court was not to receive a clear answer from Marriott anytime soon. This was assured in May, 1983, when, in a separate court finding, the Appellate Division Court of the New York Third District struck down the decision of the New York DEC approving 250 condominiums at the resort site on the "condition" that sufficient water supplies were proven to exist. In a unanimous five-judge decision, the court said that proof of sufficient water supply was required first, before the DEC could approve the condos. Drew, the Administrative Law Judge who had granted the conditional approval, confirmed that the appellate decision meant that "full-scale" environmental hearings would be required to resolve the water-supply question. Marriott's Bednarz expressed concern that his company "cannot justify additional expense to get all that's needed done to fully develop the property." Marriott claimed to have spent $1.5 million during four years of project planning and preparation, and although it still had a four hundred–unit hotel and fifty condominiums on the table, it did not want to spend additional money on drilling wells in the hope that enough water could be found for the additional condominiums. The project was becoming economically untenable for Marriott.

With the project in doubt, new players appeared. Marriott announced that the Investors Management Group of Baltimore and the Tokyo-based AOKI Construction Company Limited were joining in the project. A coalition of environmental groups was attempting to coalesce around the Trust for Public Land in an effort to purchase the 1,300-acre Phillips property. After speculation in the press about various "investors" newly arrived on the scene, none seemed to muster the dollars or real commitment needed to make a serious bid for the property. With no "white knight" in sight, the judge in the bankruptcy proceeding approved the exclusive right of Marriott and its recently recruited investment allies to close the long-awaited transaction within one year.

Castro received good news in February, 1984. In a three-to-one decision, the New York Court of Appeals upheld the lower court's verdict affirming the legal right of the PIPC to amend its conservation easement. Whether the easement would actually be amended depended on further discussions with Marriott and a final vote by the commissioners. The commissioners and Castro were not at all sure that the vote would be favorable to Marriott. Still, the Court of Appeals's ruling represented "a step closer to the goal line for the Marriott project," according to PIPC Deputy Executive Director Stewart.

The Sierra Club and Appalachian Mountain Club took the next legal step available to them; they appealed the state ruling to the U.S. Circuit Court of Appeals. Almost a year later, the court handed down its ruling, finding in favor of the plaintiffs and overturning the judgment of the state courts. The 239-acre conservation easement owned by the PIPC, but purchased with matching federal funds, could not be amended without federal approval, said the U.S. Court of Appeals.

A headline in *The New York Times* on November 23, 1981, confirmed, "Marriott Calls Off Plans To Revive Ulster Resort." The resort investors had determined that they needed more than the original 590 acres the Phillips family had agreed to sell in order to reconfigure their project. They wanted to purchase more than one thousand acres and, to accommodate water needs, tap into the Peterskill, a dancing stream that flowed from Lake Awosting through Minnewaska State Park and the Phillips property before plunging off the Shawangunk Ridge to the flatland below, where it joined the Wallkill, a tributary of the Hudson River. Bednarz, speaking for Marriott, said that the company "could not conclude an acceptable agreement" with the Phillips family on the purchase of additional acreage. Even if an agreement had been reached, Bednarz knew that a redesigned project and more water questions guaranteed a return to the hearing arena, as required by the State Environmental Quality Review Act (SEQRA), and probably back to court. In a comment months later to Diana Shaman of *The New York Times,* Bednarz confirmed that the federal court's ruling on the conservation easement was "the straw that broke the camel's back." Still faced with bankruptcy, the Phillips family was left without a major resort investor.

Responding to obviously strong public support and following through on the purposes of their respective agencies, Caccese and Castro entered again into direct contact with Phillips, Sr. On October 22, 23, and 24, 1985, Caccese and Castro spent twenty-six hours in negotiation with Phillips, Sr., and his attorneys. (During this marathon negotiation, Caccese accepted an invitation to stay overnight at the Phillipses' home. Unprepared for the stay, Caccese was lent pajamas and underwear, and served breakfast in bed. When the negotiations concluded, Phillips told Caccese that he did not have to return the borrowed underwear.) On October 29, the state made an offer of $3 million for the 1,200-acre property. Phillips declined. With the property again under threat of the auction block, the state initiated eminent-domain proceedings against Lake Minnewaska Mountain Houses, Inc., in December, 1985.

Almost symbolic of the last hope for massive new resort development at Lake Minnewaska, the uninsured Wildmere Hotel, closed and vacant since 1976, caught fire in June, 1986, and like its predecessor, the Cliff House, burned to the ground.

New York Governor Cuomo stood at a cliff-side location overlooking Lake Minnewaska a year and a half after the eminent-domain proceedings commenced to accept a deed to the Phillips property from Frank D. Boren, president of The Nature Conservancy. To avoid more months of the condemnation proceedings, in which claim and counterclaim for the value of the Phillips family's holdings would be batted back and forth, the Conservancy had stepped forward to assist as it had done before on the Shawangunk Ridge, bringing along its substantial checkbook. Working with Caccese and Castro under an agreement that ensured eventual reimbursement to the Conservancy from bond-act funds approved by New York voters, a final accord was reached with the Phillipses to buy their entire property for $6.75 million. Cuomo referred to Minnewaska as an "environmental heirloom," and he reminded those in attendance that "at issue was the limited capacity of this beautiful and fragile land to absorb private development."

Lehman and Castro confirmed that the newly acquired property would be opened to the public for hiking, picnicking, and scenic enjoyment within a matter of days. They credited the steadfast organizations and individuals that participated in the seventeen-year effort to bring the Phillips holding into Minnewaska State Park. Mentioned were Hinchey, the Mary Flagler Cary Charitable Trust, The Nature Conservancy, the Catskill Center, the Open Space Institute, the Regional Plan Association, the Friends of the Shawangunks, the New

York–New Jersey Trail Conference, Mohonk Preserve, Inc., the Citizens to Save Minnewaska, the Cragsmoor Association, the Trust for Public Land, the Appalachian Mountain Club, Scenic Hudson, the Sierra Club, David Sive, Alfred and Albert Smiley, and Bernard Brennan. As part of the purchase agreement, seventy-six-year-old Kenneth Phillips, Sr., and his wife, Lucille, were granted life-tenancy rights, allowing them to remain in their artistically designed home overlooking Lake Minnewaska.

All of the property acquired by Alfred Smiley more than a century earlier was now encompassed within 13,000-acre Minnewaska State Park. (Additional acreage would be added in succeeding years.) The PIPC, acting on behalf of the State of New York and the federal government, had gained permanent stewardship of one of the premier park ecosystems in the eastern United States.

17.
Sterling Forest

October 15, 1951.

Dear Mr. Rockefeller: The Sterling Lake area, a tract of 17,000 acres to the southwest of Bear Mountain-Harriman Parks, has been placed on the market by the Harriman interests (Sterling Iron and Railway Company). Once the real estate promoter takes hold, the tract will be gone forever. In addition to the need for this wild land for recreational use, the area must be preserved for water supply purposes. . . . The purpose of this letter is to inquire whether you or one of your sons would be moved to look further into this subject. If the subject does interest you, even to the extent of considering a conditional gift in cooperation with certain New Jersey communities now so concerned with protection of their water supply, I should be glad to confer with any representative you might appoint. Very truly yours, Ridsdale Ellis, Chairman, New York–New Jersey Trail Conference.

February 2, 1986.

To the Editor: There is an exciting possibility to preserve an important part of the Town of Warwick—and a large cost if we fail to act. Many . . . residents take it for granted that Sterling Forest . . . will always be accessible to the public. Sterling Forest is now for sale and there is no guarantee that any of its 19,995 acres will be protected for future enjoyment. . . . We need help to plan an educational campaign on the watershed and recreational importance of the land. We hope that community support will ensure that our children can enjoy Warwick's beauty fully. We owe that to them. JoAnn L. and Paul R. Dolan.

". . . Sterling Forest was nearly saved last year," wrote Bill McKibben in the November-December, 1996, issue of *Audubon Magazine,* "but by a bill that would have paid for the land's purchase by selling 55,000 acres of federal grassland in Oklahoma. Even the New York and New Jersey congressmen and women crazy for a deal wouldn't do that, nor would they tie their bill to one that would have opened Utah's Redrock Wilderness to commercial exploitation. The bill died. If one of the bills now before Congress doesn't pass soon, the developers may get to work."

Malcolm Borg's *Record* referred to Sterling Forest as a "sleeping giant waiting for a future." "For the land, nothing has changed—yet," stated a companion article. "Twenty thousand acres, much of it pristine, barely 40 miles from New York City. Bare, black trees against the snowbound knolls, rags of ice fringing the steel-colored lakes, a pair of hawks flat against the wind, hungry deer stripping the low branches of cedars. Here also, curved into the dips and rises, are handfuls of houses and a half dozen sleek research laboratories." But, said the article, "Sterling Forest is on the razor's edge." The *Record* suggested "in an ideal world" that New York and New Jersey should purchase the property from its current owner, Home Insurance Company. The City Investing Corporation had owned the property for twenty-five years, hoping to develop a new community "blended into the lovely woods" that would "attract scientists and statisticians who could walk to their jobs in laboratories and raise their families in idyllic settings." Unfortunately, the City Investing dream fell victim to economic vagaries, local politics, and the tough, uncompromising nature of the Sterling Forest landscape. The corporation liquidated in 1985, ceding its assets to the insurance company that had been its subsidiary. The vast forest property was "on the razor's edge" because Home Insurance wanted to get rid of it as quickly as possible. If events were allowed to "take their course," according to *The Record,* "ticky-tacky sprawl that mars so much of the landscape will swallow Sterling Forest."

Sterling Forest was the last great, single-owner tract within sight of New York City's skyscrapers. By the standards of the western United States, where open-space acreage is commonly measured in multiples of a hundred thousand or even a million, twenty thousand acres might not seem particularly significant, but to the residents of the nation's most densely populated metropolitan region, the intrinsic value of such a sweep of unbroken, wild land is inestimable. So taken for granted were the high ridge lines, steep rocky slopes, sequestered valleys, lakes, ponds, streams, wetlands, and marshes that the 1986 edition of the *Hagstrom Atlas* depicted Sterling Forest in the color of publicly owned parks. Hunters had roamed the forest for years. Anglers knew of the rich treasure trove of native trout swimming in Sterling Lake, a sparkling natural water body that formed the centerpiece of the entire property. Those who ventured into the deep forest were rewarded with a step back in time—a step away from the rumbling city onto woodland paths leading toward quiet vales where the sounds of soft breezes easily join with bird songs, rustling leaves, and tumbling clear water, all gracefully in tune—time measured not in radio talk shows and jagged calendar days flashing by, but in eons.

But Sterling Forest, once part of a vast eastern-seaboard wilderness, was no longer pristine. The forest had not escaped the stone implements, axes, flintlocks, and zeal of Native Americans and early European explorers. Anyone roaming the soft forest pathways in the 1980s was walking through centuries of history. Evidence of prehistoric settlement dating back at least twelve thousand years had been found on the shoreline of Sterling Lake. Native Americans logically would have chosen the remote lake, abundant with fish, and the surrounding woodlands, equally plentiful with wild game, edible plants, and building materials, as

Sterling Forest Lake, New York.
(Courtesy of PIPC Archives)

a suitable place to live. The disruptions of colonial settlement had left silent the Native American sites at Sterling Lake by the time Scotsman Cornelius Board entered the forest in 1736, bringing men who were carrying tools to uncover extensive iron-ore deposits precious to the struggling colonies of North America. Board's discovery set the course for exploitation of iron-ore resources for the next 150 years as ore was pulled from mine shafts driven deep under the forest floor. Some shafts extended downward, then drove laterally under the bottom of the lake. Mining transformed the forest into a colonial-era industrial site. Ore, pried with hand tools from scores of dark tunnel walls, was muscled to the surface, there to be melted down into pig-iron ingots. Large stone furnaces, used to melt the ore and standing three to four stories high, were fueled by trees felled from the mature hardwood forest as rapidly as woodsmen could urge their ox teams to drag the logs to the furnaces. Latter-day hikers strolling in the late twentieth century through a recovered, seemingly untouched Sterling Forest would have been flabbergasted by the despoilment that logging, skidding trails, and the clutter and grime of mining, machinery, and ore processing had visited on the forest in the eighteenth and nineteenth centuries.

In 1740 most of the forest came into the ownership of William Alexander, heir to the Scottish title Earl of Stirling. Alexander's son, James, known to his colonial neighbors as Lord Stirling, and William and Abel Noble, other claimants to portions of the forest, were swept up in the events of 1776. Even though the name Sterling Forest (a corruption of Stirling) might have seemed symbolic of the distant and loathed authority of the British Crown, Lord Stirling, a Whig, became a major general and served with distinction in the Continental Army. He likely played a key role in making Gen. George Washington keenly aware of the strategic value of Sterling Forest. When war came to the Hudson River Valley, Washington sent contingents of Continental Army troops and militiamen to defend the logical routes that British troops would follow from New York City should the redcoats attempt to capture the iron mines and furnaces.

Washington's strategic defense of the forest was transformed into one of the boldest acts of the Revolutionary War when the iron masters at the forges were ordered to produce individual links of chain, each link two feet long and weighing about 180 pounds, to be hauled overland to the Hudson River. Link by link, enormous chains, intended to span a distance of five hundred yards, were assembled on the shoreline near New Windsor, then transported by barge downstream to the Hudson River narrows. Floated from shore to shore on a line of rafts stretching across the river, and secured on each end by twelve-ton anchors, the chains, conceived by Thomas Machin, an engineer serving in the Continental

Army with Col. James Clinton, were intended to prevent British ships from attacking northward up the Hudson. The first chain was anchored at Fort Montgomery, the second at West Point. Despite herculean efforts by the iron masters and farmers-turned-militiamen, the daring tactic failed; British ships broke through the first chain during the Battle of Forts Clinton and Montgomery in 1776 and, a year later, smashed through at West Point.

The spectacular attempt to chain the Hudson is a dramatic moment in the history of Sterling Forest but was only a brief departure from the production of iron to meet the market demand from growing cities and towns, the maritime industry, railroaders, and entrepreneurs who kept the furnaces glowing night and day, year after year. National crisis again reaffirmed the strategic importance of the iron mines in and near Sterling Forest during the War of 1812 and the Civil War. Peter Parrott, owner of the mines and forges on the eastern edge of Sterling Forest during the Civil War, sent pig iron to the Cold Spring Foundry, just across the Hudson from West Point, for production of the "Parrott Rifle." This "rifle" was actually a newly designed cannon with spiraled groves cut into the bore. The spinning projectile blasted from the Parrott Rifle, supplied to Union Army artillerymen, had more range and accuracy than the cannonballs shot from old smooth-bore artillery pieces used by Confederate troops, giving the Federals a tactical advantage they used with deadly results. But Parrott, though a hero of the Civil War, was first and foremost a businessperson, and his business went sour. Wartime honors could not save the Parrott family business when abundant deposits of iron ore, more easily mined and less costly, were discovered in Minnesota. Forced to sell their holdings, members of the Parrott family saw E. H. Harriman prevail in a land auction in 1890 when he bought 9,500 acres of their land for $52,500, forming the core of what would become Harriman's vast estate of more than thirty square miles.

Although Harriman claimed that the Parrott property was "more land than he really needed," he followed this acquisition in 1895 by gaining complete control through stock purchases of the Sterling Iron and Railway Company, a business entity that, like the Parrott family's enterprise, was no longer competitive in the iron-ore market. The company owned more than twenty thousand acres of Sterling Forest that it had purchased in 1864 from the heirs of William Townsend. Through control of the company, Harriman could look west and east from Arden House, the baronial mansion that he built high on a ridge line of the vast estate, and see almost nothing but his own land stretching to the horizon. Except for Arden House, which years later was donated to Columbia University, the former Parrott property remains largely in the hands of the Harriman family heirs. Not so the Sterling Iron and Railway Company land holding (Sterling Forest). Despite pleas by Ridsdale Ellis to conserve the forest, it was sold in 1953 for $452,000 to City Investing and subsequently placed with a subsidiary, the Home Insurance Company of Hartford, Connecticut, for real-estate development purposes. In 1951, when Ellis wrote to Rockefeller, Jr., to suggest that Sterling Forest be conserved, the PIPC did purchase 1,200 acres of land in the vicinity that was owned by the Tuxedo Park Association, thanks to contributions by W. Averell Harriman and George W. Perkins, Jr., but two years later the PIPC's annual report stated, "Aside from land acquired for parkway purposes—the only land acquired during 1953 was a small parcel purchased with gift funds—comprising 0.22 acres."

Using the Sterling Iron and Railway Company land as a launch point, City Investing added to its holdings over the years and attempted various real-estate development schemes, none of which was more than marginally successful. One bright spot was the opening of Sterling Gardens in 1958, a 125-acre site planted with 1.5 million tulips. Princess Beatrix of the Netherlands presided at the opening ceremonies. Other forest parcels were sold piecemeal to companies and institutions interested in the isolated character of the property, a factor that was particularly appealing for research and data-storage purposes. Among the purchasers were IBM, International Paper, Union Carbide, International Nickel, Xicom, Wehran EnviroTech, and New York University. Union Carbide operated a small nuclear reactor in Sterling Forest for medical-research purposes (later operated by Cintichem). New York University maintained a primate center in association with research on infectious diseases.

For more than thirty years, the Ellis plea to protect the remaining open land went unheeded until Paul and JoAnn Dolan, joined by a small corps of compatriots, took up the cause of Sterling Forest once again. This slice of wildness so close to New York City, and seemingly adrift toward yet undefined development stratagems, had been examined by Arthur T. Ross, professor of Planning at Yale University, who reported to the Tri-State Transportation Committee that "Sterling Forest would become a major new community of 500,000 persons and will encompass a prime area of 100 square miles." Ross's predicted time line had all but passed when, in 1985, the forest's future seemed to be put especially at risk. City Investing, caught in the economic scandals and excesses of the 1980s, was flattened financially and forced to liquidate. By default, City Investing's former subsidiary, Home Insurance, found itself owner of the mortgaged property and placed it on the market for sale-asking price, $50 million. The insurance company, now disconnected from City Investing and freestanding, created a subsidiary of its own, the Sterling Forest Corporation (SFC), to sell or develop the property, whichever avenue promised the most lucrative result.

Paul Dolan, thinking the time might be right for the states of New York and New Jersey to step forward as willing buyers, surfaced the concept of a twelve-mile-long "green belt," extending from the Appalachian Trail on the northern edge of the forest to the New York–New Jersey state line in the south, that would protect watershed resources crucial to both states. Dolan formed the Greenwood Trust and began actively lobbying for the purchase of at least nine thousand acres of SFC's holdings by New York. He urged that New Jersey should purchase an additional two thousand acres of contiguous SFC land on its side of the border. The New York–New Jersey Trail Conference endorsed Dolan's plan. James D. Rogers, planning director for Passaic County, New Jersey, was also quick to note Dolan's initiative and offered encouragement, confirming that the SFC holding was located just above a reservoir system that was being developed by the state to provide drinking water for 2 million people, 25 percent of New Jersey's population.

Dolan, editorial manager for ABC-TV's *20/20* television news magazine, had purchased a half-interest in a log house on the western fringe of Sterling Forest at Greenwood Lake as a weekend getaway. When the other share became available in 1978, Dolan gained full ownership of the house. He and his future wife, JoAnn, hiked in the forest on their first date, sharing a common admiration for the rustic trails, delicate wetlands, secretive wildlife, and rocky vistas. They shared, too, in complementary professional activities. She was a freelance writer developing educational materials for people with disabilities; he directed the One-to-One Fund, a charitable organization that championed civil rights for people with disabilities and served as a watchdog against abuse at mental and medical institutions. JoAnn subsequently became executive director for the New York–New Jersey Trail Conference, and Paul joined the world of television news, steadily advancing within ABC-TV.

The routine of using the log house as a pleasant weekend getaway was unhappily complicated for the Dolans in May, 1985, when their newborn son, Jamie, was diagnosed with Down's Syndrome. For a time, Jamie's very survival was in doubt, but he fought through the early crisis in his life, allowing the Dolans to begin taking him on outings along their favorite woodland paths. "Even though he can't walk," Paul Dolan said to a reporter for *The Record,* "he responds to the winds and the birds and leaves and he lights up. He lights up. He watches everything." The Dolans credit Jamie for converting their private experiences found in Sterling Forest to an activist campaign to save the forest from what appeared to be almost certain fragmentation at the hands of real-estate subdividers. Using their home as a rendezvous, the Dolans began organizing a series of walks into the forest for anyone willing to participate. Among the handful of friends plotting a strategy to protect Sterling Forest was John Humbach, a law professor at Pace University. The small group, closely aligned with the New York–New Jersey Trail Conference, gained welcome encouragement from Hooper Brooks of the highly regarded Regional Plan Association, an organization respected for its reasoned analyses of growth patterns in the tri-state metropolitan region.

In a matter of a few months, this small group of friends and colleagues sparked to life enough media and political interest to prompt New Jersey and Passaic County officials to take the first major step toward preserving the last great open space in the metropolitan region. In September, 1986, New Jersey Governor Thomas Kean approved a $2 million grant from the state's Green Acres Fund to Passaic County for the purpose of purchasing the 2,074 acres of SFC's holdings on the New Jersey side of the border. The county's obligation was to match this amount. Water was the motivating factor. On its side of the border, New Jersey had acted swiftly to do what it could to protect clean, unpolluted, abundant, free-flowing water. Governor Kean looked northward with the hope that the remaining 17,500 acres held in corporate ownership in New York would be similarly protected.

Before the question of whether New York might follow New Jersey's lead could be answered, the Sterling Forest FOR SALE sign was taken down. In March, 1987, Robert L. Woodrum, vice president for the Home Group [Home Insurance], announced, "We are sitting on an appreciating asset." SFC President James Tomai refused to elaborate further to members of the press, but the message was clear. The owners of Sterling Forest were opting for a development scenario, encouraged, in part, by proposed construction of a new $5 million interchange on the New York State Thruway that would funnel traffic directly into the forest. Watching from south of the state line, U.S. Congressman Robert G. Torricelli spoke for his constituents and many others by saying, "This is the last chance for the states of New York and New Jersey to plan for a greenbelt around the metropolitan area. It should have been done a century ago." Elaborating in a lengthy article in *The New York Times,* Torricelli labeled Sterling Forest an "irreplaceable asset for the entire metropolitan region that is almost without parallel."

Applauding fellow New Jersey Congressman Robert A. Roe for bringing symbolism to the hills that rolled like stationary waves for about a hundred miles between the Hudson and Delaware Rivers by referring to the region as the "Skylands," Torricelli referred to the "livability of old world cities" in England and France, contrasting them to "a loss of open space" adjacent to city centers in the

United States "that has reached crisis proportions." He argued that urban sprawl must be controlled and said, "There is no better place to start than Sterling Forest," adding that "the Palisades Interstate Park Commission stands ready to assist." Torricelli's reference to the PIPC was no coincidence; his neighbor in Englewood, New Jersey, was Malcolm Borg, whose newspaper, *The Record,* was on the Sterling Forest story from the moment City Investing began to liquidate. Wearing his commissioner's hat, Borg was to become a key champion in the PIPC's struggle. Borg and his neighbors in New Jersey did not have far to look to understand the implications of the "crisis" declared by Congressman Torricelli. They had only to look at their water taps. James Dao, writing for *The Record,* captured the message when he reported that

> amateur geologist Jerome Wyckoff stalks the narrow road into Sterling Forest like a detective hot on a criminal's trail. About a mile up, after the road has turned to mud, he finds his first clue: sandstone. What the rock tells him is this: eons ago, a glacier ripped it from the New York ridge and deposited it in the granite hills of Ringwood. There, it was polished by centuries of rainwater rushing inexorably toward the Atlantic. To Wyckoff, this explains why Sterling Forest is so important. . . . "You can't fool water," Wyckoff says. "Sooner or later, it will find its way to the ocean." He might have added, water and effluent.

Ella Filippone, also watching from the New Jersey side of the border, would put the matter more sharply, "Building sewer plants in the high headwaters of any stream and river system is ludicrous." Filippone, executive director of the Passaic River Coalition, a small not-for-profit organization, was being pulled like so many others into a full-scale battle for the future of Sterling Forest. In Filippone, allies and opponents alike would discover a splendid master of the political process.

The scale of the contest was suggested in 1988 when the corporate owners of Sterling Forest refused to attend a gathering called by the Regional Plan Association and the New Jersey Audubon Society to explore options for the future of the forest. David A. Wilkinson, speaking on behalf of the Home Group, said, "The forest has immense economic value" and pegged the asset at $150 million, a threefold jump from the $50 million estimate expressed by corporate representatives only two years previously. Time had passed since Governor Kean had approved Green Acres funding for the acquisition of the Home Group property in Passaic County. Republican Richard DuHaine, an elected county official, reported that negotiations with the Home Group for a willing-seller, willing-buyer purchase had failed. "They told us point-blank they were going to develop the property," DuHaine said of his efforts to persuade Home Group representatives to sell to the county. In October, 1988, the Republican-controlled Passaic County Freeholders (elected officials) voted to take immediate title to the Home Group property just south of the state border. On November 1, 1988, county officials exercised eminent-domain authority and wrested ownership of the land from the corporation. A prerequisite of this action was for the county to deposit with the court an amount judged to be fair compensation. Based on a $1,200 per-acre valuation, the county deposited $2.5 million. Home Group representatives claimed that the land was worth $15.5 million based on their $7,500 per acre claim of value. Company and county attorneys headed to court to argue. The 2,074 acres, though, were safely removed from the development chessboard.

About a year later Home Group hired Robert E. Thomson to assume duties as the new chair of SFC. Thomson's résumé included five and a half years as chief deputy attorney for Los Angeles County and a stint as campaign manager when Los Angeles Mayor Thomas Bradley ran unsuccessfully for governor of California. On arrival in the Hudson River Valley, Thomson said, "If modern land use planning means anything, it means citizen involvement" and pledged to meet with Humbach, now president of the Dolan-inspired Sterling Forest Coalition, and others. In a single article in the *Times Herald Record,* Thomson's expressed willingness to meet with Humbach was juxtaposed with a quote from Michael Manley, president of SFC's parent company, the Home Group. Asked about working with those who sought to conserve the remaining 17,500 acres of corporate holdings as open space, Manley said, "I don't know who they are. I don't know whether they've ever been on the property. If they have been, they've been trespassing." Manley added: "I'd be very pleased to sell the whole thing for a reasonable price," which he now claimed was $200 million, up by $50 million in only five months. Manley's statement was followed a few weeks later by the release of a traffic study, sponsored and paid for by the SFC, that reaffirmed the need for construction of a new interchange on the New York State Thruway to feed traffic directly into the property, a step guaranteed to enhance the value of the corporate holding at taxpayer expense, perhaps even to a level approaching Manley's claim of value.

Local businesspeople and representatives of the Orange County Chamber of Commerce, who pledged to seek renewed advocacy for the $5 million interchange project from Governor Cuomo and Comptroller Edward V. Regan, welcomed the study. The reaction in Albany was underwhelming. A spokesperson for the Thruway Authority, the agency that would be responsible for constructing the interchange, said, "The project remains on hold indefinitely." At Bear Mountain, Nash Castro and his PIPC staff were withholding public comment pending a detailed review of the study, but the position they would take was predictably clear—the proposed interchange would take an enormous bite out of Harriman State Park, thereby requiring approval by the PIPC. The prospect that the commissioners would agree to slice off a chunk of the park was somewhere on a scale of slim to none. Thomson was nonetheless planning to make a vigorous push for the interchange within the context of overall development potential for the Sterling Forest property. With concurrence from AmBase, Inc., now the parent company of the Home Group, Thomson retained the services of Sedway Cooke Associates, a respected but distant San Francisco–based planning firm. A principal with the firm, Thomas Cooke, said, "The land tells you what to do," and he began flying back and forth to listen to Sterling Forest.

With SFC's development planning in high gear, *The Philadelphia Inquirer* carried a lengthy article on June 26, 1989, headlined, "Open Space Around Our Cities Is Shrinking." The article was written by Democratic U.S. Congressman Peter H. Kostmayer, representative of Bucks and Montgomery Counties, Pennsylvania. As chair of the House of Representatives Interior Subcommittee on Oversight, Kostmayer had developed a deep personal concern for what he saw happening on the edges of cities across the nation. Echoing Congressman Torricelli's similar message in *The Times*'s article, he wrote: "A single day's drive through our congested suburban landscape demonstrates that the traditional fragmented and strictly local approach to controlling development has failed. We need a new ethic in this country that acknowledges the value of preserving a national landscape." Citing greenbelt protection around London, and farmland conservation in France and the Netherlands, Kostmayer scheduled seven subcommittee hearings around the nation to examine in detail the issue of open-space protection near urban areas. First on his list was a hearing in Tuxedo, New York, intended to closely examine Sterling Forest, which was rumored to be the site of the largest residential and commercial real-estate development project on the drawing boards anywhere in the United States.

About two hundred people attended the hearing on October 3, 1989. Congressional members Torricelli (D), Marge Roukema (R), and Benjamin A. Gilman (R) were in attendance. Gilman, the senior New York Republican member in the House of Representatives and chair of the powerful House Foreign Relations Committee, represented the New York congressional district in which the 17,500-acre property owned by SFC was located. Roukema's New Jersey district, which included parts of Passaic County where more than two thousand acres of SFC property had already been taken by condemnation, was Gilman's immediate congressional neighbor to the south. JoAnn Dolan was there, representing the New York–New Jersey Trail Conference as executive director, as was the Passaic River Coalition's executive director, Filippone. So, too, was, Humbach, there to speak for the Sterling Forest Coalition. The PIPC's Castro was in attendance, as were representatives of The Nature Conservancy, Sierra Club, New Jersey Conservation Foundation, North Jersey District Water Supply Commission, New Jersey Audubon Society, Environmental Defense Fund, Scenic Hudson, Orange County Chamber of Commerce, and representatives of various local communities and businesses.

Thomson was among the first to comment during the five-hour session. Questioned by Kostmayer about the rumored large-scale housing development, Thomson responded, "Do I envision it? No. Is it an option? I'm not ready to say." Those who spoke for the business community urged development of the forest "because we need ratables," which prompted Humbach to counter that for every $1.00 in taxes generated from residential developments, communities ended up paying $1.36 to provide for police, fire, educational, transportation, medical, and utility services. Humbach repeated this point when quoted in a *New York Times* article, citing the Cornell University Cooperative Extension Service and the American Farmland Trust as his sources of statistical information. Another person at the hearing put the issue of a promised property-tax windfall in terms of the city a few miles away: "If property taxes were the financial answer for communities, New York City would never be in debt." Filippone, continuing to express concern about the impact of immense development in the Sterling Forest watershed, said, "We cannot afford to have massive amounts of siltation, lead, chlorides, pesticides, and fertilizers pollute the rivers, streams, and creeks flowing from the forest." Congressman Gilman expressed the hope that well-managed development could co-exist in a "pristine environment."

This is where I entered the PIPC scene. Several months earlier I was fortunately chosen by New York Department of Environmental Conservation (DEC) Commissioner Thomas Jorling to become one of his deputies and subsequently appointed to the position by Governor Cuomo. Jorling selected me based on my twenty-five years of experience with the National Park Service (NPS), including an assignment as superintendent of Yosemite National Park, and because of the assistance I provided in the late 1960s to Mrs. David (Peggy) Rockefeller when she established the Maine Coast Heritage Trust. When I arrived in Albany in February, 1989, Jorling handed me a management portfolio that included oversight of New York's 1986 bond-act fund for land acquisition. Under Jorling's leadership, the monies were being spent aggressively to purchase land throughout the state. Wonderful properties were being aquired to enhance state parks, wildlife areas, and forests and to improve public access to river, lake, and ocean shore-lines. Particular emphasis was placed on large privately owned tracts in the Adirondack and Catskill Parks. Among properties already purchased was land in the Mongaup Valley, several miles west of Sterling Forest, that had been acquired from the Orange and Rockland utility company. The property includes nesting sites for bald eagles. Thousands of acres were being similarly added to the state's impressive inventory of public lands, but the bond-act funds were decreasing accordingly.

When I arrived at the Kostmayer hearing to testify on behalf of the state regarding Sterling Forest, only $35 million of the $250 million bond fund remained uncommitted. Within the DEC we had developed A-, B-, and C-lists for the use of these remaining funds. The A-list consisted of properties where appraisals were in hand and purchase was imminent. The B-list included prop-erties where strong willing-seller signals had been received. The C-list included scores of other desirable properties whose owners apparently were disinterested or had expressed outright opposition to state land-acquisition inquiries. The remaining $35 milion was insufficient even to cover the properties on the A- and B-lists. Sterling Forest was on the C-list. A complicating factor was that federal Land & Water Conservation Fund (L&WCF) monies that might have been used to match a state financial commitment to Sterling Forest had all but dried up, shrinking from $23 million in 1979 to $800,000 in 1989. I so testified to these prob-lems at the hearing, to the obvious disappointment of Kostmayer, Torricelli, Roukema, and the many citizen advocates for Sterling Forest protection who were in attendance. Kostmayer concluded the hearing by proposing further study by the U.S. Forest Service of the New York–New Jersey "Skylands" region.

Many people in the hearing room at Tuxedo that day would be wedded together during the last decade of the twentieth century by the vexing ques-tion of what was to become of Sterling Forest. I had no idea that I would be joining them at a level of intensity that would personally challenge my endurance like nothing I had ever encounted in my professional career, or could even have imagined.

Only two days after the session, another person appeared on the scene who would become the point man for SFC. Louis Heimbach, a native of the region, farmer, and businessperson, had served for twelve years as the elected Orange County Executive for New York State's fastest growing county. According to the *Times Herald Record,* Heimbach was reputed to be "a promoter of development in the mid-Hudson Valley." Heimbach had been recruited to assume responsibilities as president and chief operating officer of SFC. Thomson would continue in his role as SFC chair.

Just a few days later, news spread rapidly through the Hudson River Valley that Castro was choosing to retire after twenty years with the PIPC. In addition to the artful management guidance he had provided for the PIPC, Castro was leaving behind two special contributions. In negotiation with the Orange and Rockland Utilities over an easement, he won a financial settlement for the PIPC of $3.5 million, marking the first instance in which the Commission could benefit from the equivalent of an endowment fund. He also wrote the PIPC's *Second Century Plan,* a guiding document that celebrated the history of the Commission and anticipated the demands and opportunities that it would face in the coming century. Wrote Castro,

> The first history of the Palisades Interstate Park System, published in 1929, makes the proud boast: "The Palisades Interstate Park of New York and New Jersey," it begins, "is the most notable example in the United States of interstate cooperation for the conservation of outstanding scenic features and the promotion of outdoor recreation. It was a bold claim 60 years ago, but in subsequent years the cooperation has continued unabated. . . . The park has . . . withstood relentless growth at its boundaries, encountered unprecedented demands, adapted to rapid changes, and still managed to maintain the essential integrity of 85,000 acres of open space."

Castro was retiring after a half-century of public service. His long-standing friendship and professional association with Laurance S. Rockefeller would continue, highlighted by the establishment in 1998 of the Marsh-Billings-Rockefeller National Historical Park in Woodstock, Vermont.

The commissioners held the decision by Castro to retire in confidence for several months while a search for his successor proceeded quietly. The search committee consisted of Commissioners J. Martin Cornell and Borg. Castro also served on the committee. During my months with the DEC, I had occasionally spoken with Castro about various state land-conservation matters. I had known of Castro for years. He was twenty years my senior and nationally recognized as a distinguished administrator of parks and historic sites. Yet when he made a surprise telephone call inviting me to Bear Mountain to stand as a candidate to succeed him, I declined. I had been with the DEC for less than a year, admired the tenacity and skills of Jorling, and was grateful for the opportunity he had given me. But Castro was not to be dissuaded. On a gray December day I was interviewed by Borg and Castro, and subsequently by Cornell. Borg made a point during the interview of assuring me that if I were selected he would "be there" whenever I needed to reach him for advice about the history, hopes, challenges, and expectations of the PIPC. His word proved to be his bond.

In mid-April, 1990, I joined the PIPC's staff, just two months after SFC released a plan announcing its intention to build 14,500 residential units and 7.4 million square feet of commercial and light industrial space, all of which was to be scattered throughout the forest in clustered locations. Thomson later described the plan as "compact siting of development using the model of a New England town center and European mountain villages." Advocates for the preservation of Sterling Forest variously described the plan as "fracturing the forest," "Swiss cheese," and "a shotgun blast at the heart of the Highlands." Lee Wasserman of the Environmental Planning Lobby captured the thoughts of many when he asserted, "It is simply fantasy to expect that you could drop a city of 35,000 to 40,000 people into the last privately owned forested open space in the metropolitan region without forever destroying the magnificent ecological benefits it provides."

Despite the development plan, the ground shifted somewhat under Thomson and Heimbach because of the financial struggles of the corporation's parent company, AmBase. The net second-quarter loss for AmBase in 1990 was $106 million, caused in part by unpaid debt owed to AmBase by Drexel Burnham Lambert. In the third quarter of 1990 AmBase was the second worst performer on the New York Stock Exchange. Before the end of the year, SFC had become a subsidiary of a new ownership group. For $970 million, AmBase sold its holdings in the Home Group, Gruntal Financial, and SFC to a consortium of investors led by Trygg-Hansa AB, Sweden's second largest insurance company. Other investors included London-based Vik Brothers, International Insurance Advisors, and New York City–based Donaldson, Lufkin, Jennrette. Humbach, watching the transaction on behalf of the Sterling Forest Coalition, said, "I'm not sure whether they will pursue development or liquidate Sterling Forest as an asset. I know they didn't acquire Sterling Forest with the view of donating the land as a national park." In response, David McDermott, speaking for the SFC, said, "There will be no change whatsoever." The change fervently hoped for by those seeking protection for the forest was encompassed in New York's 1990 Environmental Quality Bond Act, a funding package amounting to $1.975 billion that was actively promoted by Governor Cuomo. The package included $800 million for land acquisition. The PIPC and other state agencies were standing by, ready to immediately seek bond-act funds for their highest priority land-protection projects, with Sterling Forest and a handful of land-protection opportunities in the Adirondacks sharing top billing. Thomson was repeating the corporation's mantra: "We will sell for a fair price." New

York residents, almost always inclined to approve bond acts that promised an improvement of environmental quality, this time failed to do so in the November 6, 1990, off-year election. By a 51 percent to 49 percent margin in light voter turnout, the Environmental Quality Bond Act was rejected.

By May, 1991, Gordon Bishop, writing for the *New Jersey Star-Ledger,* labeled the Sterling Forest situation a "last chance effort" and reported that Congressman Kostmayer had won bipartisan support from members of the New Jersey congressional delegation to push through $250,000 in funding for the U.S. Forest Service's promised study of the 1.1-million-acre Highlands region, with Sterling Forest included. Kostmayer found ready bipartisan support from Democrats Torricelli, Roe, Frank Lautenberg, and Bill Bradley and Republicans Roukema, Dean Gallo, and Richard Zimmer. Congressman Gilman (R-NY) thought the study unnecessary, given that SFC was still in the process of refining its development plan, and for a brief moment in the congressional process knocked the Kostmayer funding out of an appropriations bill. But later convinced by his Republican colleagues from New Jersey, Gilman relented. Joseph A. Michaels, a seasoned veteran with the U.S. Forest Service, was tapped to lead the team. For the PIPC, I added Park Ranger Tim Sullivan to the team. Sullivan's selection surprised some members of the PIPC's staff, who had assumed that someone with more planning experience might be better qualified for the task. Sullivan, though, proved more than worthy to the challenge. For forty years he had been serving on the PIPC's staff, and he had been the first person assigned to Minnewaska when that park was created. A highly skilled woodsman, who in my opinion could hold his own with any ranger in the nation, Sullivan is a self-taught naturalist, search-and-rescue expert, forest-fire specialist, deeds and records authority, and master of the Hudson Highlands terrain. No trail in Harriman and Bear Mountain State Parks has escaped Sullivan's attention, and he expanded his firsthand knowledge far and wide into the Highlands on the premise that a response to emergencies is much more effective if familiarity with the land is already in the hip pocket. Sullivan, a ranger's ranger, brought a wealth of local knowledge to the U.S. Forest Service deliberations. He did not have to guess about the watercourses, rocky slopes, valleys, and ridge lines of Sterling Forest; he had been there, on his feet.

While the Forest Service inquiry was under way, Humbach continued to deliver the environmental message on behalf of the Sterling Forest Coalition. In a May, 1991, article published in the *Times Herald Record,* Humbach contended that the corporation's comprehensive plan "is a fine example of advanced urban planning. That is not, however, the issue. The question is whether, as a matter of rational, far-sighted planning, a special regional asset like Sterling Forest ought to be developed at all." Humbach continued:

> Two major impacts of pursuing the comprehensive plan are immediately apparent: First, it will constrict and fragment a key link in the Delaware-to-Hudson greenway corridor, permanently altering and degrading the forest's traditional high-grade wildlife habitat, recreational space and natural lands. Second, development in the watershed of the North Jersey District Water Supply Commission will replace a historically reliable source of clean, safe drinking water used by two million people with permanent dependency on government-mandated sewage treatment machinery.

Speaking to an SFC contention that almost 75 percent of the 17,500-acre property would remain as open space, Humbach said,

> More than 100 separate, discrete areas or chunks of development will be distributed within the forest. Extensive portions of the surface area shown in green are, in reality, nothing more than buffers interlaced among chunks of development. This network of green membranes would be quite considerable if lumped together. As a latticework, however, it no more retains the open, wild character of Sterling Forest than the wooded medians in the Thruway.

Returning to the watershed issue, Humbach reminded his readers that "three million gallons of treated sewage" would flow from the new Sterling Forest development each day. "The development of Sterling Forest according to the comprehensive plan means forcing two million people in New Jersey to give up their naturally clean sources of drinking water. It means forcing these people to depend instead, for the rest of time, on the good grace of New York town officials to maintain sewage plant machinery at the expense of their New York constituents."

As U.S. Forest Service representatives learned in nine public hearings, hundreds of people agreed with Humbach. Speaker after speaker approached the microphone in packed meeting halls to echo the message about the potential loss of recreational open space, wildlife habitat, and watershed. Thomson and his representatives countered with arguments about the sensitivity of their comprehensive plan, the economic benefits to local communities, and the risk to Sterling Forest if, in the absence of public funding for a "willing seller" transaction, the forest was simply thrown on the open market and subdivided in keeping with existing zoning ordinances.

* * *

With the demise of New York's 1990 Environmental Quality Bond Act and with continuing signals from SFC that development plans were in motion, a loose alliance of people involved with environmental organizations and government agencies began to form to meet the crisis. At Bear Mountain, the telephone was glued to my ear. With its interstate structure, the Commission seemed the public agency best suited to become the acquisition agent in the attempt to save Sterling Forest. Telephone calls were flying among Humbach, the Dolans, Filippone, and myself. This group quickly expanded to include Village of Tuxedo residents Helmet Nimke and Al Ewert; Klara Sauer, executive director of Scenic Hudson; Robert Pirani, a senior staff member with the

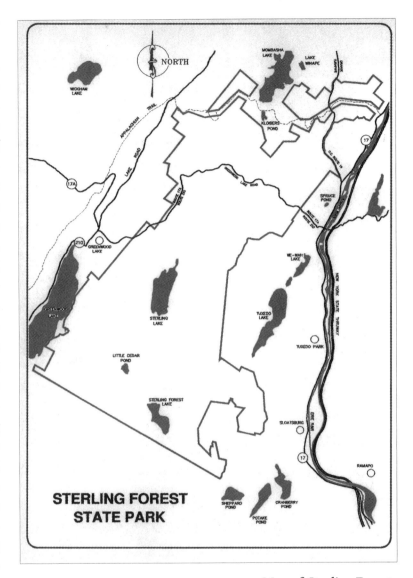

Map of Sterling Forest.
(Courtesy of PIPC)

Regional Plan Association; Judy Noritake, on Congressman Kostmayer's staff; Dean Noll, chief engineer for the North Jersey District Water Supply Commission; Olivia Millard of The Nature Conservancy; the Appalachian Mountain Club's Jennifer Melville; Environmental Defense Fund senior attorney Jim Tripp; and John Gebhards, who had been recruited to become the sole staff member of the Sterling Forest Coalition (subsequently renamed Sterling Forest Resources).

Within the PIPC, strength of purpose was solid among the commissioners. The Commission's president in 1991, Martin Cornell, a highly regarded trial attorney from New City, New York, was ready to lend his steady hand, optimistic outlook, and keen legal counsel to any PIPC action that might protect all or part of Sterling Forest. Barnabas McHenry, appointed to the Commission in 1987 and serving as its vice president, signaled that he was ready to go anywhere, anytime, to talk with anyone, organize any event, communicate in every way possible, and work day and night, if necessary, to find a way to save the forest. Malcolm Borg was in the treasurer's slot and, obviously, had placed Sterling Forest as a high personal priority that matched the most pressing demands within his large corporation. He was instantly responsible and accessible to anyone who needed his involvement to advance the cause. Larry Rockefeller, who had worked successfully on the Alaska lands issue of the 1970s, an initiative that led to the protection of millions of acres in the nation's largest, wildest state, brought this same interest and skill to the Sterling Forest test. Mary Fisk and Anne Cabot, respectively representing the Harriman and Perkins families, signaled their strong commitments to a venture that, in scale and difficulty, promised to test their personal resolve against the highest standards set on behalf of the PIPC by their parents and grandparents. Nash Castro had stepped away from day-to-day Commission activities, but not very far. He, too, was eager to assist.

Sadly, a key person would be absent from the fight. On January 31, 1992, David P. McCoy, assistant director of the PIPC, adept landscape architect, and devoted professional, died from complications of melanoma. The gentle, artistic, and unpretentious McCoy had provided a steady hand and guidance during the first months of my tenure with the PIPC. Kenneth Krieser, a park veteran who had transferred to the PIPC's staff in 1980 from his position as assistant director for the Thousand Islands Park Region on the St. Lawrence River, succeeded McCoy. He brought to his new assignment a sharp analytical ability and firm pragmatism that proved invaluable to McHenry and me.

An overarching problem faced the alliance of individuals beginning to coalesce around the increasingly urgent need to find an environmentally sound future for Sterling Forest. Thomson would "sell for a fair price," pegging the value at $150 million, but the PIPC and its collaborators had exactly zero dollars with which to negotiate a purchase. This was not exactly a strong bargaining position. Somehow, funds would have to be cobbled together from many sources so that a serious purchase offer could be made before the corporation pulled the trigger on its development shotgun.

Melville, watching from her Appalachian Mountain Club office in Boston, was concerned about different financial numbers. In various presentations, representatives of SFC were suggesting that local communities would receive a $35.5 million tax windfall from the proposed development. In alliance with the PIPC, Melville retained the services of Vermont-based Ad Hoc Associates to examine the tax-windfall promise. The Associates reported that school and municipal costs of almost $34 million were not included in the corporation's numbers, nor were the increased costs of treating the effluent that would begin to flow down from the forest into New Jersey's Monksville and Wanaque Reservoirs. Water company engineer Noll estimated these additional costs at $150 million over a twenty-year period.

A *Wall Street Journal* article appearing in September, 1991, seemed to confirm these findings. Under the headline "Boom County, Bust Budget," David Bergman, writing about a study of DuPage County, west of Chicago, said, "Curiously, the belief that development is lucrative may be one of the reasons it isn't. Across the country, developers have been able to thwart growth management movements by arguing that development is the only way to check rises in property taxes. If the association between taxation and development suggested by the DuPage study is confirmed, a powerful new argument for managing growth may be emerging." Bergman described how a hoped-for tax windfall in economically strong DuPage County never materialized. As job growth and development increased in the county, so did property taxes. He found that in the postindustrial United States, the pattern was to seek less expensive land on the periphery of metropolitan areas for development, thus adding to municipal costs for everyone. He could have been describing Sterling Forest.

SFC had already made clear that it would fade away once environmental approvals for its vast project were in hand. Thomson put the matter in simple terms: "We're not planning to build anything higher than a curb," he said. The corporation's business strategy was to rough in the road and utility systems, then sell off the approved development sites to other builders and exit as swiftly as possible. In the judgment of the corporate hierarchy, up-front planning, public relations, advertising, and time spent to move through New York's demanding Environmental Quality Review Act process would bring a substantial return-on-investment when building sites throughout the forest were ready to be marketed to other companies. The up-front costs were already reaching toward $7 million, according to Thomson, and the building plan would extend over two decades, but SFC intended to leave to other contractors the network of curb-lined roadways for construction of the largest new urban community between New York City and Albany.

The Regional Plan Association reported that population growth in the New York/New Jersey metropolitan region in the past thirty years had increased by only 6 percent, while the urbanization of land around the city had grown by 60 percent. SFC was intent on adding mightily to these already unbalanced statistics. To no one's surprise, the Forest Service found, on release of its 1991 draft "New York–New Jersey Highlands Regional Study," that the region offered potentially huge outdoor recreational benefits to 22 million nearby residents, 20 percent of the nation's population. These findings reflected similar conclusions reached in three parallel studies, "Communities of Place: Interim State Development and Redevelopment Plan" by the State of New Jersey; "Skylands Greenway—A Plan for Action" by the New Jersey Governor's Greenway Task Force; and "Conserving Open Space in New York State" by the New York Department of Environmental Conservation. Congressman Kostmayer, now chairing the House Subcommittee on Energy and the Environment, used the Forest Service study as a springboard to ask for a $25 million federal appropriation to help acquire Sterling Forest, contending that the forest was "a pearl in a necklace of linear greenways . . . stretching through the northern tier of states." Congressman Gilman promptly made known his opposition to the appropriation, arguing in favor of SFC's development plan and pointedly stressing that Kostmayer had no business getting involved in a "local matter" in Gilman's congressional district. From his neighboring congressional district in New Jersey, Congressman Torricelli favored the appropriation and firmly maintained that all 17,500 acres of the corporate holding should be conserved. In this contest, Gilman prevailed; a House appropriations subcommittee denied Kostmayer's request.

Despite this setback, the persistent Kostmayer scheduled a June, 1992, hearing before his subcommittee to further debate the fate of Sterling Forest. After hearing from Thomson about the comprehensive plan, the unimpressed Kostmayer responded, "You can't preserve a forest intact as an ecological unit if you break it up. . . . It won't be a forest anymore. . . . [You can] call it Sterling Acres, Sterling Vistas, or Sterling Meadows, but don't call it a forest because it won't be a forest." JoAnn Dolan and Filippone were there to remind subcommittee members of the strategic environmental importance of the forest ecosystem. Representing the PIPC, McHenry confirmed that the Commission, the New York Office of Parks, Recreation and Historic Preservation (OPRHP), and corporate representatives were in contact, trying to find some means of ensuring environmental protection for at least the most environmentally sensitive portions of the forest, prompting Congressman Gilman to say, "If both the PIPC and the SFC can come to some reasonable agreement, I promise to do all I can to acquire the funding, as questionable as it may be, for such an acquisition." Later, in response to comments by Torricelli that appropriations should be "pursued doggedly," Gilman said a push for a major slice of federal funding was "pie in the sky" thinking. Gilman had reason for pessimism; taxes had been cut, defense spending was up, and the nation was in a severe economic slump. Congress was in no mood to add more red ink to an already crimson financial ledger.

Outside the hearing room, Dolan, Filippone, McHenry, and I were at work with Kostmayer, Torricelli, Roukema, and New Jersey Republican Congressman Gallo, a member of the House Appropriations Committee. Judy Noritake, Kostmayer's staff assistant, was particularly effective in her work with friends and colleagues among the staff corps on Capitol Hill through her knowledge of how to deliver convincing messages and gain commitments within the intricate political web on the Hill. Using the Forest Legacy Fund as a financial vehicle, Kostmayer and his allies won a favorable House vote for a $5-million appropriation earmarked to acquire Sterling Forest lands. In the face of the entrenched budget-cutting mood in the 103rd Congress, a House-Senate Conference Committee subsequently lowered the amount to $3 million, far from the number demanded by Thomson and Heimbach as the basis for serious discussions of a sale by the corporation. The SFC's representatives made clear that they had no intention of selling off their holding piecemeal; $3 million was close to a frivolous amount as far as they were concerned. Still, the Kostmayer initiative represented a glimmer of hope that the drive to protect Sterling Forest warranted national attention.

While the effort was under way in Washington, Richard Curley, a land-acquisition specialist with the New York OPRHP, gained professional real-estate appraisals of SFC's property with the cooperation of Thomson, and with the full endorsement of OPRHP Commissioner Orin Lehman. The appraisals confirmed that the value of SFC's land holdings was far below the $150–$200 million range that had been mentioned in press quotes attributed to Thomson. The appraisals were showing a per-acre value of about $3,500—a total value in the range of $60 million. With this figure in hand, Lehman encouraged a park team to hold discussions with Thomson's group to determine whether an agreement-in-concept might be reached on the acquisition of enough contiguous acreage to allow for the creation of a new state park in at least a portion of Sterling Forest. Assuming agreement for a partial purchase of corporate holdings, the idea was that the park team, including the PIPC, would then try to gain the needed acquisition funds from federal, state, and private sources. This cart-before-the-horse approach was variously ridiculed and found to be somewhat amusing by the Thomson group. Heimbach kept challenging, "Where is the money?" All eyes were turned toward the PIPC to produce or shut up. Very few people truly seemed to believe that millions could be found somewhere, from some source, for a legitimate purchase of thousands of costly, privately owned acres already on the development drawing board.

Careful coordination among various environmental advocates seemed to offer the only hope for success, but competition of considerable scale is not uncommon among established environmental organizations. They have their own agendas and compete for charitable dollars, political compatriots, and members, sometimes tripping over one another in the process.

To guide Sterling Forest into a sheltered environmental harbor was going to take an extra-special effort fashioned to tap into the best strengths of a variety of organizations and individuals already engaged in the Sterling Forest debate, opening a pathway to an exercise in collective wisdom that would supersede the best efforts of any single entity. With encouragement from the PIPC commissioners and the Trail Conference board, JoAnn Dolan and I decided to reach for the collective brass ring by calling a meeting to urge everyone to work together and share information, allowing group dynamics to identify the person or persons best suited to pursue the immediate priorities—tapping hard for wisdom and strength while staring across the environmental-development divide toward a well-organized, generously funded, politically adept, self-assured opponent. Samuel F. Pryor III, chair of the Board of the Appalachian Mountain Club and senior partner at Davis Polk & Wardwell, a prestigious New York City–based law firm, provided the meeting place. Pryor is an avid outdoors person and for years placed his skills and prestige on the line in the contest to assure similar opportunity for others, that the joy and satisfaction of meeting nature on its own terms would be there for anyone to discover.

The PIPC took responsibility for scheduling the meetings. Larry Rockefeller agreed to extend the meeting invitations. Mixed with the stream of employees arriving at the law office in early 1992 was a group headed for a conference room reserved by Pryor. The conference room was large, handsomely decorated with lightly toned wood panels, a sweeping conference table to match, built-in kitchenette, comfortable chairs, and almost magical acoustics. A person standing at one end of the long room could talk in normal tones and be heard easily by those at the other end. Hidden in the ceiling were speakers for the telephone system—anyone calling in could be heard in godlike style by those in the room, the voice drifting down from above. It was hard not to stare up at the ceiling when someone was participating by telephone. At Davis Polk, ranked among the very best law firms in the nation, an entire floor was devoted to conference-room accommodations, large, medium, and small. The environmentalists, more accustomed to folding tables, modest rooms, and paper cups, settled in. There would be no bylaws for this group, no officers, no minutes to document discussions. The participants were coming together as a brain trust to fight for Sterling Forest. As expressed by Humbach, the group had four general purposes:

1. Identify sources of public and private funding for the purpose of acquiring Sterling Forest.
2. Monitor and participate in the Environmental Impact Statement process.
3. Educate and inform the public.
4. Cooperate with one another.

Along with coats and hats, the members of the group instinctively left their egos and turf concerns outside the conference room. From the first moment an unstated rule applied—no prima donnas. At the suggestion of Nash Castro, who, though retired, was in attendance, the group chose to name itself the Public-Private Partnership to Save Sterling Forest (PPP). In Washington, a small corps of congressional staff members, encouraged to become involved by Noritake and, beginning in 1993, expertly cajoled by Chris Arthur, staff aide to newly elected Congressman Maurice Hinchey, would mirror and reinforce the Hudson River Valley contingent.

Extending a compliment to the PIPC after the first meeting, JoAnn Dolan wrote,

> It would have been fun to be around in the Major Welch years, but I imagine that this is the first time since the Welch era that a state park agency has acted so purposefully in a partnership with the public. Your leadership and steadfastness, from the very beginning, have given great credibility to the Sterling Forest project. . . . [You] have been the energizing force for many groups to work in harmony. . . . A partnership like this can be a very dynamic process, but rarely happens.

The gathering of the PPP (see appendix C) came at a time of transition in Washington. With the election of Bill Clinton to the presidency, and despite Democratic gains across the nation, Congressman Kostmayer, the first elected official to gain funds for the preservation of Sterling Forest, was defeated in his home district in Pennsylvania. In the Hudson River Valley, Maurice Hinchey, stepping away from his influential position as chair of the Natural Resource Committee in the New York Assembly, was elected to the U.S. Congress by a hair's breadth. President Clinton appointed Bruce Babbitt, former governor of Arizona, as Secretary of the Interior. All eyes in the PPP turned toward Babbitt, anxious to convince the new secretary that the federal government should legitimately join in a financial partnership to purchase Sterling Forest. To make the point, the PIPC produced an analysis of appropriations from the Federal L&WCF for federal and state land-acquisition projects. Elizabeth Gordon, a bright intern who was assisting the PIPC, prepared a paper entitled, "Why Does California Get So Much?" The Gordon paper confirmed that over a recent five-year period, California had received $248 million in L&WCF appropriations, mostly for federal projects such as Santa Monica National Recreation Area on the outskirts of Los Angeles, while New York had received $9 million. Put another way, as calculated by Gordon, per capita spending from the fund for Californians was $8.33; for New Yorkers, $0.03. New York was not the only eastern state being shortchanged. Gordon found a letter to a congressman that stated, "I am writing to ask for your help in support of an amendment to the Land & Water Conservation Fund Act. The proposed amendment would reestablish the formula by which annual L&WCF appropriations are divided between federal and state governments." The letter was signed by the former governor of Arkansas, Bill Clinton.

With the arrival of Babbitt in Washington, expectations ran high that the PPP might gain sympathy and support for the plight of Sterling Forest, especially when George Frampton agreed to leave his post as executive director of the Wilderness Society to assume responsibilities under Babbitt as Assistant Secretary of the Interior. Frampton's portfolio would include oversight of L&WCF expenditures. The PPP anticipated that Frampton, widely respected within the environmental community, could be quickly convinced to join in the initiative to protect rare open space within sight of the Empire State Building.

I was especially optimistic. In 1986 Frampton and I had participated in the formation of a not-for-profit corporation designed to win the concession contract for Yosemite with the intent of reinvesting profits in park stewardship. We did not succeed, but this camaraderie with Frampton led me to believe that he would be quick to accept my rationale that federal matching funds should be funneled as soon as possible toward the Sterling Forest acquisition initiative. Frampton, though, proved to be a tough sell. In a meeting with him in 1993, Frampton counseled me that money in the coveted L&WCF should be used almost exclusively for federal projects. He recognized and appreciated that the fund, as originally envisioned, would be shared about fifty–fifty between the federal and state governments but explained that not enough money was being appropriated by Congress for even the most urgent federal projects of highest national importance. There simply was not enough federal funding to help with state-level projects like Sterling Forest, he asserted.

On the shoreline of Sterling Lake, a different dialogue was taking place. With appraisals in hand, serious discussion continued in May, 1993, between a New York State Parks–PIPC negotiating team and SFC's crew. The purpose was to try to determine through confidential discussions how much acreage the corporation would be willing to sell, and at what price, even though the Parks–PIPC team had no visible means of financial support. A sluggish economy was one incentive for continuing the dialogue. Speculation in *The New York Times* was that SFC might rather have some money in hand than a grand development plan on the table. But almost before the negotiators were out the door after their confidential meeting, and more to the surprise of Borg than anyone, *The Record* broke the story that the two groups were exploring a 13,000-acre purchase for between $30 and $40 million, leaving the corporation 4,500 acres for the development of six thousand houses and 4 million square feet of commercial space. Someone had leaked. *The Record* and other media sources, however, did not know about the major obstacles being encountered behind the closed doors of the negotiating room. As part of the deal, Thomson wanted airtight assurance that the hoped-for interchange on the New York State Thruway would be constructed. Added to the interchange problem was the major question of value. The Parks–PIPC team had a confidential appraisal that took exception to Thomson's claims of market value. Appraiser Kenneth Golub of American Properties, Inc., reported to the PIPC that the corporation's projection of housing market–share in the metropolitan region was "highly optimistic." Analyzing housing-market trends, Golub thought that the time frame for selling 14,520 housing units at Sterling Forest would approach seventy years, not the twenty-five years projected by SFC's planners. Finding that a viable community could be seen only in the hazy future, if at all, Golub said, "It would be difficult to find retail stores to locate in Sterling Forest even if their spaces were provided free of charge." He added, "Enormous capital outlays will be required before any positive cash flow appears." Golub's opinions hung silently in the air on the Parks–PIPC side of the table while Thomson and company continued to assert that they were sitting on a golden real-estate egg, with emphasis on the gold.

Still, the leaked news that some kind of an acquisition compromise might be near encouraged Congressmen Gilman, Torricelli, and Hinchey to introduce House Resolution 2741 that would appropriate $35 million to the PIPC for Sterling Forest acquisition purposes. Gilman, who had earlier applauded the full Sterling Forest development package, expressed support for a compromise that would create a park while leaving significant acreage for a scaled-down development. New Jersey's Senator Bradley, working closely with Torricelli, introduced a companion bill, S-1683. The rationale was that the PIPC, as an interstate agency functioning under a 1937 Compact approved by Congress and the President of the United States, could receive federal appropriations. The interstate structure of the PIPC positioned it to receive funds from Congress, channeled through the Department of the Interior, that neither New York nor New Jersey could receive directly. Congresswoman Roukema was alert to the same possibility. She introduced her own version of an appropriations bill, asking for $25 million to be matched by New York and New Jersey, making clear that her bill was not intended as a substitute for the Bradley-Gilman-Torricelli-Hinchey legislation but a complement to it.

The PIPC was hoping that Thomson might express active support for the funding initiatives being taken in Washington if, in fact, the corporation wanted payment now, not later. But Thomson's lobbyist, Leon Billings, dashed that hope. Billings was well regarded as the author of the 1979 Clean Air Act, while serving on the staff of Senator Edmund Muskie, but responding to the *Times Herald Record* in June, 1993, Billings, referring to the full build-out scheme for thirteen thousand houses, explained, "I would not have taken the SFC as a client if I didn't think that their plans were environmentally defensible." Then, assuring the *Times Herald's* reporter, "I have absolute admiration for wilderness," Billings added, "We're not talking Glacier National Park here; this isn't even farmland in Virginia; this is an area that was at one time industrialized. . . . There's significant urbanization, power lines, roads." JoAnn Dolan did not agree. Writing directly to Billings, she said, "In this most crowded urban area in the United States, where there is no virgin land, people are holding on to the shreds of their sense of place. We hope that you will not write off the urban areas because you can only relate to preserving things on a grand scale . . . like Glacier National Park, which is so far away from the maddening crowds." Echoing Dolan's sentiment, I said to the *Star-Ledger's* Bishop, "We must save this space where the fresh green meets the dull gray of urban sprawl," adding, "Protection of clean water is good conservation and good economics," framing the choice at Sterling Forest to be "buy the land or buy the infrastructure." Then, to remind Billings and others that a park system actually does exist in the metropolitan region, I added, "The PIPC accommodates 8 million people a year, compared with Yellowstone's 2 million."

Week by week, the Sterling Forest conservation message was gaining support. On a campaign swing with New Jersey's Governor Jim Florio in September, 1993, Secretary of the Interior Babbitt stood at a scenic vista on the Palisades overlooking the Hudson River and expressed his general support for the initiative to acquire Sterling Forest. Florio was in a tough campaign with Christine Todd Whitman, and he was well known to Babbitt through their earlier contacts at the National Governors' Conferences. Even a casual reading of public sentiment confirmed that Sterling Forest was a good campaign issue in northern New Jersey. Florio wanted Babbitt standing by his side on the issue, and Babbitt was happy to oblige. Keen observers at the event, although delighted by Babbitt's expressed interest in saving the forest, noticed that he did not mentioned any amount or source of federal funding to help with the acquisition. But the very fact that a member of the president's cabinet was even talking about Sterling Forest provided hope that the Clinton administration was about to join the bipartisan coalition in Congress to push forward the $35 million appropriations bill. The PPP needed a funding breakthrough.

The breakthrough came, but not in Washington. In the midst of a winter ice storm, PIPC Commissioner Borg and I drove down to Trenton to meet Florio and his staff to discuss their Sterling Forest strategy. Scott A. Weiner, counsel to the governor and a former Bergen County resident who knew about the PIPC and its accomplishments, had been searching for funding sources for Sterling Forest. His exploration uncovered an almost-forgotten Water Conservation Bond Act approved by New Jersey voters in 1969 that still held $16 million in nonobligated spending authority. Funds from the bond act could be made available for Sterling Forest through routine financial procedures administered by the New Jersey Department of Environmental Protection. Weiner, with the governor's approval, advised us that at least $10 million of the amount should be so used, assuming that New York State and the federal government came aboard to help prove to SFC that serious acquisition money was on the table. This delightfully welcome news proved to be a parting message of encouragement to the PIPC from Governor Florio. He had not prevailed in the November election. The incoming Whitman administration would have to be convinced of the wisdom of using the Water Conservation Bond money as proposed. Thanks to Weiner's detective work, though, Florio was handing a relatively uncomplicated choice to Governor Whitman. With financial authority already provided by statewide vote, even if that vote was dated by twenty-four years, the new governor had a clear opportunity to provide acquisition funding for Sterling Forest, if she chose to do so.

The timing of the discovery seemed good. Before the end of 1993, *The Wall Street Journal* was reporting that Trygg-Hansa, the parent company of SFC, was recapitalizing. After three years of struggle to staunch the flow of red ink from Home Insurance, Trygg-Hansa took the insurance company public, hoping to raised $350 million in a stock offering. The result was disappointing. Only $127 million was raised, forcing Trygg-Hansa to increase debt for Home Insurance from $100 to $280 million. The debt-to-equity ratio stood at 70 percent. In addition, Thomson confirmed that the annual carrying costs for Sterling Forest were in the range of $2 million. The bad corporate financial numbers raised the expectation that the corporation's interest in selling Sterling Forest might be enhanced.

All signals were "go" in early 1994 when Sauer of Scenic Hudson convinced twenty-five of her environmental colleagues to sign a letter to Governor Cuomo, urging him to strengthen his position on Sterling Forest. "A powerful team of public and private, state and federal, interests already has emerged in a collaborative effort to protect the precious natural landscape," Sauer wrote, "but, frankly, the right coaching and captain are still missing." Referring to the promise of funds from Congress, New Jersey, and the private sector, Sauer concluded: "We cannot stress strongly enough how these real and potential funding commitments depend—or are contingent upon—the State of New York becoming a key player and demonstrating that Sterling Forest is a priority." Sauer had reason for optimism in approaching the governor. In addition to people in Washington and New Jersey, the PIPC and New York–New Jersey Trail Conference were hard at work raising funds to ensure that experts could be retained to comment during the public review of SFC's Environmental Impact Statement (EIS). With Nash Castro's assistance, the PIPC raised more than $165,000 for this purpose. The principle contributors were Borg, George Perkins, Jr., the James H. Ottaway Jr. Revocable Trust, the Gladys and Roland Harriman Foundation, the National Fish and Wildlife Foundation, the George W. Perkins Memorial Foundation, the Geraldine R. Dodge Foundation, the Mosaic Fund, and the Victoria Foundation.

Castro was also in a position to be of immense help in the search for major acquisition funding. He was one of five trustees of a Lila Acheson and DeWitt Wallace charitable fund that specialized in Hudson River Valley conservation activities. Through the fund, Scenic Hudson and the Open Space Institute received annual grants totaling millions of dollars to protect land. The two organizations normally functioned independently, but Sauer for Scenic Hudson and Kim Elliman for the Open Space Institute, both of whom were very active PPP participants, signaled that they would be willing to combine financial resources in the attempt to save Sterling Forest. Sauer and Elliman convinced their respective boards of directors of the need for combined monetary strength on this matter, giving Castro the opportunity he needed to deliver this message to his fellow Wallace Fund Trustees. The trustees quietly indicated that a linked $5 million grant to Scenic Hudson and the Open Space Institute to help acquire the forest would receive favorable consideration.

At the same time, Filippone was performing some political magic in New Jersey. She had noticed that the PIPC owned about 78,000 acres of land in New York and only 2,400 acres in New Jersey. Wondering why, Filippone learned that since 1900 the PIPC had been restricted in its New Jersey activities to the "highest elevations of the Palisades," a narrow north-south strip running parallel to the Hudson River. Working with her friend Phyllis Elston, a staff assistant for New Jersey Assembly Speaker Chuck Haytaian, Filippone drafted legislative language that would expand the PIPC's land-protection authority into the 1-million-acre New Jersey Highlands Region. Her motivation was that New Jersey should be positioned to take full advantage of the interstate structure of the PIPC, especially to carry forward the momentum in watershed protection that might be achieved at Sterling Forest. With Elston's help, Filippone convinced Haytaian and cosponsor Maureen Ogden, chair of the Assembly's Environmental Committee, to introduce the legislation.

Filippone and I testified before Ogden's committee, which gave unanimous endorsement of the PIPC bill. The influence of Haytaian and Ogden promised favorable action by the Assembly, but Filippone knew that a possible stumbling block existed in the person of Robert Littell, chair of the Budget Oversight Committee in the New Jersey Senate. Littell, a fiscally conservative Republican reputed to be unenthusiastic about most environmental initiatives, had to be convinced if the PIPC legislation was to prevail. Filippone wasted no time. She and I went straight to Littell with a presentation about the potential financial and environmental benefits of bringing the PIPC into the Highlands. Littell made one demand: he did not want his county, Sussex, included in the legislation. Otherwise, he gave it his blessing. In late April, 1994, the Assembly unanimously approved the bill that allows the PIPC to function in Bergen, Passaic, Morris, Somerset, Hunterdon, and Warren Counties, New Jersey, a highlands swath of hundreds of thousands of acres extending southwesterly from the New Jersey–New York border to the Delaware River. Senate endorsement and the governor's signature followed. After almost a century, New Jersey invited the PIPC to step far beyond the Palisades, bringing along its traditions for acquiring and managing parklands and historic sites. Filippone could easily translate the word *park* to *watershed*. For her, the distinction was small; parks are generally good sponges, soaking up and filtering rainfall essential to all life-forms.

In Washington, events were not progressing so smoothly. Senator Bradley scheduled a hearing in May, 1994, to garner support for the $35 million federal appropriations legislation. Torricelli, Gilman, Hinchey, and Roukema were there to record their support. Governor Cuomo, convinced by Sauer and the PPP, sent a letter to every member of the New York and New Jersey congressional delegations, expressing his backing for the federal initiative and pledging assertive follow-up by New York. Thomson reconfirmed SFC's willing-seller posture. The PPP was strongly represented. The mood and expectation in the hearing room were very positive, until Marie Rust took the microphone.

Rust was the Northeast Regional Director for the National Park Service (NPS). Appearing in uniform, she was carrying testimony vetted through the Department of the Interior and the Office of Management and Budget, the keeper of budget strategies for the White House. To the stunned audience, Rust's testimony slammed the collective effort to save Sterling Forest. She testified that any federal funding directed toward the acquisition of Sterling Forest lands "ignored" important NPS priorities. "With a current backlog in land acquisition of some $1.1 billion," she said, "we should not divert what limited funds are available to projects outside the system." Adding that no federal interest would be served by protecting Sterling Forest, despite the fact that a brand new park would be attached to the NPS-owned Appalachian Trail, Rust claimed that "a dangerous precedent" would be set if Congress appropriated money for Sterling Forest. She did offer a limp carrot by suggesting that the NPS would be willing to "study" Sterling Forest for a year and come back to Congress with recommendations.

Everyone in the room knew that Secretary of the Interior Babbitt had stood on the Palisades with then-Governor Florio only a few months earlier and pledged support for the Sterling Forest protection initiative. Roger Kennedy, director of the NPS and a fan of the Hudson River Valley, had offered similar strong assurances in an earlier meeting with McHenry and me. Questioned a day later by one of his own reporters, Borg was diplomatic: "It is our belief that if the Federal government takes a leadership role in this, private funding will follow." (Borg knew about the quiet, $5 million approach to the Wallace Fund.)

Torricelli was also quoted: "We are at a loss to understand how the Park Service could fail to see the federal interest in preserving this tract." Feeling the heat from Torricelli, Bradley, and other elected officials, a spokesperson for Babbitt offered the disingenuous remark that the secretary's staff was trying to "track down" what happened between "last fall," when Babbitt expressed support for Sterling Forest, and the NPS's expression of opposition, now flapping like a red cape. Congressman Hinchey dispatched his staff aide, Chris Arthur, to the Interior Department to investigate. Cuomo personally telephoned Babbitt. The steam from Torricelli was clearly evident. The *Record* carried an editorial declaring, "New Jersey got a kick in the teeth from the National Park Service." One pundit said Babbitt's words were "chiseled in Jell-O." Referring to the gross imbalance between L&WCF money spent in the West versus the East, a *Rockland Journal News* editorial said, "Maybe the National Park Service is so blinded by the beauty of California redwoods . . . that it has written off the equally spectacular eastern part of the nation." The PPP took on a war-room mentality.

Flak was still flying and telephone lines burning the following week, when the Commission's president, Cornell, appeared on behalf of the PIPC before the House Subcommittee on National Parks, Forests, and Public Lands. To the general relief of Cornell, Dolan, Filippone, Tripp, and our PPP colleagues, word circulated in advance of the hearing that the NPS had changed its position. In place of Rust, who had been delegated the unpleasant task of delivering the earlier message, an NPS assistant director explained the reversal. He testified that the NPS would support a $17.5 million appropriation for Sterling Forest, but with strings attached. The NPS would make its own deal with SFC, he suggested, by buying land adjacent to the Appalachian Trail. The spokesman said that the Interior Department reserved the right to pay no more than 25 percent of the total purchase price for Sterling Forest lands. Assuming a total price of $55 million, the NPS would be obligated for $13.5 million.

Although the PIPC and its allies were encouraged that a major level of federal financial support now seemed possible, the attached strings were unthinkable. The three towns that claimed portions of Sterling Forest for property-tax purposes had swung strongly in the direction of the PIPC's acquisition initiative, in large part because property and school taxes would continue to be paid on the acquired land but very few municipal services would be required in return. In the long-ago days of Perkins, Sr., foresighted political decisions had been made to keep almost all the PIPC's lands on the local tax rolls rather than move them to tax-exempt status, as was the custom with parklands. Over decades, this strategy greatly aided the expansion of the park and historic-site system. The rationale was that the payment of property and school taxes on open space was less costly to taxpayers in the long run than the escalating tax demands required to indefinitely cover the costs of an aging infrastructure left in the wake of development. In 1993 the New York General Fund had paid more than $6.5 million in taxes to towns in which PIPC holdings were located. In the Town of Tuxedo, the PIPC's lands provided the largest single source of tax revenue. By contrast, any land at Sterling Forest that the NPS might acquire under the strings-attached scenario would be promptly removed from the tax rolls. The specter of the NPS's vying head-to-head with the PIPC for Sterling Forest acreage would also position SFC to play off one buyer against the other. To snip the strings, more trips to the nation's capital, telephone calls, faxes, letters, and entreaties were required of the PIPC and PPP. Congressman Hinchey's staff assistant, Arthur, was spending more time at the Department of the Interior than he was in his office on Capitol Hill. His boss personally consulted with Secretary Babbitt about the problem. Torricelli, Roukema, Bradley, and Lautenberg pitched in. The mood of the New York and New Jersey congressional delegations was that no new and restrictive federal rules should suddenly be invented for Sterling Forest, when no such restrictions had been draped on other L&WCF projects.

In the meantime, Filippone was continuing to work with State Senator Littell, even though many of her environmental allies took a dim view of her willingness to collaborate with someone they considered to be a political enemy. She shrugged off these criticisms, judging that if she could not work effectively with the chair of the Senate Budget Committee, then any hope for funding from New Jersey, to be spent in New York, would be dead on arrival. Littell was key, and he delivered. To the amazement of many of Filippone's friends, Littell's Budget Committee unanimously approved the expenditure of $10 million in New Jersey funds for Sterling Forest acquisition purposes. So persuasive was his influence in the state budget process that the full Senate followed suit, voting in July, 1994, to support the appropriation. The vote was thirty-seven in favor, one opposed. New Jersey was standing on the threshold of protecting Sterling Forest, putting its money where its clean water was and ringing a signal bell for New York and Congress that would be hard to ignore.

Thomson would not be around to see where the New Jersey lead would take the acquisition initiative. Abruptly and without fanfare in mid-August, 1994, he left his position as president and C.E.O. of SFC to "pursue other interests." Heimbach immediately took Thomson's place. Only three weeks later, SFC released its Environmental Impact Statement, all thirty-one volumes and four thousand pages. Imposing though the EIS was, and supposedly filled with objective data, it delivered one clear and simple message: the real-estate development project was in full gear and racing forward. In the section of the EIS that required a listing of "alternatives," should the entire development package not be approved, no mention was made of any possible public acquisition of the property. As far as the corporation was concerned, the only legitimate alternatives were development or slightly less development. The "preferred alternative," around which all the data spun, affirmed that thirteen thousand housing units and 8 million square feet of commercial space could be constructed in Sterling Forest with only slight, inconsequential environmental effects. The commercial space alone would be equivalent in size to 240 football fields.

The PPP was scrambling to keep up. Against the millions claimed to have been spent by SFC on the statement, the PPP was turning to universities, various environmental organizations, pro-bono lawyers, and a few paid consultants to try to gather well-documented and scientifically defensible facts on hydrology, water supply, ecological fragmentation, endangered species, wetlands, transportation, scenic quality, and fiscal impact.

At Bear Mountain, Jack Focht, director of the Trailside Museums and Wildlife Center, had been watching the contest unfold. Knowing that SFC was diligently guarding its land against trespassers, especially those who might be too curious about some of the conclusions reached in the EIS, Focht gathered together his Volunteer League of Naturalists, a loosely arranged group of academicians, businesspeople, retirees, docents, and students who shared a common love of natural history. Focht sent them for weekend walks along the section of the Appalachian Trail that passes through Sterling Forest. Mostly confining themselves to the narrow Trail corridor, the naturalists invested a few days of volunteer time compiling a list of 369 different species of plants, birds, insects, fish, mushrooms, mammals, reptiles, and amphibians. The list included the rare American chestnut tree, dainty Queen Anne's lace, wild licorice, red-throated and common loons, wood ducks, bald eagles, wild turkeys, American woodcock, great horned owls, ruby-throated hummingbirds, and belted kingfishers. Twenty-two species of warblers were found and fifteen species of butterflies. Beaver were at work and white-tailed deer, red fox, and various shapes and sizes of turtles were abundant, and the naturalists knew that black bears roam the forest. From high points, a few of Focht's troopers could study the World Trade Center, glimmering on the horizon in a city dominated by pigeons, while their feet were planted in a veritable wilderness. Forest fragmentation, the shotgun blast that SFC was aiming at this intact and amazingly fruitful ecosystem, was predicted to leave only a relic of what the volunteer naturalists found all around them.

Despite Focht's initiative, the effort in Washington to gain approval of an appropriation for the forest was beginning to run up against the headwinds of a midterm election. By a sixteen-to-four vote, the Senate Energy and Natural Resources Committee endorsed a $17.5 million appropriation in August, 1994, adding the legislation to a truckload of bills trundling toward final action, but in jeopardy because senators and members of the House of Representatives were anxious to adjourn as soon as possible to attend to campaign needs. Months of intense effort by the PPP had been narrowed to a few weeks, then to the last hours of the 103rd Congress. In early October, I was glued to CSPAN, watching as senators passed to and fro in front of the television camera, conferring in small groups, asking for procedural votes and claiming parliamentary privileges. At one point, Senator Bradley could be seen chatting with Senator Richard Shelby, Democrat of Alabama, who was objecting to legislation about a historic site in Pennsylvania that was packaged with Sterling Forest and other public-lands bills. Was Bradley trying to convince Shelby to let the Sterling Forest legislation go forward on its own? Only they knew. No question remained, though, when Senate Minority Leader Robert Dole, acting at Shelby's request, formally objected to the legislative package. Based on the clubby rules of the Senate, objection by the Minority Leader killed the package. Moments later, the 103rd Congress went out of business. A new Congress would be elected in November, and the PPP would have to start all over again. Shrugging off the missed opportunity, Heimbach was quoted in the *Times Herald Record* as saying, "It's a major setback, sure, but we didn't really have anything before."

For those seeking to preserve Sterling Forest, the November, 1994, election brought more change. In New York, Governor Cuomo, seeking a fifth term, lost to State Senator George Pataki. On the national stage, the Republicans took control of both Houses of Congress for the first time in decades. Newt Gingrich, the incoming Speaker of the House, would control leadership positions on the various committees and subcommittees. In New York, Joan Davidson, had succeeded Lehman when he voluntarily retired with great honor after years of service as New York's Commissioner of OPRHP. Davidson expressed immediate support for the Sterling Forest initiative, but she, in turn, was replaced only a few months later by Bernadette Castro (no relation to Nash Castro) when Pataki prevailed in the 1994 election. Castro, heir to the Castro Convertible Sofa company, agreed to run in the 1994 election in a bid to unseat Senator Daniel Patrick Moynihan. Her bid was unsuccessful, but she nonetheless established strong credentials within the Republican Party and subsequently was appointed by Pataki to the OPRHP post.

For the PPP, Pataki, Castro, and a whole raft of new people in Albany and Washington would have to be convinced of the increasingly imperative need to save Sterling Forest. The exception to this new test was in New Jersey. Governor Whitman and other state officials watched the election results from the sidelines. Except for the congressional races, New Jersey operated on a different election-year calendar. Only a few ripples occurred on the New Jersey political pond. Republican Rodney Frelinghuysen, who, until the Gingrich sweep, served in the State Assembly as chair of the Appropriations Committee, won against his

Democrat opponent and joined the 1994 "freshman" class in Congress. In his position as the Assembly Appropriations chair, Frelinghuysen heard testimony from Filippone and me and, in keeping with his otherwise strong environmental credentials, strongly supported the Sterling Forest acquisition initiative. The State Assembly, taking its cue from Frelinghuysen and reflecting similar action in the State Senate, approved $10 million for the Sterling Forest purchase by a fifty-eight-to-twelve vote.

For the PPP, Frelinghuysen's move to Congress was delightfully good news, spiced even more by the discovery that he had been honored at the national level with a coveted appointment to the House Appropriations Committee. Frelinghuysen more than landed on his feet in Washington. He was right where the purse strings were controlled. Joining Frelinghuysen in the 1994 freshman congressional class was another Assembly colleague, Bill Martini, who rode the Republican wave to success in a normally Democratic district in New Jersey.

Soon after the election, on November 22, 1994, Governor Whitman, addressing an audience at Drew University, delivered an undeniably clear message about her position on Sterling Forest:

> . . . Most of you know that I recently took positive action on legislation that will bring us very close to preserving Sterling Forest. . . . I am committing upwards of $10 million toward this effort. I am counting on the State of New York and the Federal Government to commit their fair share of funds to complete this project. I pledge to you this evening that I will work with our new Congress and with Governor-elect Pataki to make this vision a reality as soon as possible. Sterling Forest naturally cleanses the water supply for some two million New Jerseyans, and it does this for a song. If we lose the forest to development, expensive treatment plants will take its place. New Jersey taxpayers would feel the pain, and pay the price. That would be crazy! Once again, the right environmental choice is also the best economic policy!

The North Jersey District Water Supply Commission's Chair Robert Rubino confirmed the price that Governor Whitman had in mind if Sterling Forest were not protected. Rubino, on a track parallel to the PIPC's as an activist in the battle for Sterling Forest, had made trips to and from Trenton and Washington to testify for acquisition funding. Speaking to the financial numbers, he reported that if the forest were to be developed as proposed, chemical-treatment costs for drinking water would leap at full build-out of the massive project from $3.1 million to a projected $77 million per year, calculations for inflation not included. The cost of granular activated carbon treatment, currently not required at the reservoirs in northern New Jersey, would jump from zero to $60 million annually.

In early 1995 Governor Whitman wrote to New York's governor: "Dear George: As you know, last month I signed legislation essential to the preservation of Sterling Forest. With confidence that you share my strong interest in protecting the natural resources of the Highlands region and safeguarding . . . vital aquifers, I urge you to champion passage of similar legislation in your state. Your support of this important interstate effort can ensure its success. . . ." Governor Pataki's response came quickly; "Thank you for your letter expressing your strong support for the preservation of Sterling Forest. As an avid outdoors man, I am personally familiar with the property and I feel, as you do, that it must be protected." Pataki meant what he said. He was a son of the Hudson River Valley, having grown up on a farm near Peekskill, New York. He and his family had been frequent visitors over many years to Bear Mountain and Harriman Parks and had hiked along the Appalachian Trail in Sterling Forest. Pataki closed his letter to Governor Whitman by pledging his enthusiasm for "cooperative ventures between our two great States—beginning with Sterling Forest." Whitman also acknowledged a letter to her from Larry Rockefeller: "I appreciate the support and strong interest of the Public-Private Partnership to Save Sterling Forest. . . . As you know, the next steps are for New York and Congress to pass similar legislation."

In a March, 1995, letter to Pat Noonan, now president of The Conservation Fund, I tried to express my own view that something special might be happening in the partnership effort to save the forest:

Perhaps most importantly, the effort to acquire Sterling Forest may be taking on aspects which could apply in a positive manner to major land conservation initiatives in the 1990s. The informal, but increasingly effective "partnership" which has materialized in pursuit of the acquisition goal suggests how federal-state-private alliances can capture the attention of a Congress otherwise challenged by deficits, political positioning, internationally intertwined economies, foreign policy, and a quickly approaching Presidential election. The proof is in actions of recent date. In mid-January, New Jersey Governor Christine Todd Whitman approved appropriation of $10 million to help acquire Sterling Forest Corporation lands, all of which are located on the New York side of the border. Last week, the Senate Committee on Energy and Natural Resources advanced a $17.5 million Sterling Forest Authorization Bill on a favorable 13 to 3 vote. The convergence of two states, the Federal government, and the private sector in pursuit of a common land acquisition goal is not necessarily unique, except that in this case it is happening in the crowded northeast, a section of our nation not well known for this type of initiative, and it is happening in the '90s. Our hope is that the Swiss will be in a position to focus on selling of a non-performing asset, but the local managers remain resistant and continue to tell the public that they truly want to construct 13,000 residential units and 8 million square feet of commercial space in phases over the next 25 years on a rocky, steeply sloped, and wet landscape.

New York Parks Commissioner Castro, rapidly learning about the parks/historic-site portfolio handed to her by Governor Pataki, attended a spring meeting of the PPP held in one of the Davis Polk conference rooms. She came away impressed, sensing, as she put it, that Sterling Forest might become a worthy environmental prize to be claimed during the first four-year term of the Pataki administration, and one that would be a mark of personal success for the governor. Her impression was reinforced during her visit to Bear Mountain. I was unaware that Castro was less than enthusiastic about questionable-looking contraptions that flew through the air and had arranged for an aerial view of Sterling Forest. Only after the helicopter had safely returned to the great lawn at Bear Mountain did Castro confirm that she had just completed her first helicopter flight. She did like the bird's-eye view of the vast forest, though, and told me, "If I have to rent an apartment in Washington to lobby this thing through, I will."

While the transition was under way in Albany, the Zurich Insurance Group, successor to Trygg-Hansa as owners of Home Holdings and SFC announced that a $30 million line of credit was available to initiate the proposed development. However, the media were characterizing Home Holdings as a financial millstone, reporting $264 million in losses in the first quarter of 1995. Continuing speculation that this red ink might tempt the Zurich group to unload Sterling Forest at a bargain price proved to be wishful thinking. When the New York DEC announced that hearings would be held on SFC's Draft Generic Environmental Impact Statement, Heimbach welcomed the news, reaffirming that public dialogue was a necessary prelude to the development.

Anticipation of the hearings may have prompted a Freedom of Information (FOI) demand directed at the PIPC by a law firm representing SFC. The corporation wanted access to all the PIPC's files from January 1, 1992, to December 31, 1994, including "all letters, memoranda, calendars, telephone logs, and diaries" that had anything to do with the PIPC's involvement in the effort to save Sterling Forest.

The burden for pulling out files fell primarily on Kathryn Brown and Elizabeth VanHouten, my administrative assistants. At one point, two SFC attorneys were sitting in our office at Bear Mountain, taking notes as rapidly as possible, with stacks of files strewn everywhere, while people were coming and going on other business. They seemed to be searching for proof that the PIPC was darkly in cahoots with not-for-profit environmental organizations with the intent of taking unfair advantage of a subsidiary company whose parent owner claimed assets of over $40 billion. To our relief, Bernadette Castro stepped forward to remove the FOI burden. In an Albany meeting, she convinced Heimbach to drop the demand.

During the spring of 1995, the DEC held four public hearings in the communities adjacent to Sterling Forest. James Ahearn, writing for *The Record,* described the first hearing:

> When the hearing got underway, eight of the two dozen witnesses were from the Town of Tuxedo. The town supervisor, Joseph Ribando, was the only witness who was not unreservedly opposed to the plan. The hearing was in a gymnasium, hung with red-and-white banners celebrating championship seasons in girls' soccer and boys' basketball. The microphone did not work. Until a replacement was found, witnesses had to stand with their backs to the hearing office and bellow. The audience included many New Jerseyans, concerned about downstream effects of development. There were lots of green and white lapel buttons saying, "Keep Sterling Forest Green." The room, packed with 200 people, became warm. Big ceiling fans were turned on, creating a tremendous racket. The crowd, unable to hear the speakers, shouted protests. The fans were turned off. Doors to the outside were opened to admit fresh air, revealing an orange-and-white dog chained to an exit stairway. The dog began lunging at his chain and barking ferociously, drowning out the witnesses. It was, all in all, a Tuxedo, not Tuxedo Park, event.

This first hearing lasted almost until midnight. People were still waiting their turn when the exhausted hearing officer called for adjournment. The succeeding three hearings mirrored the first.

Heimbach was among the two hundred people packed onto the gymnasium floor, there to listen, not to speak, as would be his style at all four hearings. Gebhards of Sterling Forest Resources, a spare man with a graceful presence and granite resolve, would also attend all four hearings, and he did speak. Gebhards deserved much of the credit for the packed hearing rooms. Sterling Forest Resources was the local, grassroots organization that, with a budget even more spare than its leader, served as the counterweight to the corporation's public-relations campaign. Gebhards's low-budget newsletter, combined with his willingness to speak in any forum, visit schools, talk with neighbors, debate with

Heimbach, lead hikes, gather facts, refine strategy, respond to the media, reason with elected officials, and urge informed citizens to become activists, won him great admiration and respect within the Tuxedo community and among his PPP peers. Many of the speakers at the hearings were exceedingly well informed because Gebhards made certain that they were.

By numbers alone, the public voice proclaimed overwhelming opposition to the development of Sterling Forest. Mary Yrizarry, a local resident and Gebhards's friend, said, "We're being asked to buy a pig in a poke. . . . We may be left with the remnants of a grandiose scheme that will become burdensome to the entire region. . . ." The PIPC argued tax benefits, flatly contending that acquisition of the forest for park purposes would be tax positive to the local communities, while "Swiss cheese" development would clearly be tax negative. Describing the hidden costs of development, the PIPC reported that a transportation consultant had pegged the need for road improvements alone at $41 million. Harvey Stoneburner, a mathematical economist at Hunter College, challenged the conclusions reached by SFC in its Environmental Impact Statement as being based on a "selective approach to data." Labeling corporate assumptions about the type of lifestyle to be created at Sterling Forest as "utopia," another speaker said, "People who will inhabit the forest will be among the most unique human beings on the planet: They will have fewer children, fewer cars, ride more buses and create less garbage than anyone yet known."

David Startzell, representing the Appalachian Trail Conference, pointed out that SFC's statement suggested that a way to mitigate the impact of development near the Appalachian Trail was to "move the trail." Another local resident, Geoffrey Welch, a professional musician and self-taught water expert, criticized the corporation for what he judged to be its cavalier approach to water issues and defended his own carefully reasoned hypothesis about the true impact on water quality should the development go forward.

Dr. Richard Lathrop, a Rutgers University associate professor, used computer modeling to examine SFC's claim that the thousands of residences and acres of commercial space it intended to introduce into the forest ecosystem still would leave "75%" of the land as "open space." Lathrop found that 86 percent of the property would be "severely or very severely" impacted. He did discover that 10 acres of the 17,500-acre property could be safely placed in the "slightly impacted" category. Martin Lavenhart, using simple logic, remarked, "We have a forest. No assumptions are necessary to keep it a forest." Speakers ranged from eight-year-olds to almost ninety-years-old. Hundreds of pages of written testimony were stacking up on the hearing table, all requiring detailed review by the DEC's staff.

The Environmental Defense Fund's Tripp questioned in detail the legal suffi-ciency of the Environmental Impact Statement. Tripp, Larry Rockefeller, McHenry, Pryor, JoAnn Dolan, Filippone, Timothy Dillingham, and the rest of the PPP knew that the road ahead would likely lead straight to court if the hear-ings failed to produce major corrections in what they judged to be faulty EIS data, assumptions, and conclusions. Heimbach, listening throughout, characterized the hearings as "part of the process" and suggested that sound and reasonable answers to all the concerns brought forward at the hearings, emotional and fac-tual, could be found in the EIS and the corporation's frequently reiterated intent not to damage the forest ecosystem. In this stance, Heimbach was distinctly in the minority. Later in the year, when Tuxedo Supervisor Joseph Ribando and two Town board members, considered to be overly sympathetic to SFC's develop-ment scheme, stood for reelection, they were voted out of office.

Another "part of the process" continued to play out in Washington. In July, 1995, Senator Bradley telephoned Borg with good news: the Senate had autho-rized an appropriation of $17.5 million for Sterling Forest acquisition purposes. After months of maneuvers, steps and missteps, and optimism dashed by disap-pointments, the powerful and legislatively skilled New Jersey senator, joined by his equally adept colleague, Senator Lautenberg, had scored mightily on behalf of forest conservation. The authorization bill was the first step of a two–step process. Authorization was the green-light legislation needed to provide any legitimate hope that appropriations—money in the bank—would follow in a sep-arate legislative action. Without authorization, there was almost no hope that funds would be appropriated. The authorization bill placed the Senate squarely on record in favor of the necessary appropriation. This achievement caused expectations to run high on the House side of Capitol Hill when a hearing was held before the subcommittee on National Parks, Forests and Public Lands to consider a similar authorization bill. Congresswoman Roukema and her staff had been working hard behind the scenes to convince her Republican colleagues that protecting Sterling Forest was in the national interest. In this effort, she was joined by Gilman, Frelinghuysen, Martini, Sue Kelly, and other Republican mem-bers of the New Jersey and New York congressional delegations. Hinchey and Torricelli were carrying the flag for the House Democrats. Chairing the hearing that day was James Hansen, R-Utah. Other participating subcommittee members included Wes Cooley, R-Oregon; Wayne Allard, R-Colorado; Richard Pombo, R-California; and Hinchey, D-New York.

Allan Freemeyer, counsel to the Republicans on the subcommittee, set the tone by referring to Sterling Forest as "radioactive." Bernadette Castro, testifying for the first time before Congress, tried to make the case for federal participation in the forest preservation initiative. Pombo, a rancher from the San Joaquin Valley in California and first-term member elected to Congress in 1994, made an obvious point of chatting with a staff aid while Castro testified. Speaking on behalf of the PIPC, I attempted to explain that the Commission functioned under a 1937 mandate approved by Congress and signed by the president, but fared no better. The Western congressmen made no secret of their distaste for what they deemed to be a misguided attempt to use federal money to buy a "state park." Reminded by Hinchey that the initiative to save Sterling Forest enjoyed strong bipartisan support within the New York and New Jersey delegations, the Western members were unimpressed. "Just local pressure," one said. Hansen, enjoying his new post as subcommittee chair, was a well-known advocate for mining, grazing, hunting, trapping, logging, and off-road motor-vehicle access to public lands; he was equally suspicious of environmental motives, disdainful of wilderness protection, and resistant to expansion of the public land base. "I can hardly wait for the full committee to get this one," he said. His meaning was clear. The Committee on Resources, to which Hansen referred, was chaired by Don Young, R-Alaska, a former taxidermist and kindred spirit to the subcommittee chair.

The fate of federal funding for Sterling Forest was likened to a "high-stakes poker game." Passage of the authorization bill in the Senate put pressure on the House to follow suit. Senator Bradley made known that if the House did not act favorably on Sterling Forest, he would bottle up fifty or so bills being sought by Hansen and Young that required Senate endorsement. Roukema, the senior member of the New Jersey Republican delegation, decided to work around Hansen's subcommittee by appealing directly to Speaker Newt Gingrich. In a campaign swing to the Hudson River Valley several months earlier to aid Kelly in her successful bid for election to Congress, Gingrich had applauded the idea of protecting Sterling Forest. None other than the intrepid Filippone had counseled him about the forest preservation effort. While in Washington on other business, Filippone had impulsively decided to swing by Gingrich's office to try to talk with a staff person about Sterling Forest. Telephoning me afterward, she said, "I went into the office, asked if I could see Gingrich or a staff person, and the next thing I knew, I was talking with Gingrich."

Now, weeks after the Speaker's campaign visit with Kelly, Congresswoman Roukema wanted to remind him of his stated support for the Sterling Forest conservation initiative. She did so by sending him a letter, signed by thirty-eight members of the New Jersey and New York congressional delegations, urging that funds be appropriated to purchase the forest. But, then, to Roukema's utter surprise, her fellow New Jerseyan, Congressmen Martini, and his 1994 freshman-class colleague from California, Richard Pombo, put a bid on the political poker table. They proposed that the federal government auction off 56,000 acres of national grasslands in Oklahoma and use the proceeds to help buy Sterling Forest. Added to the bid was that a 326-acre Washita National Battlefield Site would be established in Oklahoma to commemorate the deaths in 1868 of 150 Cheyenne, surprised while sleeping and killed by Cavalry troops under the command of Lt. Col. George Armstrong Custer. Martini and Pombo thought they had found a creative trade-off that would respond to a conservation need in the northeastern United States while lowering the inventory of federal land in the West.

The Cheyenne and Arapaho tribes in Oklahoma did not agree. They had a stake in the grasslands based on tradition, spiritual meaning, and personal enjoyment. Neither did the Oklahoma Wildlife Federation, joining in this instance in an unusual alliance with the National Audubon Society. From different perspectives, the two organizations saw risk in losing access to and use of 5 percent of the public land in the state, known particularly as excellent pronghorn antelope and quail habitat. Oklahoma hunters, backed by the New Jersey State Federation of Sportsmen's Clubs, saw the proposed grassland auction as a "land grab" by ranchers. Roukema believed that she was making progress with Gingrich, but the Oklahoma component produced a sudden complication that threatened to bring momentum to a halt. At the Department of the Interior, Secretary Babbitt left no doubt about his view: "Throwing public land on the auction block to generate revenue for other conservation projects would set a very bad precedent," he contended. Major environmental organizations quickly concurred. But bringing the heavy weight of his influence to bear, Gingrich stepped forward to express support for the Pombo-Martini maneuver, claiming that it offered to pay for the Sterling Forest purchase "in a way that fits in with getting a balanced budget."

Enough thrust was being developed for Sterling Forest funding, however it might be garnered, to convince Heimbach to sit down and begin serious negotiation of a possible purchase. All the dialogue in Washington and elsewhere still had not provided an answer to the logical question "How much acreage at what price?" Speculation about purchase price was running all over the chart. To reel in federal, New York, and additional private money, a precise answer was required. At one of the early PPP meetings, I sought out Rose Harvey and asked her whether the Trust for Public Land would be willing to join with The Nature Conservancy, the Open Space Institute, and Scenic Hudson to form a private-sector negotiating team that would work with New York and New Jersey to hammer out a purchase price for Sterling Forest. Harvey said yes, but ground under the negotiating-team concept shifted when Heimbach made known to Bernadette Castro that any purchase discussions must be draped in strictest confidentiality and that the PIPC, in particular, was not welcome at the table. Castro thereupon turned exclusively to the Trust for Public Land (TPL)'s Harvey and the Open Space Institute (OSI)'s Elliman to negotiate with Heimbach, sending them off for the next several months on a behind-closed-doors odyssey about which those left on the outside could only speculate.

Harvey and Elliman recruited Steve Horowitz, a talented attorney with the law firm of Cleary, Gottlieb, Steen & Hamilton, to provide what proved to be thousands of dollars of pro-bono counsel for the team. TPL and OSI lawyers Phyllis Nudelman and Robert Anderberg were immersed in the negotiations, as was OSI's Katie Roberts, the niece of former PIPC Commissioner Frederick Osborn. "Grinding" was the best word to describe the process. On occasion, a negotiating team staff member or lawyer would check with the PIPC on details related to park-management needs, but otherwise the shades were drawn. Harvey and Elliman stopped attending PPP meetings. The scores of people who had worked so hard to raise hope that enough funding could be found to protect the forest were left to speculate about what was going on in the negotiating room.

While negotiations proceeded in relative secrecy week after week, the Sterling Forest-for-Oklahoma-grasslands deal fell of its own controversial weight, only to be replaced by an even more questionable tactic. In early February, 1996, I arranged for a series of meetings in Washington for Bernadette Castro. McHenry and I rode the train yet again to rendezvous in the hallway just outside the office of Utah's Hansen with Castro and Mary Ann Fish, widow of former Congressman Hamilton Fish, Jr., and a member of Governor Pataki's congressional liaison staff. After exchanging pleasantries with Hansen and Freemeyer, counsel to Hansen's subcommittee, we were informed of an entirely new legislative strategy for Sterling Forest. Hansen was proposing a stratagem intended to open millions of acres of federally owned wilderness in southern Utah to mining, dams, and off-road vehicles. He asserted that the only chance for Sterling Forest rested with support by the New York and New Jersey congressional delegations for the Utah maneuver.

No one in the room yearned for Sterling Forest preservation more than McHenry. He had devoted countless volunteer hours to the bid for environmental common sense in the Hudson Highlands, had always been available at a moment's notice when needed, was carrying around a personal calendar filled with appointments and meetings about Sterling Forest, was sending out letters to anyone and everyone who might be nudged toward the preservation camp, and was striding forward with the growing legion of advocates for forest protection with unshakeable perseverance. He and I had made such pests of ourselves that congressional and legislative staff members started calling us "Sterling and Forest." McHenry, though, reacted to the Utah ploy like someone shot from a cannon. He was on his feet, staring furiously at Hansen. "We want this very badly, but we will never sacrifice Utah wilderness to save Sterling Forest," he declared. Hansen sat back in his chair, then rose, quickly shook hands, and moved toward the door, claiming scheduled business elsewhere. He turned the meeting over to Freemeyer. Not much of a meeting was left. Freemeyer urged our group to "think about" the need to bring Western members of Congress into the Sterling Forest mix.

Hansen's Utah card was on the table. He wanted nothing less than mining and off-road access to 4 million acres of wilderness in the spectacular Redrock region of southern Utah. When the news surfaced in the media, Secretary Babbitt said he would recommend a veto if any such legislation reached the president's desk. Congressman Gilman, wise in years and service in Congress, counseled that the Utah connection would overly complicate the Sterling Forest initiative and should be avoided. Hinchey, serving in the minority on Hansen's subcommittee, joined actively with Western-based environmental organizations to head off the Utah wilderness ploy and keep Sterling Forest from becoming entangled in a legislative package that would be vetoed.

The Hansen card was still in play in March, 1996, when Speaker Gingrich agreed to return again to the Hudson River Valley to host a reception in Fishkill, New York, for his colleague Congresswoman Kelly. The Speaker was then scheduled to travel by van to the Monksville Reservoir in New Jersey to make an announcement about Sterling Forest. Congresswoman Roukema had ensured that the Monksville visit was added to the fund-raiser itinerary. On learning of the Speaker's plans, I took a chance and telephoned Rob Hood, a Gingrich staffer who was frequently in the chain of Sterling Forest communications, and suggested that Bernadette Castro be given a seat in the van for the hour-and-a-half drive from Fishkill to the Monksville Reservoir. Hood agreed. On the day of the fund-raiser, the PIPC's Krieser spotted the location of the van and alerted Castro. Krieser and Castro maneuvered through the crowd to the van as the event concluded. Gingrich and his staff were still involved with photographers and well-wishers. Castro hesitated to jump in the van, not knowing with certainty whether the Speaker even knew of Hood's agreement that she could be a passenger for the drive to the Monksville Reservoir, but the opportunity was just too good to pass up. When Gingrich and his staff arrived, the van doors closed, and the passengers, including Castro, were on their way to New Jersey.

A reporter for *The Record* wrote,

Waiting for Newt Gingrich, we heard the northwest wind whistling. After it discovered our mass huddled in the slushy parking lot and invaded our puny jackets, leaving our blood curdled, the wind could be heard merrily whistling at a job well done. An hour late, Gingrich de-vanned and strode to the little rubber mat laid down to protect North Jersey's tundra from the depredations of politicians' feet. "We are going to save Sterling Forest," a beaming Gingrich announced, warming the crowd. . . .

The Speaker assured the gathering that a bill "is going to pass this year" and would not be "held hostage" in Congress. Castro, standing with a group close behind the Speaker, was also beaming; the van ride had provided her a much better forum than the one experienced in Hansen's office. Governor Whitman, Congresswoman Roukema, and Congressmen Gilman, Frelinghuysen, and Martini were there to add their enthusiastic endorsements to the Speaker's message.

Even so, the Sterling Forest roller coaster continued. Bradley, who had announced his plan to retire from the Senate, mounted a three-day filibuster against an "omnibus" package of parkland legislation that included more than fifty mostly noncontroversial bills, but they also embraced the Sterling Forest–Utah link. When it became obvious that sixty-one votes could not be mustered among the senators to break the filibuster, Majority Leader Dole withdrew the entire package. Then, over in the House, Western members of Hansen's subcommittee inserted a provision in the much-sought-after $17.5 million authorization that would require Sterling Forest to be declared a wilderness and approved it on a straight ten-to-seven party-line vote. "Senator Bradley stands up there and says how great wilderness is," Freemeyer was quoted as saying. "Well, here is an opportunity to create some in his back yard." If written into law, the wilderness designation would require roads, power lines, and buildings to be taken out of Sterling Forest. One subcommittee staffer gleefully crowed that local residents who commuted on the existing roads through Sterling Forest would have to go "on foot or horseback." Roukema termed the amendment "absolutely absurd." Hinchey's staff member, Arthur, kept saying, "I want to get this thing off my desk" and dug even deeper by networking with other congressional staff colleagues to gain approval of a clean appropriations bill in what had become a West-versus-East political contest.

With flak flying around in Washington, Elliman, Harvey, Horowitz, and their teammates emerged bleary eyed from the shadows of confidentiality in May, 1996, after nine months of on-again, off-again negotiating sessions to announce that they had initialed a purchase agreement with SFC. The corporation would retain about 2,220 acres of its holdings. For a purchase price of $55 million, it would sell 15,280 acres and eventually donate another 525 acres when the transaction was completed. The corporation would retain the right to draw millions of gallons of water from Sterling and Blue Lakes, but draw-down limits were imposed on both lakes; two feet at Sterling Lake, one and one-half feet at Blue Lake. Logging contracts already in place would be allowed to run their course, even if title were to be transferred before the contracts expired. Heimbach signaled that he anticipated higher-density development on the retained 2,220-acre parcel, and he put safeguards in the agreement to protect the corporation's right to the higher densities. A $5 million down payment was required.

Finally, the purchase price was out there for everyone to see, and the clock was ticking on an escrow agreement and final closing. The question, How much is this going to cost? had been answered. Heimbach wanted the closing within a year, two years maximum. Working with Sauer at Scenic Hudson, Elliman's Open Space Institute was prepared to accept title to 1,400 acres when the down payment was made. The Lila Acheson and DeWitt Wallace Fund would be the source of the $5 million down payment. New Jersey was still standing tall with its $10 million commitment to the project. But that was it. The Washington roller coaster had yet to land on anything resembling firm ground; New York's pledge had yet to result in a dollar commitment. The negotiators came out of the room with an agreement, but the conservation bank account was $40 million short.

Despite the financial shortfall, three strong ingredients had become part of the chemistry of Sterling Forest. The handful of conservation advocates who had met in the home of Paul and JoAnn Dolan almost a decade earlier had expanded into the hundreds of thousands. The ambition to save Sterling Forest had truly taken on a life of its own, as reflected by hundreds of news stories, scores of supportive editorials, and solidly bipartisan political backing in New Jersey and New York, all reflecting an undeniable public consensus that the intact forest should never be chopped into fragments. This life-of-its-own was now fueled by the Elliman-Harvey negotiating success, including the ticking clock. The fuel's octane was increased by 1996 presidential-election-year pressures on Republicans and Democrats to reaffirm their environmental credentials.

Even though Governor Pataki and the New York Legislature had yet to write a check for Sterling Forest, the governor's resolve to match or exceed New Jersey's $10 million was unquestioned. Pataki frequently expressed his comfort with the conservation legacy of Theodore Roosevelt and seemed to be judging the need to protect Sterling Forest based on his personal knowledge of the area and his strongly evident Roosevelt-style environmental convictions. High on Pataki's first-term list of achievements was a $1.75 billion Clean Water/Clean Air Bond Act he confidently intended to place before New York voters for approval in the November election. Money for Sterling Forest would come from the bond act, if approved, or from other state sources, if not approved. In Washington, the once ridiculed venture to protect this "ragged collection of trees somewhere in the northeast" had taken on such high profile that it was beginning to attract unpopular riders, like the "rangelands management act," an attempt to open public lands to more intensive cattle grazing on the assumption that protection of Sterling Forest, carrying endorsements from President Clinton and Speaker Gingrich, had become almost politically unstoppable. Fortunately, this rider, too, fell by the wayside like the Oklahoma grasslands and Redrocks gambits.

In early July, I was able to advise the PPP that "the latest word from Washington is that the 'soft earmark' for Sterling Forest . . . is considered a great breakthrough success. . . . Dialogue apparently is underway between House and Senate members to determine whether the Senate will follow the House and also affirm the earmark. . . ." Three key sections were driving the omnibus package of park-related legislation forward. One was Sterling Forest. The others were the proposed transfer of the Presidio in San Francisco to NPS stewardship. The third was a proposed federal-private land exchange in Utah in preparation for the 2002 Winter Olympics. Importantly, the omnibus package, as now configured, had won the support of Democratic leaders Babbitt, Bradley, Lautenberg, Torricelli, Hinchey, and Congresswomen Nita Lowey, opening the way to a presidential signature should the legislation reach Clinton's desk, especially given the strong bipartisan support from the Republican side of the aisle. During this critical time, Lautenberg, Bradley, Torricelli, Roukema, and Martini were regularly in contact with Borg; New Jersey remained in the driver's seat. On July 7, 1996, the House of Representatives approved the $17.5 million Sterling Forest authorization bill. The House also voted favorably on a $9 million appropriation for the acquisition, with the stated intent of adding the remaining $8.5 million in 1997. Congressman Martini, in particular, must have breathed a sigh of relief. He had timed his election to Congress perfectly, joining the 1994 sweep when the Republicans took over on Capitol Hill, but Martini knew, nonetheless, that he was in for a tough reelection bid in a district centered on Paterson, New Jersey, where registered Democrats significantly outnumbered Republicans. Delivering on Sterling Forest, for which Martini could take some of the credit, was a feather in his cap. Gingrich wanted all of the Class of '94 Republicans reelected. Martini's vulnerability in a swing district was part of the reason why the Speaker opened the door for Sterling Forest. Sterling Forest helped Martini, but not enough—he lost in the November election.

On the Senate side, the national election was fast approaching, adjournment was in the air, and Senator Bradley was retiring. These factors didn't make the legislative track any easier. Senators were exercising all sorts of parliamentary privileges, slowing legislation, blocking legislation, speeding legislation, ignoring legislation, hooking on amendments to the most popular bills. Somewhere in this flux, surfacing from time to time, was the omnibus package that enfolded Sterling Forest, the Presidio in San Francisco, the Utah land exchange, and a long list of other park and public lands projects targeted to benefit forty-one of the fifty states. Most threatening to the bill in the final hours was a provision to extend logging for fifteen years in the Tongass National Forest, Alaska. The Alaska provision prompted yet another veto threat from the White House. Bradley spent his last days in Congress brokering a two-year logging deal on the Tongass that Senator Frank Murkowski of Alaska found acceptable. The veto threat was removed. During this final Senate endgame, Bradley was in contact with PIPC Commissioner Borg, at one point confirming that he was holding forty-seven bills on his desk that other senators wanted passed, to ensure that the Sterling Forest legislation was not again maneuvered to the sidelines. In the predawn hours on October 3, 1996, the very last piece of legislation passed by the 104th Congress, supported by the very last vote cast by Senator Bradley, was the omnibus bill, including a $17.5 million authorization for Sterling Forest.

The Sterling Forest acquisition purse, once containing only moths, had increased to $32.5 million, counting $10 million from New Jersey, $5 million from the Lila Acheson and DeWitt Wallace Fund, and $17.5 million from the federal government. In the November, 1996, election, New York voters approved Governor Pataki's Clean Air/Clean Water Bond Act, providing a source for the money he had pledged for Sterling Forest. Based on counsel offered by Bernadette Castro, Elliman, and Harvey, Governor Pataki provided an impressive $16 million for Sterling Forest, bringing the purse to a substantial $48.5 million. Three of the financial legs were firmly on the stool, and Elliman and Harvey were working hard to cement the fourth leg by finding enough private-sector contributions to close the remaining $6.5 million gap. The New Jersey–based Victoria Foundation, already on record with a timely contribution to the PIPC in response to the earlier Environmental Impact Statement challenge, responded again, this time with a $1 million contribution. The Trust for Public Land, the

New York–New Jersey Trail Conference, Sterling Forest Resources, and the PIPC were regularly receiving contributions large and small. Students and faculty from the E. G. Hewitt High School, Ringwood, New Jersey, contributed $1,034.74. Students at the Dwight D. Eisenhower Middle School, Wyckoff, New Jersey, donated $158.00 in lunch money. Harvard student Jamie Fitzgerald organized an "Ocean-to-Ocean" cross-country bicycle trek with the intended goal of raising $12,000 for the Sterling Forest purchase. Only days after graduating from Harvard, the twenty-two-year-old Jamie, along with his Harvard classmate, Alan Ferency, twenty-two; Jamie's nineteen-year-old sister, Shannon, a Cornell University junior; and Patrick Farley, twenty, a neighborhood friend from the Village of Palisades, New York, set out from Seattle, Washington, toward their destination, the summit of Bear Mountain. When they arrived two months later, lean, sunburned, and happy, Governor Pataki was there to greet them. As symbolized by the bicyclers, many people dug into their pockets and contributed to the Sterling Forest cause.

Private contributions, small and large, all welcome, closed the gap to $5 million, and there the purse stood as Elliman and Harvey turned to the Doris Duke Charitable Foundation. The Foundation, with assets of $1.25 billion and ranking it in financial strength among the top ten in the nation, had recently resolved difficult organizational problems and was seriously considering a request for funding to create the new park. The Foundation retained the Conservation Fund's Noonan for a due diligence review of the Sterling Forest funding request. Noonan dispatched a staff colleague to the PIPC's New Jersey office to spend most of a day grilling Elliman and me about the details of the project. Noonan was not about to allow friendships and shared environmental concerns to buffer the search for provable, factual details about Sterling Forest. In early December, 1997, with the Conservation Fund findings in hand, Joan Spero, president of the Doris Duke Charitable Foundation, speaking on behalf of the trustees, announced a $5 million grant for Sterling Forest. In response, Bernadette Castro and the PIPC's commissioners agreed that a one thousand–acre portion of the forest would be designated the Doris Duke Nature Sanctuary and that this section of the forest would be permanently closed to hunting. The funding gap was closed—the four-legged stool was in place.

The devil-in-the-details of the $55 million acquisition fell into the exceedingly capable hands of New York's Assistant Attorney General Henry DeCotis. DeCotis sits at an intersection within New York State government through which all land transactions must pass. He supervises a real-property staff of twenty-three attorneys, fourteen title-search specialists, and thirty-two additional support personnel. Working with attorney Megan Levine and real-property specialist Steve Lewis, representing the New York OPRHP; Jim Economidies, an effervescent lawyer with the New York DEC; and Donald King, chief of the Land Acquisition Field Office for the NPS, DeCotis labored straight through the December holidays and into the new year to pull together the blizzard of real-estate closing documents.

On February 5, 1998, I sat quietly with various lawyers for several hours signing documents in SFC's office. The mood was businesslike and subdued, with papers being shuffled from one signatory to the next. With all signatures in place, notarized, and deeds ready to be filed, handshakes ended the session. The PIPC was owner of an incredible new park, "the largest to have been created in the northeastern United States in the last half-century," as one of the participants put it. The new park promises unending benefit for warblers and wanderers, historians and ecologists, children and grandparents, hikers and poets, frogs and flowers, people of the region, people from afar—inhabitants, temporary and permanent, of a gentle, timeless, intact forest ecosystem.

The PPP dissolved just as it had been born, easily and without fanfare. Standing in its place is a living monument to the conservation ethic. There were many moments in the Sterling Forest saga when just giving up might have been the rational choice. Every person involved was busy with other responsibilities; Sterling Forest was not anyone's entire life. But there was the forest, and it needed rescue. A rescue operation is not necessarily rational. The PPP had a clear goal even if that goal was framed against almost hopeless odds. It forged ahead, improvising, gathering allies along the way, finding a kind of collective chemistry and common purpose that overcame the nasty little critters called "ego" and "turf," and finally placed safely in the hands of the public thousands of acres of natural beauty in a most unlikely location, megalopolis. Most of the people who roam the forest in years to come will not be aware of the details of how Sterling Forest State Park was created. What they should appreciate is that no place is conserved by accident. Grit is essential. It helps, too, to be a little bit crazy at times.

18.
Looking Ahead

On December 12, 2000, *The New York Times* reported that an additional 1,065 acres of Sterling Forest Corporation land was acquired for $7.89 million to become part of the park. The acquisition leaves the corporation with about 5 percent of its original 19,500-acre holding.

The four-legged financial stool was again in place for this final transaction. New York committed $4 million; New Jersey pledged an additional $1 million; the Clinton administration promised $2 million from the Forest Legacy Fund; the remaining amount came from the PIPC and private sources, including an anonymous member of the New York–New Jersey Trail Conference. In addition to the lands acquired from the Sterling Forest Corporation, 209 acres have been acquired from Sears Hunter and the Lawrence Copans Trust and another 659 acres from New York University. The list of other protected lands in the forest includes the Indian Hill tract, a strategically located 490-acre parcel acquired independently by Scenic Hudson.

When that "slip of an Irish girl," Alice Haggerty, pushed a plunger in 1898 to dynamite the Indian Head, "one of the most widely known and splendid pieces of scenery in North America," she symbolically set in motion an experiment in conservation in the Hudson River Valley and beyond that spanned the twentieth century.

The PIPC is responsible for the stewardship of almost one hundred thousand acres of parkland and historic treasures that honor the past, invite the current generations to cherish and enjoy life, and stand as a symbol of respect for those who will inherit the products of our society, good and bad. Carol Ash has taken over the PIPC's helm. She stands with an organization that is looking south toward the 1 million-acre New Jersey Highlands, a region that ranks among the nation's premier scenic landscapes. The PIPC has been summoned to help conserve portions of the Highlands. Much work must be done, and new partnerships formed. For the PIPC, the turn of the century is business as usual.

At Bear Mountain, a new merry-go-round is being donated by the grandchildren of George W. Perkins, Sr. The century-long involvement of the Perkins family with the PIPC could not be more delightfully represented. The merry-go-round will welcome the next wave of park visitors, in every sense bringing smiles and joy, wonder and discovery. To saunter alone or with friends and family, soak in the views, share space with wild birds and animals, explore and learn, gather lifetime memories, or just ease along with Mother Nature, the people's park beckons.

APPENDIX A

PALISADES INTERSTATE PARK COMMISSION PARKS
AND HISTORIC SITES

Bear Mountain State Park, N.Y.	5,067 acres
Blauvelt State Park, N.Y.	590 acres
Bristol Beach State Park, N.Y.	53 acres
Goosepond Mountain State Park, N.Y.	1,543 acres
Harriman State Park, N.Y.	46,613 acres
Haverstraw Beach State Park, N.Y.	73 acres
Highland Lakes State Park, N.Y.	3,086 acres
High Tor State Park, N.Y.	565 acres
Hook Mountain State Park, N.Y.	676 acres
Lake Superior State Park, N.Y.	1,409 acres
Minnewaska State Park, N.Y.	11,630 acres
Nyack Beach State Park, N.Y.	61 acres
Palisades Interstate Parkway Right-of-Way	1,475 acres
Palisades Interstate Park, N.J.	2,452 acres
Rockland Lake State Park, N.Y.	1,079 acres
Sterling Forest State Park, N.Y.	16,380 acres
Storm King Mountain State Park, N.Y.	1,888 acres
Tallman Mountain State Park, N.Y.	687 acres
Knox's Headquarters State Historic Site, N.Y.	48 acres
New Windsor Cantonment State Historic Site, N.Y.	120 acres
Senate House State Historic Site, N.Y.	3 acres
Stony Point Battlefield State Historic Site, N.Y.	87 acres
Washington's Headquarters State Historic Site, N.Y.	7 acres
Underwater Rights	1,426 acres
Total acreage	97,018 acres

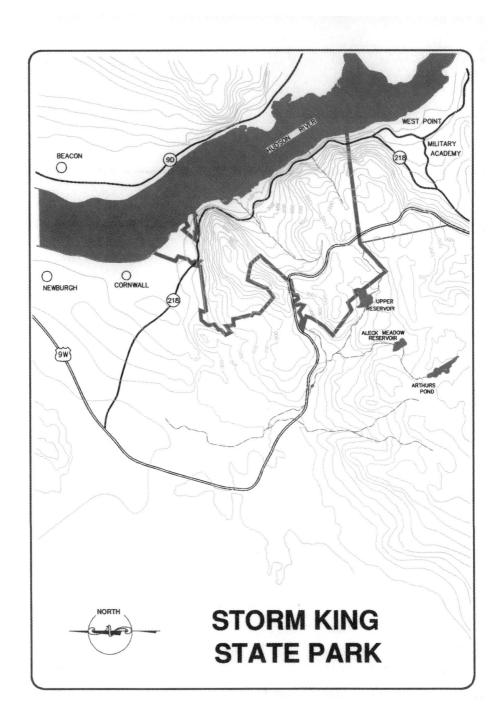

STORM KING
STATE PARK

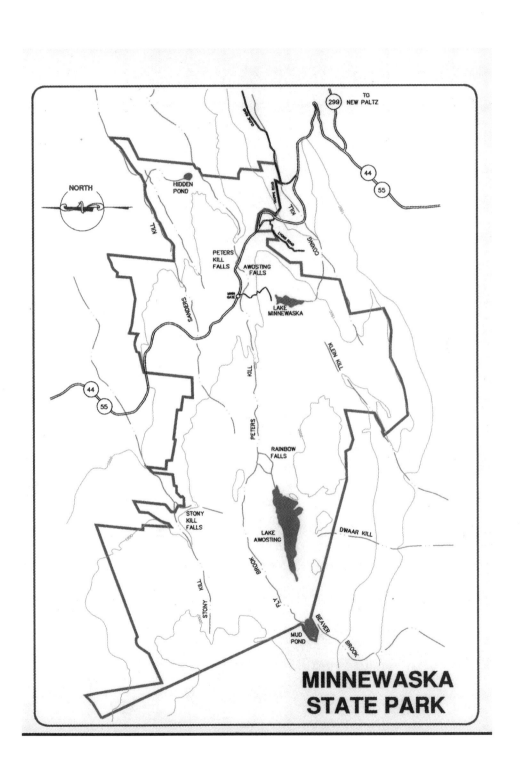

MINNEWASKA
STATE PARK

APPENDIX B

COMMISSIONERS OF THE PALISADES
INTERSTATE PARK COMMISSION

George W. Perkins	1900–1920	William Childs	1926–1933
Abram S. Hewitt	1900–1902, 1915	Frederick Osborn	1927–1971
		Edmund W. Wakelee	1929–1943
D. McNeely Stauffer	1900–1912	Alfred E. Smith	1930–1943
Edwin A. Stevens	1900–1914	Victor H. Berman	1935–1953
J. Dupratt White	1900–1938	Reg Halladay	1938–1953
Franklin W. Hopkins	1900–1928	Catesby L. Jones	1938–1955
Ralph Trautman	1900–1903	Laurance S. Rockefeller	1939–1978
William A. Linn	1900–1912	Albert R. Jube	1941–1970
Nathan T. Barrett	1900–1914	Horace M. Albright	1944–1961
Abram DeRonde	1900–1912, 1932–1937	Theodore Boettger	1946–1967
		Donald G. Borg	1953–1973
William B. Dana	1903–1909	W. Roland Harriman	1955–1958
William Porter	1905–1926	Thomas A. Byrd	1956–1978
Richard V. Lindabury	1910–1924	Phelps Phelps	1956–1970
Edward L. Partridge, M.D.	1913–1929	Carl O. Gustafson	1962–1963
Frederick C. Sutro	1913–1931	Mrs. Linn Perkins	1962–1973
Charles Whiting Baker	1913–1940	Conrad L. Wirth	1964–1972
Mornay Williams	1914–1918	David Van Alstyne, Jr.	1970–1976
John J. Vorhees	1915–1921	Charles A. Agemian	1971–1981
W. Averell Harriman	1915–1954, 1959–1973	Peter Dudan	1971–1982
		Richard Drukker	1971–1973
Myron W. Robinson	1919–1922	Edward A. Jesser, Jr.	1973–1980
Otis H. Cutler	1921–1922	George R. Lamb	1973–1976
George W. Perkins, Jr.	1922–1960	George W. Perkins, III	1973–1988
George T. Smith	1922–1934	Mary A. Fisk	1974–1996

Malcolm A. Borg	1974–	Anne P. Cabot	1990–
Dr. Mamie Phipps Clark	1976–1983	Gus D'Ercole	1991–1994
Ugo J. Lisi	1976–1984	Donald Aronson	1991–1995
Jon F. Hanson	1978–1984	Kevin J. Collins	1995 –
Larry Rockefeller	1979–	J. Fletcher Creamer	1994–1996
George E. Imperatore	1980–1992	James E. Hanson, II	1995–
Sidney Silverstein	1981–1988	Lawrence M. Manus	1995–1997
J. Martin Cornell	1984–1998	Maureen Ogden	1996–1999
Alfred N. Sanzari	1985–1994	Ann O'Sullivan	1998–
Paul C. Petrillo	1985–1990	Philip H. White	1998–
Barnabas McHenry	1987–	Samuel F. Pryor	1998–
David Poskanzer	1989–1990	Kathryn Porter	2000–

APPENDIX C

THE HUDSON RIVER VALLEY CONTINGENT OF THE
PUBLIC-PRIVATE PARTNERSHIP TO SAVE STERLING FOREST

Bob Binnewies—Palisades Interstate Park Commission
Malcolm Borg—Palisades Interstate Park Commission
Nash Castro—Palisades Interstate Park Commission (retired)
Charles Clusen—Natural Resources Defense Council
Martin Cornell—Palisades Interstate Park Commission
Tim Dillingham—New Jersey Sierra Club
JoAnn Dolan—New York–New Jersey Trail Conference
Kim Elliman—Open Space Institute
Ella Filippone—Passaic River Coalition
Wilma Frey—New Jersey Conservation Fund
John Gebhards—Sterling Forest Resources
Rose Harvey—Trust for Public Land
John Humbach—Sterling Forest Coalition
Andrew Lawrence—New York Sierra Club
Barnabas McHenry—Palisades Interstate Park Commission and
    Hudson River Valley Greenway Council
Jennifer Melville—Appalachian Mountain Club
Olivia Millard—The Nature Conservancy
David Miller—National Audubon Society
Louis V. Mills—Orange County Land Trust
John Myers—New York–New Jersey Trail Conference
Bill Neil—New Jersey Audubon Society
Dean Noll—North Jersey District Water Supply Commission
Jerry Notte—North Jersey District Water Supply Commission
Rob Pirani—Regional Plan Association

Samuel F. Pryor III—Appalachian Mountain Club and Palisades Interstate Park Commission

Larry Rockefeller—Natural Resources Defense Council and Palisades Interstate Park Commission

Steven Rosenberg—Scenic Hudson

David Sampson—Hudson River Valley Greenway Council

Klara Sauer—Scenic Hudson

David Startzel—Appalachian Trail Conference

Jim Tripp—Environmental Defense Fund

Richard White-Smith—New York Parks & Conservation Association

Neil Woodworth—Adirondack Mountain Club

Neil Zimmerman—New York–New Jersey Trail Conference

SOURCES

Note: Either copies or originals of all sources listed are located in the Palisades Interstate Park archives. The author thanks the Rockefeller Historical Archives, located in Tarrytown, New York, for granting permission to copy and use much relevant information.

Chapter 1: Boss Blaster

"'Indian Head Destroyed.'" *The New York Times* (March 5, 1898).

Mack, Arthur C. *The Palisades of the Hudson*. 1909; reissued by Walking News, Inc., 1982.

"Palisades Interstate Park 1900–1929: A History of Its Origin and Development." PIPC: 1929.

Chapter 2: The Commission

Books

Bradley, Stanley W. *Crossroads of the Hudson: The Story of Alpine, New Jersey*. Alpine Bicentennial Committee.

Foord, John. *The Life and Public Services: Andrew Haskell Green*. DD, Page and Co., 1913.

Garraty, John A. *Right-Hand Man: The Life of George W. Perkins*. Harper and Bros., 1957.

Howat, John K. *Hudson River and Its Painters*. American Legacy Press, 1983.

Humphrey, J. A. *Englewood: Its Annals and Reminiscences*. J. S. Ogilvie Publishing Co., 1899.

Lattimer, John K., M.D., Sc.D. *This Was Early Englewood*. Englewood Historical Society, date unknown.

O'Brien, Raymond J. *American Sublime: Landscape and Scenery of the Lower Hudson Valley*. New York: Columbia University Press, 1981.

Rybczynski, Witold. *A Clearing in the Distance*. New York: Scribner, 1999.

Serrao, John. *The Wild Palisades of the Hudson.* Plind Publications, 1986.

Strouse, Jean. "Annals of Finance: The Brilliant Bailout." *The New Yorker* (November 23, 1998).

Pamphlets and Periodicals

"A Century of Service." Englewood Woman's Club, 1995.

"A Century of Challenge." New Jersey State Federation of Women's Clubs, 1995.

"The Palisades Interstate Park 1900–1929: A History of Its Origin and Development." PIPC, 1929.

"Preserving the Palisades." *American Monthly Review of Reviews* (date unknown).

Brown, Edward F. "Perkins: Park Builder." PIPC Archives, 1919.

Hopkins, Franklin W. "Preservation of the Palisades." *American Scenic and Historic Preservation Society* v.2 #3 and 4 (December 1930).

Martin, Neil S. "Saving the Palisades." *Gannett Westchester Newspaper Sunday Magazine* (January 7, 1979).

Strouse, Jean, "Annals of Finance: The Brilliant Bailout." *The New Yorker* (November 23, 1998).

Newspapers

"To Save the Palisades." *The New York Times* (November 25, 1894).

"A Light Legislative Day." *The New York Times* (February 15, 1895).

"For the Protection of the Palisades." *The New York Times* (July 13, 1895).

"The Palisades of the Hudson." *The New York Times* (July 29, 1895).

"To Save the Palisades." *The New York Times* (August 27, 1895).

"Save the Palisades from Ruin." *The New York Times* (September 29, 1895).

"Park, Not Military Post." *The New York Times* (October 7, 1895).

"Preserve the Palisades." *The New York Times* (October 8, 1895).

"New Plan for Palisades." *The New York Times* (October 9, 1895).

"To Save the Palisades." *The New York Times* (September 23, 1897).

"Question of the Palisades." *The New York Times* (October 29, 1897).

"To Save the Palisades: Recommendations to Include Them in a Public Park." *The New York Times* (January 18, 1900).

"For a Palisades Park." *The New York Times* (January 20, 1900).

"Outlook for the Palisades." *The New York Times* (January 14, 1900).

"And 'Fishermen's Village' of Undercliff." *Sunday Star Ledger* (March 31, 1963).

Correspondence

Files: Greenbrook Nature Sanctuary, Palisades Interstate Park.

From William Welch, March 13, 1929.

"35th Anniversary of PIPC." Raymond Torrey press release, June 12, 1935. PIPC Archives.

Chapter 3: Upriver

Books

Fosdick, Raymond B. *John D. Rockefeller, Jr., A Portrait*. Harper and Bros., 1956.
Muir, John. *Edward Henry Harriman*. Doubleday, Page & Company, 1912.

Reports

"Palisades Interstate Park Commission Financial History 1900–1927." PIPC.
"6th Annual Report" American Scenic and Historic Preservation Society, 1901.

Pamphlets and Periodicals

Journal: American Scenic and Historic Preservation Society v.2 #3 and 4 (December, 1930).
"The Preservation of the Highlands of the Hudson First Publicly Advocated by Edward Lasell Partridge, M.D." *The Outlook* (November, 1907).

Correspondence

PIPC Minutes and Correspondence, 1900–1907.
John D. Rockefeller to Governor O'Dell, March 18, 31, 1902.
George W. Perkins to Governor O'Dell, March 31, 1902.
James P. McQuade to John D. Rockefeller, Jr., March 14, 21, 1902.
Starr J. Murphy to Timothy L. Woodruff, March 10, 1906.
Starr J. Murphy to John D. Rockefeller, Jr., March 22, 1906.
From Mrs. Barrie Tait Collins, January 6, 1998.

Newspapers

"Palisades League Formed." *The New York Times* (May 4, 1900).
"Palisades Plans in Danger." *The New York Times* (January 27, 1901).
"Palisades Bill Signed." *The New York Times* (March 23, 1901).
"The Palisades Park." *The New York Times* (April 26, 1901).
"White in a Dilemma." *The Observer* (May 5, 1901).
"Was Mr. Morgan's Gift." *The New York Times* (May 15, 1901).
"Palisades Interstate Park: A Landscape Engineer Employed to Study and Preserve the Rocks." *The New York Times* (October 23, 1901).
"Abram S. Hewitt Dead." *The New York Times* (January 19, 1903).
"The Majestic Park on the Palisades." *Nyack Evening Star* (August 1, 1903).
"To Save the Palisades." *The New York Times* (January 14, 1906).
"William B. Dana." *The New York Times* (October 11, 1910).
"Dr. E. L. Partridge Dies at 77 Years." *The New York Times* (May 8, 1930).
"Abram DeRonde Dies in South, 88." *The New York Times* (February 24, 1937).
"J. DuPratt White, Former Park Head Dead." *Journal-News* (July 14, 1939).
"Governor in Tribute to White and Stagg." *The New York Times* (July 1, 1939).

Chapter 4: Harriman

Books

Abramson, Rudy. *Spanning the Century: The Life of W. Averell Harriman 1891–1986*. William Morrow and Co., Inc., 1992.

Myles, William J. *Harriman Trails: A Guide and History*. NY–NJ Trail Conference, 1992.

Reports

13th Annual Report, American Scenic and Historic Preservation Society, 1908.

PIPC Minutes, 1908–1910.

8th Annual Report, PIPC, March 9, 1908.

10th Annual Report, PIPC, January 1, 1909.

"Report of the Work of the Commissioners of the Palisades Interstate Park Made by George W. Perkins, President of the New York State Commission on the Occasion of the Dedication of the Park at Alpine, New Jersey, September 27, 1909."

"Highlands of the Hudson Forest Reservation." 15th Annual Report, New York State Forest, Fish and Game Commissioner, 1909.

11th Annual Report, PIPC, January 31, 1911.

17th Annual Report, American Scenic and Historic Preservation Society, March 28, 1912.

"Dedication of Palisades Interstate Park," The Hudson-Fulton Celebration.

Pamphlets and Periodicals

Hopkins, Franklin W. "Preservation of the Palisades." *Scenic and Historic America* (June 1930).

"Dr. Edward Lasell Partridge Passes." *Scenic and Historic America* (June 1930).

"To Improve the Harriman Forest." PIPC Archives, 1899.

Correspondence

Of J. DuPratt White, 1908, 1909.

Of Leonard Smith, 1909.

George W. Perkins to General Woodford, June 22, 1909.

From William Welch, October 20, 1936.

Newspapers

"Blasting Away of Bear Mountain." *City and Country* (February 11, 1908).

"The Patriotic Effort to Save River Scenery." *Rockland County Messenger* (March 23, 1967).

"Palisades Park Opened." *The New York Times* (September 28, 1909).

"60-Mile River Park Insured to the State." *The New York Times* (January 6, 1910).

"The Proposed Park in the Highlands." *City and Country* (January 22, 1910).

"Killed in Senate." *City and Country* (May 28, 1910).

"Palisades Park for the People." *City and Country* (May 28, 1910).

"The Voters Say Yes to Park Bond Issue." *The New York Times* (October 1, 1910).

"Harriman Park Passes to the State." *The New York Times* (October 30, 1910).

Chapter 5: Legend and War

Books

Bedell, Cornelia A. *Now and Then and Long Ago in Rockland County.* The Historical Society of Rockland County, 1968.

Dunwell, Frances F. *The Hudson River Highlands.* New York: Columbia University Press, 1991.

Leiby, Adrian C. *The Revolutionary War in the Hackensack Valley.* New Brunswick, N.J.: Rutgers University Press, 1962.

Reports

Carr, William H., and Richard J. Koke. "Twin Forts of the Popolopen: Forts Clinton and Montgomery." PIPC Archives, July 1937.

Chapter 6: Welch

Books

Garraty, John A. *Right-Hand Man: The Life of George W. Perkins.* Harper and Bros., 1957.

Reports

PIPC Minutes, 1910–1912.

Pamphlets and Periodicals

"Frank Eugene Lutz, 1873–1943." *Journal of the New York Entomological Society* v. LII (March 1944).

"Frank E. Lutz." *American Museum of Natural History* v. 22 #5 (May 1997).

Garraty, John A. "Millionaire Reformer: The Progressives Part II." *American Heritage* (February 1962).

Correspondence

PIPC Correspondence, 1910–1912.

From J. DuPratt White, in *The New York Times* (March 19, 1911).

Samuel Broadbent to George W. Perkins, October 16, 1911.

George W. Perkins to John D. Rockefeller, Jr., November 9, 1912.

Newspapers

"Perkins Retiring at End of Year From J. P. Morgan and Company." *The New York Times* (December 11, 1910).

"Commission Buys the Hook." *Rockland Journal News* (March 11, 1911).

"South Mountain to the Public." *Rockland Journal News* (October 28, 1911).

"George W. Perkins Dies in 58ᵗʰ Year." *The New York Times* (June 19, 1920).

"Welch to Get Gold Medal." *Rockland Journal News* (December 16, 1935).

"Major Welch Dies, Builder of Parks." *The New York Times* (May 5, 1941).

Chapter 7: Bear Mountain

Books

Abramson, Rudy. *Spanning the Century: The Life of W. Averell Harriman 1891–1986.* William Morrow and Co., 1992.

Pamphlets and Periodicals

"Maintenance of Order." PIPC Archives, PIPC.

"Financial Data Prepared for Inspection Trip: June 11ᵗʰ, 1914." PIPC.

"Palisades Interstate Park." *American Scenic and Historic Preservation Society* (April 19, 1915).

"Proceedings of the National Parks Conference." Government Printing Office, 1917.

"In Memoriam: Frederick Charles Sutro." *Your Parks.* New Jersey Parks and Recreation Association (December 1964).

Correspondence

Of Leonard Smith, 1913.

George W. Perkins to John D. Rockefeller, September 18, 1913.

William Welch to the Superintendent of Yellowstone National Park, July 27, 1914.

H. Percy Silver, Chaplain, U.S. Military Academy, West Point, to J. DuPratt White, October 3, 1914.

Frederick C. Sutro to George W. Perkins, December 5, 1914.

George W. Perkins to Frederick C. Sutro, December 11, 1914.

George W. Perkins to Abby Barstow Bates, Secretary, Appalachian Mountain Club, December 11, 1914.

George W. Perkins to John D. Rockefeller, June 2, 1915.

John D. Rockefeller, Jr., to George W. Perkins, June 18, 1915.

William Welch Files, 1916–1918, PIPC Archives.

Of Elbert W. King, 1916–1918.

Nathan F. Barrett to George W. Perkins, March 1, 1916.

Between Reverend Lee W. Beattie and George W. Perkins, March 24, April 19, 1917.

John D. Rockefeller, Jr., to John D. Rockefeller, April 17, 1917. Rockefeller Family Archives.

Col. A. C. Dalton to George W. Perkins, April 30, 1918.

Theodore Horton to George W. Perkins and Dr. Hermann M. Biggs, September 17 and October 21, 1918.

Reports

PIPC Minutes, 1913–1918.

Newspapers

"Palisades Park Commission To Be Sulerized Next." *Newburgh Daily News* (June 12, 1913).
"Perkins Denies Palisades Charges." *The New York Times* (June 13, 1913).
"Inquiry Into Interstate Park." *Rockland County Journal* (June 21, 1913).
"No Road for Palisades." December 1914 newspaper article found in PIPC Archives.
"Governor Dedicates Park." *Rockland County Times* (June 3, 1915).
"Approves $2,650,000 Award." *The New York Times* (May 3, 1916).
"Perkins To Be Made Food Commissioner." *The New York Times* (August 5, 1917).
"Hatch & Perkins Clash on Bathing." *The New York Times* (August 21, 1918).
"R. V. Lindabury Dies on Horseback Ride." *The New York Times* (July 16, 1925).
"Charles W. Baker, Engineer 55 Years." *The New York Times* (June 7, 1941).
"Ex-Gov. Averell Harriman, Adviser to 4 Presidents, Dies." *The New York Times* (July 27, 1986).

Chapter 8: Perkins

Books

Garraty, John A. *Right-Hand Man: The Life of George W. Perkins*. Harper and Bros., 1960.

Reports

Adams, Dr. Charles C. "Natural History Survey of Palisades Interstate Park." *Empire Forester* v.5. New York Sate College of Forestry (1919).
Perkins, George W. "Sight Seeing Buses on the Palisades." *State Service*. Governor of the State of New York, 1919.
"Directory of Encampments-1919." PIPC Archives.
"Appropriations Made To Palisades Interstate Park Commission." Rockefeller Family Archives.
Senate Act Nos. 1764, 1905 Rec. 425, April 8, 1919, State of New York.
PIPC Minutes, 1919, 1920.
Clyne, Patricia Edwards. "Iona Island." *Hudson Valley* (April 1985).

Correspondence

PIPC Correspondence 1919, 1920.
George W. Perkins to Richard V. Lindabury, January 28, 1919.
George W. Perkins to William Welch, January 28, 1919.
Brig. Gen. Brice P. Disque, U.S. Army, to Director, Bureau of Aircraft Production, Washington, D.C., February 11, 1919.

William Welch to George W. Perkins, February 22, 27, 1919.

Edward F. Brown to William Welch, March 5, 1919.

William Welch to Edward F. Brown, March 7, 1919.

Elbert W. King to J. DuPratt White, March 5, 1919.

Edward F. Brown to Franklin W. Hopkins, March 20, 1919.

Edward F. Brown to Edward L. Partridge, M.D., March 20, 1919.

William Welch to Abram Deronde, March 27, 1919.

From William Welch, March 27, 1919.

R. B. Potter to J. DuPratt White, March 26, 1919.

Elbert W. King to William Welch, April 2, 1919.

William Welch to Dr. Hugh Baker, October 10, 1919.

William Welch to Miss Marjorie B. Jones, April 10, 1919.

William Welch to A. M. Herbert, April 19, 1919.

Elbert W. King to A. M. Herbert, April 29, 1919.

J. DuPratt White to Elbert W. King, May 1, 1919.

William Welch to Files, May 1919. Welch Files.

Edward F. Brown to William Gee, May 26, 1919.

George W. Perkins to William Welch, June 5, 1919.

William Welch to F. Kingsbury Curtis, June 12, 1919.

Frederick Law Olmsted, Jr., to William Welch, June 18, 1919

Maurice M. Lefkowitz to William Welch, June 24, 1919.

Mrs. Tannebaum to William Welch, July 9, 1919.

Edward F. Brown to George W. Perkins, July 9, 1919.

Smith Riley to Edward F. Brown, July 12, 1919.

Charles B. Webb to PIPC, no date (mid-August 1919).

Fred K. Stuart Greene to William Welch, August 27, 1919.

Edward F. Brown to George W. Perkins, August 30, 1919.

Enos A. Mills to William Welch, October 14, 1919.

William Welch to George W. Perkins, November 26, 1919.

F. L. Fisher to William Welch, December 5, 1919.

John D. Rockefeller, Jr., to George W. Perkins, January 28, 1920.

Between John D. Rockefeller, Jr., and George W. Perkins, February and March 1920.

Stephen T. Mather to William Welch, February 16, 1920.

George W. Perkins to Commissioner Lindabury, March 18, 1920.

William Welch to Jay Downer, March 24, 1920.

From George W. Perkins's secretary May, June 1920.

H. W. Jenkins (mayor, Englewood Cliffs, New Jersey) to PIPC, June 2, 1920.

William Welch to Dr. George F. Kunz, June 19, 1920.

Newspapers

"Bath Houses and Lunch At Hook Mountain This Year." *Nyack Evening Journal* (April 4, 1919).

"Provide Mothers' Rest Stations." *The Messenger,* Haverstraw, New York (August 7, 1919).

"Making Others Happy." *The Rockland County Times* (August 1919 [exact date unknown]). PIPC Archives.

Benson, Captain William O. "Memories of a Visit to My Brother on the 'Onteora.'" *Sunday Freeman* (August 27, 1972). PIPC Archives.

Chapter 9: Jolliffe

Reports

"Bear Mountain—Harriman Attendance Reports for Entire Season."

"New Jersey Attendance Reports for Entire Season 1920." PIPC Archives.

"1920 Values (Purchased)." PIPC Archives.

PIPC Minutes, 1920–1921.

"PIPC Annual Report." 1921.

Correspondence

George W. Perkins's secretary to Richard Lindabury, June 24, 1920.

Between W. H. Radcliffe and William Welch, June 23, 25, 1920.

Fred Schiebelhuth to William Welch, August 3, 1920.

Elbert W. King to Peoples Bank of Haverstraw, August 14, 1920.

William Welch to Enos Mills, August 30, 1920.

Elbert W. King to Dr. Edward L. Partridge, September 2, 1920.

William Welch to PIPC, September 9, 1920.

Boy Scouts of America to William Welch, September 17, 1920.

Elbert W. King to William Welch, September 18, 1920.

Between William Welch and Dr. Edward L. Partridge, September 20, October 3, 1920, and January 25, 1921.

William Welch to Horace M. Albright, September 28, 1920.

Between James M. Lynch, New York State Department of Labor, and PIPC/William Welch, September 28, 30, October 4, November 8, 1920.

William Welch to Mary Ethel McAuley, September 30, 1920.

William Welch to Frederick C. Sutro, October 11, 1920.

Edward F. Brown to Dr. Edward L. Partridge, October 13, 1920.

George A. Blauvelt to William Welch, October 13, 1920.

F. Martin Brown to William Welch, October 22, 1920.

Elbert W. King to William Welch, October 23, 1920.

Between Stephen Mather and William Welch, October 23, 30, December 4, 1920.

Elbert W. King to Charles Whiting Baker, December 1, 1920.

Elbert W. King to P. V. D. Gott, December 3, 1920.

Everett G. Griggs to William Welch, December 27, 1920.

PIPC Correspondence, 1920–1921.

William Welch to A. J. James, February 21, 1921.

Elbert W. King to Committee on the Advisability of Selling the Dana Property, February 25, 1921.

Elbert W. King to Capt. James Conway, March 3, 1921.

George D. Pratt, Commissioner New York State Conservation Commission, to William Welch, March 4, 1921.

Between Mrs. Henry H. Dawson and William Welch, March 1921.

Elbert W. King to Mr. Deyo, March 28, April 18, 1921.

Elbert W. King to Richard V. Lindabury, April 14, 1921.

Elbert W. King to William Welch, April 18, 1921.

Elbert W. King to William Welch, April 26, 1921.

Elbert W. King to J. DuPratt White, April 27, 1921.

Elbert W. King to Dr. Edward L. Partridge, April 28, 1921.

Elbert W. King to Messrs. Blauvelt and Warren, April 30, 1921.

Elbert W. King to John F. Daschner, May 5, 1921.

William Welch to J. L. Ryan, May 17, 1921.

Elbert W. King to William Welch, May 20, 1921.

Elbert W. King to Charles W. Baker, May 21, 1921.

William Welch to Miss Jolliffe, May 24, 1921.

Elbert W. King to William Welch, July 7, 1921.

Elbert W. King to William Welch, October 6, 1921.

William Welch to Averell Harriman, October 7, 1921.

William Welch to Otis H. Cutler, December 19, 1921.

Newspapers

"Interstate Park Commissioners' Map Opens Forest Roads For Tourists." *New York Evening Post* (September 10, 1920).

"May Drill For Oil Under Palisades." *The New York Times* (May 17, 1921).

Chapter 10: Trail and Bridge

Books

Myles, William J. *Harriman Trails: A Guide and History.* New York–New Jersey Trail Conference, 1992.

Waterman, Laura and Guy. *Forest and Crag: A History of Hiking, Trail Blazing and Adventure in the Northeast Mountains.* Appalachian Mountain Club Books, no date.

Pamphlets and Periodicals

"The Growth of the Appalachian Trail." PIPC press release, no date. PIPC Archives.

Caro, Robert. "Annals of Biography: The City-Shaper." *The New Yorker* (January 5, 1998).

Dickinson, H. V. "The Bear Mountain Bridge." *Parks and Recreation* (March/April 1927).

MacKaye, Benton. "Progress Toward the Appalachian Trail." *Appalachia* vol. XV, no. 3 (December 1922).

———. "The Appalachian Trail: A Guide to the Study of Nature." *Scientific Monthly* vol. XXXIV (April 1932).

Place, Frank. "Raymond H. Torrey." *Yearbook of the Appalachian Club* (January 1939).

Scherer, Glenn. "A Celebration of Vision, Planning, and Grass-roots Mobilization: Paying Homage to Benton Mackaye." *Appalachian Trailway News* (March/April 1997).

Reports

"Proceedings of the Second National Conference on State Parks." May 22–25, 1922.

28th Annual Report American Scenic and Historic Preservation Society. April 12, 1923.

DeWan, George. "The Master Builder: How Planner Robert Moses transformed Long Island for the 20th Century and Beyond." http://www.lihistory.com/7/hs722a.htm .

PIPC Minutes 1921, 1922.

Annual Report 1923. PIPC.

PIPC Minutes April 12, November 20, December 28, 1923.

Correspondence

Elbert W. King to William Welch, January 3, 1922.

Elbert W. King to William Welch, January 10, 1922.

William Welch to Dr. E. L. Partridge, January 25, 1922.

Elbert W. King to Otis H. Cutler, February 24, 27, 1922.

Elbert W. King to Leib Deyo, March 15, 1922.

Elbert W. King to John E. Robinson, editor, New York Amsterdam News, March 20, 1922.

Elbert W. King to Dr. Edward L. Partridge, April 8, 1922.

Elbert W. King to William Welch, August 9, 1922.

Elbert W. King to J. Finley Bell, M.D., August 25, 1922.

Elbert W. King to Richard V. Lindabury, September 12, 1922.

Elbert W. King to Carl Bannwort, October 5, 1922.

Elbert W. King to William Welch, January 8, 1923.

Elbert W. King to J. DuPratt White, February 24, 1923.

To PIPC, February 27, 1923.

Elbert W. King to William H. Porter, March 26, 1923.

Edward L. Partridge and Franklin W. Hopkins to PIPC, April 10, 1923.

Elbert W. King to J. DuPratt White, April 11, 1923.

J. DuPratt White to Dr. Ernest Stillman, April 12, 1923.

Elbert W. King to Senator Blauvelt, April 13, 1923.

Raymond H. Torrey to Frederick C. Sutro, January 26, 1932.

Newspapers

"Would Span Hudson at Bear Mountain." *The New York Times* (February 9, 1922).

"Motorists Urge New Bridge to Bear Mountain." *New York City American* (March 4, 1922).

"Winter at Bear Mountain." *Peekskill Union* (February 8, 1922).

"Bill Authorizes Huge Suspension Bridge Over Hudson." *Brooklyn New York Eagle* (February 8, 1922).

"Harrimans Back New Park System." *New York City World* (February 13, 1922).

"New Bridge Plan Endorsed by Westchester Interests." *New York City Telegram* (February 16, 1922).

"Mrs. Harriman Backs Hudson Bridge Plan." *Newburgh News* (February 18, 1922).

"Westchester Park Plan." *The New York Times* (February 19, 1922).

"Both Farmers and City Dwellers Gain By New Bridge Across the Hudson." *Brooklyn New York Citizen* (February 26, 1922).

Chapter 11: Uncle Bennie

Pamphlets and Periodicals

VanIngren, W. B. "A Wilderness Transformed." *The New York Times Magazine* (September 7, 1924).

Reports

Adolph, Eleanor Bazzoni. "The Man Who Is Uncle to All the Boys of America." No date. PIPC Archives.

PIPC Annual Reports, 1924–1927.

Snead, J. E. "That Fair and Ancient Land: Archaeology and Society in the American Southwest, 1890–1915." \amnh\hee3dr.doc Draft (March 3, 1997).

PIPC Minutes, April 28, May 20, September 23, 1924.

PIPC Minutes, March 11, 17, and October 20, 1925.

Correspondence

Robert Moses to J. DuPratt White, May 21, 1924.

Robert Sterling Yard, executive secretary, The National Parks Association, to Maj. W. A. Welch, July 15, 1924.

Press Release from PIPC, July 31, 1924.

Elbert W. King to Frederick C. Sutro, August 19, 1924.

Elbert W. King to Miss Marvin, September 3, 1924.

Elbert W. King to George W. Perkins, Jr., September 11, 1924.

Elbert W. King to Hamilton Ward, September 12, 1924.

Frederick C. Sutro to PIPC, September 15, 1924.

Elbert W. King to PIPC, October 16, 1924.

W. A. Welch to Laura Spelman Rockefeller Foundation, November 3, 1924.

Kenneth Chorley to Col. Arthur Woods, November 11, 26, and December 20, 1924.

Internal Rockefeller, dictated by Mr. Chorley, December 13, 1924.

W. A. Welch to Col. Glenn H. Smith, December 4, 1924.

W. A. Welch to Secretary of the Interior Hubert Work, December 12, 1924.

W. A. Welch to Col. W. B. Greeley, February 7, 1925.

Harold Allen to Maj. W. A. Welch, February 25, 1925.

Elbert W. King to Paul H. Tichnor, March 12, 1925.

Elbert W. King to Major Welch, March 14, 1925.

Telegram of Elbert W. King to Vincent B. Murphy, comptroller, March 20, 1925.

Elbert W. King to Mr. Knowles, April 10, 1925.

Allegeny State Park Commission to Maj. W. A. Welch, April 11, 1925.

Arthur Woods to W. A. Harriman, April 17, 1925.

Elbert W. King to PIPC, May 13, 1925.

Elbert W. King to Scott R. Knowles, May 15, 1925.

Arthur Woods to Mr. Fosdick, May 22, 1925.

W. A. Welch to P. H. Elwood, Jr., June 4, 1925.

Elbert W. King to Scott R. Knowles, August 12, 1925.

Elbert W. King to Major Welch, October 28, 1925.

Elbert W. King to William Shepherd Dana, December 24, 1925.

Newspapers

"Trail Typhoid Peril To Palisades Brook." *The New York Times* (July 16, 1924).

"Bond Issue May Go Into Courts." *New York City Sun* (October 20, 1924).

"Cardinal Hayes Endorses Park As Aid to Children." *New York City Evening World* (October 20, 1924).

"Battle Over Parks at Albany Hearing." *The New York Times* (February 12, 1925).

"Big Engineering Feat Now Going On In This County." *Nyack Evening Journal* (April 21, 1925).

"R. V. Lindabury Dies on Horseback Ride." *The New York Times* (July 15, 1925).

"City Migrates To Camps." *The New York Times* (August 9, 1925).

"Mather And Welch Enroute To Park Are Fresh From Dynamiting Big Saw Mill in Glacier National Park; Inspect Tetons." *Livingston (Montana) Enterprise* (August 12, 1925).

"Welch To Get Gold Medal." *Journal-News* (December 16, 1935).

"'Uncle Benny' Hyde Dies of Injuries; In Crash." *Santa Fe New Mexican* (July 17, 1933).

"Dr. Stillman Gives 600 Acres to Park." *The New York Times* (May 26, 1922).

"Call Storm King Motor Highway Triumph of Road Construction." *The New York Times* (June 10, 1923).

"To Move a Mountain For a Great Park." *The New York Times* (July 11, 1923).

"It Seems To Be All Right." *The New York Times* (July 12, 1923).

"Commission Will Inspect New Bear Mountain Span Wednesday." *New York City Herald* (October 5, 1924).

"Novel Honeymoon Trip." *The New York Times* (November 15, 1924).

"Mrs. E. H. Harriman Opens Bear Mountain Span." *The New York Times* (November 26, 1924).

"Bear Mountain Bridge Formally Opened Today for Thanksgiving." *Middletown Daily Times Press* (November 26, 1924).

Chapter 12: Black Thursday

Reports

Bradley, Stanley W. *Crossroads of the Hudson: The Story of Alpine, New Jersey.* Alpine Bicentennial Committee.

Haugland, Gary. "Thomas A. Edison." Trailside Museum and Zoo, Historical Papers #H-3/93. PIPC archives.

Minutes of Southern Appalachian National Park Commission, January 8, 1926.

Jones, Mark M. "Palisades Interstate Park." (February 15, 1926).

PIPC Annual Reports, 1926–1928.

PIPC Minutes, April 19, June 21, 1927.

Program: "Outdoor Speed Skating Handicap Meet, Conducted by Bear Mountain Sports Association at Bear Mountain Park Sunday February 6th, 1927."

Program: "New York State Ski Jumping Championship Tournament Sanctioned By the Eastern Amateur Ski Association Under Auspices of Swedish Ski Club of New York At Bear Mountain Palisades Interstate Park Sunday, February 13th, 1927."

PIPC Minutes, June 6, August 21, October 9, October 11, December 28, 1928.

PIPC Minutes, March 19, May 21, 1929.

Correspondence

Address by Frederick Sutro on the "Occasion of the Dedication of the Memorial Women's Federation Park April 30, 1929."

Proclamation by Franklin Roosevelt, August 30, 1929.

Mark Jones to Rockefeller Staff, January 7, 1926.

William Welch to Mark Squires, January 19, 1926.

DeHart H. Ames to William Welch, January 20, 1926.

Elbert W. King to Miss Young, January 21, 1926.

Frederick C. Sutro to Governor Silzer, January 27, 1926.

Raymond H. Torrey to Franklin D. Roosevelt, February 14, 1926.

Elbert W. King to Mr. E. C. Wallin, International Newsreel Corporation, February 19, 1926.

Elbert W. King to Franklin W. Hopkins, March 2, 1926.

Elbert W. King to Major Welch, March 13, 1926.

Elbert W. King to Miss Marvin, March 16, 1926.

Elbert W. King to Oscar R. Ewing of Messrs. Hughes, Rounds, Schurman and Dwight, March 16, 1926.

Elbert W. King to Mr. Hopkins, April 1, 1926.

Elbert W. King to Mr. L. O. Rothschild, April 5, 1926.

Elbert W. King to J. DuPratt White, April 5, 1926.

Elbert W. King to Miss J. A. Marvin, May 4, 1926.

W. P. Davis to Maj. William Welch, May 14, 1926.

From Kenneth Chorley, May 7, 1926.

Elbert W. King to Maj. W. A. Welch, October 25, 1926.

Elbert W. King to J. DuPratt White, December 1, 1926.

A. J. Joseph to PIPC, January 5, 1927.

Mrs. H. Pleus to William Welch, undated.

Elbert W. King to Franklin Hopkins, February 2, 1927.

William A. Welch to Mr. P. H. Elwood, Jr., professor of Landscape Architecture, Iowa State College, February 23, 1927.

J. DuPratt White to Governor A. Harry Moore, March 16, 1927.

Elbert W. King to Commissioner George T. Smith, March 24, 1927.

Elbert W. King to Frederick Osborn, March 25, 1927.

Elbert W. King to Mr. Richards of Messrs. Hughes, Rounds, Schurman and Dwight, August 2, 1927.

Elbert W. King to Maurice Marmer, June 24, 1927.

Willis G. Corbitt to Mrs. George Leviston, September 14, 1927.

John D. Rockefeller, Jr., to Major Welch, September 26, 1927.

William A. Welch to Edsel B. Ford, November 21, 1927.

William A. Welch to Daniel P. Wine, January 12, 1928.

John D. Rockefeller, Jr., to Mr. Cammerer, January 23, 1928.

William A. Welch to George Leviston, February 29, 1928.

E. Childs to Maj. W. A. Welch, March 6, 1928.

Howard J. Benchoff to Maj. W. A. Welch, March 8, 1928.

Raymond H. Torrey to Maj. W. A. Welch, March 12, 1928.

Howard H. Parsons to Maj. Wm. A. Welch, March 14, 1928.

Harold M. Lewis to Maj. Wm. A. Welch, March 15, 1928.

Elbert W. King to Mrs. William H. Osborne, April 18, 1928.

W. S. Richardson to John D. Rockefeller, Jr., May 24, 1928.

Elbert W. King to L. H. Harrison, June 2, 1928.

Elbert W. King to Mr. J. F. Verrips, June 22, 1928.

Between Major Welch and Mrs. S. C. Eristoff, July 1, 20, 1928.

Elbert W. King to Major Welch, July 16, 1928.

John D. Rockefeller, Jr., to Arthur Woods, August 22, 1928.

Thomas W. Lamont to Mr. Debevoise, August 24, 1928.

Arthur Woods to John D. Rockefeller, Jr., August 31, 1928.

Elbert W. King to Major Welch, October 3, 1928.

Charles Heydt to John D. Rockefeller, Jr., November 8, 1928.

Elbert W. King to William Welch, March 11, 1929.

Elbert W. King to Department Superintendents, March 28, 1929.

W. A. Welch to the International Olympic Committee, March 28, 1929.

W. A. Welch to Christine C. Heis, April 10, 1929.

Elbert W. King to Frederick C. Sutro, July 31, 1929.

John Hays Hammond to W. A. Welch, September 1, 1929.

W. A. Welch to Mrs. Henry Fairfield Osborne, September 10, 1929.

Newspapers

"Wm Childs Dead; Restaurant Man." *The New York Times* (November 26, 1926).

"Parks and Nature Study." *The New York Times* (October 31, 1926).

"Hook Mountain Park To Be Picnic Ground." *The New York Times* (November 26, 1926).

"W. H. Porter Dead; Stricken in Street." *The New York Times* (December 1, 1926).

"Park Museum Under Way." *The New York Times* (May 5, 1927).

"Frederick Osborn, A General, 91, Dies." *The New York Times* (January 7, 1981).

"Bear Mountain Case Heard." *The New York Times* (July 30, 1927).

"Bear Mountain Ban Upset." Newspaper unknown (July 31, 1927).

"Trail Hut Now Open For Hikers." *The New York Times* (October 23, 1927).

"Park Invites Fox Hunters To Shoot 500 Which Kill Game." *The New York Times* (March 5, 1928).

"Foreword To A Plan." *The New York Times* (May 19, 1928).

"Consider Parkway To Save Palisades." *The New York Times* (May 21, 1928).

"Regional Plan Sees Big Jersey Growth." *The New York Times* (May 30, 1929).

"Jury Lists Palisades High in Artistic Parks." *Herald Tribune* (January 10, 1929).

"Park Commission Sued." *The New York Times* (March 26, 1929).

"Palisades Board Loses Land Ruling." *The New York Times* (June 8, 1929).

"Governors Praise Park Cooperation." *The New York Times* (August 7, 1929).

"High Court Reverses Palisades Case." *The New York Times* (February 25, 1930).

Chapter 13: The Compact

Reports

"History of the New Jersey State Federation of Women's Clubs 1927–1947." New Jersey State Federation of Women's Clubs.

PIPC Minutes, March 6, November 6, 1930.

PIPC Minutes, July 9, December 3, 1931.

PIPC Annual Report, 1932.

PIPC Minutes, October 5, November 2, 1933.

"July Excursions 1934." Report in PIPC files.

"Business Booked For Summer Season—1934 (Up to June 27[th,] 1934)." Report in PIPC files.

PIPC Minutes, September 13, 1934.

PIPC Minutes, September 10, 1935.

PIPC Minutes, January 8, May 14, December 10, 1936.

New York State Council of Parks Minutes, March 6, 1936.

White, J. DuPratt. "Statement of J. DuPratt White, President, Commissioners of the Palisades Interstate Park, at hearing on November 21, 1936 before Committee on Interstate Cooperation regarding Proposed Compact between New York and New Jersey to create Palisades Interstate Park Commission."

PIPC Minutes, 1937.

Resume of Te Ata (undated).

60 Years of Park Cooperation. Palisades Interstate Park Commission, 1960.

Pamphlets and Periodicals

Delavan, D. Bryson, M.D. "Long a Valued Member of Scenic Society—Originated Movement for Conservation of Hudson Highlands." *Scenic and Historic America* vol.II, no.2 (June 1930).

"To the Ladies." *Liberty Magazine* (August 17, 1935).

Legislation

"An Act to provide for the creation by interstate compact of the Palisades Interstate Park Commission as a joint corporate municipal instrumentality of the states of New York And New Jersey with appropriate powers and thereby to continue the Palisades Interstate Park." State of New York No. 828 Int. 791 In Assembly January 30, 1936.

"An Act to Provide for the creation by Interstate compact of the Palisades Interstate Park Commission as a joint corporate municipal instrumentality of the states of New York And New Jersey with appropriate rights, powers, duties and immunities, for the transfer To said commission of certain functions, jurisdiction, rights, powers and duties together With the properties of the bodies politic now existing in each state known as 'Commissioners Of the Palisades Interstate Park' and for the continuance of the Palisades interstate park." State of New York No. 1973 Int. 1758 In Assembly March 10, 1937.

Correspondence

Charles O. Heydt to John D. Rockefeller, Jr., February 14, 1930.

Charles O. Heydt to Mr. Rockefeller, February 10, 1930.

Elbert W. King to Frederick C. Sutro, May 5, 1930.

E. W. King to Frederick C. Sutro, June 13, 1930.

W. A. Welch to Robert Moses, November 21, 1930.

John D. Rockefeller, Jr., to Mr. Heydt, December 31, 1930.

Elbert W. King to Mrs. Brobst, February 2, 1931.

E. W. King to Mrs. J. F. Dashner, April 22, 1931.

Chief Clerk to George W. Perkins, May 25, 1931.

Chief Clerk to Mr. Vincent J. Kennedy, June 10, 1931.

Ruby Jolliffe to Upper Cohasset Camps, August 25, 1931.

J. DuPratt White to Winfield Scott, September 28, 1931.

Edmund W. Wakelee to Governor Morgan F. Larson, December 3, 1931.

Frederick C. Sutro to Charles Whiting Baker, January 21, 1932.

Frederick C. Sutro to Edmund W. Wakelee, June 8, 1933.

J. DuPratt White to John D. Rockefeller, Jr., June 30, 1933.

John D. Rockefeller, Jr., to the commissioners of the Palisades Park, July 7, 1933.

Raymond H. Torrey to Frederick C. Sutro, October 21, 1933.

W. A. Welch to President Franklin D. Roosevelt, October 24, 1933.

Carola Lehrenkrauss to Mr. Sutro, April 16, June 19, October 2, December 19, 1934.

Frederick C. Sutro to Dan F. McAllister, August 14, 1935.

Robert G. Mead to Thomas M. Debevoise, August 23, 1935.

Thomas M. Debevoise to PIPC, November 29, 1935.

W. A. Welch to Frank Storer Wheeler, December 7, 1935.

Robert Moses to Jay Downer, November 16, 1936.

J. DuPratt White to Thomas M. Debevoise, March 30, 1937.

John D. Rockefeller, Jr., to J. DuPratt White, April 6, 1937.

J. J. Tamsen to K. T. Ross, June 18, 1937.

Press Releases

Torrey, Raymond H. "Beware Picking Flowers in the Bear Mt. Park." Book 1 (1939).

————."Naturalization of Artificial Lakes in Harriman State Park." Book 2 (August 5, 1931).

————."A Promising Experiment in Rehabilitation of Down and Outs." Book 4 (March 1, 1933).

————."Civilian Conservation Corps Work in Palisades Interstate Park." Book 4 (July 5, 1933).

————."Delay in Re-Opening Dyckman Street Ferry." Book 5 (April 24, 1935).

————."Storm King Mountain Now Preserved in Interstate Park." Book 6 (April 1, 1936).

————."Bronze Elk Head Dedicated in Bear Mountain Park." Book 6 (May 7, 1936).

Newspapers

"Ask State to Bar Dam as a Peril." *The New York Times* (January 20, 1930).

"Alfred E. Smith is Appointed a Member of Palisades Interstate Park Commission." *The New York Times* (May 26, 1930).

"Jersey Confirms Smith." *The New York Times* (May 28, 1930).

"A Mountain Folk in New York's Shadow." *The New York Times* (July 27, 1930).

"Better Vegetation Along the Hudson." *The New York Times* (July 26, 1931).

"Jobless Build Road on Bear Mountain." *The New York Times* (December 2, 1932).

"State Relief Programs Stress Work." *The New York Times* (December 25, 1932).

"Mrs. Roosevelt to Unveil Plaque at Bear Mt. Saturday Afternoon." (publication unknown) (May 25, 1933).

"Mather is Honored By Park Leaders." *The New York Times* (May 28, 1933).

"Big Tract Donated By Rockefeller, Jr. To Save Palisades." *The New York Times* (July 12, 1933).

"Beer By Nearly 2-1 Voted in Oklahoma." *The New York Times* (July 12, 1933).

"A New Move to Preserve the Palisades." *The New York Times* (July 16, 1933).

"Treasure Hunters Blast Mountain in Mysterious Quest in Palisades." *The New York Times* (November 9, 1934).

"Log-Cabin Pioneers of Ramapos Driven Out by Man-Made Lake." *The New York Times* (February 18, 1935).

"Rockefeller Gives Land on Palisades." *The New York Times* (June 26, 1935).

"Privations of WPA Workers At Bear Mountain Revealed." *Citizen-Register, Ossining* (December 12, 1935).

"Joint Board Urged on Palisades Park." *The New York Times* (January 27, 1936).

"White Urges Interstate Park Treaty." *Rockland Journal-News* (March 18, 1936).

"New Jersey Assembly Votes a Luxury Tax; Approval of Senate Is Expected Tonight." *The New York Times* (April 14, 1936).

"Assembly Rejects 2 Palisades Bills." *The New York Times* (May 15, 1936).

"Moses & Smith Oppose Park Plan." *The New York Times* (November 22, 1936).

"Palisades Park Bill Passed at Albany Setting up a Corporate Bi-State Board." *The New York Times* (March 24, 1937).

Chapter 14: The Palisades Parkway

Reports

PIPC Minutes, 1938–1945.

Fischer, Louis. "Report of Louis Fischer to the Palisades Interstate Park Commission." March 31, 1941.

PIPC Minutes, January 1, 1941.

PIPC Minutes, April 21, 1943.

PIPC Minutes, December 13, 1944.

PIPC Minutes, June 16, 1945.

Ward, Gene. "Man of the Mountain: Big Jack Martin." 1946.

PIPC Minutes, January 10, November 9, 1948.

PIPC Minutes, September 11, 1951.

PIPC Minutes, April 21, 1952.

PIPC Minutes, January 12, December 21, 1953.

PIPC Minutes, January 17, May 26, July 9, 1956.

PIPC Minutes, August 19, 1957.

PIPC Minutes, May 24, June 28, 1958.

PIPC Minutes, March 23, November 11, 1959.

PIPC Minutes, February 2, 1960.

Pamphlets and Periodicals

Lamont, Corliss "The Palisades—3d Call." *Survey Graphic* (July 1945).

Correspondence

Robert Moses to Laurance Rockefeller, August 9, 1939.

George W. Perkins to A. K. Morgan, November 14, 1939.

To Palisades Interstate Park Commission, February 1, 1940.

Frederick C. Sutro to A. K. Morgan, May 19, 1941.

Edmund W. Wakelee to A. K. Morgan, October 11, 1943.

Robert Moses to George W. Perkins, February 6, 1945.

Bill Carr to A. K. Morgan, April 15, 1945.

A. K. Morgan to General Osborn, May 3, 1945.

John D. Rockefeller, Jr., to Governor Edge, July 20, 1945.

Robert Moses to A. K. Morgan, August 10, 1945.

A. K. Morgan to Col. George W. Perkins, August 25, 1945.

John D. Rockefeller, Jr., to A. K. Morgan, November 27, 1945.

Ellen W. Rionda to Senator Van Alstyne, Jr., January 1, 1946.

Emma G. Foye to Colonel Perkins, January 18, 1946.

Governor Edge to John D. Rockefeller, Jr., February 8, 1946.

Ridsdale Ellis to John D. Rockefeller, Jr., October 15, 1951.

Ida W. Certo to John D. Rockefeller, Jr., May 5, 1952.

A. K. Morgan to Laurance S. Rockefeller, July 1, 1952.

Josiah M. Hewitt to Francis V. D. Lloyd, September 23, 1952.

A. K. Morgan to George W. Perkins, February 19, 1953.

Transcript of E. W. Kilpatrick to A. K. Morgan, February 16, 1953.

A. K. Morgan to George W. Perkins, March 8, 1954.

A. K. Morgan to John D. Rockefeller, Jr., March 23, 1954.

A. K. Morgan to George W. Perkins, November 24, 1954.

William Kean to Governor Harriman, February 7, 1955.

Averell Harriman to George Perkins, March 2, 1955.

Donald G. Borg to Ambassador George W. Perkins, May 4, 1955.

A. K. Morgan to Laurance S. Rockefeller, November 10, 1955.

A. K. Morgan to George Perkins, January 10, 1958.

Dana S. Creel to George W. Perkins, April 23, 1958.

Dana Creel to George W. Perkins, December 5, 1958.

Lt. Col. J. B. Meanor, Jr., to A. K. Morgan, June 1, 1959.

A. K. Morgan to Robert Moses, June 2, 1959.

Col. Miles H. Thompson to George W. Perkins, June 10, 1959.

George W. Perkins to A. K. Morgan, June 25, 1959.

Newspapers

"High Tor in the Hudson Being Sought for a Park." *The New York Times* (November 15, 1942).

"On Palisades Park Board." *New York Herald Tribune* (March 23, 1945).

"Bird's-Eye View of Palisades Parkway Shows This Rolling Bomb Gathered Moss 10 Years." *Bergen Evening Record* (November 8, 1945).

"Rockefeller Gives Views on Parkway." *The New York Times* (December 7, 1945).

"Palisades Parkway Project Defended at Public Forum." Newspaper unknown (probably the end of 1945).

"Expert Cites Many Reasons for Parkway." *Englewood Press* (January 3, 1946).

"Good Faith and Bad on Parkway." *Bergen Evening Record* (August 8, 1946).

"New Nature Unit Gets Welcome From Commission." *Englewood Press* (November 7, 1946).

"Driscoll Pens Name To Bill For Parkway." *Bergen Evening Record* (April 22, 1947).

"Tamed Josephine Returns to Museum; Pilot Black Snake Toured for 10 Years." *The New York Times* (August 10, 1947).

"Laurance S. Rockefeller Gives Dunderberg to Palisades Park." *New York Herald Tribune* (October 17, 1951).

"'Save Palisades' Campaign Opens in Fort Lee As Boro Views Offer For Cliff-Top." *Fort Lee Sentinel* (April 17, 1952).

"May Raze Riviera." *Newark Sunday News* (June 8, 1952).

"Bear Mountain Uranium Hunters Put Ski Jump Among Filed Claims." *The New York Times* (September 8, 1954).

"Cops to Guard Palisades Zone Hearing." *New York Daily News* (March 13, 1955).

"Fantastic Jersey Estate." *Newark Sunday News* (April 24, 1955).

"Fort Lee Ordered To Sell 1776 Site." *The New York Times* (January 30, 1956).

"Fort Lee To Fight Sale Order." *The New York Times* (February 1, 1956).

"Fort Lee Sale Stayed." *The New York Times* (February 7, 1956).

"Rockefellers, Harrimans Get Praise at Parkway Dedication." *Newburgh News* (August 29, 1958).

"A F 'Invaded' Area in '59." *Cornwall Local* (September 30, 1992).

Chapter 15: Storm King

Reports

PIPC Minutes, February 2, March 21, June 18, August 15, 1960.

McKeon, Warren H. "Recommendations For a Deer Management Program in the Bear Mountain State Park Area." June 1960.

PIPC Minutes, February 27, March 20, November 27, 1961.

PIPC Minutes, May 19, 1962.

Brochure: "Restoration and Power: Creative Conservation at Cornwall-On-Hudson." Con Edison, probably 1962.

Legal Brief: Doty, E. Dale. "Brief Opposing Exceptions of the Scenic Hudson Preservation Conference." October 8, 1964.

"PIPC A History 1900–1973." PIPC.

PIPC Minutes, April 15, May 18, October 21, November 18, 1963.

PIPC Minutes, February 17, 1964.

Report to the Members: John D. Dale to the Hudson River Conservation Society, May 10, 1964.

Tamsen, John J. "Testimony Before Joint Lesislative Committee." November 20, 1964.

PIPC Minutes, March 23, May 15, 1965.

PIPC Minutes, February 17, 1966.

PIPC Minutes, April 17, December 18, 1967.

Memorial Tribute: Lembo, Margaret. 44th Annual Camp Director's Conference Bear Mountain Park, New York. March 30, 1968.

PIPC Minutes, September 16, 1968.

PIPC Minutes, December 16, 1968.

Prepared testimony of Conrad L. Wirth, March 24, 25, 1969.

PIPC Minutes, May 17, June 14, November 17, 1969.

PIPC Minutes, June 20, October 19, November 16, 1970.

PIPC Minutes, February 16, March 15, June 5, 1971.

PIPC Minutes, January 17, June 26, September 25, 1972.

Correspondence

Telegram of Robert Moses to Hon. Nelson A. Rockefeller, January 3, 1960.

Robert Moses to Hon. Nelson A. Rockefeller, January 14, 1960.

Laurance S. Rockefeller to Hon. Nelson A. Rockefeller, February 6, 1960.

Telegram of A. K. Morgan to Mrs. George W. Perkins, March 23, 1960.

A. K. Morgan to G. W. Perkins, March 15, 1960.

A. K. Morgan to Dr. Carl O. Gustafson, February 6, 1961.

Albert R. Jube to Laurance S. Rockefeller, September 1, 1961.

J. Willard Marriott, Jr., to Donald Borg, November 27, 1961.

A. K. Morgan to files, September 24, 1962.

A. K. Morgan to Mr. L. L. Huttleston, October 11, 1962.

J. O. I. Williams to A. K. Morgan, January 2, 1963.

Frederick Osborn to A. K. Morgan, January 15, 1963.

A. K. Morgan to J. K. McManus, C. A. Marks, T. LeNoir, February 4, 1963.

Robert Moses to Mr. H. Philip Arras, April 12, 1963.

L. O. Rothschild to Hon. William J. Ronan, April 23, 1963.

Harry J. Gommoll to Hon. Richard J. Hughes, May 23, 1963.

A. K. Morgan to J. O. I. Williams, May 24, 1963.

A. K. Morgan to Hon. Robert Moses, May 31, 1963.

L. O. Rothschild to Hon. Harold G. Wilm, Commissioner of Conservation, May 31, 1963.

Laurance S. Rockefeller to Lelan F. Sillin, Jr., July 17, 1963.

Laurance S. Rockefeller to Mr. Harland C. Forbes, July 17, 1963.

Carl O. Gustafson to A. K. Morgan, July 30, 1963.

Leo Rothschild to Hon. William J. Ronan, July 19, 1963.

Carl O. Gustafson to A. K. Morgan, October 8, 1963.

A. K. Morgan to Mr. Carl O. Gustafson, October 10, 1963.

A. K. Morgan to Laurance S. Rockefeller, November 27, 1963.

A. K. Morgan to J. K. McManus and E. Van Houtin, January 31, 1964.

William J. Ronan to A. K. Morgan, March 26, 1964.

Between Mrs. Alexander Saunders and Robert Moses, April 3, 13, 1964.

Randall J. LeBoeuf, Jr., to A. K. Morgan, April 10, 1964.

Dale E. Doty to A. K. Morgan, April 10, 1964.

A. K. Morgan to Randall J. LeBoeuf, Jr., April 14, 1964.

A. K. Morgan to Laurance S. Rockefeller, May 5, 1964.

Form from A. K. Morgan, May, 1964.

Mrs. LeRoy Clark to A. K. Morgan, May 17, 1964.

A. K. Morgan to Laurance S. Rockefeller, June 23, 1964.

A. K. Morgan to the Files, July 9, 1964.

R. Watson Pomeroy to Hon. Albert R. Jube, November 30, 1964.

Albert Wilson to A. K. Morgan, August 16, 1965.

Action from Scenic Hudson Preservation Conference, New York–New Jersey Trail Conference, Sierra Club, Atlantic Chapter, North Jersey Conservation Foundation, 1968.

Albert R. Jube to "People Objecting to PIPC Land for Con Ed Project," November 1968.

Henry L. Diamond to A. K. Morgan, December 4, 1968.

A. K. Morgan to Laurance S. Rockefeller, January 9, 1969.

J. O. I. Williams to Henry Diamond, February 28, 1969.

Letter and resume of Nash Castro to Robert Binnewies, November 23, 1999.

Newspapers and Periodicals

"Jube Elected President of N. Y. Park Unit." *Bergen Evening Record* (February 2, 1960).

"Palisades Tract Marks 60th Year." *The New York Times* (May 13, 1960).

"New State Beach Gets a Wet Start." *The New York Times* (June 16, 1962).

"Huge Power Plant Planned on Hudson." *The New York Times* (September 27, 1962).

"Hudson Day Line Bought By Circle." *The New York Times* (October 6, 1962).

"Businessmen Get Outline of Plans By Con Ed Aide." *The Evening News* (November 29, 1962).

"Opposition to Power Cable Registered by Garden Club." *The Evening News* (December 19, 1962).

"Power Plan Stirs Battle on Hudson." *The New York Times* (May 22, 1963).

"Court Approves Palisades Motel." *The New York Times* (May 27, 1963).

"Defacing the Hudson." *The New York Times* (May 29, 1963).

"Conservation Aid, Wife and Daughter Die in Plane Crash." *The New York Times* (October 18, 1963).

"Con Ed on Hudson Opposed." *The New York Times* (February 15, 1964).

"F.P.C. Report Backs Hudson Power Plan." *The New York Times* (March 11, 1964).

"Con Edison Hearings Expected." *The Evening News* (March 25, 1964).

"State Pushing Park Program." *Middletown Record* (May 16, 1964).

"Preserving the Hudson Highlands." *The New York Times* (May 23, 1964).

"Con Edison Plant on Hudson Backed." *The New York Times* (June 16, 1964).

"Cornwall Con Ed Plant Opposed." *The New York Times* (June 16, 1964).

"Hudson Group Plans Con Ed Opposition." *The New York Times* (June 23, 1964).

"Must God's Junkyard Grow?" *Life Magazine* (July 31, 1964).

"Armada of Foes Invades Site of Con Ed Project on Hudson." *The New York Times* (September 7, 1964).

"Protecting the Highlands." *The New York Times* (September 8, 1964).

"Saving the Hudson Highlands." *The New York Times* (November 17, 1964).

"Con Ed-on-Hudson Hearings On." *The New York Times* (November 20, 1964).

"Retreat of 1776 Noted in Jersey." *The New York Times* (November 21, 1964).

"Governor Backs Storm King Plant." *The New York Times* (December 11, 1964).

"Mr. Rockefeller's Wrong Move." *The New York Times* (December 14, 1964).

"Con Edison Plan Is Called Fatal to 2 Fish Industries." *The New York Times* (December 29, 1964).

"Housewives Picket To Preserve Manor." *The New York Times* (January 17, 1966).

"Joseph Kearns McManus, 59; Interstate Park Superintendent." *Middletown Record* (September 5, 1967).

Gill, Bo. "Stray Boots." *Newburgh Evening News* (September 27, 1967).

Dobbin, William J. "Palisades Puts Play Above Par." *The New York Times* (September 8, 1968).

"City Asks F.P.C. to Block Con Ed at Storm King." *The New York Times* (October 28, 1968).

"Hearings Reopened On Plan by Con Ed To Build in Cornwall." *The New York Times* (November 20, 1968).

Chapter 16: Minnewaska

Reports

Death Certificate: A. K. Morgan, October 16, 1969.

Memorial Service Program: Mamie Phipps Clark, 1917–1983.

"PIPC A History 1900–1973." PIPC.

PIPC Minutes, October 29, 1973.

PIPC Minutes, April 15, May 20, December 16, 1974.

PIPC Minutes, January 27, February 24, April 21, May 19, October 20, 1975.

PIPC Minutes, January 19, 1976.

PIPC Minutes, June 20, September 19, 1977.

PIPC Minutes, July 31, December 18, 1978.

PIPC Minutes, May 21, July 5, September 17, 1979.

Statement: New York Office of Parks and Recreation and the Palisades Interstate Park Commission on DEC Project No. 356-15-0080 Presented at Public Hearings Conducted in Rochester, New York, July 14, 1980.

Record of above hearing, July 18, 1980.

Statement: Findings and Closing Brief of the New York State Office of Parks and Recreation and the Palisades Interstate Park Commission on DEC Project No. 356-15-0080 March 13, 1981.

Proposed Findings of Fact, Issues and Recommendations: DEC Project No.356-15-0080 New York State Office of Parks and Recreation and Palisades Interstate Park Commission, March 31, 1981.

Reply Brief of Applicant: DEC Project No. 356-15-0080, undated.

Decision: DEC Project No. 356-15-0080, June 2, 1981.

PIPC Minutes, July 20, 1981.

PIPC Minutes, March 25, November 25, 1985.

PIPC Minutes, January 13, 1986.

PIPC Minutes, June 22, 1987.

"Minnewaska and Surrounds Historical Time Line Revised 10/06/96." PIPC.

Correspondence

Press Release: PIPC, July 18, 1969.

J. O. I. Williams to A. K. Morgan, August 28, 1969.

Albert R. Jube to Hon. William T. Cahill, June 30, 1970.

Nash Castro to Frederick Osborn, November 29, 1971.

John F. Haggerty to Laurance S. Rockefeller, September 7, 1972.

John P. Keith to Nash Castro, February 4, 1972.

Conrad L. Wirth to Nash Castro, January 13, 1972.

Christopher J. Schuberth to Donald B. Stewart, October 24, 1972.

Linn M. Perkins to Laurance [Rockefeller], September 18, 1973.

Press Release from State of New York, Executive Chamber, Nelson A. Rockefeller, Governor, September 21, 1973.

Nash Castro to Mr. Jeffrey Ketterson, June 12, 1974.

George R. Cooley to Nash Castro, November 14, 1974.

Kenneth B. Phillips to Nash Castro, August 8, 1975.

Adrienne K. Wiese to Nash Castro, August 30, 1975.

Assemblyman Maurice D. Hinchey to Commissioner Orin Lehman, September 6, 1975.

Commissioner Orin Lehman to Peter Goldmark, September 10, 1975.

Arthur Schleifer to Nash Castro, October 6, 1975.

Bradford C. Northrup to Commissioner Orin Lehman, January 5, 1976.

Richard L. Erdmann to C. Mark Lawton, January 27, 1976.

Roger W. Tubby to Richard L. Erdmann, February 11, 1976.

L. Sisk to M. O'loughlin, February 11, 1976.

Nash Castro to Roger Tubby, February 17, 1976.

Nash Castro to Bradford C. Northrup, April 15, 1976.

R. R. Paige to Nash Castro, April 20, 1976.

Nash Castro to Bradford C. Northrup, April 27, April 28, May 4, May 10, May 25, August 6, 1976.

Message from Joan to Mr. Castro, May 11, 1976.

Orin Lehman to Mr. Northrup, June 14, 1976.

David W. Burke to Commissioner Orin Lehman, August 2, 1976.

Roland R. Page to Bradford C. Northrup, September 9, 1976.

R. R. Page to Nash Castro, October 14, 1976.

Albert E. Caccese to Hon. R. Lewis Townsend, October 18, 1976.

Roland R. Page to Bradford C. Northrup, October 29, 1976.

John Crutcher to Orin Lehman, January 19, 1977.

Lucille Phillips to Nash Castro, March 1, 1977.

Ivan P. Vamos to C. Mark Lawton, September 16, 1977.

To Anthony Corbisiero, September 16, 1977.

Robert M. Watkins to William Averell Harriman, October 5, 1977.

Orin Lehman to Mr. Phillips, October 14, 1977.

Press Release: "State Parks Agency To Acquire 1,300 Acres At Minnewaska." October 20, 1977.

W. J. Kiely to Pete Lynch, November 3, 1977.

Laurance S. Rockefeller to Governor Hugh L. Carey, July 12, 1978.

Ron Karner to William Kiely, April 3, 1979.

James L. Stapleton to Nash Castro, July 20, 1979.

Edward L. Bednarz to Nash Castro, June 18, 1980.

Nash Castro to the commissioners, August 13, 1980.

Nash Castro to Kenneth Phillips, Jr., March 26, 1981.

Nash Castro to Edward L. Bednarz, June 23, 1981.

Nash Castro to Orin Lehman, July 31, 1981.

Newspapers

"$18 million project proposed for Minnewaska." *Times Herald Sunday Record* (January 12, 1975).

"Planners advise against Minnewaska condominium." *The Times Herald Record* (March 7, 1975).

"Equity Partner Sought" (advertisement). *The New York Times* (June 6, 1975).

"Foreclosure Action Is Filed Against Lake Minnewaska." *The Daily Freeman* (July 25, 1975).

"Group asks state to buy Lake Minnewaska park land." *The Times Herald Record* (August 19, 1975).

"In the Shawangunks." *The New York Times* (October 25, 1975).

"Real Property Foreclosure Sale" (advertisement). *The New York Times* (October 6, 1977).

"State makes new bid for Minnewaska land." *The Times Herald Record* (October 19, 1977).

"State agrees to buy Minnewaska land." *The Times Herald Record* (October 21, 1977).

"Minnewaska Saved." *The Newburgh Evening News, Beacon Edition* (October 22, 1977).

"29 Acre Historical Park Is Dedicated in Fort Lee." *The New York Times* (May 15, 1976).

"Fire Levels Minnewaska's Cliff House." *The Times Herald Record* (January 3, 1978).

Martin, Neil S. "The View Today." *Westchester Rockland Newspaper Co.* (January 7, 1979).

"Rochester approves plan for Minnewaska building." *The Weekly Freeman* (May 1979).

"Marriott plan termed 'environmentally unsound.'" *The Times Herald Record* (August 7, 1979).

"At N. J.'s edge, a park is dying." *The Sunday Record* (September 9, 1979).

"Neglect on the Palisades." *The Record* (September 16, 1979).

"Marriott plans spring startup." *The Times Herald Record* (November 16, 1979).

"Tests polluting stream, Minnewaska opponents say." *The Times Herald Record* (January 18, 1980).

"Marriott, Ulster leaders laud resort plans." *The Times Herald Record* (January 18, 1980).

"Minnewaska sale near, Marriott says." *The Times Herald Record* (January 18, 1980).

"Archeologist urges study of Minnewaska hotel site." *The Times Herald Record* (February 1, 1980).

Haddad, Ron. "Will Marriott mar Lake Minnewaska?" *Sierra Atlantic* (February 1980).

"Court Oks Marriott land purchase." *The Times Herald Record* (April 24, 1980).

"Marriott big issue in New Paltz school vote." *The Times Herald Record* (May 3, 1980).

"'Casinos not Marriott issue.'" *The Times Herald Record* (May 20, 1980).

"Marriott studies disputed." *The Daily Freeman* (May 25, 1980).

"Citizens' group raps Marriott impact report." *The Times Herald Record* (June 7, 1980).

"DEC rejects delay on Marriott hearing." *The Times Herald Record* (July 2, 1980).

"PIPC talks result in suggessted Marriott trade-offs." *Huguenot Herald* (August 6, 1980).

"Marriott hearings turn to effect on lake." *The Times Herald Record* (August 7, 1980).

"Lawyer threatens legal action over Minnewaska records." *Poughkeepsie Journal* (August 16, 1980).

"Owner: Minnewaska interests Moon." *The Times Herald Record* (August 19, 1980).

"A Peace Treaty for the Hudson." *The New York Times* (December 20, 1980).

"Marriott ready to spring water study." *The Times Herald Record* (January 7, 1981).

"Catskill Center endorses proposed Marriott complex." *The Times Herald Record* (April 1, 1981).

"Fate of Scenic Upstate Lake Resort Hinges on a Judge's Opinion." *The New York Times* (April 11, 1981).

"Marriott challenges state report on Minnewaska plans." *Poughkeepsie Journal* (April 9, 1981).

"Marriott resort Project's opponents shifting focus to commission." *The Times Herald Record* (June 4, 1981).

"Marriott pressed to give up condominium plan." *The Daily Freeman* (June 5, 1981).

"Condominium proposal in jeopardy." *The Times Herald Record* (June 5, 1981).

"Who Speaks for us?" *The Daily Freeman* (June 5, 1981).

"Heritage pitted against Marriott." *The Daily Freeman* (June 7, 1981).

"Key opponent explains Marriott proposal stand." *The Times Herald Record* (June 9, 1981).

"Marriott backers plan support act, organizer says." *The Times Herald Record* (June 12, 1981).

"Sides argue at Marriott meeting." *The Times Herald Record* (June 16, 1981).

"Challenge mounted against Marriott." *The Times Herald Record* (August 4, 1981).

"Lawsuit filed against easement." *The Times Herald Record* (October 6, 1981).

"Marriott gets OK to build golf course." *The Times Herald Record* (November 6, 1981).

"Court order stalls disputed Marriott plan." *The Times Herald Record* (November 25, 1981).

"Judge lifts fiat blocking Marriott deal." *The Times Herald Record* (December 15, 1981).

"Obstacle cleared to Marriott's resort." *The Times Herald Record* (May 5, 1982).

"Marriott intentions probed." *The Times Herald Record* (January 21, 1983).

"Court rejects DEC approval for Marriott condos." *The Times Herald Record* (February 4, 1983).

"Marriott pulls backing in condo project." *The Times Herald Record* (February 9, 1983).

"Making a mountain of protest." *Sunday Times Herald Record* (April 3, 1983).

"Lake Minnewaska resort plan revived." *The Times Herald Record* (May 25, 1983).

"Small-scale Minnewaska plan offered." *The Times Herald Record* (June 1, 1983).

"Marriott golf site gets legal green light." *The Times Herald Record* (February 3, 1984).

"Marriott Calls Off Plans to Revive Ulster Resort." *The New York Times* (March 13, 1985).

"Battle Lines Drawn at Lake Minnewaska." *The New York Times* (October 6, 1985).

"Albany Considering Minnewaska's Fate." *The New York Times* (June 28, 1986).

"State to Acquire an Upstate Lake." *The New York Times* (November 25, 1986).

"Lake to Be a State Park, Ending a 17-Year Battle." *The New York Times* (June 3, 1987).

Chapter 17: Sterling Forest

Correspondence

JoAnn Dolan to Mr. Leon G. Billings, July 26, 1993.

Robert O. Binnewies to Assistant Secretary–designate George T. Frampton, Jr., April 7, 1993.

JoAnn Dolan to Robert O. Binnewies, February 26, 1993.

Bob Binnewies to Bob Thomson, July 9, 1993.

Klara B. Sauer, Robert Augello, Kim Elliman, and Olivia Millard to Hon. Mario M. Cuomo, January 19, 1994.

Bob Binnewies to the Public/Private Partnership to Save Sterling Forest, March 25, 1994.

Jim Tripp to Rob Pirani, April 20, 1994.

Bob Binnewies to the Public/Private Partnership to Save Sterling Forest, October 7, 1994.

Bob Binnewies to "Mac" [Commissioner Malcolm Borg], November 30, 1994.

Bob Binnewies to Rob Pirani, December 9, 1994.

JoAnn Dolan to Robert O. Binnewies, January 10, 1995.

Robert O. Binnewies to Dr. Edward Kubersky, January 31, 1995.

Governor Christine Todd Whitman to Hon. George Pataki, February 3, 1995.

Governor Christine Todd Whitman to Mr. Larry Rockefeller, February 23, 1995.

Robert O. Binnewies to Mr. Patrick F. Noonan, March 24, 1995.

Governor George Pataki to Hon. Christine Todd Whitman, April 6, 1995.

Barnabas McHenry to Commissioner Bernadette Castro, April 14, 1995.

Robert S. Davis to Hon. Bernadette Castro, June 15, 1995.

Bob Binnewies to the Public/Private Partnership to Save Sterling Forest, July 3, 1995.

Bob Binnewies to the Public/Private Partnership, April 19, 1996.

Bob Binnewies to the Public/Private Partnership, June 14, 1996.

Bob Binnewies to the Public/Private Partnership, July 10, 1996.

Bob Binnewies to the Public/Private Partnership, October 18, 1996.

Reports

"Sterling Forest Fund Receipts As Of 2/1/96."

"Sterling Forest Fund Expenditures As Of 2/1/96."

"Proposed Agreement for Acquisition of Sterling Forest." November 1, 1996.

"Sterling Forest: Impact of Development in Reservoir Watershed." North Jersey District Water Supply Commission.

Newspapers

"Would protect a portion of Sterling Forest." *Advertiser Photo News* (February 5, 1986).

"Future of Sterling Forest Stirs Imaginations." *The Bergen Record* (February 23, 1986).

"Don't spoil Sterling Forest." *The Bergen Record* (March 7, 1986).

"Monroe-West Milford green belt proposed." *The Bergen Record* (March 8, 1986).

"Activist's plan borne out of love for forest." *The Bergen Record* (April 13, 1986).

"$2M grant to help buy woodlands." *The Bergen Record* (August 28, 1986).

"They're mapping the 'greenway.'" *West Milford Argus* (September 7, 1986).

"Sterling Forest land deal appears near." *The Times Herald Record* (September 17, 1986).

"For sale: Sterling Forest 19,990 Acres." *The New York Times* (October 26, 1986).

"Sterling Forest off seller's block." *The Times Herald Record* (March 26, 1987).

"Sterling Forest preservation has Torricelli support." *Green Lake and West Milford News* (May 18, 1988).

"Questions About Sterling Forest." *The New York Times* (May 22, 1988).

"Sterling Forest: What's a watershed worth." *The Bergen Record* (June 20, 1988).

"Battle for Sterling Forest." *Rockland Journal News* (August 21, 1988).

"Owner to skip talks on Sterling Forest's future." *The Times Herald Record* (September 23, 1988).

"Quick seizure approved for forest tract." *The Bergen Record* (October 20, 1988).

"Passaic takes title to Sterling Forest." *The Bergen Record* (November 1, 1988).

"Sterling Forest chief to stress public relations." *The Times Herald Record* (February 6, 1989).

"Open space around Cities is Shrinking." *The Philadelphia Inquirer* (June 26, 1989).

"Exit 15A plan gets new support." *The Times Herald Record* (July 11, 1989).

"'Environmentally sensitive' firm to decide Sterling property's fate." *The Times Herald Record* (August 10, 1989).

"Sterling Forest: Feds pushed to intervene." *The Times Herald Record* (October 3, 1989).

"Development of Sterling Forest viewed as threat to North Jersey." *The Star-Ledger* (October 3, 1989).

"Forest Project Called Peril to New Jersey." *The New York Times* (October 8, 1989).

"Heimbach named Sterling president." *The Times Herald Record* (October 11, 1989).

"Palisades park appoints director." *The Times Herald Record* (November 29, 1989).

"Sterling Forest study released." *The Times Herald Record* (February 16, 1990).

"Sterling Forest plan would preserve much wilderness." *The Bergen Record* (April 23, 1990).

"Sterling Forest principal has local tie." *The Times Herald Record* (August 16, 1990).

"British firm buys Sterling Forest Corp." *Rockland Journal-News* (August 16, 1990).

"Sterling Forest sale a done deal." *The Times Herald Record* (October 2, 1990).

"Albany Looks Longingly at Land It Can't Pay For." *The New York Times* (November 25, 1990).

"Sterling Forest land plan unveiled." *The Bergen Record* (March 28, 1991).

"Environmentalists Criticize Plan for Sterling Forest Development." *The New York Times* (March 31, 1991).

"Last chance effort." *The Star Ledger* (May 12, 1991).

"Clock is running on Sterling Forest." *The Times Herald Record* (May 15, 1991).

"You can't see the forest for the buffers." *The Times Herald Record* (May 28, 1991).

"Boom County, Bust Budget." *The Wall Street Journal* (September 25, 1991).

"Sterling Forest plan errs on costs: report." *The Times Herald Record* (October 5, 1991).

"Democrat fights Sterling Forest development." *The Times Herald Record* (February 29, 1992).

"Selling Sterling Forest." *The Times Herald Record* (March 30, 1992).

"Fund match for Sterling ruled out." *The Times Herald Record* (May 7, 1992).

"Lawmakers clash over Forest land." *The Times Herald Record* (June 24, 1992).

"Gilman opposes Sterling Forest purchase." *Rockland Journal-News* (June 24, 1992).

"House panel OKs Sterling Forest funds." *The Bergen Record* (June 30, 1992).

"DEC to oversee Sterling Forest review." *The Times Herald Record* (July 1, 1992).

"State seeks Sterling Forest deal." *Rockland Journal-News* (August 22, 1992).

"Preserve forest, citizen group's survey finds." *The Times Herald Record* (September 4, 1992).

"War of Woods." *The Bergen Record* (February 14, 1993).

"Economy Aids a Compromise Over Developing Forest Land." *The New York Times* (April 27, 1993).

"Sterling Forest, U. S. dealing." *The Bergen Record* (April 28, 1993).

"Protection for NJ Highlands." *The Bergen Record* (May 15, 1993).

"Steps taken for U. S. To buy Sterling tract." *The Times Herald Record* (May 27, 1993).

"$35 million sought to save Sterling Forest." *The Bergen Record* (July 27, 1993).

"$25 million sought for Forest purchase." *Green Lake and West Milford News* (August 22, 1993).

"NY 'new city' project threatens Jersey water." *The Star Ledger* (August 22, 1993).

"Babbitt calls Sterling land-buy a first step." *The Times Herald Record* (September 29, 1993).

"Trygg-Hansa Recapitalizing Its Home Unit." *The Wall Street Journal* (December 20, 1993).

"Park panel enlisted in fight for Highlands." *The Bergen Record* (April 26, 1994).

"National Park Service dampens $35 million plan to buy SF." *The Star Ledger* (May 19, 1994).

"Setback in plan to safeguard Sterling Forest." *The Bergen Record* (May 18, 1994).

"Congressmen ask Babbitt to rescue Sterling Forest bill." *The Bergen Record* (May 19, 1994).

"Saving Sterling Forest must be a top priority." *The Bergen Record* (May 20, 1994).

"Park Service does grave disservice to Highlands." *The Bergen Record* (May 22, 1994).

"Park Service now backs Sterling Preservation." *The Times Herald Record* (May 24, 1994).

"Sterling Forest parkland plan may get $17M federal boost." *Rockland Journal-News* (May 24, 1994).

"Strings tied Sterling Forest aid." *The Bergen Record* (May 26, 1994).

"Sterling Forest can be preserved." *Rockland Journal-News* (May 26, 1994).

"Panel OKs NJ funds to acquire woodland." *The Bergen Record* (June 3, 1994).

"State Senate OK's $10M for Sterling Forest." *The Bergen Record* (July 1, 1994).

"Sterling Forest funding backed." *The Bergen Record* (August 4, 1994).

"Heimbach moves up." *The Times Herald Record* (August 11, 1994).

"Sterling Forest funding moves ahead." *The Bergen Record* (August 22, 1994).

"SFC goes generic with its EIS." *Green Lakes and West Milford News* (September 7, 1994).

"10M OK'd for Sterling Forest." *The Bergen Record* (September 27, 1994).

"Senate kills quartet of bills dealing with New Jersey issues." *The Bergen Record* (October 11, 1994).

"Senate backs Sterling Forest proposal." *The Bergen Record* (December 16, 1994).

"Sterling Talk put to rest." *The Times Herald Record* (February 11, 1995).

"Forest short listed." *Green Lake and West Milford News* (March 1, 1995).

"Newt favors buying forest." *The Bergen Record* (March 10, 1995).

"DEC clears way for Sterling hearings." *The Times Herald Record* (April 12, 1995).

"SF: A search for answers." *The Times Herald Record* (April 19, 1995).

"Park Chief backs forest buy." *The Times Herald Record* (May 5, 1995).

"Development opposed." *The Times Herald Record* (June 16, 1995).

"For Tuxedo, A Big Decision on Sterling Forest." *The Bergen Record* (June 21, 1995).

"Editor's Corner: Reality Check." *Green Lakes and West Milford News* (June 21, 1995).

"Forest DGEIS blasted in Tuxedo." *Green Lake and West Milford News* (June 21, 1995).

"House panel fires away at Sterling Forest plan." *Rockland Journal-News* (September 29, 1995).

"Gingrich Backs Buying Tract on Jersey-New York Border *The New York Times* (December 13, 1995).

"Gingrich's New Deal: Buy Sterling Forest." *Rockland Journal-News* (December 14, 1995).

Chapter 18: Looking Ahead

Books

Abbott, Arthur P. *The Greatest Park in the World*. Historian Publishing Co., 1914.

Correspondence

Bob Binnewies to Henry DeCotis, Megan Lesser Levine, Steve Lewis, and Jim Economides.

Newspapers

"Another Victory for Sterling Forest." *The Sterling Messenger* (February 2000).

"Saving Sterling Forest." *The Bergen Record* (February 10, 2000).

INDEX

Abercrombie & Fitch, 107–8
Abramson, Rudy, 46–48
Adams, Charles C., 102
Adams, Thomas, 204
Addams, Priscilla, 79
Ad Hoc Associates, 323
Adirondack State Park, 8
Adolph, Eleanor, 164–66
African Americans: on Commission, 283; use of parks, 76, 134, 139, 150–51, 208, 214, 232
Ahearn, James, 342
Albright, Horace M., 114, 125, 188, 203, 218, 221, 270
Alexander, James, 307
Alexander, William, 307
Alexander Hamilton, 276
Algonquin nation, 58
Allard, Wayne, 344
Allis, J. Ashton, 142
Allison estate, 229–30
Allison Land Company, 26
AmBase, Inc., 314, 318
AMC. *See* Appalachian Mountain Club
American Canoe Association, 30
American Museum of Natural History, 69–71, 164, 166–67, 222
American Scenic and Historic Preservation Society, 12, 44, 67, 98, 150
Ames, DeHart, 177
Anderberg, Robert, 347
Anderson, E. Ellen, 26

Anderson, Maxwell, 217
André, John, 104, 197
Anthony, Susan B., 18, 30
AOKI Construction Co. Ltd., 300–301
Appalachian Mountain Club (AMC), 91, 299, 301, 321
Appalachian Mountains, geology of, 57–58
Appalachian Trail, 141–43, 158
Appalachian Trail Conference (ATC), 143, 343
Appropriations, 43, 53–54, 75, 114–15, 140, 188; controversy over, 161–62, 184–85; federal, 240–41; of land, 17; for Parkway, 231; for Sterling Forest, 311, 337–38, 344–46. *See also* Land acquisitions
Arapaho tribe, 346
Archbold, John D., 53
Arden (Harriman estate), 45–46, 49, 51–52, 130, 308
Arizona-Sonora Desert Museum, 217
Arnold, Benedict, 104
Arthur, Chris, 327, 334–36, 349
Ash, Carol, 356
ATC. *See* Appalachian Trail Conference
Atomic Energy Commission, 254–55
Audubon, Victor, 6–7

Babbitt, Bruce, 328, 331, 334–35, 346, 348, 351
Bacon, Robert, 20

Baker, Charles Whiting, 81, 102, 107, 126, 134–35, 195, 211
Baker, George F., 53, 124, 169
Baker, Hugh, 104
Baker Camp, 169, 175
Ball, Florence, 131
Banks, Henry W., 26
Barbara, Philip, 292
Barber Asphalt Company, 72
Barrett, Nathan T., 17, 40, 82, 96
Bartlett, Charles L., 14
Bartlett, Willam, 6
Beal, Gifford, 280
Bean, Ernest D., 91
Bear Mountain Bridge, 143–46, *146*
Bear Mountain docks, *109,* 183
Bear Mountain Inn, *92,* 113, 213, 241, 288; dancing at, 104–5, 125; development of, 90–92, 96
Bear Mountain prison stockade, 44–46, *45,* 51, 54–55
Bednarz, Edward, 298–302
Bell, W. W., 142
Benchoff, Howard J., 181
Benson, William O., 110
Bergman, David, 323
Berman, Victor H., 209, 219
Beveridge, John, 111
Bierstadt, Albert, 6, 27
Billings, Leon, 330
Bill Miller's Riviera, *227,* 227–28
Binnewies, Bob, 315–18, 325, 328–30, 338–41, 345–48, 353–54

Bishop, Gordon, 319, 330
Black Mountain, 59
Black Rock Forest, 260
Blauvelt, George A., 82, 85, 126, 136, 151, 163
Blauvelt Park, 87, 90, 95
Board, Cornelius, 307
Boardman, Walter, 254
Boating, 30, 137, 138
Bond issues, 53, 159–62, 318–19, 351
Boren, Frank D., 302
Borg, Donald G., 228, 229–30, 270, 293, 317; and Marriott, 244, 257, 278; and Parkway, 221–22, 224, 228–29
Borg, Malcolm A., 228, 278, 332; and Sterling Forest, 312, 322, 331, 334, 344, 351–52
Bouton, Mrs. Dale, 246
Boyle, Robert H., 261–62
Boy Scouts, 87, 117, 162
Bradley, Bill, 319, 330, 333–34, 338, 344–45, 349, 351–52
Bradley, Mary T., 74
Bradley, Steven Rowe, 72, 74
Bradley, William C., 74
Brennan, Bernard, 303
Britt, Albert, 134
Britzke, Ron, 247, 249–50
Broadbent, Samuel, 74
Brooklyn Dodgers, 213
Brooks, George, Mr. and Mrs., 249
Brooks, Hooper, 311
Brown, Edward F., 103, 113, 122, 129–30
Brown, Kathryn, 341
Brown & Fleming, 7, 33
Bugbee, Emma, 119–20
Bull Moose Party, 77–78
Burgoyne, Johnny, 62–63, 66
Burnett, Cora Timken, 225, 230
Burnett, John Clawson, 220–21, 225–27, 230
Burroughs, John, 50
Butzel, Albert, 266, 296
Byrne, Brendan, 278

Cabot, Anne, 322
Caccese, Albert E., 285, 294–97, 299, 302
Caldwell's, 58–59
Cammerer, Arno B., 181
Campbell, Mungo, 65
Campfire Girls, 87

Camping, 30, 38–40, 87–88, 94
Carey, Hugh, 281, 289
Carmer, Carl, 254, 259
Carnegie, Andrew, 41, 53
Caro, Robert, 154
Carpenter, Senator, 31
Carpenter Brothers, 1, 4, 7, 13, 19
Carpenter Brothers Quarry, 9, 12, 26, 152, 168
Carr, William, 167, 179, 199, 217
Cars, 137–38, 150
Castro, Bernadette, 338, 342, 344–45, 347–49, 352–53
Castro, Bette, 270
Castro, Nash, 269–71, 317, 341; and Minnewaska, 275–77, 279–96, 299, 301–3; and Sterling Forest, 313–15, 322, 327, 332
Cataldo, Joseph C., 295
Catholic Charities, 159
Central Hudson Gas & Electric Corporation, 250, 266
Central Hudson Steamboat Company, 106
Certo, Ida W., 224
Chaco Canyon, 166–67
Chapman, Augusta B., 74
Charitable organizations, 40, 113, 120, 151–52
Chestnut blight, 44
Cheyenne tribe, 346
Chiang Kai-shek, Mme., 214
Child care, 112
Childs, E., 178
Childs, William, 171
Choate, Joseph H., 41
Chorley, Kenneth, 162
Christy, Bayard H., 132
Church, Frederic, 6
Citizens to Save Minnewaska, 292, 297–99
City Investing Corporation, 305, 309
Civilian Conservation Corps, 197, 197–98
Clarence Fahnstock State Park, 259
Clark, Mamie Phipps, 283, 283
Clark, Mrs. Leroy, 259
Clark, Preston, 139
Clean Water / Clean Air Bond Act, 351
Clermont, 109, 109–10, 116, 120–22, 182–83, 213
Cleveland Rams, 213
Cliff House (Hotel), 268, 271–72, 273,

279, 281, 288
Clinton, Bill, 327
Clinton, George, 62–65
Clinton, Henry, 63–64, 66
Clinton, James, 63, 65, 308
Clinton, Sir William, 59
Clinton Point Quarry, 88
Coe, George S., 26
Cole, Thomas, 6
Coley, George R., 279
Columbia River Gorge, 128
Commissioners of PIPC, 17, 358–59; in 1908, 40; in 1912, 82; in 1945, 219; in 1960, 239–40; in 1974, 278–79
Concessions, 85–86, 108, 124–25, 127, 213
Cone, Edward Payson, 43
Conklin, Ramsey, 192
Conservation ethic, 40, 48–49, 54, 74, 98, 223, 249, 257, 275, 354
Conservation Fund, The, 340, 353
Consolidated Edison Company of New York, Inc. (Con Ed), 239–68, 251, 296
Cooke, Thomas, 314
Cooley, Wes, 344
Cooper, Edward, 29
Cornell, J. Martin, 317, 322, 335
Cornell football team, 214
Cornwallis, Charles, 30, 61–62
Cornwallis Headquarters, 42, 43, 203
Cornwall-on-Hudson, 246, 248–49, 254, 261
Cortland Conservation Society, 261
Coyotes, 234
Croes, J. J. R., 9
Cropsey, Jasper Francis, 6
Cunningham property, 83–84
Cuomo, Mario, 302, 313, 318, 332, 334, 338
Curley, Richard, 325
Curry, Mrs. D. A., 112
Custer State Park, 112
Cutler, Otis H., 147

Dana, William, 18
Dana, William B., 30, 40, 81
Dana property, 26, 99, 102–3, 136–38, 140–41, 168, 182, 189, 205
Dancing, 104–5, 125
Dao, James, 312
Davidson, Joan, 338
Davis, Clelland, 136–37

Dawson, Ida W., 139–40
Dayliner, 276
Dayliners, 86, 95, 106, *109,* 109–10,
    116, 120–22, 134, 182–83, *209,* 276
Debevoise, Thomas M., 212
DEC. *See* New York Department of
    Environmental Conservation
DeCotis, Henry, 353–54
Deer, 177
Delaney & Galligan, 33
Delano, Frederic A., 179
Delavan, D. Bryson, 37
Delaware-Hudson Steamship
    Company, 183
Demarest, Elizabeth, 34, 43, 97,
    106–7, 185
Dempsey, Jack, 214
Department of the Interior, 287
De Ronde, Abram, 17, 34, 40, 72, 78,
    80–81, 104, 196
Development, 180, 249; of
    Minnewaska, 275–303; profitabil-
    ity of, 323; of Sterling Forest,
    304–54
Devil's Horse Race, 36, 58, 63
Devoe, Frederick W., 43
DeVries Colony, 6
DeWan, George, 154
Dewey, Thomas E., 218, 230–31
Diamond, Henry, 257
Dickinson, Robert L., 142
Disabled persons, use of parks by, 194
Disque, Brice P., 100
Dix, John A., 76
Dobson, Meade C., 132–34
Dodge, Cleveland H., 33, 43, 53, 124,
    135
Dodge, Cleveland, Jr., 204
Dodge, William E., 44
Dolan, Jamie, 310–11
Dolan, JoAnn L., 304, 309–11, 315,
    324–25, 327, 330
Dolan, Paul R., 304, 309–11
Dole, Robert, 338, 349
Donahue, Michael J., 261
Doodletown, 64, 192–93
Doris Duke Charitable Foundation,
    353
Doty, Dale E., 257–59
Douglas, James, 75
Downer, Jay, 118, 160–61, 193, 210–11
Drew, Robert S., 294, 296–98, 300
Driscoll, Alfred E., 222, 224, 228–29
Duggan, Stephen and Beatrice, 254

DuHaine, Richard, 312–13
Dunderberg Mountain, 152
DuPont, Colman, 124
DuPont property, 83, 152, 168, 182
Durand, Asher, 6
Dwight D. Eisenhower Middle
    School, 353
Dyckman Street Ferry, *95,* 139, 144,
    207
Dyke, Victoria, 103

Economidies, Jim, 354
Edge, Walter E., 101–2, 114, 220–21
Edison, Charles, 152, 218, 240
Edwards, Edward, *108,* 114, 135
Egemeier, Stephen J., 291
Eggert, Charles, 261
E. G. Hewitt High School, 353
Eisenhower, Dwight D., 241
Elk, 114, 213
Elliman, Kim, 332, 347, 349–50,
    352–53
Ellis, Ridsdale, 224, 304, 309
Ellis Island, 243–44
Elston, Phyllis, 333
Elwood, P. H., Jr., 168, 175
Emery, Henry G., 107
Empire National Bank, 272–73
Englewood Garden Club, 34
Englewood Women's Club, 11–12
Environmental Defense Fund, 321
Environmental planning, 179–80, 265
Environmental Protection Agency,
    266
Environmental Quality Bond Act,
    318–19
Environmental Quality Review Act,
    323
Eristoff, Anne Tracy, 185
Ermeti, Achille, 168, 182
Ewert, Al, 321

Faerber, Frederick, 280
Farley, Patrick, 353
Federal Power Commission (FPC),
    257–58, 263–65
Ferency, Alan, 353
Fiedler, James F., 80
Filippone, Ella, 312, 315, 324–25, 333,
    336, 339, 345
Finley, John H., 132
Fish, Con Ed and, 261–63, 266
Fish, Hamilton, Jr., 186
Fish, Mary Ann, 347

Fish, Stuyvesant, 47–48
Fisher, George J., 132
Fisk, Averell Harriman, *234, 235*
Fisk, Mary, 278, *279,* 283, 322
Fitch, Wilson, 145
Fitzgerald, Jamie, 353
Fitzgerald, Shannon, 353
Flacke, Robert, 298
Florio, Jim, 330
Focht, Jack, 129, 337
Fokker, Anthony H. G., 19, 128–29,
    134–35, 141
Forbes, Harland D., 253
Ford, Charles T., 83–84
Ford, Edsel B., 180–81
Forest Legacy Fund, 325
Forest management, 44–46, 201
Forest-of-Deane Iron Mine, 44
Forest Preservation Act, 44–45, 56
Forest Service, 324
Fort, J. Franklin, 43, 56
Fort Clinton, 62–63, 65, *65,* 67, 90,
    178–79
Fort Lee, 27–28, 60–62, 67, 244, 257,
    278; development attempts,
    224–25; Visitor Center, 267, 289
Fort Montgomery, 62–64, *65,* 67, 90
Fort Washington, 61–62
Fosdick, Raymond B., 28
FPC. *See* Federal Power Commission
Frampton, George, 328–29
Freemeyer, Allan, 344–45, 347–49
Frelinghuysen, Rodney, 338–39, 344,
    349
Fremont, John C., 7, 73–74
Friends of Marriott, 299
Friends of the Shawangunks, 292,
    297–300
Fulton Centennial, 41–43
Funding for land acquisitions, 140,
    168; for Minnewaska, 274–75, 282,
    293–94; for Parkway, 204–5; for
    Rockland Lake, 233; for Sterling
    Forest, 313, 318–19, 322–23,
    325–26, 344–46, 350, 355
Fund raising, 52–53, 124, 147, 152–53;
    Perkins Sr. and, 94–95, 101,
    115–16, 119; for Sterling Forest,
    326–28, 332–33, 350, 352–53;
    Welch and, 162–63

Gaines, Cecelia, 11, 13, 16–17, 24, 43,
    185, 203
Gallagher, P., 7

Gallo, Dean, 319, 325
Garden Club of America, 258
Garraty, John A., 13–14, 20–21, 71, 77–78
Gates, Horatio, 62, 66
Gebhards, John, 321–22, 342–43
General Services Administration, 242–43, 256
Geological Survey, 29
George, Henry, 29
George Washington Bridge, 182, 228
George W. Perkins Memorial Foundation, 332
George W. Perkins Memorial Highway, 196–97, 202–3, 206
Geraldine R. Dodge Foundation, 332
Ghost stories, 30, 59
Gilbert, Cass, 204
Gilbert, Henry V., 90
Gilchrist, S., 84
Gill, Bo, 267–68
Gilman, Benjamin A., 314–15, 319, 324–25, 329, 334, 344, 348–49
Gingrich, Newt, 338, 345–46, 348–49
Gitlen, Phillip, 294, 298
Glacier National Park, 169
Gladys and Roland Harriman Foundation, 332
Goldmark, Peter, 282, 285
Golub, Kenneth, 329
Gordon, Elizabeth, 328
Gordon, H. A., 117
Gould, Edwin, 169
Gould, Helen Miller, 53
Grabouski, count, 65
Grant, C. W., 111
Grant, F. D., 41
Grant, Ulysses S., 18, 29
Gray, E. H., 53
Great Depression, 188, 192–99, 207–8
Great Smoky Mountains National Park, 158, 180–81
Greeley, W. B., 158
Green, Andrew H., 12, 43
Green, George, 26
Green Bay Packers, 213
Greenbrook Park, 96, 259
Greene, Nathanael, 61
Greenwood Trust, 310
Greycliff, 18, 102–3, *103*
Griffith, Earl, 260
Griggs, Everett G., 128
Group camps, 87, *88–89,* 95–96, 103, 120, 129, 131, *132,* 151–52, 159–60, 162, 241

Guido, Alfred T., 289
Gustafson, Carl O., 253–54
Gyra, George, 205

Hackensack nation, 6
Haggerty, Alice, 1–4
Half Moon, 1, 134
Hamilton House Settlement, 40
Hand, Marie, 246
Handy, Albert, 132
Hansen, James, 344–45, 347–48
Hanson, Jon F., 299
Harding Camp, 175
Harkness, Edward S., 124
Harriman, Carol, 50, 54
Harriman, Cornelia, 50
Harriman, Edward Henry, 36, 38–51, 47, 145–46
Harriman, Edward Roland, 50, 93, 145, 230, 233, 236
Harriman, Mary, 50
Harriman, Mary Averell, 37–56, 47, 144–46
Harriman, William Averell, 49–51, 54, 55, 56, 93, 130, 186, 209–10, *234,* 263, 281; and Bear Mountain Bridge, 145–46; as commissioner, 70, 93, 122, 169, 236, 239, 270, 278; as governor, 230–31, 235; war service, 214
Harriman estate, 304–5, 308–9
Harvey, Rose, 346–47, 349, 352–53
Hayes, cardinal, 159
Haytaian, Chuck, 333
Hazard, R. G., 94
Heald, Henry, 263
Hedges, General, 28
Heimbach, Louis, 316–18, 326, 336, 338, 342, 344, 346–47, 350
Heiskell, Marion, 263
Henry Hudson Drive, 71–72, 75, 91, 140
Herbert, Andrew M., 84–85
Hewitt, Abram S., 17, 28–30
Hewitt, Sarah Cooper, 29
Heydt, Charles O., 186, 189–90
Higgins, Frank W., 31
Highland Lakes State Park, 255
Highlands, *356;* geology of, 57–58; history of, 57–68; New Jersey portion of, 333; preservation act, 44–45, 56; residents of, 191–92
Highlands Park, 36, 41, 56
High Tor, 217–18, 255–56
Hiking, 95, 131–32

Hinchey, Maurice D., 282, 296, 327–30, 334, 344–45, 348, 351
Historic preservation, 8, 224–25, 357
Hoffman, Harold G., 210
Holland, Cecelia Gaines, 11, 13, 16–17, 24, 43, 185, 203
Holland, John, 24
Home Group, 311–13
Home Holdings, 341
Home Insurance Company, 305, 309–10
Homer, Winslow, 7
Hone, Phillip, 6
Hood, Rob, 348
Hook Mountain, 72, 232; development of, 103–4, 174; quarrying at, 32, 40, 152–53
Hopewell, E. S., 146
Hopkins, Franklin W., 17, 24, 40, 43, 82, 101–2, 153, 163
Hopkins, Mary Alden, 116
Hopper, Irving, 72
Horewell, Ellis, 185
Horowitz, Steve, 347, 349
House Resolution 2471, 329–30
Howard, Charles E., 44, 46
Howe, William, 59–61
Hudson, Henry, 1, 36, 203
Hudson, Paul, 229–30
Hudson River, 75–76, 261–62; chaining, 307–8
Hudson River Conservation Society, 218, 259
Hudson River Day Line Steamship Company, 106, 183
Hudson River Fishermen's Association, 263
Hudson River School, 6–7
Hudson River Valley Commission, 262–63
Hudson River Valley Contingent for the Preservation of Sterling Forest, 360–61
Hudson Tercentenary, 41–43
Hughes, Charles Evans, 43, 51–53, 56, 174
Hughes, Richard J., 257
Humbach, John, 311, 313, 315, 319–20
Hunting, 95, 126–27, 177—78, 275–76, 353
Huntington, Archer M., 218, 255–56
Huttleston, L. L., 246
Hyde, Benjamin Talbot Babbitt, 164–70, *165*

Hyde, Frederick, 166

Ice harvesting, 232–33, *233*
Ickes, Harold, 203
Indian Head, 1–4
Indian Hill tract, 355
Inness, George, 6
Interstate compact, 189–212
Interstate issues, 9, 23, 101–2, 173, 243–44
Investors Management Group, 300–301
Iona Island, 179, *242*, 242–43, 256–57; ammunition depot, 98–99, 110–11
Iroquois nation, 43
Isseks, Abraham S., 300

Jackson Hole Preserve, 233
Jaeger, H. A., 39
James, Arthur, 124, 135
James, Eileen F. and Arthur Curtiss, 53
James H. Ottaway Jr. Revocable Trust, 332
Javits, Jacob K., 262
John Ellison House, 67–68
Johnson, Addison, 72
Johnson, Jim, 65
Johnson, Lady Bird, 269–70
Johnson, Nathan T., 6
Jolliffe, Ruby M., 129–31, *130*, 138, 162, 175, 199–201, 215, 217
Jones, Mark M., 172–73, 211
Jones Report, 169, 172–74
Jordan, John, 163
Jorling, Thomas, 315–16
Josephine, 222–23
Jube, Albert R., 218–19, 240, 264
Juet, Robert, 1
Julliard, Frederic A., 156, 175

Kafin, Robert, 294–97
Karner, Ron, 290
Katz, Samuel, 218
Kean, Thomas, 311
Kellogg, Paul U., 204
Kelly, Sue, 344–45, 348
Kennedy, Robert F., Jr., 262
Kennedy, Roger, 334
Kidde, Walter, 204
Kihm, Mary, 122
King, Donald, 354
King, Elbert W., 122, 126, 134–37, 147, 150–51, 155, 172, 190; and

administration, 160–61, 185, 194–95; correspondence, 163, 167–68, 175, 182–83; death of, 195
Kipling, Rudyard, 7
Knowles, Scott R., 168
Kohm, William J., 226
Kostmayer, Peter H., 314–15, 319, 324–25, 327
Krieser, Kenneth, 322, 348
Kunz, George F., 43, 56, 122
Kutschera, Peter, 280
Kykuit, 27–28

Laborers, 84–85, 117, 126, 196–99
La Guardia, Fiorello, 207
Laidlaw, Reverend, 24
Lake Awosting, 275
Lake Minnewaska, 268–303
Lake Mohonk, 271
Lake Te Ata, 201
Lake Welch, 244–45
Lamb, Frederick S., 24, 43
Lamb, Joseph, 18
Lamb, Mrs. Frederick, 24
Lambert, C. E., 44
Lamont, Corliss, 218–20
Lamont, Thomas W., 184, 204, 218–19
Land acquisitions, 13, 22, 26–27, 33, 40, 72, 126, 272; controversy over, 86–87, 106; Depression and, 209–10; Jones Report on, 173; for roads, 83–84; of Sterling Forest, 353–55; during WWII, 217. *See also* Funding for land acquisitions
Land & Water Conservation Fund (L&WCF), 240, 273, 316, 328
Larson, Morgan F., 186–88, 190, 194, 196
Lasker, Loula D., 180
Lathrop, Richard, 343
Laura Spelman Rockefeller Memorial Fund, 109–10, 116, 152, 162–63, 179; Jones Report to, 172–74
Lautenberg, Frank, 319, 344, 351
Lavenhart, Martin, 343
Law enforcement, 30–31, 34, 94, 104, *105*, 105–6, 155, 201, 288; Palisades Parkway Police, 277–78; and traffic, 137–38
Lawrence, Lydia G., 43, 72
Lawrence Copans Trust, 355
League for the Preservation of the Palisades, 23

Leahy, Frank, 214
Leavitt, Charles W., Jr., 75–79
LeBoeuf, Randall J., Jr., 258
Lee, Charles, 60–61
Lefkowitz, Maurice M., 104
Legal issues of PIPC, 24–25, 113, 127, 184–85; and Con Ed, 263–68; Freedom of Information demand, 341–42; with Minnewaska, 285–86, 294–303; with Parkway land gift, 205
Legislative issues of PIPC: Environmental Quality Review Act, 323; Forest Preservation Act, 44–45, 56; House Resolution 2471, 329–30; Limitation Bill, 16; NJ Assembly Bill 546, 135; Peck Bill, 106
Lehman, Herbert, 210
Lehman, Orin, 282, 284, 287, 299, 302–3, 325
Leiby, Adrian C., 59–60
Levine, Megan, 354
Levitt, Charles W., Jr., 26
Lewis, Harold M., 179–80
Lewis, Steve, 354
Lewis, Supervisor, 103
Lexow, Senator, 7
Liberty Pole Tavern, 62
Lieb, H. C., 56
Limitation Bill, 16
Lincoln, Abraham, 29
Lindabury, Richard V., 81, 101, 117, 124, 126, 136–37, 152, 170
Linn, William A., 17, 40, 43, 72, 81
Linrud, Ruth, 105
Littell, Robert, 333, 336
Locklin, Bruce, 292
Lockwood, F. D., 85–86
Loeks, C. David, 282
Loomis, Mrs. Chester, 11
Low, Seth, 41
Lowey, Nita, 351
Lowry, Paul, 298
Luce, Charles, 296
Lutz, Frank E., 69–71
L&WCF. *See* Land & Water Conservation Fund
Lysle, John S., 26

McAllister, Dan F., 208
McAllister Steamboat Company, 86, 106, 183, 193
McAneny, George, 204

McAuley, Mary Ethel, 127
McCabe, Mike, 113
McClave, S. Wood, 43
McCoy, David P., 322
McDermott, David, 318
McHenry, Barnabas, 287, 322, 324–25, 347–48
Machin, Thomas, 307–8
Mack, Arthur C., 51
McKay, William J., 54–55
MacKaye, Benton, 141–42, 181
McKeon, Warren, 292
McKibben, Bill, 305
McLean, James, 53
McManus, Joseph Kearns, 267–68
McPherson, Mrs. Edward R., 203
McQuaide, James P., 28
Macy, V. Everitt, 53
Magee, J. H., 40
Mahan estate, 26
Mailler, assemblyman, 210
Mandigo Property, 186
Manhattan Trap Rock Company, 72
Manley, Michael, 313
Marriott, J. Willard, Jr., 244
Marriott Corporation, 225, 244, 257, 278, 288–89, 291–92, 294–303
Mars, J. C., 129
Marsh-Billings-Rockefeller National Historical Park, 317
Martin, Jack, 213–14
Martini, Bill, 339, 344, 346, 349, 351
Marvin, Jessie A., 195
Mason, Frank, 139
Mastick, Seabury C., 144
Matching gifts, 116, 124, 134, 152, 156, 181, 228, 233
Mather, Jane T., 203
Mather, Stephen Tyng, 96, 99, 112, 117, 128, 148, 157–58, 169, 188, 203
Meanor, J. B., Jr., 236–37
Melville, Jennifer, 321, 323
Merck, George and Friedrike, 239
Meyner, Robert B., 230, *234, 235*
Michaels, Joseph A., 319
Middleton, Mrs. Joseph M., 76
Mid-Hudson Pattern for Progress, 282
Miles, Mrs. E. B., 31
Millard, Olivia, 321
Miller, Mannix, Lemery & Kafin, 297
Miller, Nathan, 139, 146–47, 228–29
Milliken, Albert E., 290–91

Millionaire's row, 18
Mills, Abraham G., 43
Mills, Enos, 96–98, 112, 128
Milne, May, 87
Moffat, assemblyman, 210
Mohonk Mountain House, 271
Mongaup Valley, 316
Montgomery, Richard, 63
Moodna Tunnel, 263
Moore, A. Harry, 81
Moore, James D., 137–38, 171
Moran, Thomas, 7
Morgan, A. K., 224, 228, 245, *246,* 249, 251, 257–58, 268; and Con Ed, 258–60, 266; correspondence, 230–31, 239, 254–55
Morgan, John Pierpont, 22, 41, 48; donations by, 43, 53; and Perkins, 13–15, 20–21, 71
Morgan, John Pierpont (Jack), 119, 124
Morgan, Kenneth, 215–16
Morgan, Mrs. J. Pierpont, 54
Morgan, Mrs. Leonard, 218
Morrow, Dwight, 204
Morschauser, Joseph, 183
Morse, Harrison B., 12
Morse, Waldo G., 9
Mortimer, David Harriman, *234, 235*
Morton, Levi P., 9, 11, 41
Morton, Rogers C. B., 289
Mosaic Fund, 332
Moses, Robert, 143, 154–55, 160–61, 193–94, 232, 244–45, *246;* and Con Ed, 258; correspondence, 192; interference by, 158–59, 239; and interstate compact, 188, 210–11; and Parkway, 218–20, 227, 231, *234, 235;* and PIPC, 215–16; and SCP, 173, 249–50
Moynihan, Daniel Patrick, 338
Muir, John, 23, 50–51
Munsey, Frank A., 53, 77, 123
Murkowski, Frank, 352
Murphy, Starr J., 31–32
Murray, Amy, 217

National Audubon Society, 256, 346
National Conference on State Parks, 148–49, 202
National Fish and Wildlife Foundation, 332
National Geographic Society, 114

National League of Urban Conditions Among Negroes, 76
National Park Service, 79, 96–98, 127–28, 243–44, 269, 334–35
National Recovery Administration, Public Works Sector, 205
Native Americans, 6, 43, 58, 111, 166–67, 306–7; Princess Te Ata, 199–200, *200*
Natural Resources Defense Council (NRDC), 254
Nature Conservancy, The: and Con Ed, 253–54, 257; and Minnewaska, 272–73, 275, 279, 282, 284–85, 302; and Sterling Forest, 321
Newburgh Address, 67
New Jersey Department of Environmental Protection, 331
New Jersey Federation of Women's Clubs, 11–12, 17, 76, 203, 221
New Jersey Parks and Recreation Association, 81
New Jersey Riparian Board, 25
New Jersey State Federation of Women's Clubs, 31, 97
New Windsor Cantonment, 67
New York Department of Environmental Conservation (DEC), 139, 294, 299, 316, 342
New York Department of Transportation, 281
New York Fine Arts Commission, 178
New York Giants, 213
New York–New Jersey Trail Conference, 142, 304; and Con Ed, 250, 254, 257; formation of, 132–34; and High Tor, 218; logo of, *142;* and Sterling Forest, 224, 310, 315, 353, 355
New York Office of Parks and Recreation, 282
New York Office of Parks, Recreation and Historic Preservation (OPRHP), 324, 338
New York State Industrial Commission, 127
New York State Thruway, proposed interchange, 311, 313, 329
Niagara Falls, 8
Nimke, Helmet, 321
Nobel, Alfred, 75
Noble, William and Abel, 307
Noll, Dean, 321, 323
Noonan, Pat, 272, 284, 340, 353

Nordhoff, Charles, 19
Noritake, Judy, 321, 325, 327
North Jersey District Water Supply Commission, 321, 339
Northrup, Brad, 284–85
Northside Center for Child Development, 283
Notre Dame football team, 214
NRDC. *See* Natural Resources Defense Council
Nudelman, Phyllis, 347

Ochs, Adolph S., 180
Odell, Benjamin, 23–24, 28, 31–32, 56
Ogden, Maureen, 333
Oklahoma grasslands, 346–47
Olcott, E. E., 124
Older, Obediah and John, 34
Olmsted, Frederick Law, 7–8, 36, 74
Olmsted, Frederick Law, Jr., 108–9
Onteora, 109, 109–10, 116, 120–22, 182–83
Opdyke, Charles W., 26
Open Space Institute, 288, 332, 347, 350
OPRHP. *See* New York Office of Parks, Recreation and Historic Preservation
ORRRC. *See* Outdoor Recreation Resources Review Commission
Osborn, Frederick Henry, 172, 186, 210, 256, *267,* 270–72, 274
Osborn, Mrs. Frederick, 259
Osborn, William Church, 259
Osborn, William H., 259
Osborne, Mrs. William H., 185–86
Osborne, William Henry, 48, 189–90
Ottinger, Richard, 262
Outdoor Recreation Resources Review Commission (ORRRC), 240–41
Owen, Steve, 214

Palisades, *2;* geology of, 2–3, 57–58; upriver properties, 22–37
Palisades, 95
Palisades Improvement Company, 26
Palisades Interstate Park Commission (PIPC): administration of, 33–34, 287–88, 292–93; and Con Ed, 239–68; dedication of, *42,* 42–44; expansion of, *333;* finances of, 24, 33–34, 38, 51, 91, 113, 117, 126, 135–36, 155–56, 185, 202; forma-

tion of, *5–21;* future of, *355–56;* interstate compact and, 212; legislative issues of, 16, 44–45, 56, 106, 135, 323, 329–30; meetings of, 293; mission of, 18, 101; offices of, 34, 117, 138, 188; parks and historic sites, 357; popularity of, 38, 94–96, 98, 108, 119–20, 125–26, 160, 186, 207–8, 241–42; *Second Century Plan,* 317. *See also* Funding for land acquisitions; Legal issues of PIPC
Palisades Interstate Parkway, 35, 180, 191, 203–4, 213–38, *236,* 281; dedication of, *234, 235*
Palisades Mountain House, 5, 18
Palisades Nature Association, 223, 259
Palisades Parkway Police, 277–78
Parker, Alton B., 41
Parks, national and state, 7–9; budget patterns for, 115, 294; management of, 9, 40–41, 74, 79, 97, 112, 140, 186, 265, 275–77; regulations, 39, 94; services, 111–12; Welch's recommendations on, 127
Parkway concept, 35, 204
Parrott, Peter, 49, 308
Partridge, Edward Lasell, 35–37, 41, 82, 83, 126, 133, 137, 139, 284; as commissioner, 150, 153; death of, 194; and Harriman, 51, 56; and Women's Memorial, 107
Partridge, T. Dwight, 255, 284
Passaic River Coalition, 315
Pataki, George, 338, 340, 350–51, 353
Peck Bill, 106
Penzato, Joseph, 299
Perkins, Dorothy, 54
Perkins, Evelina Ball, 15, 54, 122
Perkins, George Walbridge, 13–16, *14,* 42, 55, 71, 99–122; and acquisitions, 19–20, 26, 28, 33; and administration, 17, 43–44, 51–53, 56, 82, 91; correspondence, 77, 85, 87–88; donations by, *53,* 124; and fund raising, 94–95, 101, 115–16, 119; and Roosevelt, 77–78; sickness and death of, 117–19, 122–23; tributes to, 55–56
Perkins, George Walbridge, Jr., 124, 145, 147–48, *148,* 214, 233, 238; as commissioner, 146–47, 153, 210–11; correspondence, 229, 232;

and Parkway, 219, 221, 228, 234
Perkins, George Walbridge III, 278, 332
Perkins, Linn M., 206, 239–40, 270, 278
Perkins Memorial Tower, 206, *207*
Phelps, William Walter, estate of, 26
Phelps property, 152
Phillips, Kenneth E., Sr., 272–74, 279–82, 284–85, 287, 303
Phillips, Kenneth, Jr., 281, 288, 294, 296–97, 299
Phillips, Lucille, 286–87, 303
Phipps, Henry, Mr. and Mrs., 53–54
Pinchot, Gifford, 44
PIPC. *See* Palisades Interstate Park Commission
Pirani, Robert, 321
Place, Frank, Jr., 134, 142
Platt, Chester C., 85
Polio, 96, 194
Polk, Davis, 327
Pombo, Richard, 344–46
Poor, Henry Varnum, 217
Porter, Horace, 41
Porter, William H., 40, 82, 171–72
PPP. *See* Public-Private Partnership to Save Sterling Forest
Pratt, George D., 139
Prison Commission, 44–46, 51, 54–55
Profit motive, 40, 74, 85–86, 108, 124–25. *See also* Development
Progressive Party, 77–78
Pryor, Samuel F. III, 326
Public opposition: to Con Ed, 246, 250, 252, 254, 258, 260–61; to Marriott, 292, 294, 297–99; to Sterling Forest, 304, 313, 342–44, 350
Public-Private Partnership to Save Sterling Forest (PPP), 327, 332, 340–41, 354
Purple Heart, 67
Pusey, Nathan M., 260
Putnam, Frederick Ward, 166
Putnam, Harrington, 132

Quarrying, 1–4, 10–11, 17, 19–21, 72, 82, 88, 106, 183–84; by PIPC, 152–53; public opposition to, 7, 28–29, 32–33; upriver, 27, 32–33, 40

Racial issues, 76, 134, 139, 150–51, 208, 214, 232
Ramapo Mountains Water, Power, & Service Company, 113

Raritan nation, 6
Recession, 276, 325, 329
Reese, Franny, 266
Regan, Edward V., 313
Regional Plan Association, 257, 311, 321, 324
Reid, Ogden, 280
Reilly, Hugh, 3–4, 21
Reilly, Mrs. Hugh, 3
Revolutionary War, 30, 57–68, 307–8
Reynolds, Paul A., 224
Ribando, Joseph, 342, 344
Rice, Diana, 191–92
Rickey, Branch, 214
Rifle range, 74–75, 87
Riker, Albert S., 136
Ringling, John, 19
Riondo, Manuel, 18–19
Riverdale Home for Children, 283
Roads, 26, 54, 78–79, 119, 137–38; acquisitions for, 83–84; George W. Perkins Memorial Highway, 196–97, 202–3, 206; Henry Hudson Drive, 71–72, 75, 91, 140; Palisades Interstate Parkway, 35, 180, 191, 203–4, 213–38, *234*, *235*, *236*, 281; Seven Lakes Drive, 84; Storm King Highway, 149
Roberts, Katie, 347
Robinson, Beverly, 64
Robinson, Jackie, 214
Robinson, John E., 150–51
Robinson, Myron W., 155
Rockefeller, David, 70
Rockefeller, John D., Sr., 27–28, *28*, 31, 98, 224–25
Rockefeller, John D., Jr., 27–28, 109, 115–16, *190*, 219, 309; correspondence, 32, 87–88, 99, 181, 202, 215–16; donations by, 53, 77, 98, 184, 224, 228; and interstate compact, 211–12; and Jones Report, 174–75; and Parkway, 189–91, 203–5, 218, 220–21; and Rockland Lake, 232–35
Rockefeller, Larry, 289, 293, 298–99; and Sterling Forest, 304, 322, 326, 340
Rockefeller, Laurance S., 93, 239–40, *245*, 249, 257, 269–70, 275, 317; and Con Ed, 259–60, 262; and conservation, 270–71, 289; donations by, 289; war service, 214
Rockefeller, Mary, 270

Rockefeller, Nelson, 93, 236, 239–45, *245*, 251–55, 262, 273, 275–76
Rockefeller, Peggy, 315
Rockefeller, William, 53
Rockefeller Brothers Fund, 233
Rockefeller Foundation, 94–95
Rockland County Conservation Association, 217
Rockland Lake, 232–35
Rockland Lake Championship Golf Course, 198, 234
Rockland Lake Trap Rock Quarry, 88
Rockland Park, 73
Rocky Mountain National Park, 128
Roe, Robert A., 252, 311, 319
Roebling, Mrs. W. A., 24
Roebling, W. A., 24
Rogers, James D., 310
Ronan, William J., 240, 243, 250
Rondout Valley Sportsmen Club, 280
Roosevelt, Eleanor, 79, 127, 131, *132*, 200, 203–4, 206
Roosevelt, Franklin D., 96, 127, 180–81, 204, 206, *206;* as governor, 186–88, 191, 194, 196; and group camps, 131, 215
Roosevelt, Theodore, 29, 101, 149; and Bull Moose Party, 77–78; as governor, 12–13, 16–17; and Harriman, 48–49; as vice president, 22–23
Ross, Arthur T., 309
Ross Dock, 128–29, 134–35, 141
Rothschild, Leo O., 182, 250–52, 261
Roukema, Marge, 314, 319, 325, 334, 344–46, 348–49, 351
Rubino, Robert, 339
Rulison, Mildred, 130–31
Runyan, William, 114
Russell Sage Foundation, 179
Rust, Marie, 334

Sage, Margaret Olivia, 53
SAGE. *See* Semi-Automatic Ground Environment
St. George, Katharine, 238
St. Leger, Barry, 62–63, 66
St. Michael's Convent, 76
Sandler, Ross, 296
Sandyfields, 191–92
Sanhikan nation, 6
Sarno, Mrs. John R., Jr., 255
Satterlee, Herbert L., 119
Satterlee, Mrs. Herbert, 54
Sauer, Klara, 321, 332, 350

Sauzade, Mrs. K. J., 12
Savage, Arthur, 299
Scarlet fever, 163
Scenic Hudson Preservation Committee, 254, 257, 261, 265–66, 288, 321, 332, 350, 355
Schuyler, Philip, 62
Schwartz, Steve, 280
Schwarzkopf, Herbert Norman, 155
SCP. *See* State Council of Parks
Sears Hunter, 355
Sedway Cooke Associates, 314
Selby, Norman ("Kid McCoy"), 97
Semi-Automatic Ground Environment (SAGE), 237
SEQRA. *See* State Environmental Quality Review Act
Seven Lakes Drive, 84
Seward, Frederick W., 41
SFC. *See* Sterling Forest Corporation
Shaman, Diana, 301
Shawangunk Ridge, 268–303
Shea, Daniel, 288
Shelby, Richard, 338
Shenandoah National Park, 158, 180
Sierra Club, 23, 261, 298–301
Sigaud, Louis A., 224
Sight-seeing, 107
Signs, 112, 148, 201, 276
Sillin, Lelan F., 253
Silver, H. Percy, 90
Silzer, governor, 153, 155, 171
Sisters of Peace, 40
Sive, David, 303
Ski jump, 149, 175—77, 178
Skunk Hollow, 18
Smiley, Albert and Alfred, 271, 303
Smiley, Albert F., 295–96
Smith, Alfred E., 101–2, 106, 119, 152–54, 159, 173, 210; as commissioner, 194, 211–12
Smith, George T., 147
Smith, Leonard Hull, 25–26, 38, 82, 84
Smock, John, 7
Snead, J. E., 166–67
South Mountain, 73–74
Spaniards, 58–59
Spero, Joan, 353
Speyer, John, 31–33
Squires, Mark, 180
Stalter, Elizabeth "Perk," 193
Standard Oil property, 217
Standard Trap Rock Corporation, 183–84

Stapleton, James J., 291
Startzell, David, 343
State Council of Parks (SCP), 154–55, 159, 169, 173, 184–85, 211, 232, 240, 249, 259
State Environmental Quality Review Act (SEQRA), 301
Staub, Mrs. Albert W., 87
Stauffer, D. McNeely, 17, 40, 81
Steamboat Agent C. T. Mallory, 106
Steamboats, 86, 90, 95, 106, *109*, 109–10, 116, 120–22, 182–83, *209*, 276
Sterling, Adaline, 11
Sterling Forest, 224, 304–54, *321*
Sterling Forest Corporation (SFC), 310–11, 316–18, 323–24, 329, 335; Environmental Impact Statement, 332, 336–37, 341, 343–44
Sterling Forest Resources (Coalition), 313, 315, 322, 342, 353
Sterling Gardens, 309
Sterling Lake, 306, *306*
Stetson, Francis L., 41
Stevens, Edwin A., 17, 40, 78–79, 82
Stewart, Donald B., 290, 301
Stillman, Calvin W., 247, 259
Stillman, Ernest G., 138, 150, 238
Stillman, James, 19–20, 53
Stillman, John, 138–39, 150
Stoneburner, Harvey, 343
Stony Point Battlefield, 27, 31, 67
Storm King Highway, 149
Storm King Mountain, 90; acquisition of, 209–10; Air Force and, 236–38; Con Ed and, 239–68, *251*, 296
Stotesbury, E. T., 53
Stout, Captain, *108*
Straus, Nathan, 158–59
Straus, Oscar S., 41
Sullivan, John L., 111
Sullivan, Tim, 319
Sulzer, William, 80, 83, 86–87
Sutro, Frederick C., 81, 91, *108*, 215–17; as commissioner, 102, 114, 126, 153, 155, 160–61; correspondence, 163, 203; as staff, 195, 202, 207–8
Sweet, T. C., 117

Taft, William Howard, 77–78
Tallman Mountain, 183, 217
Tamsen, John J., 208, 261
Tappan nation, 6

Taxation issues, 39, 82–83, 118, 224, 249; and Sterling Forest, 315, 323, 335–36
Te Ata, Princess, 199–200, *200*
Tench, Frederick, 145
Thomas, Lowell, 263
Thompson-Seaton, Mrs. Ernest, 24
Thomson, Robert E., 313–15, 318–19, 323–24, 329, 336
Tiorati Workshop for Environmental Learning, 287–88
Tokle, Torger, 215
Tomai, James, 311
Tongass National Forest, Alaska, 352
Torrence property, 152
Torrey, Raymond H., 132, 142–43, 181, 193–94, 198, 201–2, 217
Torricelli, Robert G., 311–12, 314, 319, 324–25, 329, 334–35, 344, 351
Townsend, R. Lewis, 285, 287
Traffic, 137–38
Trail shelters, 177
Trailside Museum, 70–71, 178–79, 199, 203
Train, Russell, 296
Trautman, Mrs. Ralph, 24
Trautman, Ralph, 17, 24
Treavor Brothers, 7
Tripp, Jim, *321*
Trust for Public Land, 301, 346–47, 352
Trygg-Hansa, 331–32
Turnbull, George, 65
Turner, Albert M., 148–49
Tuxedo Park Association, 309
Tweed Boulevard, 73
Twombly, Hamilton, Mr. and Mrs., 43
Typhoid, 163

Udall, Stewart, 263
Ulster Sportsmen's Federation, 280
Undercliff, 18
United States, 90
United States Hotel, 117, 138
U.S. Air Force, 236–38
U.S. Army, 90; and park management, 8
Uses of parks, 30–31, 34, 40, 69–71, *121*, 129, 178–79, 231–32, 275–76
U.S. Forest Service, 44
U.S. Military Academy, West Point, 36, 45, 90, 241
U.S. Supreme Court, 184–85
Utah, Redrock Wilderness, 305,

347–49
Utility companies, 113, 246–68

Van Alstyne, David, Jr., 221–22
Van Brunt Properties, 26
Vanderbilt, Arthur, 229
Vanderbilt, William K., 53
VanHouten, Elizabeth, 341
Van Ingen, W. B., 159
Van Orden, Elmer, 217
Van Rensselaer, William B., 41
Van Wort, Isaac, 197
Vermilye, Elizabeth, 11, 13, 16–17, 23–24, 43, 51, 185
Verrazano, Giovanni da, 3
Victoria Foundation, 332, 352
Volunteer League of Naturalists, 337
Voorhees, Daniel S., 39
Voorhees, Foster M., 12–13, 17, 23, 29
Voorhees, John J., 93–94, 147

Wakelee, Edmund W., 44, 54, 202, 215
Wallace, DeWitt, 287
Wallace, Lila Acheson, 259, 287
Wallace Fund, 332, 350, 352
Wallin, B. C., 175
Washington, George, 8, 30, 60–63, 67, 307; headquarters of, *66, 67*
Washington, Martha, 67
Water: flooding, 201–2; at Minnewaska, 291–92, 294, 301; pollution, 75–76; and Sterling Forest, 311–12, 320, 339–40, 343; treatment of, 104, 163
Water Conservation Bond Act, 331
Watkins, Robert M., 286
Watson, Tom, 263
Wayne, "Mad" Anthony, 57, 197
Weiner, Scott A., 331
Welch, Camille, 102
Welch, Geoffrey, 343
Welch, Jessie, 146
Welch, William Addams, 79, 91, 95, *108*, 112, 114, 123, 143, 177, 190, 215–16; and administration, 117–18, 122, 124–25, 138–39, 177–78, 206; as consultant, 96–97, 108–9, 127, 140, 169, 175; correspondence, 157, 168, 176, 192; and fund raising, 152–53, 155, 162–63; and Jones Report, 172, 174; and Tallman Mountain, 185; and Trail Conference, 132–34; war service, 99–101

Wells, Mrs. John A., 11
Werts, George T., 7, 8, 11
Wetherill, Richard, 166
Wetmore, Jacob S., 26
White, J. DuPratt, 17, 22, 25, 33–35, 52–53, 159, 172, 215, 241–42; and administration, 24–26, 38–39, 103–4, 135; as commissioner, 82, 126; correspondence, 69, 74–75; and fund raising, 152–53, 183–84; and Henry Hudson Drive, 71–72; and interstate compact, 202, 204, 210–12; and Parkway, 204–5; on Perkins Sr., 55–56; and women's memorial, 31, 106, 139–40
White House Historical Association, 289–90
Whitman, Christine Todd, 331, 339–40, 349
Whitman, Walt, 209
Whyte, Herbert, 95
Wilbur, C. P., 142
Wildlife: coyotes, 234; deer, 176; elk, 114, 213

Wildmere Hotel, 271–72, 279, 281, 294, 302
Wilkinson, David A., 312
Wilson, J. G., 41
Wilson, Malcolm, 278
Wilson, Woodrow, 76, 78, 196
Wine, Daniel P., 181
Winter sports, 149–50, 175–77, 186
Winton, H. D., 8–9
Wirth, Conrad, 256, 264–65, 270–72, 277
Witte, Sergei, 14
Women: on commission, 239; education of, 164, 166; on staff, 130, 162; use of parks, 87, 95, 120, 151–52, 194
Women's Memorial, 31, 34, 43, 76, 97, 106–7, 139–40, 185–86, 187
Woodford, Stewart L., 41–43
Woodruff, Lieutenant Governor, 28
Woodruff, Timothy L., 31–32
Woodrum, Robert L., 311
Woods, Arthur, 162, 184
Work, Hubert, 157–58

Work Relief Program, 196–97
Works Progress Administration (WPA), 198–99
World War I, 97–101
World War II, 213–15
WPA. *See* Works Progress Administration
Wyckoff, Jerome, 312

Yard, Robert Sterling, 157
Yellowstone National Park, 7, 8, 38, 90
Yosemite National Park, 7–8, 112
Young, Don, 345
Young Women's Christian Association, 87
Yrizarry, Mary, 343

Zimmer, Richard, 319
Zoning, 32
Zukor, Adolph, 218
Zurich Insurance Group, 341